NETWORK PERIMETER SECURITY

Building Defense In-Depth

OTHER AUERBACH PUBLICATIONS

The ABCs of IP Addressing
Gilbert Held
ISBN: 0-8493-1144-6

The ABCs of LDAP
Reinhard Voglmaier
ISBN: 0-8493-1346-5

The ABCs of TCP/IP
Gilbert Held
ISBN: 0-8493-1463-1

Building an Information Security Awareness Program
Mark B. Desman
ISBN: 0-8493-0116-5

Building a Wireless Office
Gilbert Held
ISBN: 0-8493-1271-X

The Complete Book of Middleware
Judith Myerson
ISBN: 0-8493-1272-8

Computer Telephony Integration, 2nd Edition
William A. Yarberry, Jr.
ISBN: 0-8493-1438-0

Electronic Bill Presentment and Payment
Kornel Terplan
ISBN: 0-8493-1452-6

Information Security Architecture
Jan Killmeyer Tudor
ISBN: 0-8493-9988-2

Information Security Management Handbook, 4th Edition, Volume 1
Harold F. Tipton and Micki Krause, Editors
ISBN: 0-8493-9829-0

Information Security Management Handbook, 4th Edition, Volume 2
Harold F. Tipton and Micki Krause, Editors
ISBN: 0-8493-0800-3

Information Security Management Handbook, 4th Edition, Volume 3
Harold F. Tipton and Micki Krause, Editors
ISBN: 0-8493-1127-6

Information Security Management Handbook, 4th Edition, Volume 4
Harold F. Tipton and Micki Krause, Editors
ISBN: 0-8493-1518-2

Information Security Policies, Procedures, and Standards: Guidelines for Effective Information Security Management
Thomas R. Peltier
ISBN: 0-8493-1137-3

Information Security Risk Analysis
Thomas R. Peltier
ISBN: 0-8493-0880-1

Interpreting the CMMI: A Process Improvement Approach
Margaret Kulpa and Kurt Johnson
ISBN: 0-8493-1654-5

IS Management Handbook, 8th Edition
Carol V. Brown and Heikki Topi
ISBN: 0-8493-1595-6

Managing a Network Vulnerability Assessment
Thomas R. Peltier and Justin Peltier
ISBN: 0-8493-1270-1

A Practical Guide to Security Engineering and Information Assurance
Debra Herrmann
ISBN: 0-8493-1163-2

The Privacy Papers: Managing Technology and Consumers, Employee, and Legislative Action
Rebecca Herold
ISBN: 0-8493-1248-5

Securing and Controlling Cisco Routers
Peter T. Davis
ISBN: 0-8493-1290-6

Six Sigma Software Development
Christine B. Tayntor
ISBN: 0-8493-1193-4

Software Engineering Measurement
John Munson
ISBN: 0-8493-1502-6

A Technical Guide to IPSec Virtual Private Networks
James S. Tiller
ISBN: 0-8493-0876-3

Telecommunications Cost Management
Brian DiMarsico, Thomas Phelps IV, and William A. Yarberry, Jr.
ISBN: 0-8493-1101-2

AUERBACH PUBLICATIONS

www.auerbach-publications.com
To Order Call: 1-800-272-7737 • Fax: 1-800-374-3401
E-mail: orders@crcpress.com

NETWORK PERIMETER SECURITY

Building Defense In-Depth

CLIFF RIGGS

AUERBACH PUBLICATIONS

A CRC Press Company

Boca Raton   London   New York   Washington, D.C.

Library of Congress Cataloging-in-Publication Data

Riggs, Cliff.
    Network perimeter security : building defense in-depth / Cliff Riggs.
        p. cm.
    Includes index.
    ISBN 0-8493-1628-6 (alk. paper)
        1. Buildings—Security measures. I. Title.

TH9705.R54 2003
005.8—dc21

                                                                        2003056278

Visit the Auerbach Publications Web site at www.auerbach-publications.com

© 2004 by CRC Press LLC
Auerbach is an imprint of CRC Press LLC

No claim to original U.S. Government works
International Standard Book Number 0-8493-1628-6
Library of Congress Card Number 2003056278
Printed in the United States of America 1 2 3 4 5 6 7 8 9 0
Printed on acid-free paper

Contents

Chapter 1
Introduction

1.1 Who Is This Book For?

I previously worked for a networking company that specialized in designing and installing Windows NT systems for customers who did not have their own IT staff. I was constantly haunted by our company's complete lack of security awareness regarding our customer installations. The network to our own company's Internet connection had absolutely no packet filtering or other security mechanisms of any type installed on our routers — and search as I might, there was no indication of a firewall anywhere on our own network.

When I inquired of management about not consulting with customers about their own network security and the frightful lack of any on our own network, I received an interesting response: "Customers are not interested in paying for security consulting." Why customers were not interested in paying was explained by management's response to the second half of my question. "We don't have a firewall because it is too expensive — and then I'll have to pay for someone to configure it."

Today, this *laissez-faire* attitude toward network security is thankfully becoming increasingly rare. While many network security experts give a knowing nod and an "I told you so!" every time there is another high-profile computer crime — the press has begun to make our jobs a lot easier. No longer are top-secret government agencies the only organizations interested in the state of their network security. Any customer my company consults with, from the smallest SOHO start-up business to Fortune 500 ISPs, now has network security on the top of the priority list.

Despite this awareness and the abundance of press, the task of securing networks has not gotten any easier over the past few years. Increasingly connected networks, cheap high-speed Internet access, and complex applications requirements have made the task of securing networks more complicated than ever before. Network security is becoming more complex because our networks are becoming more complex. Each time a network professional increases the security on his or her network, a network hacker is taking the time to figure out a new weakness to exploit.

This book will help both the novice and experienced network administrator and manager determine the appropriate defenses to incorporate into their network. While network security is complex, the network "bad guys" can be slowed down quite a bit with a thoughtfully laid-out security policy.

I purposefully used the term "slowed down" in the previous paragraph. If you are new to the network security game, here is something to remember: in general, the more money you spend, the more you can secure your network. At the same time, no matter how much money you spend, you will never completely secure your network.

Network security will cost money; but be clear, no matter how much money you spend, you will never have a 100-percent secure network. It is this slight bit of doubt, the wondering what the other guy is doing, that keeps the job interesting for security professionals. While interesting for people like me, this truism creates a particular problem for those attempting to implement their own security policy. How much should I spend on security so that I can secure my network? But how do I know how much "too much" is? In other words, what is the point of diminishing returns for my network security program?

The first section of this book helps to answer this question. We review what steps can be taken in the creation of a security policy. This process will help determine how much what we are trying to protect is worth. From that value, we will then examine the various elements that go into implementing the security policy — otherwise known as the security model. This examination will assist us in creating a security policy that will not only satisfy a network security professional, but also make the accounting department happy.

1.2   The Path to Network Security

A secure network is not an accident. Secure networks generally are not the product of random changes, additions, and additional network functionality. While there is no doubt that someone would be able to point to a friend or associate who has a "secure" network that happened to "organically grow" out of years of trial and error and switching things around according to the zodiac, this is really the exception. Secure networks are built out of a solid understanding of how networking works: How *does* a packet of information get from a client to a remote server? What happens at the server to make it return another packet to the client? How does this return packet of information get back to the client?

A secure network is built from policy. I am the type of person who cringes when I hear the term "policy." Sometimes, Dilbert-esque policies leave me mystified as to their intent and reason, other than to annoy the average end user. Despite this policy aversion of my own, I am the first to ask a customer to help me create their security policy. This ensures that you and your customer/client/boss/management all understand what you need to do. A security policy is a broad statement of principle. Once the policy is completed, then the security model can be implemented. This is the step-by-step guide that puts the principle into practice. Chapter 2, "Managing Network Security," addresses the critical issue of creating a security policy. It also provides critical tips to avoid your transformation into the pointy-haired manager type as well. By creating a policy that has input, is well understood, and is fairly enforced, most of the negative connotations of "policy" will disappear.

In my experience, the most difficult part of creating a security policy is this initial step. This step needs the most participation, the most research, the most input, and the most thought. Done correctly, implementing the security model is a relatively straightforward matter of choosing the hardware, placing it in strategic points in your network, configuring it, and continually testing and monitoring it. Simple enough. Right?

Without a basic understanding of this process, it is difficult to create a system that can reliably secure your network. If you are missing this information or feel that you could stand a refresher, Chapter 3, "The Network Stack and Security," will be a good place to start. One place that I find even some seasoned security professionals failing is a solid understanding of routing and routing issues. Chapter 3, in addition to the normal presentation of network hardware and protocol operation, such as TCP/IP, also examines some of the more commonly encountered routing protocols and how they can play a part in the secure network.

While there is no shortage of obscure and confusing acronyms, protocol types, hardware, and software vendors to confuse the issue of implementation, for the most part, all of network security only uses about half a dozen different technologies. While the names of who wrote the programs and the decals on the side of the hardware may change, network security uses the same basic ideas over and over again. A series of chapters on access-control, firewalls, VPNs (virtual private networks), and intrusion detection systems cover all of the basics of each technology. Once the basics are reviewed, we then examine how they fit into our network security policy: how do they assist us in creating our security model? It is in these chapters that we will learn the amount and type of protection that each technology affords us and, more importantly, how to wisely invest in the technology to maximize security for minimum cost.

In addition to the material covering the common security technologies, we also examine some network applications and designs that, while not directly related to security, do affect the security of our network through their very operation. Wireless networking — all the rage for its ease of deployment and user friendliness — is one example. How can a wireless network with security that has been demonstrated over and over again to be faulty be part of the "secure" network? We examine our options and explore other applications that need special consideration in Chapters 4–11.

Comparing our security policy with the technologies available to us will then allow us to examine a number of case studies to put all the pieces together. For four networks, ranging from a small SOHO to enterprise-class networks, we examine the process of creating a sample security policy and then build a security model around that policy.

Finally, the book concludes with perhaps the most satisfying element of network security — penetration testing. When you attempt this on some-one else's network, you are considered a criminal; but when you test your own network for vulnerabilities, you are providing valuable insight into your own network because you see it as it is seen by the rest of the world or by others utilizing your internal network. By performing network pene-tration testing — either through a contracted third party or by yourself — you ensure that the fruits of your labor, starting with the first meeting that discussed security policy, have been worth your time and effort. Chapter 12, "Network Penetration Testing," discusses the process of testing your own network, points you in the direction of some common tools (which changes frequently) and techniques for penetration testing, and discusses what to expect from a third party if you were to hire them to test the secu-rity of your network.

1.3 Who Should Read This Book?

I hope that the primary value of the book will be to those who are entrusted by others to provide network security to their organization, company, or club. Network security is commonly complicated but it does not need to be. By following some commonly known best practices, you can safely secure your network under budget yet still allow yourself a good night's sleep. This book will show you how.

This text is not intended to serve as a study guide for any security cer-tification. That said, most security certifications have a "common body of knowledge" on which they test. This common body of knowledge may be quite extensive yet not very deep, as in the case of the ICS^2 CISSP — or very deep yet not broad, as in the case of the SANS GIAC certification. If you are already a CISSP, you will likely not find much new in terms of information in this text. However, if you are already a CISSP, then you did not purchase this book to use as a study aid. The primary value of this book to those who already hold security certifications is to assist them in the process of work-ing with and educating others who may not have the same level of exper-tise. If you are in the process of obtaining either of the above security cer-tifications, this book will either instruct or reinforce the most common and critical elements of network security.

This book also does not extensively cover any particular technology or provide detailed configuration steps for each product. In the process of obtaining my own networking certifications, I have a stack of books for each discipline, each of which is taller than my own 6'5" frame. The number of Linux books alone fills a number of bookshelves in my home office. Each of these texts taught me valuable information; however, I find the ones most likely to collect dust are those that provide specific command references for a particular application. Not only does the technology move too fast to keep those books valuable for more than a month, but through the process of reading, consulting, working closely with clients implementing their own security policies and complex network needs, I have come to realize that although the checkboxes may change and the command-line interface or GUI may look different from box to box, what really matters when working with various networking products is knowing *how* the technology works and *why* I would be checking an option box in the first place. Sometimes, I even feel that some books use the screen shots to bump up their page count, with little long-term benefit to the reader. There is simply no substitute for learning the technology through trial and error and research. In this book I minimize the learning curve for you if you are new or otherwise thrust into the role of providing network security. To do this, I explain how things work and give you the information you need to compare one product against another. From there it is up to you to research the vendor's documentation to learn how to configure a given product.

Chapter 2
Managing Network Security

Let us clarify something right from the beginning. Technology alone is not going to secure your network. A trip to your local networking superstore will not necessarily make your network secure, even if you have to back up the minivan to take everything back to the office. The problem is that underlying all security technologies is a single inconsistency that tends to skew all of our hard work and planning — people. That is correct — you, I, and that guy or gal down the hall who is constantly dumping his or her trash in your trash bin. People screw things up. Of course, that is also part of our charm; but people will misconfigure firewalls, tell friends their passwords, make a programming error that causes a server to crash when unexpected input is entered; and odds are that it was another person who typed in the unexpected input in the first place!

The point of this is that we cannot rely on technology to protect our network because the people who create the technology are not perfect. We cannot expect technology to protect us against computer crime. Crime and technology have a long history together. The invention of the wheel did not eliminate crime; it just made it easier to get away from the scene. We should not fool ourselves into thinking that we have finally arrived at *the* generation that has finally figured out a way to make us immune to crime through the use of technology.

When we start thinking about network security, we need to think about security as a system — not a single technology. By reading this book, you will hopefully be convinced that your information is secured through the use of your information security policies, and not any single piece of technology that you are using. Sadly, I have had more than one conversation with a customer that went like this:

"Well, we have a firewall. Won't that make my network secure?" the client responds.

"It certainly is a good start, but a firewall does not imply a secure network. We can't, however, determine what you *need* for security until we can determine what you need to secure," I counter, sitting down to a conference table and giving my pen a twist to expose the tip.

> A couple of scratches on the notepad later and I am confident that the pen is working. I look up to see the customer still looking at me.
>
> "What do you mean, what we want to secure? We want to secure our network against hackers."

Most people clearly understand the need to secure their network. Looking at any poll of IT professionals, CIOs, and managers, the need to secure their network against "hackers" generally tops the top-three concerns that these people have about their network. Unfortunately, this high priority generally leads to technology that drives the security.

When technology drives the security, you have a situation in which the IT staff looks around and thinks, "What do I have that can secure my network?" In general, their gaze eventually falls upon a firewall — perhaps even a VPN (virtual private network). While I will never be one to argue that a firewall is *not* a good idea to include in a security model, this is not the proper approach to creating network security. It creates a security model that is built around what security a particular device can provide, rather than the security the network needs. I counsel my clients that, instead of talking about hardware and software, the first order of business should be to create a security policy. A security policy is a high-level statement of principle and describes the needs of the network. Once we know what we need to do, we can then discuss the security model. The security model is the actual hardware, software, and configuration guidelines that will be used to enforce the policy.

2.1 The Big Picture: Security Policies from A to Z

One of my hobbies is amateur bodybuilding. This hobby also happens to provide a good nontechnical example of the difference between a policy and a model. I am often asked by people in the gym, "How can I make good gains from working out?" The questioner then typically modifies the query by defining what "gains" means to them, either losing fat or gaining muscle mass. Either way, I can respond to them with a *policy*, "Eat well. Work out consistently."

My *policy* on maximizing gains is clearly a high-level statement of principle. It broadly defines how the questioner should obtain his goal of "good gains." Rarely, however, do people nod knowingly when I tell them this and run off to put it into practice. They also need a *model*. The model is a series of steps that defines "eat this many calories per day; eat this many meals per day; ensure you get this much protein per day; work out this many times per week; do these exercises; etc." The person can agree in principle to the policy, but to actually implement the policy, that person needs a model to follow.

A properly constructed security policy has a very specific structure. The security policy is the high-level document that describes the philosophy, business environment, and goals of the organization. To implement these goals, specific steps must be taken. This is the role of security standards and procedures. A high-level policy statement such as "All financial transactions between business partners will remain confidential and arrive with guaranteed integrity" is pretty broad. Our standards and procedures may further state that "Confidentiality between networks utilizing the public Internet will employ either (1) an IPSec VPN with 256-bit AES or equivalent security. Identity will be established through the exchange of RSA signatures via a secure mechanism and validated by a third party certification authority; or (2) an MPLS-based VPN between business partners that share the same service provider. Null-encryption with the MD5 hash algorithm shall be used on such connections to assure the integrity of any transmissions." This statement offers a couple of specific ways to provide the confidentiality and integrity between your site and remote business partners.

Even then, standards and procedures are not enough to actually implement the solutions. For this, a configuration guide is required. As the name suggests, the configuration guide is a step-by-step guide that shows which options to enable, what values to fill in the provisioning order, etc. This is the step-by-step guide that is used to put the security policy into place. Together, the structure of a security policy looks like the diagram shown in Exhibit 1. The process of creating the security policy can be broken down into nine distinct steps, with additional optional steps as required. These nine steps are listed below:

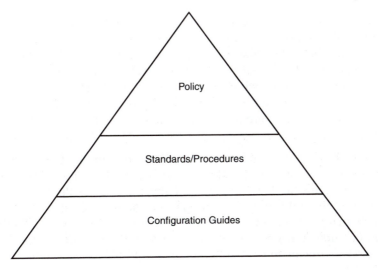

Exhibit 1. The Security Policy Model

1. Obtain management support
2. Identify information assets
3. Draft policy statement
4. Perform risk analysis
5. Select countermeasures
6. Create security standards
7. Create configuration guides
8. Implement
9. Review

Each of these steps is discussed in detail as the chapter progresses.

2.1.1 Getting Management Buy-In

Sometimes it can be difficult to explain to management why the time and effort must be spent in constructing a security policy. At the same time, without this important step, the remainder of the security policy process is somewhat pointless. By the end of this chapter it should be clear that this is a step integral to the successful implementation of network security. Until that point, when a baseline of security has been established on the network, getting the process rolling can be a Sisyphean task.

There are practical and legal reasons that management must be involved with the top-down construction of the security policy from the beginning. Remember: you cannot simply drop a bunch of technology into a network and expect to achieve security. The best improvement in information security is obtained when the behavior of individuals can be modified as well. To do this, the authority of management is essential.

Creating a security policy from the bottom up, where several concerned IT employees get together to discuss ways to secure the network, is ineffective in practice. The view of company priorities of the IT staff will most likely differ from that of management staff. When these two perspectives come into conflict, guess which one wins most often? The practical reason for obtaining management support is simply that without it, the security policy will quickly become marginalized and a point of frustration for all involved.

The legal rationale is much more complicated. In most countries, the management of an organization has a financial responsibility to the owners of a company. In a publicly traded company, this is the shareholder. When considering the liability that a company or senior executives may face when security is breached, there are several concepts with which one should become familiar. In no particular order, they are *due diligence, due care*, and the *prudent man rule*.

Many times, it is a natural instinct to consider that all computer crimes are solely the fault of hackers. After all, it was they who broke the law. From a legal perspective however, it is only part of the story. If the company is publicly traded and senior management did not take any steps to protect important company data or otherwise made it easy for an attacker to walk away with the crown jewels due to their inaction, in the U.S., senior management may be held personally liable for up to $290 million under the 1997 Federal Sentencing Guidelines. When determining the guilt or innocence of such an individual, the above-mentioned terms of due diligence, due care, and the prudent man rule will be carefully weighed against the facts of the case.

Due diligence pertains to activities that ensure that network protection mechanisms are continually maintained. This means making sure that the network is protected on an ongoing basis and that the IT and information security staff roles and responsibilities are defined.

Due care refers to the steps that a company has taken to show that it has accepted responsibility for actions that occur within, its resources, and its employees. Of course, parts of those resources are the network components. Most modern companies have a large amount of their value tied up in the data that they store on their network. Not protecting that information is not exercising due care.

Finally, the *prudent man rule* is a rule that management must follow when determining if due diligence and due care have been exercised properly. The prudent man rule states that management is required to perform those duties that "prudent" people would normally take, given similar circumstances. Due diligence can be proven with the existence of a security policy that has been properly implemented. The principle of due care outlines steps that must be taken to enforce the security policy and the network resources. Finally, a security policy that has demonstrated a thorough risk analysis will prove that, given the nature of the resources to protect, prudent steps were taken to protect them.

The concept of the prudent man rule as it relates to a security policy is worth a bit more discussion. Can managers approve a firewall installation and claim that they were meeting their legal responsibilities to the company? That depends. If the objects they were trying to protect (i.e., data, hardware, personnel, even their own reputations) were of a non-critical nature and the threats that the network were vulnerable to were largely of a packet-based nature over an IP network, then it can be argued that the prudent man rule had been followed. On the other hand, if the network contained objects of a critical nature that attracted the attention of well-financed and patient criminals or even foreign governments who could launch a wide variety of attacks, then it would be difficult to argue that the prudent man rule had been applied correctly because, clearly, a firewall alone could not provide the level of protection warranted by the data.

The question then becomes: how does this fated manager determine if the prudent man rule has been applied correctly? To do this, a risk analysis must be performed.

2.1.2 Identify Information Assets

I have yet to begin studying for an MBA; but if I do, I am confident that the studies will go well because I have one fundamental element of business management already under my belt. An *asset* is anything of value that the company has. This may be intellectual property, trade secrets, copyrights, databases, workstations, servers, routers, and printers. To know what the security policy must refer to, we need to know what the priorities are on our network. To obtain this information, a detailed inventory should be performed of all hardware and software assets, along with interviews with the management structure, to obtain a clear priority of what resources are priorities in the company.

2.1.3 Regulatory Expectations

In some cases, there may not be a lot of flexibility regarding what the emphasis of the security policy should be. There may be times when information security requirements are legislated or enforced through industry and trade groups. Before drafting a security policy, ensure that all regulatory requirements have been met. Some of the most common regulatory sites are described below.

- *Health Information Portability and Accountability Act (HIPAA).* Regulations regarding the treatment of patient healthcare information. If your work is in any way related to the health-care industry, you have heard about this act. Find more information at www.cms.hhs.gov.
- *Gramm–Leach–Bliley Act (GLBA).* What HIPAA is to patient privacy, the Gramm–Leach–Bliley Act is to financial institutions regarding consumer rights. Most people who know about the GLBA are familiar with it for the requirement of "opt-in" marketing instead of the "opt-out" marketing that most Web sites tend to engage in when you provide them with any personal information. Find more information on GLBA requirements at www.ftc.gov.
- *Federal Deposit Insurance Corporation (FDIC).* Providing deposit insurance for millions of households, the FDIC is a staple of the American banking industry. As can be imagined, there are a number of suggestions that relate to privacy, E-banking, and other online transactions. Find out more at http://www.fdic.gov.
- *1974 Privacy Act.* Stemming from the Watergate era, the 1974 Privacy Act seeks to balance national interests with the need for personal

privacy. It provides guidelines on keeping individual's records and on individual rights to review such documents. Find information regarding these requirements at http://www.usdoj.gov.

- *Department of Defense Information Technology Security Certification and Accreditation Process (DITSCAP).* This security document is used by the U.S. Department of Defense (DoD) in the certification and accreditation of all IT systems. Policy related to the DoD must meet its guidelines. Find a copy of DITSCAP at http://mattche.iiie.disa.mil.
- *Federal Communications Commission (FCC).* The FCC is involved with most facets of communication, including information systems. It has guidelines for everything from the Freedom of Information Act to initiatives on Homeland Security. Find information regarding the FCC and information security at www.fcc.gov.
- *ISO 15408.* Even if we call these by their more common name, the "Common Criteria" Specifications may not be all that well-known to many. While the Common Criteria is not a strictly U.S initiative as all the other resources are, it does represent a best practice and common language describing the security capabilities of technology. The Common Criteria represents an attempt to standardize the way we evaluate information security products across vendors and even technologies. Find information on the Common Criteria at www.commoncriteria.org.
- *ISO 17799.* These ISO recommendations are controls that describe the current consensus on best practices in information security. All alone, it is an extremely useful guide for those interested in implementing their own information security policy. Find information on ISO 17799 at www.iso-17799.com.

This is, of course, only the tip of the iceberg regarding organizations and legislation that may affect your company security policy. Other than the inclusion of the ISO, the list above is conspicuously United States-centric. Those readers in other countries should research their own applicable laws and regulations.

2.1.4 Draft Security Policy

Before discussing risk analysis and the creation of policy, some vocabulary lessons are in order. What follows is a general discussion of terms that often find their way into a security policy. We discuss later that a good security policy is written in terms that end users can easily understand; but when discussing our security policy with other professionals, we should make sure that we get our vocabulary right.

In creating a security policy, we must first consider what to achieve. This should seem simple — a more secure network, of course! But what defines a secure network? Security professionals like to describe a secure network as one that supports three essential goals:

1. *Confidentiality.* Simply put, this is the expectation that private data will remain private. This can apply to data in several forms. It might pertain to a database in which certain data elements are available only to those who possess the proper permissions. It might mean that those who capture packets over a network cannot decipher the information in them. It might mean that users' personal files on a file server or desktop computer cannot be read by those without proper permissions. A company is generally not excited about some-one reading all of its user data, as recent cases involving E-commerce, credit card numbers, and lax corporate security illustrate. In each of the above instances, there is an expectation of confidentiality, but the way that confidentiality is achieved in each case will be different. A security policy must consider under what circumstances confidentiality is expected from the users. One that uses IPSec to create a VPN between two points will do nothing to protect data already stored on a file server. Enforcing file access permission levels will do nothing if an authorized user sends the information over a network where it can be read by anyone with a packet sniffer.

2. *Integrity.* Integrity is the expectation that the data the user is reading is in its original, authorized, unmodified form. This does not mean that data can never change. If that were the case, little data would be of use to us for any significant length of time. It does mean, however, that data that changes can only be changed by those authorized. As an example, data sent over a network, such as an important e-mail, could be captured, changed, and then resent — or a forged piece of e-mail could be sent to begin with! Either way, the e-mail recipients would like to be aware that all is not as it seems. Another example is files on a file server that house student records. A criminal in this case might be more interested in altering data than simply reading it — to reduce debt or change grades. As with confidentiality, the above examples were all related to a user's expectation of user data integrity, but each would have to achieve integrity in a different way.

3. *Availability.* Availability is ensuring that data is available when users expect it. One of the simplest ways to disrupt a network that many rely upon for work and information is to simply render the network unavailable. While compromising confidentiality and integrity generally takes knowledge and skill on the part of an attacker, denying access to network resources (otherwise known as a denial-of-service [DoS] attack) can be fairly straightforward and inelegant. Availability can be disrupted in a number of ways, and each needs a different countermeasure to reduce the risk. Locking out their user names,

or rendering their PCs inoperable through a virus or Trojan can prevent user access to their own PCs. Disabling a switch, reconfiguring a router, or simply flooding the network with more traffic than it can otherwise handle can attack the network itself that is used to communicate with remote servers. Finally, attacking the endpoint of the communication process by disabling the remote server will also effectively DoS the network users. Availability can even be affected by something as simple as shutting off a power switch on a server. Clearly, there are many elements to consider when ensuring that network resources are available to users. Each of these risks and their accompanying responses are different. They all must be considered when writing a security policy.

As we move on in our discussion of security to discuss the major threats that a network faces, we will see that most network threats are also threats that affect one of the above goals of our security policy.

A security policy appears in many formats; the one presented below is just a suggestion. Regardless of the format, however, there should be several characteristics that every security policy should have.

First and foremost, it should be easy to read and navigate. Most people's experience with legal documents, such as mortgage loans and medical prescriptions, make them think that in order to be valid, a document must be presented in the most confusing way possible with a great many references to items in the third person. This is not the case. A security policy should spell out the policy as plainly as possible — the clearer, the better. The security policy should also attempt to be precise without being redundant. There will be instances when someone will challenge the security policy in defense of their own actions. The basis of that challenge will be ambiguity in the wording of the policy or vagueness in the definition of a term.

With that in mind, a security policy typically has the following sections:

- *Introduction/Abstract.* The introduction (or Abstract) describes the document and its purpose — to provide information regarding the position of the organization regarding information security.
- *Context/Operating Assumptions.* Any influence on the creation of the security policy should be stated here. For example, "As a publicly traded corporation, we have a responsibility to...." Additionally, any laws or regulations that may affect the security policy itself can be introduced in this section.
- *Policy Statement.* This is the main section of the document. Remember that this is a high-level statement of policy; thus, it is rare to find a policy statement more than a couple of pages in length. Words such as "confidentiality," "integrity," and "availability" should be emphasized here, along with the organization's information assets.

For example, "Our business relies upon the uninterrupted services of Internet and internal e-mail. The integrity of all communications originating from our company should not be called into doubt. Furthermore, the confidentiality that our clients place in our communications shall not be misplaced."

- *Definitions.* Anything that can be disputed in the policy itself should be defined here. The primary purpose of this section is to maintain the ease of readability of the policy statement itself and allow users to easily find information clarifying policy statements.
- *Authority/Responsibilities.* A security policy is only going to be as good as the support it receives at the top. The security policy should clearly state who at the top supports it. This section may also detail the enforcement and implementation responsibilities of the security policy. Finally, penalties associated with noncompliance of the security policy can be outlined here. It is important to include arbitration procedures if penalties are going to be assigned.
- *Review.* A security policy changes over time. There should be regularly scheduled reviews of the entire policy at least annually. Reviews should also be considered after any computer incidents have been resolved, as it is likely that the reason the incident occurred in the first place is due to an omission or oversight in the security policy. At some point, users of the network may request a change to the security policy to facilitate a new service that their job requires. Thus, the review process should also address the issue of change management and detail how a user makes a request for change to the security policy.
- *Distribution.* Ideally, if I were to walk into your organization, I should be able to ask any employee, "Where is a copy of your security policy?" and they would respond with a sure answer. It is the responsibility of those creating the security policy to ensure that the document is accessible to all employees of the organization and that they are duly noted of changes and updates to the policy itself.

A security policy may be accompanied by several other supplementary documents supporting information security. The most common documents include the acceptable use policy (AUP), the incident response policy, and the disaster recovery/business continuity plan. Each of these documents is created in a manner very similar to the creation of the security policy. The difference is that the security policy should be considered the master plan, and each of the supporting polices supports the overall goals of the security policy. In a sense, each of the above policies is a separate standards and procedures document describing how the goals of the security policy are ultimately met.

2.1.5   Assessing Risk

Part of the process of creating an information security policy is *risk assessment.* We cannot accurately create a security policy that reflects our business requirements and reduces risk to an acceptable level until we have a clear picture of what the risks are that threaten our assets.

In this section we discuss the art and science of determining risk. When done properly, risk assessment is an important way to determine the appropriate response in dollars and effort in the implementation of a security policy. The construction of a security policy is a multi-stage process. The primary step in creating a security policy is first determining what you are trying to protect, and then determining who you are trying to protect your data from and the likely risks that your network will face.

This preliminary work is known as a risk analysis. Risk analysis can be categorized into two major groups: (1) a *quantitative* analysis that attempts to add up the value of an asset and compare it with the cost of an associated threat; and (2) a *qualitative* analysis that essentially asks the people most knowledgeable about the company, "What do you think?" Both approaches have their advantages and, in the end, a compromise between the two will end up as the basis for the security policy.

To properly discuss risk, there are several terms that must be explained. The first is the term "risk." A risk is defined as the probability of a *threat* taking advantage of a *vulnerability.*

A *vulnerability* is a weakness that can be exploited by an attacker. When considering the entire range of network security, the number of vulnerabilities is just staggering. Unlocked doors to server rooms are vulnerabilities; unnecessary services running on a server or even host computer can add unnecessary vulnerabilities due to flaws in either the program itself or the security protecting the program. Data backups that are not regularly performed, checked, and stored in secure locations are vulnerabilities. Easy-to-guess passwords are a vulnerability, but forcing users to use hard-to-guess — and hard to remember — passwords creates another vulnerability when the user sticks the password to the side of the monitor or under the keyboard.[1]

A *threat* is any danger to the organization's assets. This can be a person — an unsuspecting employee or malicious hacker, a natural disaster, or a foreign nation. Each of these threats results in a violation of the company's security policy. While the hacker may seek to subvert the confidentiality of information, the unsuspecting employees, in an attempt to make their daily jobs more productive, could violate the integrity of the data. An earthquake in San Francisco, on the other hand, could seriously affect the availability of specific data for users all around the world.

When a threat has a chance to exploit a vulnerability, there is risk that needs to be addressed. The vulnerability of an unlocked server room door, with the threat of a malicious insider, creates a risk that could affect confidentiality, integrity, and availability all at once. On-site storage of backups coupled with a catastrophic fire creates a risk that seriously affects the availability of data.

To summarize:

$$\text{Threat} + \text{Vulnerability} = \text{Risk}^2$$

When a company suffers losses from a threat, this is known as an *exposure*. When the malicious insider (threat) walks through the unlocked server room door (vulnerability) and shuts off all the servers, the company that left the door open now has an exposure on its hands. In short, exposures are what most companies try to avert upon recognizing a combination of threats and vulnerabilities.

To mitigate the chance of exposure, *countermeasures* are implemented. A countermeasure reduces the chance of exposure from a given vulnerability/threat combination. A countermeasure to the vulnerability of an unlocked door would be one of the most cost-effective methods of physical site security yet developed: a lock. Note that in this instance the countermeasure was successful in eliminating the vulnerability (locking the door) and therefore reducing the chance for exposure. Our countermeasure, however, had no effect on the threat. In general, this is true no matter the application. Vulnerabilities are weaknesses that can be countered. Threats, on the other hand, are potential dangers of any type. A threat can never be fully eliminated, only planned for.

From this discussion one should infer that vulnerabilities are factors that are within the realm of control of the network owners. Threats are those elements outside the realm of control of the network owners. Prudence would dictate that vulnerabilities are discovered and countermeasures implemented. Threats must be considered and, through interactions with vulnerabilities, their impact assessed.

Just because there is a risk does not mean that it is something that needs to be addressed in a security policy. Strictly speaking, there is the risk that a threat such as an invading species of intelligent marsupials from another solar system could exploit the vulnerability of our building's lack of shielding against energy weapons. However, addressing the risk of protecting our corporate headquarters against such a risk would be very expensive and difficult to explain at a shareholders meeting. While this is an admittedly fantastic example, other cases might not be so cut and dry. The events of September 11th, 2001, are a case in point. On that day, a number of risks that seemed unlikely suddenly became within the realm of possibility. Can you defend your network against every possible risk now that airplanes can be used as weapons? There needs to be a way to allow security professionals and network managers to determine which risks are worth protecting against and which are not. This process is known as *risk analysis*.

Risk analysis allows us to sort our risk exposure and, based on the possible damage from an exposure, justify the cost of the security. Once the risks are identified and our possible loss from exposure is defined, we can then begin the process of *risk management*. Risk management is the process of reducing risk to an acceptable level, transferring the risk to another entity such as an insurance company, rejecting the risk outright, or accepting the risk.

As mentioned, risk analysis can be grouped into two broad approaches: the first is the quantitative approach and the second is the qualitative approach. Each has advantages, and each will be discussed in turn.

Long before entering the field of networking, I was a high school teacher. The quantitative/qualitative discussion would surface many times, generally in reference to student performance. When quantitative assessment was called for, the result would be a number of correct answers combined in some ratio with the number of incorrect answers. From the student's point of view, the assessment was cut and dry and answers were right or wrong (not withstanding partial credit!). At the end of the test, they received a number that was their score. Qualitative assessment was much more difficult to grade. Students had to meet a number of criteria for which success was somewhat subjective and depended on the perspective of the teacher doing the evaluation. Qualitative assessment in many ways was superior to quantitative assessment in that it could require a number of skills on the part of the student to successfully complete assignments and as long as the evaluation criteria was clearly laid out it could be quite fair — as long as the same instructor did the grading for every test. For this single reason, quantitative assessment is still the norm in education. Many people are comforted by the "right" answer and will not dispute the results on assignments.

When doing risk assessment, you will find that the same prejudices hold true. When justifying the expense needed for risk management, a number is the final answer that many are interested in seeing. Of course, as we explore the process of quantitative risk analysis, it will become clear that some subjective (qualitative) processes will need to occur. For the purposes of a security policy then, the quantitative and qualitative processes should be seen as complementary; both need to be understood for effective risk analysis.

At a high level, the process of risk analysis involves three steps:

1. Assign value to assets.
2. Assign cost to risks.
3. Choose countermeasures appropriate to the value of the asset and cost of risk exposure.

2.1.5.1 Assign Value to Assets. This includes such common-sense items as the cost to maintain and replace the asset, but also some not-so-clear items such as the value of the asset to the competition or the value of the asset to the company. All these elements should be considered when determining asset value. At one particular meeting, I was working with management to decide on a value for its database. The going was tough, so I presented the situation in two simple scenarios. First, I held up a CD-RW that I had taken out of my briefcase. "This is a copy of your customer database and your business plan for the next five years. How much are you willing to pay to get it back?" Then I picked up a conveniently located computer and held it over my head. "This is your customer database and I am about to destroy it. How much are you willing to pay to get me to put this back on the table?"

While the demonstrations were primarily for dramatic effect, they did illustrate to the customer the need for considering all possibilities when determining an asset's value to a company. In this particular case, when I presented the problem as such, the customer realized that most of the value of the company was locked up in that customer database and to lose it would essentially cause the company to have to shut its doors. In this case, the value of the asset to the customer was the value of the business itself. Realistically speaking, there were other assets that contributed to the value of the business; but for this customer, the perceived value was very closely tied to its customer database.

Not all assets have such an impact on a business. Consider a network connection. Another customer I have worked with noted that he lost $100,000 per hour in orders and productivity every time his Internet connection failed. In this case, the company could survive as long as its data was intact and could withstand an Internet outage of several days, but there was a clear value assigned to its connectivity that was determined by closely examining the daily online business volumes and the payroll of staffers that normally handled the E-commerce orders. It became much easier to evaluate our options for risk management once these values were known.

Information may have to come from more than one source when evaluating the value of an asset. The finance department is a good place to start to get acquisition, maintenance, and replacement costs for hardware and software. The finance department can also give a good idea of the business that relies on network objects. The IT staff is a good place to check when determining the costs of outages and the damage that a particular threat agent could pose to the systems.

In some cases, important value to the business cannot be determined based on a line in a financial statement. What is the value of a company's reputation? Some companies have lost more than a billion dollars in market capitalization because of the public perception of the company after a high-profile attack. Many businesses do not even bother to report computer crime because they feel that public trust of the company itself will deteriorate if this information were to become public. If your company offers online purchases, what would be the cost to the company if it were determined that its Web site had been hacked? Because you were, of course, storing customer data on another server (of course you were!), none of the customer data was compromised, yet how do you convince your customers that this was the case and restore their confidence in your ability to keep their secrets secure? In this case, the value is tangible to your company, but assigning a dollar value can be more difficult.

2.1.5.2 Assign Cost to Risks. The official term in risk assessment when assigning a cost to a particular risk is known as determining the *single loss expectancy* (SLE). Based on a per-exposure comparison, how much would the realization of each risk cost your network assets? In English, that means how much would it cost you if someone dropped a network server out a window? How much would it cost to recover that data? What would be the value of the lost productivity? Because there are a number of risks, each with a varying degree of associated cost, there will be a number of risks defined for each asset. Recalling our definition of risk, we can provide some examples to solidify our understanding for assigning cost. If a threat such as a hacker was able to compromise our Web server through vulnerability in the HTTP server software, at a minimum we would have to restore the server from original media or a known, good backup. This may take several hours, during which time the server is unavailable for use. What would be the cost associated with recovering from this risk if there were an exposure?

Another example would be the threat of a virus infecting the client host systems due to out-of-date virus scanning software. In a system of 25 end users, what would be the cost associated with removing the virus software from the host PCs? At a very minimum, the anti-virus signatures would need to be updated, and each person would be required or taught how to run the anti-virus software. The costs associated with this exposure would be primarily the time required to employ effective countermeasures and lost productivity on the part of the end users. This estimation would be optimistic in that it assumes that no further damage had been done to the host operating system.

When evaluating the cost associated with a risk, knowing how much a single exposure will cost you is not enough to make a financial or resource decision. How often the exposure will occur, or how likely the exposure is, also needs to be considered. A meteorite large enough to destroy a city may hit the Earth every 100,000 years. Couple that with the chances that this meteorite will also happen to hit your city and then the chance of exposure may drop to one in 100,000,000 years.[3] While the cost of exposure may be the value of the company, dividing that number by 100,000,000 gives you an average estimate for how much this risk will cost your company annually.

Happily, such catastrophic risks are rare. Other risks may happen with more frequency. Consider the case of the e-mail virus. Over the past five years, there have been an average of two major e-mail attachment viruses per year, with other smaller outbreaks here and there. This is a risk that your company will be exposed to and one that will require appropriate countermeasures. Likewise, your network will be the focus of automated network attacks, perhaps several per day. The annual rate of occurrence for exposure to this threat would be high.

2.1.5.3 Choose Countermeasures Appropriate to the Value of the Asset and the Cost of Risk Exposure. By comparing the average annual cost of each risk with the value of the asset, a meaningful dollar value can be established that allows a company to determine how much it should spend each year to protect its assets from the various risks to which it may be exposed. Hypothetically speaking, if a company establishes that each virus outbreak that its network is exposed to cost $25,000 and the company knows from its own records and observations of the industry that it will be exposed to two attacks per year, then this risk will end up costing the company an average of $50,000 per year. This then becomes the maximum budget for implementing countermeasures to the risk of viral infection. If the faithful and hardworking IT director and his or her stalwart group of network engineers can find a way to reduce the risk for less than $50,000, they have just made the accounting department happy. If, for some reason, it is determined that the risk cannot be reduced for an annual price of less than $75,000 a year, then the company has a decision to make. From a purely financial point of view, this solution does not make sense, given that the company would save $25,000 each year by simply doing nothing other than cleaning up virus infections as they occur. Several factors, notably the annualized rate of occurrence rising, may change this. There would only need to be, on average, one additional company-wide virus infection per year to make the $75,000 solution make sense. In some cases, the cost of reducing the risk to an acceptable level is going to be more than the value of the asset we are trying to safeguard. While in most instances the goal of risk analysis is to allow an intelligent reduction of risk through the use of countermeasures, in some cases the most intelligent thing to do is to assign the risk to another party, or simply accept it.

When the cost of the countermeasure is too high for a company to bear the fiscal responsibility on its own, it may choose to assign the risk to another party. In common parlance, this is referred to "getting insurance." For most individuals, the total cost of employing countermeasures to protect their primary asset, their home, against fire is too much for them to take on as individuals. At the same time, the cost of a single exposure to the threat of fire will ruin most families. In this case, the risk is assigned to an insurance company that assumes the risk for a price. The same strategy can apply to network resources. If the cost of replicating the network for use in a catastrophic event is too high for a company to maintain, they can assign that risk to an insurance company that will reimburse the company if such an exposure occurs.

When accepting risk, a decision can also be made that if exposure should occur, the company would simply assume the costs. Accepting risk may be appropriate if the cost to reduce the risk is too high, as is the cost of assigning the risk. The risk may be considered to have such a low annualized rate of occurrence, or will cost so much to protect against, that countermeasures are simply unrealistic to implement. The previously stated risk of invasion from an alien species is most likely one that is so low that most reasonable and prudent people simply accept the risk.[4] There is an element of chance in this approach, however. Choosing to accept a risk simply because it is the easiest solution to risk management may mean that if that risk were ever realized, you are out of business.

No matter which approach is taken to respond to risk, a thorough risk analysis will serve two purposes: (1) it will allow security managers and financial officers to determine the proper, financially responsible response to risks facing the network; and (2) it can serve as evidence of prudent action on the part of management to protect the company's resources.

Before moving on, let us summarize the new information discussed thus far:

- To determine how much to spend on information security, you first need to evaluate the value of your information assets.
- Enumerate the likely risks that these assets would face and the likely cost if one of the risks were to materialize.
- Choose countermeasures to the risks you have identified based upon the effectiveness and cost of the countermeasure relative to the cost of the risk.

2.1.6 *Quantitative Risk Analysis*

Having discussed the basics of risk analysis, we can now examine some specifics.

The first step in risk analysis is gathering data. In the end, our decisions will be based on the initial data we gather. To avoid the unpleasant situation of "garbage in, garbage out" being applied to a security policy we are responsible for, the process of data gathering must be done methodically. The first step is to create a list of all the assets in the company. Each asset needs to be assigned a dollar value. Remember to include more than just the purchase price. This means the cost to replace the asset, the value of the asset to competitors, the impact that the asset has on the profitability of the company, etc.

I am often asked *how* to list assets. When working with customers, they might give me a number such as "Database server: $53,274.42." While I appreciate the preciseness of such a value and the effort that must have gone into obtaining it, it is in the interest of the customer to break down the functions of the server as much as possible. In this case, the database server may be the server itself with a value of $15,000. The database, on the other hand, has an estimated value of about $45,000 to the customer. The reason for the distinction is that each may have different vulnerabilities and different threats that need risk analysis. While a fire or explosion may destroy both, risk management may determine different countermeasures for each asset — the database may be backed up incrementally each evening with an image stored off-site. The server, which is a platform the company has standardized upon, may have a single standby server in a "warm standby" state, which also serves as a backup server for the company's 15 other servers.

Granularity in defining assets allows controls to be more accurately chosen. While more granularity is the goal for defining assets, do not go too far to the other side of the spectrum. I have run into more than one customer who had so many discrete assets that actually working with the information turned out to be more than a human can reasonably keep straight.

For each asset, the risks that the asset may be exposed to need to be enumerated, as does the potential for loss from each risk. These are hard numbers. Evidence that an unauthorized person such as a hacker has accessed the machine means that, at a minimum, the system needs to be reformatted and built from the original media or backed up from a copy with known integrity. For the sake of argument, let us assume that this cost is $2000 in labor, along with $10,000 in lost productivity from those who rely on the server for their daily operations. Your risk analysis spreadsheet may have a line in it that reads:

Server 1   Hacker $12,000

This value of $12,000 is known as the *single loss expectancy* (SLE) from the risk "Hacker." Another risk that we might add as an example is damage to the system board due to an electrical power surge. In this case, the data and OS may be intact but the server is offline until the system board can be replaced and tested. For purposes of discussion, let us assume that the cost in parts in labor creates a potential loss for this risk of $2000 and lost productivity amounts to another $15,000. Your asset sheet would contain another line:

Server 1   Hardware Failure — critical $17,000

As a final example for use later on in the risk analysis process, we will also include a natural disaster, a tornado. In this case, a tornado may simply destroy the entire server, dump it in a river, or even send it to Oz. In either case, the hardware will be unusable by our company and must be replaced. The hardware must be replaced and any information on the server must be backed up from a backup (which is hopefully stored far away from the affected site and not sitting in Oz with your server at the time the backups are needed).

Server 1   Natural Disaster — tornado $45,000

Another way to determine the SLE, and one that you might run across if pursuing a security certification is this equation:

$$\text{Asset} \times \text{Exposure factor (EF)} = \text{SLE}$$

While I prefer the more intuitive method, both will return the same results. The asset value is the same total value of the asset that we have discussed. The exposure factor (EF) is a fraction of the asset value that is lost per risk (i.e., the exposure factor percentage of value lost of the asset per risk exposure). When a server loses 50 percent of its value due to a worm attacking its SQL database, then we would say that the EF of such an incident is 0.5. If we assume that the total asset value of our database is $45,000 and that the EF for a hacker attack is 0.3, then

$$\$45,000 \times 0.3 = \$13,500$$

In this case, the SLE would be $13,500. While academically — and according to risk analysis theory — this is the correct method to determine the SLE, when working with customers, users, managers, and finance and IT departments to determine these values, it is easier to get them to think in terms of total dollars of potential loss when considering a risk. The following conversation may be one such example:

> "So Jerry, we have discussed the importance of your database to the overall operation of your business and we have provided an asset value of $45,000 once we consider all of the ways that this database contributes to your business. Now let's look at some specific risks. If a hacker were to compromise the server that housed the database, what do you think the exposure factor for the database would be? 0.2? 0.4? Higher? Come on, think!"

People have a difficult time thinking of their resources in these terms, especially if they are new to the process of risk analysis. It is far easier to work with Jerry to evaluate the potential loss by working with him to determine the steps and expenses that need to be in place to recover from the risk. The primary benefit of using the EF to determine the SLE is that the highest EF value you can have is "1." An EF of unity means that the SLE per risk would be the entire value of the asset. If Jerry were to describe to me $65,000 worth of work that would need to go into the recovery of the database due to a hacker, then either the value of the database has been underestimated to begin with, or Jerry needs to better understand his recovery processes.

A simpler way to determine the SLE is to calculate what it would cost to restore an asset to its original operating state prior to the incident. Jerry may say that the value of a particular server is $45,000. If the OS (operating system) needs to be reinstalled from a backup because of an attacker gaining unauthorized access to the system, then it is generally easier for people to figure out the dollar value than to estimate an exposure factor. In this case, Jerry might tell me that it normally takes four hours to restore a system from a backup and twelve hours to restore it from the original media. Accounting for the lost productivity and the hours spent restoring it, Jerry can estimate that the SLE from a database compromise would be, at the most, $25,000. That is a 0.55 EF, but Jerry does not need to know that.

Knowing the SLE, we can now perform a threat analysis. Recall that a threat can be human, natural, or technological in nature. Threats affect our systems through vulnerabilities. What must be determined is how often we can expect, on a yearly basis, to be exposed to particular threats if no countermeasures are put into place. This value is known as the *annualized rate of occurrence (ARO)*. The ARO is represented as a frequency from 0.0 representing a chance of occurrence of 0% to any given high number integer. The 0.0 end of the spectrum means that this is a threat that will never materialize. On the other hand, an ARO of 1.0 means that it is certain that the threat will take advantage of a vulnerability within a given year. An ARO of 0.1 means once every ten years, while an ARO of 0.25 would mean the threat has an annualized rate of occurrence of once every four years.

The careful reader might note that any given risk can suffer from exposure more than once per year. The default operating system installation with standard installation options on the Internet has a life span of hours[5] before becoming the victim of an Internet attacker. Does this mean that my ARO should be 365.0 as my server could potentially be compromised 365 times in a year, and 366 times during a leap year? The ARO is correctly defined as the *frequency* with which an event will occur. Below a value of 1.0, however, this frequency is very similar to a probability. The difference is that the maximum allowable value for a probability is 1.0, meaning that the event will occur with certainty. Experts differ on whether an ARO above 1.0 is meaningful in their calculations of ARO. After all, it is presumed that the controls implemented to protect the operating system described above will apply and protect the device on more than just a single day of any given year. You will not have to implement a new security policy on the second of January after the risk to network attacks was reduced on the first of January. Combining the ARO to consider the total frequency over 1.0 can lead to incredible assessments of the cost of exposure on an annual basis. Assuming that it costs a company $50,000 in lost time and recovery costs for each network incident, an ARO of 364 would lead to an annual cost of $18,250,000. That does not mean that $15,000,000 spent protecting that operating system would be cost-effective. Instead, the ARO is typically calculated at a factor of 1.0, indicating that you can bet the bank that if you do not spend some money implementing controls to reduce the risk, you had better include at least $50,000 in the operating budget for recovery because your organization will be exposed to the risk at some point during the year.

How is the ARO determined? Again, through research. Many Web sites and security texts will explain what the ARO is, but I have yet to find a concise listing of the common network threats that details all human, natural, and technological threat agents that face our networks. Some ARO rates may be higher for one natural threat than others. In the northeastern United States, the ARO for tornados, floods, and earthquakes is quite low — not so in other parts of the world. The midwestern United States may have a much higher ARO for tornados than earthquakes, a situation that is reversed on the west coast of North America. Human threats may have to be based on company history. Can it be expected that given the opportunity, a well-meaning person could compromise an asset through deleting important files? Does the company have resources that are known to the world at large and likely to be the targets of hackers? In these cases, the ARO might be quite high. Is the company located in an urban area known for its crime rate? Is it right down the street from the local police station? All these elements contribute to the ARO of specific threats and need to be considered on a case-by-case basis. For some natural threats such as fire and flooding, the ARO can be quickly established through a conversation with a local insurance agent.

When the frequency or likelihood of the threat affecting us annually is combined with the loss that we can expect from a single exposure, we can then determine the *annualized loss expectancy* (ALE).

For those of you intending to create a spreadsheet that automatically calculates values based on columns, you can determine the annualized loss expectancy (ALE) using the following formula:

$$SLE \times ARO = ALE$$

That is, on a per-risk basis, a single loss exposure (SLE) will incur an average cost known as the annualized loss expectancy (ALE) based upon its frequency of occurring annually (ARO).

While we can conclude, based on past experience and security resources, that a machine with no protection *will* be hacked at some point, this is an event that we can count on occurring at least once a year if no countermeasures are put in place. The critical hardware failure, however, is not unheard of, but many computer systems can run for years without hardware failures affecting their performance. Based on the manufacturer's mean time between failures (MTBF) rating and our own experience, we will assume that a given server will face exposure to a critical hardware issue once every three years. Applying these values to our current risk analysis, we find annualized loss expectancies of:

> Server 1   Hacker $12,000 (SLE)
> $\times$ 12 (ARO) = $144,000 (ALE)
>
> Server 1   Hardware failure: critical $17,000 (SLE)
> $\times$ 0.33 (ARO) = $5610 (ALE)
>
> Server 1   Natural disaster: tornado $45,000 (SLE)
> $\times$ 0.01 (ARO) = $450 (ALE)

Finally we have some information we can work with to help us create our security policy. Based on our estimations we can now decide how we want to handle the risk. Recall that our three options are to reduce the risk, assign the risk, or accept the risk.

Because continually restoring a server to an operational state each day would be time consuming and expensive and companies willing to assume the risk for such an event would be rare, your company decides to reduce the risk of hackers exploiting vulnerabilities on your server.

Part of our SLE calculations for the server's hardware failure assumed that the mean time to repair could be minimized by having the available hardware close to the affected server. This may mean keeping a stash of spare parts or even a complete server on standby in case of hardware failures. For a fee, some computer manufacturers will guarantee replacement parts delivered to your company within four hours. Paying the fee for prompt replacement parts would be a method of assigning the risk for hardware failures to a third party. Keeping parts handy would be a way of reducing the risk exposure of a critical hardware failure. In this example, we will reduce the risk by keeping a spare server on standby.

Keeping a server on standby would almost certainly cost more than $5610 annually because the hardware would have to be kept up, OS and software patches must be made to match the base configuration of other servers, and thorough documentation must be maintained for all possible uses of the server so that recovery can occur quickly and with a minimum of errors. For our example, we are going to assume that the risk analysis we are performing here is only a snapshot of a larger risk analysis where there are a number of servers that this backup server could service. In this case, applying the total cost of a standby server over a number of servers, say 10 to 15, would certainly make it economical.

What if the company did not need to reduce the risk of hardware failures on 10 to 15 servers? When we begin the discussion of applying counter-measures, we will discover that a company with only one server would not be making a wise financial decision to keep a standby server ready — unless the value of that server were increased greatly by the applications running on it. In this case, the cost of the countermeasure, a spare server, is too expensive relative to the value of the asset. In this case, paying a premium for priority service from a vendor might make more sense as far as risk reduction.

Finally, noting the annualized loss expectancy of the natural disaster, your company decides to have another party assume the risk. While it would be possible to create a tornado-proof enclosure for a server, the cost can be significantly prohibitive on an annualized basis, even when assuming that a single structure could protect a number of servers. Again, this decision is making several assumptions. One is that this is the cost to retrofit an existing structure with tornado-proof reinforcements. If the company is building a new plant, the cost of incorporating these countermeasures into new construction would be significantly less. Furthermore, as far as servers and the value of assets go, we have chosen fairly inexpensive assets. Increase the value of the assets by a factor of 10 or 100 and suddenly reducing the risk may be less expensive than assigning risk.

Let us assume now that the company is located in the Green Mountains of Vermont. In this case, the ARO of a natural disaster such as a tornado will be less than 0.01. For a company located in this region, they may even choose to accept the risk from tornados. The likelihood of a tornado that is powerful enough to destroy or even seriously damage a building — and then have it be your building — is pretty rare in the state. Based on its likelihood, it may not make economic sense to either reduce or assign the risk. The company will simply accept it with the understanding that if a tornado should hit, then the company may not be able to recover from the risk exposure.

A company might also determine that a combination of reducing risk and assigning it is the most cost-effective option. My insurance company reduces the amount of premium that I pay for fire insurance because I have working fire extinguishers and working smoke detectors in my home. While I cannot totally reduce the risk of fire to zero, I can reduce it to a point where the insurance company feels that my home is at less risk for destruction by fire than similar homes without such countermeasures. The same concept applies to risk analysis. By implementing a firewall to reduce the risk of a hacker exploiting local vulnerabilities, the risk has been reduced. The risk can be further reduced by employing defense in depth and by adding access controls to the servers, employing an IDS (intrusion detection system), using encryption for sensitive data when appropriate, etc. Each one of these countermeasures reduces the risk of the hacker threat. This process can continue indefinitely; however, for every countermeasure used, there is someone sitting around thinking of ways to defeat these countermeasures. Instead of spending more and more for that final bit of security, companies can assign the last bit of that risk to an insurance company or accept it.

In the process of doing a risk analysis, some pretty large numbers can show up. It is important to iterate at this point that we have not discussed countermeasures. Some countermeasures can reduce a number of risks in one shot. For example, a single packet filtering firewall can potentially protect hundreds of systems. When discussing countermeasures, we will use the ALE information to determine which countermeasure is the most effective from a technological and economic point of view.

The primary disadvantage of the quantitative approach, despite its accuracy, is that it is very difficult to do properly. Those of you wondering where all those values and numbers come from are right to wonder. Even inserting dollar amounts is somewhat subjective and dependent upon the source of those figures. There is no common agreement in the types of threats or threat frequency among vendors and risk analysts. Thus, without a good amount of previously recorded data, the data used to obtain the quantitative results is little more than a best guess from other experts. Another serious disadvantage is that while the calculations for quantitative analysis are sufficiently straightforward, the gathering of data is complex and not really feasible using a homegrown spreadsheet. Despite its accuracy then, most corporations and security experts rely on another method of assessing information security risks — qualitative analysis.

2.1.7 Qualitative Risk Analysis

Qualitative analysis uses the experience and intuition of those that are closest to or have the most knowledge of the company's assets. This means that people in the know will use their experience to evaluate what risks threaten assets and what the best countermeasure to employ against these threats would be. This method has the advantage of being very open and easy to accomplish. By trusting the expertise of those who work with the assets on a daily basis, a suggested regime of countermeasures can be deployed.

Because qualitative analysis heavily relies on people's judgment, it is most effective when a number of individuals participate in the process. Ideally, this can be facilitated through the use of questionnaires with a 1 to 10 scale, interviews, group meetings, detailed hypothetical questions — any technique that allows individuals to express their opinions regarding threats and reducing risk; however, allowing participants to brainstorm threats and solutions at the same time will do.

In practice, the element of getting everyone with a vested interest in the eventual security policy is the benefit of qualitative risk analysis. Often, a group of knowledgeable individuals will be able to identify more risks and propose a greater range of effective countermeasures than just one person.

The process of qualitative analysis works similarly to that of quantitative analysis, except without the numbers and formulas. First, the assets to be protected are identified. Brainstorming occurs to identify the potential risks that threaten each asset. Then, the group decides on the most effective countermeasure for each risk.

Qualitative analysis differs from quantitative analysis in that the calculations are less complex, but this approach still suffers from disadvantages. The primary issue is the subjective nature of the analysis and lack of objective data regarding the relative value of assets. This can lead to widely varying results as the actual worth of an asset is either under- or overestimated and the corresponding controls implemented are based upon this information. In some ways, however, this same disadvantage is what makes qualitative analysis the more popular of the risk analysis methods.

2.1.8 Combining Qualitative and Quantitative Risk Analysis

Depending on the organizational structure, management might be satisfied with the output of qualitative analysis. Some organizations may need to justify their expenses and thus need the details that a quantitative analysis provides. In practice, elements of both are used. When determining the exposure factor or the single loss expectancy (SLE) in a quantitative analysis, there is always a qualitative element. Few institutions will be able to authoritatively predict that, on average, the exposure factor (EF) for a given asset is 0.65 versus 0.50, or that the annualized rate of occurrence (ARO) for an exposure is 0.3 versus 0.5. These numbers are best and most accurately described through discussions with experts in the industry and individuals in your own company who are generally basing their reports on their own intuitions and experience.

2.1.9 Selecting Countermeasures

By this point we know what our network assets are. We have a good idea of the risks our assets face and how much they could cost us. Now what?

Now is the time to determine what steps must be taken to protect those assets. In short, we must select countermeasures. Using the terms used in risk analysis, a countermeasure is anything that effectively reduces the exposure to a given risk. Thus, a countermeasure could reduce the SLE or reduce the ARO. Because the average ALE for any risk is based on these two values, anything that reduces either of them will effectively reduce the ALE as well.

A countermeasure can be a technical solution but it can also be an administrative or physical solution. Consider the ways that an unlocked server room can be taken advantage of. An effective countermeasure in this case might be as simple as a lock. If a lock and key are not enough to account for all those coming and going into the server room, then perhaps biometric authentication along with the lock might be sufficient. That would decrease the likelihood that the "key" to the lock will fall into the wrong hands. Here we have added a technological element to our physical lock. Perhaps this is still not enough, considering the value of our servers and the damage that anyone could do with physical access to them. Perhaps we will add the additional countermeasure of an armed guard at the door.

Before beginning the process of discussing countermeasures and the process of selecting effective countermeasures, there is an important thing to consider. When selecting countermeasures, technology alone is not the only option available. When people use the term "defense in depth" to discuss the proper implementation of information security, they are not referring to the use of four firewalls in a row. They mean: allow yourself to consider administrative and physical countermeasures as well. In some cases, these options may be more cost effective or more effective at reducing threat than technology alone.

When selecting countermeasures, we move into the implementation phase of our security policy. The risk analysis has told us what is important to protect. Countermeasures define how our assets are protected.

This is the step that most people start with when employing a network security plan. We choose what would be the best investment for the protection of our network. In choosing a countermeasure, we are looking for two elements. The first is that the countermeasure is a good value and makes good business sense to purchase. We establish this by computing a cost/benefit analysis. The second element of interest is the functionality and effectiveness of our countermeasures. If we can establish two solutions that will serve as an effective countermeasure for a given risk and both make good business sense, how can we compare these products to find the best value for our company? This section assists us in determining the cost/benefit of countermeasures and allows us to compare them as apples to apples.

2.1.10 *Cost/Benefit Analysis*

All the work that we have done up to this point has provided a background to allow us to make this critical decision — what countermeasures make the most sense with regard to network security and business sense for our network. Business sense means that the cost of the solution is less than the cost of the problem. To put it another way, it would not make good business sense to spend $100,000 a year to fix a problem that was only going to cost us, on average, $50,000 a year.

It should come as no surprise that there is a formula that helps us quantify this relationship.

> Value of countermeasure = (Pre-countermeasure ALE)
> – (Post-countermeasure ALE)
> – (Cost of countermeasure)

We can plug in some numbers to help us digest its meaning. Using examples that we have been working with in this chapter, we have established that our Web server has an ALE of $5610 with regard to critical hardware failures. Let us say that through the use of power conditioners and redundant parts, we have reduced the ALE of an exposure from a critical hardware failure to $980 annually. Our solution of $2500 in spare parts and a power conditioner for the three-year cycle gives us a yearly cost of $2500/3 = $834. This would mean that the value of our countermeasure is:

$$\$5610 - \$980 - \$834 = \$3796$$

Thus, the value of our countermeasure would add up to $3796 in value for our company. This value could then be compared with other solutions that would reduce the risk the company faces from a critical hardware failure. If another solution reduced the risk equally as well, but had a value of $4214, then we would be able to quickly evaluate which of the two options presented the greater value or ROI (return on investment) to our company.

Because the ALE has already been calculated, there are essentially two ways to influence the value of the countermeasure. The first is that the post-countermeasure ALE can be adjusted. Countermeasure "A" might reduce the post-ALE to $100, while countermeasure "B" might reduce the post-ALE to only $2000. All other items being equal, countermeasure "A" would be the best solution. As an example, in securing our network against packet-based threats from the Internet, we have found two firewalls that perform according to our network needs. Based on the total cost of ownership, we have determined that one firewall actually reduces our ALE to only $100, while the second one reduces it to $2000. We now have a case for the first firewall being the better value for our business. This is not to say that the first firewall is a faster, more feature-rich firewall than the second. In fact, the second firewall may excel in performance and features but still not apply to the needs of our network or may cost too much to provide a significant value to our security needs.

The second part of the cost/benefit equation that can be modified is the cost of the countermeasure. A cheaper countermeasure "A" will create more value than a more costly countermeasure "B," assuming that the reduction in risk is identical for the two products. When determining the cost of a countermeasure, it is important not to simply use the number that is on the invoice. *All* of the costs that are part of implementing the counter-measure must be considered. This includes training, configuration, testing, changes to the network or physical environment to accommodate the countermeasure, compatibility with existing applications, and effects on the network including throughput and productivity. While countermeasure "A" may be cheap, when the company discovers that because of incompat-ibilities with existing applications, productivity decreases by 2 percent, suddenly countermeasure "A" does not seem like such a bargain.

This full analysis of the cost of a countermeasure can have surprising effects on the overall cost/benefit ratio for a given countermeasure. I am a big proponent of Linux and BSD, and often recommend these solutions to clients in need of a quality IDS and firewall product. Because a majority (but decreasing number) of networks that I typically consult for are Microsoft-only networks, the cost of training users to operate, update, and configure the Linux servers sometimes, unfortunately, puts the very low-cost solution in the position of being a lesser value for the company. Hap-pily, this is changing but the only way to know if this is the case is to do a comprehensive risk and cost/benefit analysis using numbers as accurate as you can make them.

The selection of safeguards does not stop at determining the cost. There are a number of other factors to consider when evaluating the functionality and effectiveness of countermeasures. Some of the most important things to consider when evaluating products are described below. Going through a list like this, especially when comparing two different vendor's products, is especially helpful.

2.1.11 Consideration Points for Security Countermeasures

2.1.11.1 Acceptance by Users and Management. The countermeasure must be of a form that is not overly intrusive to the lives or job functions of the network users. While providing living DNA samples for network authentication would certainly be a tough countermeasure for preventing unauthorized access to the network, most people would balk at such use. Acceptance is particularly important because it affects how hard people work to get around the countermeasure. This does not mean that the user has criminal intent; it is just that if the countermeasure is particularly difficult or cumbersome to use, users will, in an attempt to make their own jobs easier, figure out sometimes ingenious ways to circumvent the countermeasure. One example would be the use of randomly generated 16-character passwords that must be changed every 45 days. While effective at preventing password guessing, most users will simply end up writing their passwords on a piece of paper that they keep in a convenient location. Consider a form of countermeasure that was used by many dial-up ISPs. To prevent users from monopolizing an incoming flat rate dial-up connection, ISPs will require users to reconnect after a short period of inactivity. If this time period is too short, it annoys the users to the point where they will create fake traffic simply to ensure that the link stays open. By not fully considering the needs of the users the ISP loses its user's trust and has spent its money implementing a countermeasure that does not have the intended effect.

Acceptance is particularly interesting when considering access controls. Biometrics is a particular example where the most effective forms for biometrics (palm scans, hand geometry, retina scanning, and iris scanning) are the least popular among end users, while the least effective methods of biometrics (signature analysis and keystroke monitoring) are among the most popular for end users.

2.1.11.2 Affect on Asset. Ideally, the countermeasure should not have an appreciable effect on the resource it protects. A classic example of this is the interoperability problems that network address translation (NAT) and IPSec encounter when used in some topologies. The countermeasure of implementing encryption has the undesired effect of changing the environment of the asset it is trying to protect. To get the countermeasure (IPSec) to work with the environment (NAT), reengineering the asset may be required. This increases the cost of the countermeasure, lowers its effectiveness, and introduces additional complexity that may have its own unknown effects on the network and network security.

2.1.11.3 Alerting Capability. There are two elements to consider when evaluating the abilities of the countermeasure to alert administrators of significant events. The first is the avenue through which this can be done. Does the device support e-mail messaging? What if the network were to fail? Does the device support out-of-band alerting such as dialing a phone number and sending a page? The other element is the tuning ability of the alerts themselves. Generally, during the first couple of days after a countermeasure is installed, a new network administrator will excitedly have themselves alerted when any significant event occurs. After about the eighth alert, however, this grows old. Make sure that the device has the ability to tune the alerts to only those of a specific activity or alarm level. Being able to tune alerts within an alarm level is even better. After all, some critical alerts are more critical than others. If this capability is not present in the device, most alert systems generally end up being shut off altogether after a short period of time.

2.1.11.4 Auditing. The countermeasure should support varying degrees of auditing. When troubleshooting an event or looking for a particular type of activity, verbose auditing is appropriate. Due to the size of the audit logs and the general difficulty in parsing through them looking for a specific event, the audit function should also include minimal audit reports to reduce the size of the audit information for most normal transactions.

2.1.11.5 Can Be Reset. The countermeasure should be able to be reset to its original configuration or a stored configuration with minimal effect on the device or the asset it is protecting. The ability to quickly restart the system to a saved configuration is important if there is an error condition in the device itself — Microsoft Windows has trained us all that a restart can solve most problems. There will be a time, however, when either the network environment has changed so significantly, or the documentation regarding the configuration of the asset has been lost, that a return to its default operating condition is needed. Resets and restarts apply in all of these situations. Resets might also be required when there have been personnel changes and a lack of sufficient documentation on the network. At least one major VPN (virtual private network) vendor has a VPN appliance that does *not* have a password recovery procedure. If the administrator password to the VPN gateway is lost, then the only way to reset it is to ship the entire device back to the vendor. It is difficult to imagine a scenario that is more disruptive to your asset than having to remove the countermeasure (the VPN in this case) and express ship it back to the vendor for a (normally) simple password reset. It is also difficult to imagine a scenario that is more frustrating for the customer as well.

2.1.11.6 Countermeasure Is Independent of Asset It Is Protecting. Ideally, we would like the ability to remove or change the countermeasure without affecting the asset. If the countermeasure is logically or physically distinct from the asset, this becomes easier to do. If the countermeasure is distinct, it is also easier for the device to protect a number of systems.As an example, consider a firewall system. You could purchase a single firewall and configure it as a host-based firewall — but it would only protect the host for which it was configured. If you choose to include your firewall as a stand-alone device, however, the same firewall could protect a number of hosts. This of course increases the cost/benefit analysis for a given device.

The same firewall, if host based, would by necessity disrupt the host if it needed to be upgraded or replaced. As a stand-alone system, however, a replacement could be dropped in with minimal disruption to the entire network.

2.1.11.7 Defaults to Least Privilege. In an attempt to be user friendly, some popular modern operating systems default to a very insecure state. The application developers have rightly concluded that security adds to the complexity of a system and by choosing to have all but the most rudimentary security disabled, they are making a decision that favors ease of use over security. When choosing a security countermeasure, choose the product that defaults to a secure state. In the example of a firewall, in the absence of a configuration or the failure of the device, no traffic is allowed. This will certainly be inconvenient when it occurs, but consider the alternative — the firewall fails; but because it allows all traffic to pass (defaulting to no security), nobody notices because normal traffic is unaffected. When failing to a secure state, traffic is affected, but someone will also notice and investigate that there has been a device failure on the network.

2.1.11.8 Dependence on Other Components. The ideal is a minimal dependence on other components to ensure proper operation. Complexity is regarded as the enemy of security and a countermeasure that relies on interactions with other components should be regarded in a less favorable light than those that can function independently of others. This is not to suggest that dependence and interactions are bad — sometimes, they cannot be avoided, as it may be the role of the device to interact or depend on other components. A central logging station would not serve its primary goal if it did not depend on the syslog messages that it is receiving from remote systems. Just keep in mind that when comparing two equivalent products, the one that operates the best independently should be given a higher ranking.

2.1.11.9 Differing Levels of Access. The primary criteria are ensuring that there is clear distinction between user accounts and administrative accounts. This ensures our ability to audit access to the device. Ideally, there would be the ability to assign users administrative status instead of having a single administrative account. By being able to assign users to administrative status, the auditing of user activity is made easier. Think of the confusion that might occur if someone logged into a device at 10:30 a.m. as "administrator" and started making changes. If there were four people in the organization that knew the password, then it would be much more difficult finding out who made what changes — especially if the account password had been hacked, or sniffed, or the administrators wanted to otherwise cover their tracks. If we knew that Tom logged in at 10:30 a.m. with administrative access and began making changes to the device, then we have a place to start. Either Tom has been doing something that he should not have or Tom's account has been compromised. Either way, we are able to more effectively respond to the threat — either through administrative means with Tom or by simply changing his account information.

2.1.11.10 Flexible and Functional. While this entire section is about choosing a product that is functional and effective, we are also concerned about product flexibility. Compare which options the countermeasure supports. For example, if you are evaluating VPN devices, what encryption protocols does it support? What IPSec modes are supported? As the user of the countermeasure, you should be able to configure only the options that you need and disable those do not need. The ability to easily select all options or none should also be available. It is during this stage of the evaluation that I also consider the interface that I must use to interact with the device. Do not be impressed with a pretty GUI (graphical user interface). Some GUIs greatly increase the amount of work you need to do to change configurations. Are the options logically located near each other, or do you need to wade through several screens of nested output to be able to find all relevant configuration options? Consider how you will interface with the device. Must all communications be done while physically attached to the device over a serial port? Is there a way to manage the device remotely? If the countermeasure can be controlled remotely, how can you ensure that the management session itself is secure? If the management interface is a Java-enabled Web page, will your current security policy or network configuration allow this type of traffic? Does the management interface present any significant risks of its own; and if disabled due to a risk exposure, is there a reliable way to connect to the device otherwise?

The flexibility and functionality of the device, both in its configuration options and management options, will significantly impact the training and operational costs associated with the device. It will also impact your own review of your security policy. If you invest in a device that is troublesome to work with, you will find that changes that can impact business decisions occur with less speed than desired. A prime example is a customer that has extended access lists on its routers to perform packet filtering and possibly even stateful packet inspection. While an access list can seem intimidating, a little familiarity goes a long way with them. I have run into customers with access lists more than 300 lines long. This was not because of business needs, it was because the person who first set up the list left the company and as the business needs of the company changed, the configuration of the access list changed to keep pace. This company, however, did not know how to properly modify access lists and so just kept appending new lines to allow new ports and IP address ranges through the router. All the old access remained as well. In the end, the access list became less than an effective countermeasure and more of vulnerability in its own right. This was because the users were not familiar or comfortable with its configuration.

2.1.11.11 Minimal Human Intervention Required. There are any numbers of times that we have pointed at computers and said, "Why are you doing that? It's not right!" While we may be suspicious of expert claims that a computer cannot be malicious in its own right, most of the time they are not. There has been a configuration error on the part of a human. Undoubtedly, there can be programming errors as well; but on the whole, it is much more reliable for a computer to be able to interact with its environment and obtain the configuration information it needs.From a security perspective, the errors that humans mightcreate when configuring countermeasures also create new vulnerabilities. When comparing the effectiveness of countermeasures, consider the amount of configuration that needs to occur on each device in order for it to operate properly. Ideally, we would like countermeasures to "plug and play" as much as possible in the existing environment.

2.1.11.12 Modular in Nature. Consider countermeasures that are modular in nature; they are superior to those that are not modular. This quality will allow us to install or remove the countermeasure with minimal impact on our assets or other countermeasures in the environment. The modular nature of a countermeasure may also contribute to the functionality and flexibility of the device. Consider a firewall product that also contains modules that will scan e-mail for viruses or Web traffic for suspicious content. While not all these functions may be required as part of our security policy, the ability to add them in the future, or selectively enable them as needed, can cut initial product costs and allow network administrators the flexibility to configure only countermeasures that are required for their network environment.

2.1.11.13 Output Is Easily Understandable. Ultimately, people need to be able to use the information that the countermeasure is producing. This may be during troubleshooting, auditing, or general management of the device. Output that can be read by people without any special training is going to turn out to be much more valuable than information that needs to be converted from hex. Ideally, we would also like the ability to produce this information into reports that can be adjusted to highlight what we are trying to show. Thus, we would like the ability to produce outputs that allow us a more thorough technical analysis yet have the ability to modify that report in order to present a summary to management. Most vendors, in an effort to show the user friendliness of their product, will include report output that includes a great deal of graphs and colors. There is something to be said for visually representing data in a chart or graph; just make sure this information contains information relevant to your needs and that you have the ability to easily customize them.

Ideally, the countermeasure output should not require that you be part of the "in" crowd to be able to interpret it. Many of you may have heard of an excellent and free network sniffer product known as tcpdump. If you have not, this is a very common network sniffer used on networks. Some certification tracks, such as the SANS GIAC, require that you have a great deal of familiarity with the output of tcpdump. The output, however, can be less than clear to those new to the program or those who do not use it all the time. Before you fire up your e-mail editor to fire off an e-mail about the greatness that is tcpdump, let me assure you — I agree. When consulting with clients or others who do not spend all their time poring over text output, tcpdump is an example of a program that is lean, mean, fast, and free — but because of that, the output can either confuse or intimidate some. If people are confused or intimidated by their network tools, the tools will never be utilized to their full potential. When determining the functionality and effectiveness of a countermeasure, most companies will err on the side of a product that produces good output everyone understands over one that requires additional training costs to be absorbed in order to understand what the tool is telling you in the first place.

2.1.11.14 Provides Override Functionality. Although this would seem like a dangerous feature to look for, it is often convenient to be able to override the countermeasure for certain network situations. I most commonly encounter this need when adding another asset to the network in the form of a new application or server. If something seems like it should be working correctly, but is not, it might be that the countermeasure itself is interfering with the new application. Instead of disabling the countermeasure, it is useful to override its protection for a brief period of time to isolate a network problem.If the device does provide an override function, it is also advantageous if it provides some sort of signal, visual or otherwise, that the override function has been enabled. It would be a shame to have your expensive countermeasure provide no risk reduction at all due to human forgetfulness.

2.1.11.15 Security of Device. Clearly, because we are interested in improving the security of our network with our selected countermeasures, we will want to make sure that the countermeasure itself presents a minimum of vulnerabilities. This includes how access to the device can be secured — if it contains a Web server to provide Web-based management, does the Web server have any vulnerabilities? How is communication with the device encrypted? How are users authenticated? Given the ruthless examination given to security devices by both white-hat and black-hat hackers, it would be extraordinarily rare to find a countermeasure with no known vulnerabilities. While this is an unhappy position to be in — purchasing a countermeasure that will have its own vulnerabilities — you can protect yourself by examining your vendor's response to released weaknesses. Does the vendor only release a patch when forced to by the release of an attack? Does the vendor have a history of working with security researchers and releasing patches in a timely manner and in coordination with the researcher who discovered the vulnerability?

This final point is important to consider carefully. One of the worst positions that a network administrator can be in is when an important countermeasure has an exploit released or made public by a security researcher and there is no fix available. As soon as the vulnerability is made public, there will be a number of individuals who will create automated threats that seek to exploit this weakness. These threats can be executed via scripts or simply included in the next virus/worm/Trojan variant to be released onto the Internet.

This situation often arises for two reasons. The first is that the security "researcher" is simply looking to cause a bit of trouble. There is not much you can do about that other than hope that someone tracks them down and gives them what they deserve. Happily, a great many security researchers are conscientious and play an important role in the overall security of our networks. When they discover a significant vulnerability, they will often contact the vendor of the product and establish a reasonable timeline for the release of the vulnerability. This intern period will also give the vendor time to create and test an appropriate patch. When the process is executed in this manner, all sides win. The security researcher gets the credit he or she deserves for improving the security of our networks, the vendor is perceived as responsive to the needs of network security, and network administrators can patch their networks before the automated attacks are created.

This process sometimes breaks down, however. Some companies concerned with the perception that security flaws mean that their products may be considered inferior to consumers try to downplay the security vulnerability or refuse to acknowledge it. In this case, the researcher will generally release the exploit anyway in an effort to generate publicity and force the vendor's hand. When this is the case, your network may suffer. Prevent this situation as much as possible by not only investigating the overall security of the countermeasure itself, but also investigate — by contacting the vendor if necessary — the vendor's policy on responding to vulnerabilities and working with security researchers.

2.1.11.16 System Performance. Some countermeasures can adversely impact the performance of your assets. The classic example is the IPSec VPN. Due to the complex process of data encryption and decryption on each end, network throughput can be affected.[6] Furthermore, the VPN device may only be able to handle state information for a limited number of IPSec sessions at any given time. Both of these factors can influence the perceived performance of your assets. When we discuss firewalls, we will learn that the additional processing that more "intelligent" firewalls need to perform over their simpler cousins will also create network delay.When comparing countermeasures, be sure to consider likely loads that they will face. If you have 500 remote office employees who will all be expected to

41

use the VPN during their normal work hours, you will need a system that can easily support that many and is able to burst to even more connections. If you know that your firewall device is going to serve not only as a packet filter, but also scan e-mail for viruses, Web pages for suspicious content, and serve as a proxy for your 1000 employees, then a careful examination of the vendors' specs would be in order. In the firewall section, we discuss the features of the various firewalls described in the previous sentence, so do not be alarmed if some of those terms seem new.

Given today's computing power, most of these problems can be removed through the use of more powerful processors, faster and larger hard drives, and more system memory. This, of course, would increase the overall cost of the countermeasure and should be considered in the cost/benefit analysis.

2.1.11.17 Upgradeable. It is important to ensure that the countermeasure has the capability to be tested and is upgradeable. Often, companies will try to save a few dollars in the short term and purchase hardware that is limited in expandability — only to find that their network and security needs grow as time passes. Purchasing an expandable solution in the first place may cost a bit more up front, but in the long run it will prevent the inevitable forklift upgrade.

2.1.11.18 Testable. It is important that the countermeasure be evaluated on its ability to verify or test the protection it offers. This is also known as "auditing" capabilities. If it is not easy to see what the countermeasure is providing in the way of security, how can it be assured that it is actually offering security? Look for solutions that provide easy-to-find feedback on the protection they offer. This will make both the network administrator sleep better at night and make management happy that it has spent its security dollars wisely.

2.2 Administrative Countermeasures

As mentioned, not all countermeasures need to be technical. Considering that the real unknown in network security is generally the people and not the technology, it is best to create a security policy that protects your information in a variety of ways. This section briefly discusses the types of administrative countermeasures that can be employed to add security to your network.

At the very highest level, the security policy itself could be considered an administrative control. Its existence creates the expectations for technology, facilities, and behavior with regard to information security. On an implementation basis, administrative controls are such things as personnel controls, security awareness training, testing, supervision, and other policy and procedures related to administrative tasks.

Personnel controls are procedures that control the interaction of employees and address any issues of noncompliance. The most common example of personnel controls are acceptable use policies (AUPs) that detail the appropriate use of network resources and consequences for violating the AUP.

Personnel controls typically seek to reduce risk on the network by controlling the work environment. One way to do this is by enforcing the *separation of duties* regarding critical business functions. For example, many companies have network administrators that perform all functions on the network from maintaining network security, providing technical support for users, and configuring applications. It is seldom realized how precarious a position this can put a company in. Not only does the administrator have complete access to the network, but also there are no outside checks on the administrator. Any action the administrator takes can be hidden or otherwise buried by the same network administrator. I have been to networks where the network administrator was actually using spare bandwidth and company computer resources to run his own independent business on the side. This is clearly unacceptable.

Before you start suspecting your network administrator, let me emphasize that most network administrators are conscientious, hard-working individuals who are overworked and underappreciated. When things are going well, they are forgotten; and when things turn sour, they are the first to get the finger pointed at them. Now that I have covered myself with any network administrators who may be reading this book, let me continue by saying that, whenever possible, the information security policy should support the separation of duties with regard to critical company resources. One common division of duties is breaking down network administration into three major functional roles: a network security administrator, an operations administrator, and a user administrator.

The network security administrator is responsible for enforcing the network security policy and reviews all logs and responds to all computer incidents. The operations administrator ensures that the servers and network devices are operating correctly and maintains applications and operating system patches on the servers. Finally, the user administrator is responsible for ensuring that users have the appropriate rights on the network to perform their required tasks.

Personnel controls may also address the issue of rotation of duties. Using the above example of separation of duties, periodically, the three network administrators who are fulfilling the role of security, operations, and user administrators should rotate assignments. This provides several tangible benefits in the area of information security. The first is that it encourages cross training. This allows greater availability of services should one of the other administrators quit, die, get sick, or go on vacation.

The second tangible benefit is that it becomes much more difficult to conceal inappropriate actions when job responsibilities rotate. Let us assume that the person taking on the role of the security administrator considers engaging in some legally questionable behavior. His assumption is that because he has control over all of the security logs and reports, he can remove evidence of his behavior. This is much less likely to occur if the same administrator knows that in two weeks, another security administrator will take over his job for a period of time.

When rotation of duties has been implemented as an administrative countermeasure, the only way our suspect security administrator would be able to pull off his illegal scheme would be to get other network administrators rotating into the position to collude with him. That is, they must all agree to work together to perform any illegal or deceptive activity. The combination of separation of duties and rotation of duties works together to reduce, but not eliminate, the chance of this occurring.

Implementing a security policy can be an uphill battle if end users are not adequately trained in both application of security to their job and the necessity of information security. When users are expected to interact with security controls, they should be adequately trained in not only the proper execution of their tasks, but also the reasoning behind it. Consider a simple example that is common on many networks — password policies. Instead of simply rolling out a policy that requires passwords to be ten characters in length and contain non-alphabetic characters and leaving it at that, users should be instructed as to *why* it is important to use complex passwords and then shown *how* to create passwords that fit the policy and that they can still remember. Administrative controls should thus include procedures regarding the training of network users.

While users themselves can present a threat to the security of network information, most of the time it is not because they are malicious in nature. Users have their own bosses who expect them to get their work done, and they can be incredibly clever in circumventing security policies when they find that they interfere with their own ability to get their work done. This cultural tendency cannot be changed through administrative rules alone, but it is a start. Administrative controls should also create methods to remind users how information security is benefiting them, show them the benefits, and reward them for keeping the network secure. I have found through years of teaching that a bit of sincere appreciation and recognition goes a long way toward motivating people.

Testing is covered in Chapter 12, "Network Penetration Testing." Until then, it will suffice to say that the entire information security policy should be tested from time to time. This is to ensure that the policy is still relevant and that it is providing the level of protection that the framers of the policy had intended.

Finally, administrative controls can also include the personnel hierarchy of the organization. This is an important element in enforcing accountability for the behavior of security policy users. The expectation should be that managers are directly responsible for the actions of their subordinates.

Together, administrative controls are a good illustration of how technology alone will not be enough to protect your network. We can authenticate users using passwords, but if users choose bad passwords or write them down, what have we really accomplished? We can encrypt the accounting files using strong cryptography; but if the user in accounting shares the unencrypted file with their buddy in marketing, then again, our encryption has not failed but our information security policy has. Every technical solution offered in this book should be complemented by the appropriate administrative control, where appropriate.

2.3 Physical Countermeasures

Physical countermeasures almost make up an entirely distinct discipline in information security, but we can offer some high-level recommendations to consider when defending your own network.

When discussing the common technical countermeasure, we are often concerned with defending our network perimeter against a packet-based attack. That is, there are some "bad" packets outside our network that we want to make sure cannot get in. We typically use a firewall to stop these bad packets. Physical security commonly takes the same approach, but instead of dealing with packets, keeps out the "bad" people or other threats from our network.

The most common way of doing this is with locks, chains, guards, and cameras. These all fall into the category of perimeter control. Each one of these controls would be valuable in reducing any risk to our information that is related to someone gaining physical access to our resources. Like the technology we use in our network, these countermeasures will not guarantee the security of your facilities, but they will go a long way toward slowing down any intruder.

Beyond these common physical controls we can also apply physical controls to our network. This means functional areas of our network are separated from each other. The research and development network, for example, may be a physically separate network from our administrative and user networks. This may mean physically distinct on different hubs and switches with access controlled through a firewall, or an actual distinct network complete with its own DMZ and WAN links, each configured to reflect the particular security needs of the research and development network.

Data backups are also considered physical controls. To my chagrin, I will attest that I have seen customers keep their backups sitting on top of their server rack. This will help if the server crashes, but is of little use if a fire should strike. Data backups should be kept off-site, under lock and key, and in a fireproof location. Ensuring the physical integrity of the backups most certainly qualifies as a physical control.

The list of possible physical controls continues. Controlling the work environment so that only employees of a certain department have access to a particular work area would qualify, as would including controls on the user workstations themselves. A common control on the user workstations would be to remove the floppy disk drive and disable the USB ports to prevent users from easily attaching removable media to the devices. A great number of company secrets can slip out the door on a Zip drive securely tucked into a briefcase. Some companies even go so far as to search carry-out articles such as duffle bags and briefcases.

2.4 Technological Countermeasures

Of course, what most people (other than physical security experts!) are concerned with is the use of technological countermeasures. While they play only a small part in the overall security scheme of a network, they are usually the most foreign and intimidating to the general public. There is the assumption that some sort of magic must be occurring in them that makes them the accessible only to the high wizards of networking. Not so! The most common technological controls relate to controlling access to the system, creating a secure network architecture, controlling network access, the use of encryption, and the auditing of all of the above countermeasures. Each of these is covered in a separate chapter in this book.

2.5 Creating the Security Standards Document

Knowing what countermeasures are going to be effective in securing our network assets, we are ready to begin the process of creating our standards document. This document simply outlines what technologies, administrative procedures, and physical controls we will implement in order to enforce the security policy. While the security policy statement is general, this is where we will discuss technologies such as IPSec, firewall solutions, intrusion detection systems, hiring and firing procedures, and standards for environmental controls, among others. I often explain the relationship between the standards document and the policy document by pointing out that the standards document can follow much the same format as the policy document, but in this case we will specifically spell out the steps required to enforce the policy document.

2.6 Creating the Configuration Guide Document

One of the goals and advantages of a security policy is the implementation of a consistent policy across the organization. The goals of configuration documentation are to serve as a record of the configuration of information security controls on the network and as a guide for the future deployment of such services. This document is primarily for any staff who will be responsible for the actual implementation of elements of the security policy. Here is where access lists are described, configuration options for IPSec sessions noted, allowable server services categorized, and group membership rights defined. In all likelihood, this "document" will end up being a series of documents for the various information security countermeasures, both technical and nontechnical, employed in the organization.

2.7 Pulling It All Together: Sample Security Policy Creation

The final section in this chapter is a sample security policy. Due to space constraints, the actual policy itself will be rather straightforward and somewhat abbreviated, but it will walk you through all the major steps of creating a security policy and implementing it.

The following sample describes a sample security policy that my consulting company, Proteris, might follow. For purposes of this example, Proteris is a consulting company that produces a good deal of unique intellectual property. Their most important information asset then is this data. While the materials are printed in hard copy for classes, Proteris must maintain strict controls over the digital versions of their courses lest the company lose value at the same time it loses its intellectual property.

2.7.1 Abstract

Proteris recognizes that intellectual information is the corporation's primary asset. The material value of the company itself is directly tied to safeguarding this intellectual property and, therefore, safeguarding all administrative, technical, and physical systems used to access this information is likewise critical. To support this critical asset, Proteris will create policy, standards, and guidelines to protect the confidentiality, integrity, and availability of this information.

2.7.2 Context

Proteris maintains a worldwide reputation for quality technical training and consulting. Our clients expect and receive knowledgeable, experienced instructors and high-quality training materials tailored to meet their specific technology training and consulting requirements. To consistently meet these high standards, Proteris employs state-of-the-art information management systems. As such, the security and availability of these information systems are critical to Proteris' success.

The information security policy of Proterls applies to all employees, contractors, vendors, and consultants that access Proteris information systems as part of their employment at Proteris. All information systems and information assets, including logical or physical representation of Proteris intellectual property, are covered as part of this policy.

2.7.3   Policy

Proteris will establish standards, procedures, and guidelines that support information security. Information security shall pertain to the confidentiality, integrity, and availability of information on the Proteris network. Standards, procedures, and guidelines will employ the most cost-effective solutions that reduce risk from information security threats to acceptable levels as determined by the IS staff. This includes but is not limited to creating physical, technical, and administrative controls as deemed necessary to ensure that the objectives of the Proteris security policy are met.

Acceptable levels for the purposes of this document shall be defined by the relative value of the information assets owned by Proteris versus the likely risks to be encountered by those assets as determined by the information security (IS) team.

The information technology (IT) department manager shall head the IS team. The IS team shall consist of members of the IT staff as deemed appropriate by the IS director. The department manager of all other Proteris departments shall select one member of their staff to serve as a representative on the IS team.

Implementation of the goals of this policy is described in the Proteris security standards and procedures document. The most recent copy of the Proteris security standards and procedures document is attached to this document as *Proteris Security Standards and Procedures version 2.05 4/15/03* or in electronic form at http://house.proteris.com.

In the course of network operations, employee data, including transmitted data or stored data regardless of place of storage, may be monitored or examined. This will take place under one of three circumstances:

1. IT staff observes the data during the course of normal network operations and troubleshooting.
2. The IS team will monitor employee data with the supervision of the human resources department if an employee is suspected of violating the terms of this security policy or any other associated documents.

3. The incident response (IR) team may monitor or examine stored or transmitted data in response to an information system incident to determine the cause and severity of the incident.

2.7.3.1 Administrative Security. The human resources department and IS team will establish administrative procedures at Proteris that support the goals of information security. The IS team will be responsible for the creation of administrative procedures pertaining to user interaction with network or computer systems, including but not limited to password policies, acceptable use policies, data storage policies, and remote access policies.

Human resources will create policy that pertains to all other aspects of the user work environment subject to the approval of the IS director.

2.7.3.2 Technology/Network/Computer Systems Security. The Proteris IS team will create standards and procedures that support the goals of confidentiality, integrity, and availability. These controls will be selected and implemented based on the cost-effectiveness and ability to provide adequate security to information and information systems.

2.7.3.3 Physical Security. Proteris will take such steps as deemed necessary to provide a safe working environment for Proteris employees, contractors, vendor representatives, consultants, and visitors. These steps will be selected based on cost-effectiveness and acceptable levels of risk by the human resources department. Proteris will comply with all local, state, and federal laws regarding the safety of its premises. The Proteris IS will provide physical security devices such as are required to protect information stored on or transmitted over the network. This asset protection will be installed on the basis of cost efficiencies and provided protection.

All physical assets assigned to a department shall be the responsibility of the department head in assuring the confidentiality, integrity, and availability of such assets. Physical assets related to information systems not directly controlled by a single department shall be the responsibility of the IT staff to ensure their physical security.

2.7.4 Acceptable Use Policy

Proteris employees are permitted to use the network resources to view Internet Web pages and send e-mails subject to the following provisions:

- Resources consumed by such activities are minimal.
- Employees agree that all network information, stored or transmitted, may be monitored as described above.

- Employees do not use these resources to perform any illegal or immoral actions as defined by local, state, and federal laws and the policies defined by Proteris.
- Employees do not use Proteris resources to operate any personal business or contract work.
- Employees are not permitted to perform any activity that contradicts the goals of this security policy or its associated documents.

Definitions of minimal use are at the discretion of the employee's direct supervisor with regard to time spent on such activities and at the discretion of the IT staff regarding network resource utilization.

Full terms of the acceptable use policy can be found in the attached document, *Proteris Acceptable Use Policy version 3.25 02/04/03,* or at the Proteris documentation web site http://house.proteris.com.

2.7.5   Incident Response Planning

Proteris will form an incident response (IR) team, including members of the IT staff, the IS team, and a representative of each department as selected by the department manager.

The IR team is responsible for the creation of incident response standards and procedures. These procedures will include a categorization of risk and response related to the level of risk and the significance of the target to the Proteris information systems.

The IR team will be held responsible for preparing, testing, and training in the skills required to perform efficient incident response.

Full standards and procedures of the Proteris incident response policy can be found in the attached document *Proteris Incident Response Policy version 1.03 12/15/02* or at the Proteris documentation Web site http://house.proteris.com.

2.7.6   Disaster Planning and Recovery

Proteris will develop a comprehensive disaster recovery plan that clearly defines the most critical Proteris information requirements and is able to restore them to operational status within 48 hours of a devastating disaster. This plan will cover contingencies for human, technological, and natural disasters.

The head of the disaster recovery effort shall be appointed by the chief executive officer of Proteris, and the head of the disaster recovery plan shall have the authority to designate those resources as required for the planning and execution of a disaster recovery plan.

The disaster recovery plan will be tested on an annual basis pending approval of the chief executive officer to determine readiness and assess needs.

Full standards and procedures of the Proteris disaster planning and recovery policy can be found in the attached document *Proteris Disaster Planning and Recovery Policy version 1.00 2/15/03* or at the Proteris documentation Web site http://house.proteris.com.

2.7.7 *Definitions*

Adequate security: Security safeguards will be evaluated based on effectiveness at reducing risk and a cost/benefit analysis. Adequate security shall be considered security that can reduce risk to the lowest possible level while still providing a cost benefit in the comparison of the countermeasure and the asset to be protected.

Asset: Any item, information, or person that provides value for Proteris.

Associated documents: Documents supporting the security policy, including but not limited to the Proteris security standards and procedures policy, the acceptable use policy, incident response policy, and disaster planning and recovery policy.

Availability: Assurance that information is available when the information is required.

Confidentiality: Assurance that only those with a right to view the information will have access to information.

Countermeasure: Any technology, physical control, or administrative action that can reduce the risk to information systems or Proteris personnel.

Information systems: Any device or software that assists in the storage, transmission, or processing of data, including but not limited to servers, routers, switches, network cabling, workstations, and printers.

Integrity: Assurance that information is unaltered from its original or correct state.

Users: Any individual who has access to information systems owned or managed by Proteris.

2.7.8 *Authority*

This security policy has been approved by and is supported by the chief executive officer, the chief financial officer, and the chief information officer of Proteris. All users are expected to abide by its policy, standards, and procedures. Failure to comply with this security policy will result in action suitable to the offense. Sanctions may include reprimand, dismissal, and criminal or civil action initiated by Proteris.

2.7.9 Distribution

This document and all associated documents shall be available to any employee upon request from the human resources department. Electronic versions of this document may be found on the company intranet site http://house.proteris.com.

All users will be notified of changes to this and associated documents via e-mail within 12 hours of the changes being approved and will be held responsible for any such changes within 24 hours of notification.

The Proteris IS staff is responsible for providing training to all users prior to access to Proteris information systems being granted.

The Proteris IS staff is responsible for providing ongoing security awareness training to all Proteris users on a semiannual basis at a minimum.

2.7.10 Review

This policy may change at any time at the discretion of the chief executive officer or IS team head in response to unforeseen or unusual circumstances.

This security policy and all associated documents will be reviewed on an annual basis for changes that reflect changing priorities of the Proteris business model.

Requests for changes to this security policy will follow the following sequence of events:

- The individual making the change request submits a written request to the head of the IS team. The request must explain the nature of the change, the reason for the change request, and be signed by the individual's department manager.
- The IS team will have ten working days to review the proposed change and examine its impact on the information security goals of Proteris. Requests will either receive preliminary approval or be rejected with explanation to the requester.
- If approved, the IS team will have another ten working days to test the proposed changes in the Proteris information system environment. At the end of this period, the request will either be approved or rejected with explanation.
- Upon approval, the IS team will update the appropriate portion of the security policy document and provide notification to users as described above.

The security policy as described above is fairly generic. There are a couple of points worth discussing before moving on to an example of a standards and procedures document.

The first item is the general nature of the policy. It simply states that Proteris knows that information technology is an important element of its business and Proteris needs to take steps to ensure that this information technology is safe and reliable. Worded as such, the security policy should rarely, if ever, change. What is more likely to change is how the information security that Proteris seeks is implemented. Therefore, the AUP, incident response plan, disaster recovery plan, and standards and procedures document will most likely change regularly to reflect changing technologies and business needs.

We move on now to a look at a sample standards and procedures document that will support this security policy. It is worthwhile to point out that all of the supporting documents of the Proteris security policy will have much the same format and tone. We will not include the entire document as we have with the security policy, as this document is likely to be of much greater length and detail.

2.8   Proteris Security Standards and Procedures

2.8.1   Abstract

The purpose of this document is to provide detailed information supporting the Proteris Security policy. The Proteris Security policy can be found electronically at http://house.proteris.com.

2.8.2   Context

Proteris maintains a worldwide reputation for quality technical training and consulting. Our clients expect and receive...

2.8.3   Standards and Procedures

2.8.3.1   Administrative Security: Password Standards. The confidentiality of information is a critical element in the success of Proteris' business model. To support this confidentiality, all passwords shall meet the following requirements.

- Passwords will be at least eight characters in length.
- Passwords will contain a combination of upper case (A–Z) and lower case (a–z) characters.
- Passwords will contain at least one digit or punctuation other than letters such as: ~!@#$%^&*(){}[]:";'<>?,./\ | .
- Passwords may not be words in any language or employ slang. This includes names and proper nouns.
- Passwords may not be written down...

2.8.3.2   Technology/Network/Computer Systems Standards: Router Security Standards. Routers serve a critical role in the transfer of information on the Proteris network. As such, their configuration will reflect their central nature in the confidentiality, integrity, and availability of Proteris information assets. All log-ins must be done through unique usernames and authenticated through RADIUS. In the event of an emergency or failure of the RADIUS system, local log-on to the router shall be allowed through the use of unique user names and passwords for each authorized router administrator.

- All passwords on the router will be kept in encrypted form.
- All services not essential to the forwarding and logging functions of the router will be disabled.
- All routers will display strongly worded UNAUTHORIZED USE PRO-HIBITED messages upon log-in. Such messages will indicate that all actions on the router will be monitored and shall give no indication of the make, model, software version, or position of the router in the Proteris network.
- Log-in to the router will only be allowed through encrypted sessions. Telnet access is specifically restricted...

2.8.3.3 Physical Security Standards: External Boundary Protection Standards. Information security is part of a process that includes many different elements of security. For Proteris to meet its information security requirements, it must take steps to reduce the risks of physical trespass and unauthorized entry to Proteris offices. Proteris will install lighting sufficient to illuminate the Proteris office perimeters to a minimum of eight feet in height and two feet from the external wall.

- Entrance to Proteris shall be recorded. Employees are required to show photographic identification badges upon entry.
- Visitors to Proteris are required to sign in when entering the Proteris facilities and sign out when leaving. The minimum information to be captured is the time of entrance and the purpose of the visit.
- A Proteris employee at all times shall escort visitors to Proteris in areas other than the sales office.
- Motion detectors shall be installed in all Proteris offices and activated within three hours after normal business hours end. Motion detectors will be deactivated within one hour of normal business start times...

Each of these sections would be much longer and contain details for all the security elements of their respective categories. Information in the Standards and Procedures, AUP, Incident Response, and Disaster Recovery and Planning documents should all have similar forms. This information, while discussing the specific countermeasures to be used for reducing risk to the Proteris network is still not specific enough to actually guide the implementation. Instead, a Security Configuration Guide is required. Along with the information above, a definitions section and a table of contents or index should be included as well.

Like the Standards and Procedures document, the Security Configuration Guide is broken into specific sections. For the sake of simplicity, I generally use the actual requirements set out in the Standards and Procedures document to organize the Security Configuration Guide. For example, from the section on router security, we might see something like this:

2.8.3.4 All Passwords on the Router Will Be Kept in Encrypted Form. The configuration statement service password-encryption will be included as part of the standard Cisco router configuration. For a complete sample template with annotations, refer to Cisco Router IOS 12.2(5) Proteris Secure Template ver 1.25.

2.8.3.5 All Services Not Essential to the Forwarding and Logging Functions of the Router Will Be Disabled. The following configuration statements disable unnecessary Cisco router functions:

- #(config-if)**no ip directed-broadcast** — disable directed broadcast packets.
- #(config)**no service tcp-small-servers** — disable "small" TCP servers such as echo, chargen, discard, and daytime.
- #(config)**no service udp-small-servers** — disable "small" UDP servers like echo, chargen, and discard.
- #(config)**no ip source-route** — disables source routing.
- #(config)**no ip http server** — disable HTTP configuration server.

For a complete sample template with annotations, refer to *Cisco Router IOS 12.2(5) Proteris Secure Template ver 1.25.*

The configuration guidelines would continue for this section and each countermeasure or control utilized by the network. The information would be as specific as possible for two reasons. The first is to ease configuration and installations of new systems or recover from failures. The second is to ensure that new administrators continue to configure the network to the level of security demanded by the site security policy.

A security policy is not an easy document to create. The process of identifying assets, performing risk analysis, and selecting risk management countermeasures is not a straightforward matter of "put in the numbers and out pops the answer." Properly done, an information security policy takes time, effort, and the involvement of many of the people in your company. Alone, a security policy does nothing to increase the security of your network — it is, after all, just words. Nevertheless, a security policy is the best way to ensure that the *process* of securing your network achieves the goal of information security and reduces the risk to your network while complementing your company objectives.

Notes

1. Those new to the field of network security may think that this example is one of the enduring "urban legends" of networking. Those with more experience will nod sagely and recognize this very behavior in their own network users.
2. An examination of this formula, although simplistic, shows a fundamental relationship between the elements of risk. A vulnerability without a threat does not produce risk, and a threat without a vulnerability to exploit likewise does not produce risk.
3. These are not actual statistical chances of this event occurring. Please contact your local insurance agent for current "devastating meteorite" odds.
4. The discipline of risk analysis is particularly attractive to those who have either a pessimistic streak or a macabre fixation with what *could* go wrong given the chance. Murphy was a risk analyst.
5. The honeynet project (project.honeynet.org) has repeatedly demonstrated that the life expectancy of a "default" installation of most operating systems on the Internet is less than 24 hours. Default means no patches or other security mechanisms are applied — a sorry state for a device connected to the Internet.
6. Do not let this fact alarm you too much. When we discuss VPNs, we will see that even devices with modest hardware (such as an old Pentium 133 sitting in the closet) will provide adequate throughput for links up to T-1 speeds of 1.544 Mbps.

Chapter 3
The Network Stack and Security

If you have any experience in the world of networking, much of what is covered in this chapter may be familiar to you. This chapter addresses the basics of a network: the parts that plug in together to make sure that information gets from point A to some other point B. If you are an experienced network administrator, the value of this chapter may not be so much the explanation of a hub, switch, and router, but rather the discussion that surrounds the terms and the impact your network choices will have in the overall security of your network.

The primary protocol used on the Internet is known as TCP/IP, short for Transmission Control Protocol/Internet Protocol. Otherwise known as the Internet Suite, this is a collection of protocols that every machine that attaches to the Internet must implement. Consider it a common vocabulary that allows one machine to make a request and another machine to fulfill the request.

While it is taken as a *fait accompli* that the Internet does use and will continue to use TCP/IP, it was not always the case. TCP/IP was created in the early days of the Internet for a fairly small number of nodes and a limited number of applications. The early Internet was a much friendlier place than it is today — security was not given much consideration because, for the most part, the early Internet was considered a closed user group.

The sudden popularity of the Internet placed demands on TCP/IP that the protocols were not equipped to handle. In the late 1980s, there was a push by the U.S. Department of Defense to replace the TCP/IP suite altogether with a more "modern" protocol designed for the rapidly growing and increasingly insecure Internet. The protocols that were designed were based around a conceptual model known as the OSI Model. This model stated that for computers to communicate, there needed to be certain well-defined layers. For example, the first layer of the OSI Model was known as the physical layer and this defined how manufacturers should create ones (1s) and zeros (0s) on a given piece of transmission medium, the basis for all computer communications. If we think about it for a minute, it makes sense that we can represent a one or zero in one way on a piece of fiber-optic cable as pulses of light and on a piece of copper cable as a voltage. To ensure that everyone could communicate, each one of these layers would be associated with a number of standards or even standards organizations. To keep all the protocols straight, the OSI Model would be managed and overseen by the ISO, the International Standards Organization.

This was a great idea and would have no doubt increased the scalability of the networks that we use right now, but there was a catch. By the time the ISO got everything sorted out about the OSI Model, the Internet had grown to such a size that TCP/IP was just never going to be dethroned. There was just no way to get everyone together and say, "OK, next Tuesday at 9:30 p.m., let's all shut off the Internet and turn it back on Wednesday morning using the OSI Model!" Thus, the idea of the ISO OSI protocol suite faded away.

You can still find some OSI protocols, especially in the heart of the largest and oldest ISPs in the country. For the most part, however, the OSI Model has become nothing more than a convenient way for network geeks around the world to speak a common language. When I say to you, "Well, the router will be able to do some layer 3 filtering at the border of your network," I do not need to say that "layer 3" is layer 3 of the OSI Model and that this is the same thing as the IP protocol of the TCP/IP suite. So although we never use the protocols described by the OSI Model, it has become the way that we refer to networks and network components.

3.1   Connecting the Network

3.1.1   The Physical Layer

In deference to tradition of the OSI Model and because it just makes sense, we then begin our discussion of the network elements at the first layer of the OSI Model — the physical layer.

If you want to see the physical layer, look at the back of your computer. Odds are that there is some sort of cable of fiber-optic, category 5 copper (thin, flexible cable with four pairs of copper wire inside them), a phone line, or even a wireless network card. Each of these is some type of physical medium, and each has specific hardware with instructions as to how to transmit information that will represent a one or a zero, which in turn is transmitted over the physical medium as a light wave, voltage, or radio wave.

You can rarely pick up a text about network design without considerable text discussing the relative advantages and disadvantages of each of the different types of physical media and their associated hardware. For those of you without one of those texts handy, here is a brief overview before we begin to discuss the security considerations of the physical layer.

Fiber-optic cable sets the gold standard for physical layer transmissions. Stretched from extremely pure glass or plastic, fiber-optic cable supports fantastic transmission speeds. I would quote you some incredible top end, but as of this writing the top end has not yet been determined. The problem is that the electronics that are in common use to create the ones and zeros cannot match the potential of fiber. Currently, speeds in the terabit range are common although even faster speeds are predicted for the future. From a straight bandwidth argument, fiber is the medium of choice for the foreseeable future.

While a fiber-optic bundle of cables may include hundreds of individual fiber filaments and be as big around as your little finger, in the actual transmission path in the bundle, the individual fibers are microscopic and generally cannot be seen by the naked eye. The fiber itself is extremely pure. It is said that if the ocean were as clear as optical fiber, we would be able to see to the bottom of its deepest trenches from a boat on the surface. Around each fiber is a type of cladding that has a slightly lower refractive index than the fiber core. This causes any stray light particles to bounce back toward the center of the fiber in the same manner as a mirror. Around this cladding there is a protective sheath and strengthening fabric.

Fiber optic boasts the longest cabling distances of all media without the use of repeaters to regenerate the signal. Most copper wires used in LAN networks are commonly 100 m and top out at about 500 m in older installations. Fiber is capable of running for dozens or even thousands of kilometers. Fiber also suffers the least from attenuation of all media and has an extremely low error rate.[1] If you have a need for a network that circles a small town or campus, fiber is the logical choice.

Fiber optic suffers from a serious drawback. While the fiber itself is generally cheaper to purchase than an equivalent amount of copper cabling, the connections and the specialized splicing equipment that must be used to join microscopic fiber filaments together are very expensive. This expense factor generally limits fiber-optic media to other long-haul applications where the extra expense is easily amortized, or use in server rooms to facilitate high-speed connections between servers and network devices.

Copper comes in a variety of flavors. For some time in the days of networking, coaxial cable similar to that used to provide cable service to your television was used in most local area networks (LANs). With the emergence of cable Internet access, this form of copper has seen resurgence — for wide area access. Clearly, if 100 channels of the greatest entertainment on Earth can be transmitted over a piece of copper no bigger around than a pencil, then copper must be able to support great bandwidths of data. For the most part, the thicker a piece of copper, the more information that can be sent through it. Commonly, in LANs, the copper used is much thinner and is actually a small bundle of very thin copper wires similar to telephone wires. This type of cabling is often referred to as unshielded twisted pair (UTP). The name itself refers to the twists of the copper used to reduce interference from signals traveling down the copper. There are some types of copper, not in common use on most networks, that also have a thick mesh shield that protects the copper from radio and electromagnetic interference. This shielded version is naturally known as shielded twisted pair (STP). UTP cable, commonly referred to as category 5, (cat 5) or category 6 (cat 6), is very cheap and easy to work with. Category 6 cable is very similar to category 5 cable except that it is a newer standard and has been certified to support gigabit speeds over 100-m runs. In addition to being cheap and easy to work with, there is not much going for copper in terms of transmission media. It does not support very high bandwidths[2] in gauges commonly used on LANs and it does not support long distances. Standards for copper cable are satisfied to get 100 m out of a single run of copper cable. Copper is also easily influenced by nearby radio and electrical sources — fluorescent lights and machinery are notorious for skewing the signal on a copper wire. Still, it is very cheap and very easy to work with compared to alternatives such as fiber optic.

The final major category of transmission media is wireless technology. Just as there are different types of fiber-optic and copper cabling, there are different areas of the radio spectrum reserved for data transmission. While the range and data throughput of wireless currently does not compare to those of copper and fiber, you cannot beat the ease of installation; and for most network users, the throughput rate is more than adequate.

The various physical media all have different usage considerations that range from installation, maximum useful distance, data throughput, and maintenance. From the security perspective, regarding the various physical layer media, the most pressing concern is generally how easy it for someone to read data that is being transmitted over the media. Fiber-optic media are generally considered the most difficult to "sniff," or read data as it passes through. Because the data is being transmitted as pulses of light, unless there is significant bleeding of light into the cladding of the fiber, it is virtually impossible to track information. For those that are determined enough, the fiber can be spliced and some sort of high-speed sniffer inserted mid-stream, but such an undertaking would only be a risk from the most determined and well-financed threats. Because end users are usually not directly attached to the fiber infrastructure, users' ability to put packet sniffers on their computers and access information passing over the fiber is likewise limited.

Copper, on the other hand, is easier to sniff. Due to the tendency for high-frequency waves to emanate from the copper as signals are passed along its length, a device sensitive enough to read this radiation will be able to reconstruct data although the cost of such a device is more than the average hacker would be willing to accommodate. For the convenience of end users and the occasional hacker, there are usually a number of ports along walls that provide easy access to the network itself. There have been recent reports of individuals hacking gaming consoles such as Sony's Play-Station with built-in Ethernet ports. These consoles are hacked with a stripped-down version of Linux and deposited inside a company's network. From there, inconspicuously under a desk or in a closet, they sit and listen to all network traffic.

Most users do not need to go to such lengths to sniff the traffic on a copper infrastructure. Because user workstations are connected to the copper media, a sophisticated packet sniffer showing all traffic on the local area network can be easily installed. For those who prefer a more scaled-back sniffer, sniffers that look for patterns in the observed transmissions that look like "user" and "password" and common variants of those combinations are available for downloading.

Because copper is so cheap to work with, it has become the physical medium of choice for the majority of office buildings and local area networks around the world. While excellent in many regards, all copper should be regarded as insecure from a security point of view.

The ease of reading copper, however, pales in comparison with that of wireless. Few who have wandered about the office or home with a laptop in one hand and a wireless access point some place overhead can deny that the convenience of wireless is hard to resist. For myself, it only took the first day of working from home while sitting on my deck to convince me that I had found networking Nirvana. Wireless is, however, an inherently insecure medium. With copper, someone had to at least make a half-hearted effort to find some copper to sniff from. With wireless, all transmissions are in the clear for any interested party. In some cities, it has become a hobby of some groups to mark on sidewalks the boundaries of nearby business so that passersby may know where to look for either free wireless Internet access or "free" information about the company.

The above information should be our very first lesson into the world of risk assessment regarding networking components. A medium such as fiber can be very secure due to its nature, but never 100 percent secure. Wireless and copper, on the other hand, should never be considered secure, no matter their location. The degree of exposure for each of these may vary, depending on where it is installed. If the physical plant of an organization is trusted and software controls on workstations are implemented, then copper can be considered a bit more secure. If the securing of the entire physical plant is too expensive or time consuming, consider encrypting the data on the copper — in this way, anyone who does manage to capture the data will only capture unreadable information.

Wireless, while insecure due to its broadcast nature, can be made more secure by careful positioning of the wireless devices in relationship to the outside world. Access points in the heart of your campus would be less likely to be accessed by those on the street than those hung on the outside walls of buildings. While the built-in encryption protocol of the popular 802.11b wireless networking has been shown to be ineffective, there are other options available for encrypting wireless transmission. Depending on your risk assessment and the value of your assets, the vulnerabilities of wireless data transmission may create an acceptable risk. These solutions are discussed in Chapter 11, "Wireless Network Security."

Other hardware that is generally classified as "physical layer" hardware are known as repeaters. During the days of yore on networks, when 10base5 and 10base2 coaxial copper media ruled the LAN, a common problem was the maximum transmission distances of the coaxial cable would place serious design constraints upon networks. The problem revolved around a concept known as attenuation. As an electrical signal traveled down a wire, it slowly lost strength and the receiving stations could no longer interpret it accurately until at some point the signal became so weak that it was unreadable by the receiving side.

To overcome the distance limitations, repeaters were installed on the network. As the name suggests, these devices received the digital signal in one port and retransmitted it out another port. The new signal would be just as clear and strong as the original and the several spans of coaxial cable could then be laid end to end. This process could theoretically occur a number of times until LANs of fantastic sizes could be built — were it not for the collision detection mechanisms of the data-link layer.

As the popular physical medium of the LAN moved from coaxial copper to the more flexible cat-5 UTP, the role of a repeater changed. Where coaxial-based LANs were known as "bus" topologies in that they shared a single length of coaxial cable between all stations, UTP LANs are always designed in a physical "star" topology. Because the UTP itself is even more sensitive to attenuation, and therefore distance considerations, than the coaxial cable, at the center of the star a repeater was placed to ensure that the signal from each host would be amplified enough to reach all other hosts. The two-port repeater of the bus topology gave way to multi-port repeaters of the star topology. We called these repeaters "hubs." A hub operates just like a repeater, except with multiple ports. A signal transmitted into one port of a hub is repeated without discretion out all other ports. The diagram in Exhibit 1 illustrates the common LAN topologies. For wireless and fiber-optic media, repeaters are still quite popular. Ask anyone who has shot 802.11b around a mountainside from their office to their home, or between the homes of friends — a repeater used to redirect the signal is quite handy. Long-haul fiber typically has repeaters every so many kilometers to keep

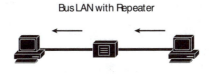

Bus LAN with Repeater

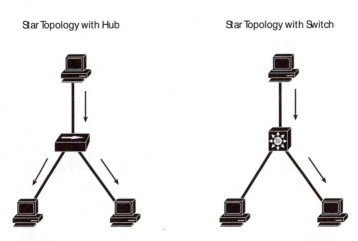

Exhibit 1. LAN Topologies

the signal strong, although these distances are increasing and nonpowered technologies such as erbium-doped fiber can, in some instances, eliminate the need for a separate repeater altogether.

In the office LAN, two-port repeaters are very rare, but the good old hub still holds a privileged spot in many workgroups. Hubs are a specific and well-known vulnerability when considering network security. Because a signal transmitted from one host can be heard by any host attached to any other port on the hub, all traffic is visible to all networked hosts at all times. The security provided by a hub alone is the equivalent of sharing secrets in a crowded room. If anyone in the room is intentionally listening for that secret, there is no way to hide it from them.

In truth, most network administrators are stuck with the physical media they have in place. A general understanding of the risks of the media itself, however, will provide the knowledge needed for a more accurate risk assessment for a corporation.

A summary of the physical layer follows:

- *Fiber optic:* High bandwidth, long distances, high cost. Generally the most secure physical medium due to the effort required in compromising it. Due to its expense, fiber is generally only used in long-haul circuits or specialized applications in server rooms and high-speed networking devices.

- *Copper:* Medium bandwidth, medium distances, medium cost. Can be compromised in any number of ways. The most complex is to read the flux in the magnetic field surrounding the copper as digital signals pass through it. Most of the time, that much effort is not required. RJ-45 ports are usually plentiful and conveniently located. If no ports are available, a network-attached host will generally suffice, providing the chance to load sniffing software onto the host. In short, suspect your copper.
- *Wireless:* Low bandwidth, low distance, and low cost. It is like having your own low-watt radio station. Anyone with a receiver that can tune into your frequency will be able to see all traffic on your network. In this respect, a wireless network can be equated to a hub in that all traffic is easily visible. Because the interloper can be some distance from the transmission sources themselves (or even the building), someone gathering packets can be difficult to detect. Wireless transmission should be considered an open book and not used without additional encryption of data at higher layers of the OSI model.

3.1.2 Data-Link Layer

The data link is the layer at which most framed protocols operate. Examples of data-link protocols include Ethernet, Token Ring, Frame Relay, ATM,[3] HDLC, and PPP. These protocols convey information from one host to another and typically operate between network nodes only. Each data-link layer is specifically tuned to a particular type of physical medium and often the standards that define the data-link layer also specify the expected operation of the physical layer. For example, Ethernet is defined in the IEEE 802.3 standard. This standard defines the operations of Ethernet from speeds of 10 Mbps to 1000 Mbps and defines protocol operation over different types of fiber and various types of copper.

Security concerns of the data-link layer, being closely tied to the physical layer, generally revolve around hardware and encryption. Because encryption is rarely performed at the data-link layer, we start our discussion with this short prelude.

Many types of physical media are vulnerable to eavesdropping. To protect against this, we can encrypt data-link layer data as it travels from link to link. This ensures that as the data is actually being transmitted, it will be very difficult for anyone to determine if the data is using some sort of device that reads the electromagnetic emanations from the media, such as a sniffer.

While this certainly sounds secure, there are several disadvantages that make this an option for only the most sensitive of data, and then only when there is no other option. First, the encryption engine adds additional expense to the network hardware, and this is generally not the type of equipment that you can purchase at an online wholesaler. Frames that travel from node to node based upon higher layer routing information need to be decrypted at each node so that a routing decision can be made upon the packet. Thus, even having the link encryption means that the packets must be in cleartext at some points as it travels through the network. The time and effort taken to encrypt and decrypt the packet at each hop add additional overhead and increase the overall delay of the network as well.

If the risk assessment determines that the data traveling over the Frame Relay links is of sufficient value and at a high risk for exposure, then link layer encryption is an option. For most of the cases involving the IP protocol that require encrypting data across the wire, there are better options. In some cases, however, link layer encryption could be considered. For example, if there is a great deal of non-IP traffic, such as SNA that is being distributed from a central hub location to remote sites over dedicated layer 2 links such as Frame Relay or X.25, clearly the option of using IP encryption does not apply.

The more common discussion of data-link security issues centers around the hardware normally found in a LAN environment. This is because unencrypted data is at the most risk because the effort required to capture it is minimal. A frame sent to one port is forwarded out all ports regardless of the ultimate destination of the frame. From a performance point of view, this is not optimal. The collision detection algorithms used by Ethernet dictate that in a shared environment, the total bandwidth over time available for any given station decreases as more hosts are added to the shared medium. Thus, ten stations sharing a 100-Mbps hub will, on average, each enjoy 10 Mbps of bandwidth available for use. When 25 stations share the same 100 Mbps and try to transmit at the same time, on average they will each have available 4 Mbps for use. This area of shared bandwidth creates what is known as a collision domain, an area of the network where hosts compete with each other to transmit their data over the network.

The initial solution to this performance problem was the bridge (see Exhibit 2). By logically breaking up a network into two or more collision domains, the number of stations that were competing for the same resources decreased. The performance for each host then increased, as, on average, more bandwidth was available for its use. A bridge would segment nodes by reading the data-link layer addresses as they passed through the bridge device. As more stations transmitted, the bridge would eventually learn the location of every host in relation to itself. Thus, when Host A sent

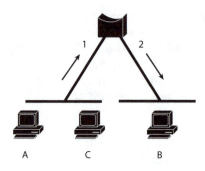

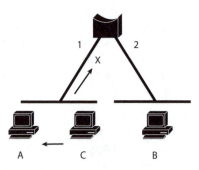

Exhibit 2. Learning Bridge Operation

a frame to Host B, the bridge, knowing that Host A was on port 1 and Host B was somewhere on port 2, would forward the frame from one port to another. At the same time, when Host C sent a frame to Host A, the bridge, knowing that they were on the same network segment, would not forward the frame between the two of them. The first bridges were expensive and simple devices that only had two ports and were used sparingly on a network. As the technology became more advanced and competition between networking vendors for Ethernet equipment heated up, the prices of bridges fell and the performance increased. By increasing the number of ports on a bridge, the Ethernet switch was created. Acting with the same logic as the bridge, the switch would rapidly learn the network topology as stations sent traffic during the normal course of business. When the switch knows the network topology, it would then only forward frames out the ports of hosts that were interested in receiving the frame. This, in effect, would give any two network hosts the illusion that they were sharing private communications facilities — much like what occurs when we make local telephone calls.

As long as the switch had the capacity to switch the traffic from port to port quickly enough, the performance of the network approached its theoretical maxima. In the common configuration of one host per switch port, the host has available to it the full transmission capacity of the medium, be it 10, 100, or 1000 Mbps.

While the cheap and available switch revolutionized our local area networks in terms of performance, they changed the security landscape — for a time. Unlike the hub, protocol exchanges between two hosts are not transmitted out all ports. Therefore, if Host A and Host B were exchanging packets, the forwarding logic of the switch would only forward information out the ports to which Host A and Host B were attached. If Host C located on another port wanted to capture traffic between the pair, it would be out of luck, as no data would be forwarded to Host C.

It would seem that, based on this, the switch was the perfect solution to combat network monitors. Considering that you could purchase a single technology that not only increased the performance of the network but also the security — then that would be a product that was worth every penny. With competition between hardware vendors dropping the price per port on a switch until they compare favorably with hubs, there is no reason not to use a switch instead of a hub.

The sense of security that switches used to provide has passed us however. There are a number of ways in which the data-link isolation provided by a switch can be circumvented. Using sophisticated spoofing techniques, an attacker is able to confuse the switch regarding the placement of network hosts.

The first method of confusing a switch is for a sniffing device to simply respond to ARP messages for IP addresses other than its own. In this manner, a sniffing host can cause a switch to forward a number of packets out the port of the sniffer.

A sniffer can also reply to ARP requests made for the router itself. This is effective because the switch then forwards packets to be routed to the sniffer, and the sniffer records the contents of the packets and then forwards them to the router with little outward indication of what has occurred. Reversing the process, the sniffer can respond to router ARPs pretending to be a local host on the network. By enabling the forwarding of IP packets on the sniffer, both directions of the communication can be sniffed despite the presence of the switch.

A host acting as a sniffer may also disable a remote host using a packet-based IP attack and take over the IP address the now-disabled host had. As far as the switch is concerned, the target host has simply switched ports and the switch dutifully begins forwarding packets to the new location — the sniffer.

Many times, the isolation offered by a switch can be defeated by flooding the switch with fake MAC addresses. A switch keeps track of the location of host and port based on a MAC address. If the portion of the switch memory allocated to retaining MAC addresses is overloaded, switches will begin to forward all traffic out all ports to ensure that traffic reaches the proper destination. In a sense, by flooding the switch with MAC addresses, an attacker can force a switch to act like a hub while it tries to recover from the attack.

Managed switches, while more expensive, are generally worth the investment because they allow the network administrator to create a number of virtual LANs (VLANs) to increase performance for small workgroups by reducing overall broadcast traffic or otherwise isolate hosts without the need for additional hardware. Managed switches, however, also allow what is known as port mirroring. While recognizing that for some troubleshooting and monitoring applications such as an intrusion detection system (IDS) the restriction on broadcasting can actually be detrimental, port mirroring allows certain ports to be configured to automatically receive or mirror traffic on any other port, group of ports, VLANs, or the entire switch. If not properly secured, the switch itself can actually facilitate the capturing of traffic. Again, we must assume that the network infrastructure is untrusted.

The amount of data that each host is allowed to transmit over a given data-link layer in a single frame is called the maximum transmit unit (MTU). The MTU is a design decision for each data-link layer and is based on several factors. The transmission speed of the data-link layer is one important consideration; links are more efficient with larger MTUs. This is because more of each frame is dedicated to data and less to overhead. Sharing characteristics are also taken into account for the data-link layer. If each host is allowed to transmit frames that are too large in a shared environment, then all other hosts need to wait to transmit their data. In small data exchanges, the large frames would cause unnecessarily long delays for small frames. The biggest factor influencing MTU selection, however, is the chip that is used to create the network interface card. One of the reasons that the MTU of Ethernet was set at 1500 octets was simply because at the time Ethernet was being developed, the cheapest, most available chip sets that could be found would support up to 1518 octets of data. While transmission speed and multiplexing of many hosts was an important consideration, the ultimate arbiter of MTU was the available hardware to support the given data-link layer.

Common MTU sizes are shown in Exhibit 3. With some restrictions, the MTU can be adjusted and, for many network media, this is often the case. Because the default MTU is also usually the maximum size that the network interface card can accept, the most common option is to set the MTU to a

Exhibit 3. Common Data-Link Layer MTUs in Octets

Media	MTU in Octets
Ethernet	1518
Gigabit Ethernet	64000 (only with Jumbo frames options selected)
Token Ring 4 Mbps	4000
Token Ring 16 Mbps	16000 (commonly set to 4000 for 4 Mbps compatability)
FDDI	4500
ATM	16000
PPP	1500 (lower values common over dial up links)
HDLC	18000 (lower values likewise common)

lower size, representing the least common denominator, to avoid fragmentation on other network media that have lower MTU values. MTU size is also an important issue for security-related reasons. MTUs that are too large may need to be fragmented somewhere in the network. This causes a decrease in network performance due to the routers' requirement of fragmentation and the hosts' requirement to reassemble the fragmented packet. As we discuss in the section on the IP layer, fragmented packets can also be a security risk. If you are concerned about IP packet fragments, changing MTU sizes on your network will eliminate them.

3.1.3 The Network Layer

At the network layer, or layer 3, the primary hardware device is the router. Routers are used to connect IP networks together, with each port on a router defining a single IP network. Generally, some sort of specialized computer with a number of network interfaces, routers make forwarding decisions based on the layer 3 addressing information in a datagram. Routers determine which interface a packet is forwarded out, based on a "routing table" (see Exhibit 4). The routing table is simply a list of all known network destinations along with the interface and next-hop IP address used to reach these destinations. In the event that there is more than one interface that would allow connectivity to a remote network, routing tables also include a metric of some sort that allows the routing process to make an objective decision as to which interface of many to use. There are two primary ways to create a routing table. The first is through static routes. This means that someone sits down in front of a router console and types in a statement that, roughly translated, would say, "To reach network 200.5.6.0/24, send the packet out the first Ethernet interface to the next router with an IP address of 135.10.15.254." This process could be repeated a number of times until all the relevant network destinations were entered. This approach, on a small scale, is very efficient. For large networks, it is time consuming, difficult to maintain as the network changes, and prone to human error.

```
R11#show ip route

       200.200.4.0/24 is variably subnetted, 2 subnets, 2 masks
O E1      200.200.4.0/27 [99/410] via 200.200.3.1, 00:08:20, Serial0.1
O E1      200.200.4.2/32 [99/410] via 200.200.3.1, 00:08:20, Serial0.1
       200.200.21.0/24 is variably subnetted, 2 subnets, 2 masks
O E1      200.200.21.0/25 [99/410] via 200.200.3.1, 00:08:20, Serial0.1
O E1      200.200.21.128/27 [99/410] via 200.200.3.1, 00:08:20, Serial0.1
       200.200.20.0/24 is variably subnetted, 7 subnets, 2 masks
O E1      200.200.20.0/25 [99/800] via 200.200.3.1, 00:11:52, Serial0.1
O E1      200.200.20.128/27 [99/410] via 200.200.3.1, 00:08:15, Serial0.1
C         200.200.20.128/27 is directly connected, Ethernet0
       200.200.1.0/27 is subnetted, 1 subnets
O         200.200.1.0 [110/780] via 200.200.3.1, 00:11:53, Serial0.1
       200.200.2.0/24 is variably subnetted, 2 subnets, 2 masks
I         200.200.2.0/24 [100/41162] via 200.200.20.130, 00:00:16, Ethernet0
O         200.200.2.0/27 [110/780] via 200.200.3.1, 00:11:53, Serial0.1
       200.200.3.0/27 is subnetted, 1 subnets
C         200.200.3.0 is directly connected, Serial0.1
       200.200.12.0/32 is subnetted, 1 subnets
O         200.200.12.1 [110/781] via 200.200.3.1, 00:11:53, Serial0.1
       200.200.40.0/24 is variably subnetted, 4 subnets, 2 masks
O E1      200.200.40.0/25 [99/410] via 200.200.3.1, 00:11:53, Serial0.1
O E1      200.200.40.128/27 [99/410] via 200.200.3.1, 00:08:22, Serial0.1
```

Destination Network   Metric   Next Hop IP Address   Next Hop Interface

Exhibit 4. A Sample Routing Table

To avoid the negative issues associated with static routes, dynamic routing protocols are often used. While there are a number of routing protocols that vary in complexity and suitability for one network type or another, in the end, each dynamic routing protocol is simply a way for a group of routers to share network reachability information with each other and create a local routing table.

When passing traffic from one IP subnet to another, a router is always used. As such, they serve as concentration points for network traffic. In this capacity, a router can be called into service to apply other needed network functions. Some examples may be firewall functions. This could include packet filtering, stateful packet filtering, network addresses translation (NAT), dynamic access-list generation, and even some higher layer protocol filtering such as is seen in application layer firewalls. Routers can also serve as Dynamic Host Configuration Protocol (DHCP) servers for the assignment of IP addresses, subnets, default gateways, and DNS servers to hosts. When connecting networks together using a VPN, routers can also serve as the physical endpoint of encryption. This means that each router will contain at least one VPN key that can be used in the encryption of VPN traffic — and its subsequent decryption.

As focal points of network traffic, routers will also be configured to track and monitor network traffic. This may simply total the volume of traffic in average bits per second, or it may mean volume and type of traffic between any two points. In a pinch, a router can also be used to load its own operating system image onto another router. This can be useful in restoring a router when the software operating system is not otherwise handy.

Few devices are more important to the idea of confidentiality, integrity, and availability than network routers. As the above description of some of the roles that a router plays in a typical network point out, several critical network functions are handled by a router.

Once a packet is en route from the host, the arbiter of that packet's fate is the router. Control of the routing tables is control of the network. For someone interested in sniffing data, careful manipulation of routing tables could direct data over a network that they have control over and have packet sniffers installed. Unless a particular issue requires troubleshooting, most users would not even notice the diversion of their traffic. Most users are accustomed to sessions timing out. If the routing manipulation occurs during an active session, users would habitually select the "reconnect" or "reload" button without a second thought.

Changing any security characteristics of the router would also severely impact the overall network security. Once again, as long as everything was working to the user's content, minor modifications to the firewall would mostly go unnoticed. The only way these changes could be detected was through the regular auditing of the perimeter security.

No attacker, unless he had access to computing resources that were greater than most in use today, would spend time trying to decrypt captured VPN traffic. Access to the routers themselves, however, may give the attacker enough information to recreate the session keys used in the VPN or even allow access to unrestricted data.

In the role of a network monitoring device, the router can also provide a wealth of information for those interested in learning more about the traffic patterns on a network. Some Simple Network Management Protocol (SNMP) configurations will even allow remote users to monitor and change the routers configuration — all of this without having to log in to the router itself.

It should be clear by now that the router should have special consideration in the overall security plan. While network connectivity may be impossible without them, a poorly configured or improperly secured router will severely compromise the security of a network.

3.2 Protocols

No serious study of network security can be accomplished without a solid understanding of the operation of the protocols used by network devices to communicate with other network devices. While there are a number of protocols used in networks around the world, when discussing a global network, the only set of protocols that is common to all networks is the TCP/IP protocol suite. On the local area network, other protocols such as AppleTalk, SNA, NetBEUI, and IPX may be encountered with decreasing frequency as the world continues to converge on TCP/IP as the networking protocols of choice.

Like the OSI Model, the TCP/IP suite is a collection of protocol layers that define the requirements of each layer of protocol communications. It is similar to the OSI Model with the exception that the top four layers of the OSI Model are represented as a single "application layer" in the TCP/IP suite. A graphic with the layers of the TCP/IP suite and associated protocols is shown in Exhibit 5. The network interface layer is roughly equivalent to the physical and data-link layers of the OSI Model. The network interface of the TCP/IP suite can be virtually anything that creates ones and zeros and has successfully (although jokingly) demonstrated to work using homing pigeons. All common data-link layer protocols are represented here, such as the various flavors and speeds of Ethernet, 802.11, PPP, HDLC, ATM, Frame Relay, X.25, and Token Ring. The major point of the network interface layer is that IP, which is responsible for getting transport layer information from point A to point B, does not care what the underlying network is created from. This transparency and adaptability is part of the enormous success of the TCP/IP suite.

3.2.1 Internet Protocol (IP)

The Internet layer of the TCP/IP suite is dominated by a discussion of a single protocol — the Internet Protocol commonly known as IP. IP is a connectionless, datagram-orientated protocol. An individual IP datagram is known as a "packet" and contains all the addressing information that the packet needs to get between points on a network. Datagram simply implies that big messages, like encyclopedias, are broken up into smaller messages for transport. By using datagrams, many packets carrying different pieces of information can share the network interface by weaving many conversations together as packets are put onto the network. Datagrams also make it much easier to recover from network errors, in that only the damaged data need be present and not the entire sequence.

There are currently two versions of IP in common use: IPv4 and IPv6.[4] Of the two, IPv4 is by far the most common protocol in use on production networks in the United States. In some European countries and Pacific Rim

TCP/IP suite layers   Sample Protocols at each layer

Application	HTTP POP3
	
	     BGP RIP RADIUS
	
	    NTP
	SMTP
	                SNMP
	FTP DNS
	
	Secure Shell Telnet DHCP
	
	      HTTPS Kerberos
	TACACS
	
	             And many, many others...

Transport	TLS/SSL TCP UDP
Internet	OSPF ICMP IP EIGRP IPSEC ARP/RARP

Network Interface	ATM
	    Ethernet HDLC
	
	Frame Relay
	       Token Ring
	
	802.11 PPP

Exhibit 5. The TCP/IP Suite and Common Protocols

nations, IPv6 is growing in popularity. In our discussion here, unless IPv6 is specifically mentioned, "IP" means IPv4.

For those interested, IPv6 offers several significant advantages over IPv4. Most often cited is the increase in IP addresses. While IPv4 allows a total of just over 4.2 billion addresses, the number of IPv6 addresses is on the order of 2^{128}.[5] It has been pointed out that there are more IPv6 addresses available than grains of sand in the world. IPv6 also offers improvements in routing efficiency, address allocation, and for purposes of this text — security. Most IPSec protocols discussed in this text are a "retrofitting" of security options built into IPv6.

"Connectionless" means that the IP layer does not keep any "state" about what packets it has sent. While the upper layers in a host, such as the transport layer or application layer in certain applications, go through a lot of effort to count packets and make sure they are reassembled in the correct order, IP sends a packet and forgets about it. When a router in a network routes an IP packet, it forgets about the individual packet.[6]

The design decision to make IP connectionless has a couple of important implications that apply to the performance and security of our networks. First, the performance. While many textbooks and vendor certifications make much to-do about the process of subnetting and configuring routing protocols, the operation of IP itself is fairly straightforward. This lends itself to a simpler network core. Instead of worrying about the sequencing of data and the path that the data takes, network devices such as routers can simply concentrate on getting data from one interface to another as quickly as possible. By simplifying the protocol as much as possible, the performance of the network is increased and the cost is decreased.

Other protocols commonly associated with IP include ARP, ICMP, and IGMP. There are others of course, but these are the most common. Each will be discussed briefly in turn.

The IP header, the data that routers and hosts use to address upper layer data, is shown in Exhibit 6. It is a common reaction, when faced with a diagram such as that in Exhibit 6, to roll your eyes up into your head and check your appointment book for important meetings discussing the value of life insurance. Regardless, understanding the header information in the TCP/IP suite is one of the most important steps in understanding the nature of network-based threats in your environment. I do not recommend memorizing the header structure unless you are forced to work in an environment that only examines packets in hexadecimal code. Instead, it is better to familiarize yourself with the fields of the header so that when examining suspicious traffic or reviewing network-based threats, you understand their operation.

As mentioned, the version number for an IP packet is currently 4. An IPv6 packet has an entirely different structure — essentially only the version field remains unchanged so that a host machine that supports both protocols will know how to read the remainder of the header after examining the first 4 bits.

The Internet header length (IHL) is the number of 32-bit words that then tell the host how long the IP header itself is. A 32-bit "word" is nothing more than a grouping of four octets of data. This format was standardized to facilitate the construction of efficient buffer space for protocol headers. TCP and UDP both follow the same format. The IHL allows the host to know

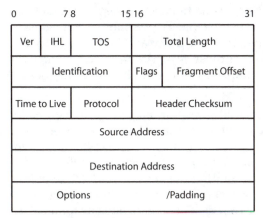

IP Header Format

Exhibit 6. The Internet Protocol Header

when to expect the next header, be it TCP, UDP, ICMP, etc. Note that the minimum that should be here is a value of 5 because the default header is a total of five 32-bit words. If the IHL has a value greater than 5, then you would expect to see a number of options added onto the IP packet header.

The type of service (TOS) field is commonly referred to as the "Quality of Service" (QoS) field. The first 3 bits of this field are used to indicate the priority of the packet and are known as the precedence bits. The next 3 bits are used to determine which type of network the packet should be routed over, if there is a choice. The options are to optimize the packet for minimal delay, maximize the throughput, or take the network path that is the most reliable.

It is a common mistaken assumption about IP that you cannot provide quality of service with it. You can provide QoS signaling in the protocol header; it is just that we generally do not act upon this QoS information in our networks. The lack of QoS is a result of a lack of agreement on how to provision the QoS mechanisms to provide scalable, end-to-end assurance that your data will meet a certain service level agreement. This is especially troublesome when routing packets over networks under diverse administrative control. The other problem facing QoS implementation is the interpretation of the precedence bits. It is difficult to get everyone to agree on what "best-effort" traffic should be and what "critical" traffic should be. Clearly, if everyone had the ability to set these values on his or her own, all traffic on the Internet would be marked as critical.

The TOS field is also not commonly utilized because to implement it in routers that could route a packet based on the delay, throughput, or reliability bits in the packet header would require the creation of multiple routing tables that is, one table for lowest delay, one for highest through-put, and one for most reliable. Furthermore, what would happen if a packet had the bits indicating low delay and high reliability set, yet the routing tables indicated that these two criteria were best met via separate paths? In the end, the complexity of the implementation doomed this effort from the start.

While the TOS field is not formally utilized as intended, it does have a number of uses for Internet traffic. There have been a number of efforts to standardize the contents of this field and define what type of traffic meets which criteria. Diffserv is the most widely deployed of these efforts. Diffserv is a specification that defines up to 64 "code-points" that define the treatment that a packet receives at each hop during its transmission. Some networks also use the original precedence bits for local traffic, but you cannot trust another network to implement these bits in the same way.

Because there is wide variation on the implementation of these bits, there are any number of combinations that can be observed in network traffic. This makes it difficult to determine if the information in this field is legitimate or not, and thus an ideal field for use as a covert channel.

Following the TOS field, 16 bits of the IP header are used to describe the overall length of the packet in octets. With 16 bits, the maximum size of an IP packet is 65,535 octets. Clearly, this is much larger than the most common maximum transmission units (MTUs) of most data-link segments. To facilitate the breaking of the IP packet into frames of the proper size for the data-link layer, IP supports the ability to be fragmented. The next 32-bit word in the IP header contains information critical to the fragmentation of the packet.

The first of the fields related to fragmentation is the identification (ID) field. Each packet that the host sends is uniquely labeled with a value from 1 to 65,535. If a packet needs to be fragmented, the ID of the original packet will be used to help the receiving host reassemble the datagram.

The next two fields of note in the IP packet are the DF (don't fragment) and the MF (more fragments) bits. As the names of these bits suggest, they relate to the process of fragmenting and reassembling datagrams.

There may be instances when an IP packet should not be fragmented. In this case, the DF bit is set. When a router or other network device determines to pass over the data-link layer on the way to the next hop, the packet must be fragmented and the DF bit is set to 1. The router does not attempt fragmentation and, instead, returns an ICMP "fragmentation needed and DF bit set" error message to the originating host. This technique is commonly used to determine the minimum MTU across multiple data links. When trying to discover the MTU across a series of dissimilar links, the sending host will send out a large packet with the "do not fragment" bit set. When the packet hits a link that has a smaller MTU than the packet, an error message is sent back to the originating host from the router, representing the link with the small MTU. The sending host then sends a smaller packet with the "do not fragment" bit set and tries again. The process is repeated with increasingly smaller packets until the packet is successfully transmitted across the network. While this adds overhead and delay to the initial transmission process, it decreases the amount of fragmentation taking place in the network.

When the MF bit is set to 1, this tells the receiving host that the packet is fragmented and the host should expect more fragmented packets sharing the same ID value to be reassembled before passing them up to the transport layer. When the router receives a packet that has the MF bit set to 0, it assumes that the last fragment has been received for the packet and attempts to reassemble the data.

To help the *receiving host* determine where in the packet the fragmented data should be placed, the fragment offset field indicates where in the *original packet* this particular fragment should be placed.

Fragmentation can be a complex process that significantly slows down the devices that must fragment and reassemble the packets. Furthermore, creating illogical packets that cannot be reassembled is a common network attack that is used to disable a remote host. In addition, this technique can sometimes be used to circumvent some firewalls.

Fragmentation slows down the routing process because of where it occurs. Consider the illustration in Exhibit 7. Host A is sending a packet that is 1500 octets to Host B. While this MTU is fine for the Ethernet segments to which the hosts are connected, the PPP connection between the two routers only supports an MTU of 576. The first router in the path that is able to transmit the packet over the PPP segment must then fragment this packet.Routers have recently begun to offer very high forwarding rates and can now operate at what is known as "line-speed" in many circumstances. This means that as fast as you can send packets to a router, it

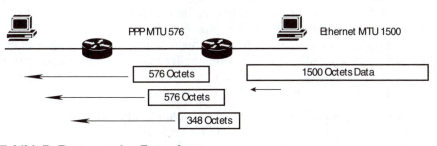

Exhibit 7. Fragmentation Example

can forward them. Previously, this feat was the province of layer 2 switches only because the forwarding logic on a router required software processing of the packet. Routers will now cache next-hop information on an interface and greatly increase their performance. This increase, however, only applies to standard IP packets. Packets that require special treatment such as fragmentation must be processed by the software functions on the router. The performance of the router decreases when it needs to fragment a great many packets.

Historically, IP stacks were written with the idea that the information that they were going to receive was going to be sane. If a host received fragmentation information that was not sane, then it might panic and crash. There are a number of ways to create troublesome packet fragments. The simplest way is to simply never send the last packet in the fragment. If the receiving host never receives that MF = 0, indicating that it was the last packet, it consumes resources waiting. Another way to confuse reassembly would be to construct packets so that the fragmentation offsets overlapped when the receiving host tried to reassemble them. Instead of fitting together like pieces of a puzzle, the overlapping fragment offsets would be equivalent to an operating system trying to put a round peg in a square hole. Finally, one could arrange the fragments so that when they were put together, the packet size was greater than the maximum IP size of 65,535 octets of data.

Most of the attacks described above have been well documented and fixed in most operating system protocol stacks. It does, however, show the danger of using fragmented packets. Instead, attackers have now moved to using fragmented packets in different ways.

When an IP packet is fragmented, only the first fragment contains the original IP header and upper layer information. For example, if a TCP segment is fragmented into five smaller packets, only the first fragment will contain the port information and control bits. Using a packet filtering firewall presents a particular problem because it is this very information that the firewall uses to make filtering decisions. When a firewall sees the separate fragments without the transport layer information included and the fragmentation bit set, it must either assume that the packet is part of a series of fragments and allow it through, or deny the fragments altogether. The first option creates vulnerability in the firewall that an attacker can utilize by just making all the traffic look like fragments. The second option could create problems for users who are using applications located on remote networks that genuinely have a need for fragmentation.

Due to the number of problems with fragmentation, its use is discouraged. The transport layer protocol TCP (Transmission Control Protocol) has a mechanism as an option known as MTU path discovery. This allows the sending host to use the DF bit in traffic to try to estimate the maximum

MTU of remote networks and send packets with that MTU, thereby avoiding fragmentation. IPv6, while not forbidding fragmentation, has put the responsibility for creating properly sized packets onto the sending host, again to avoid the need for fragmentation. Because not all hosts are configured with the MTU discovery options and for a great many in the world IPv6 is still a few years off, fragmentation is an issue that needs to be understood and dealt with today.

The time to live (TTL) field of an IP packet is normally used as a hop count. It is used to remove packets from the network that do not seem like they are ever going to reach their destinations. Without this field, packets could circle the network indefinitely. The original concept of the TTL was that each possible value in the field from 0 to 255 would represent one second. Upon implementation, however, it became clear that it was tougher than expected to estimate how much time a packet was spending in a router or in transit. If there were delay or congestion in the router, how would that be accounted for as well? The only way to do this would be to record the time the packet entered the router and the time that it left — for each packet! This clearly is too much to handle when routers process millions of packets per second. Instead, a simpler use for the TTL was devised. Each time a router forwarded an IP packet, it would decrement the TTL by a value of one (1). When the TTL reached 0 and the packet had not reached its final destination, an ICMP "time to live exceeded in transit" message would be sent back to the originating host.

Due to the current implementations of the TTL field, in IPv6, the TTL is renamed to the more accurate "Hop Count."

The popular application Traceroute (see Exhibit 8) uses decrementing TTL fields to be able to map out a network. The first packet sent by Traceroute will have a TTL of one (1). This means that when it hits the first router, the first router will decrement the TTL to 0 and return an ICMP error message to the sending host. The next packet is then sent with a TTL of 2. This second packet makes it to the second router, which then sends back an ICMP error message. Because each ICMP message has a source IP address of the originating router, this allows a listing of each router in the network path to be recorded. This is an incredibly useful tool when troubleshooting network connectivity issues. It is also an incredibly useful tool to map network devices and paths.To prevent this from occurring, some network administrators will configure firewalls and routers not to return any information when a TTL of 0 is created on their device. This lack of information, however, can be just as useful to an attacker. If I create a Traceroute to your Web server and notice that the last two hops before the server itself do not return ICMP replies, then I have a clue as to what your internal network structure is.

```
C:\>tracert www.proteris.com
```

TTL 1

Tracing route to www.proteris.com [66.113.130.206]
over a maximum of 30 hops:

Network path from host to destination

```
  1   10 ms   20 ms   10 ms  10.15.72.1
  2   20 ms   20 ms   20 ms  24.54.39.173
  3   20 ms   20 ms   20 ms  24.48.10.21
  4   30 ms   30 ms   30 ms  p1-01-02-00.r0.phl00.adelphiacom.net [66.109.4.14
9]
  5   30 ms   30 ms   40 ms  p3-00-00-00.n0.phl00.adelphiacom.net [66.109.0.12
5]
  6   60 ms   70 ms   60 ms  p3-00-03-00.n0.chi75.adelphiacom.net [66.109.0.57
]
  7   60 ms   70 ms   60 ms  p3-00-00-00.r0.chi75.adelphiacom.net [66.109.0.13
8]
  8   60 ms   70 ms   60 ms  g1-00-00-00.p0.chi75.adelphiacom.net [66.109.3.10
]
  9   60 ms   70 ms   60 ms  gigabitethernet1-0.ipcolo1.Chicago1.Level3.net [1
66.90.73.193]
 10   60 ms   70 ms   60 ms  gigabitethernet5-0.core1.Chicago1.Level3.net [209
.244.8.41]
 11   60 ms   70 ms   60 ms  so-4-0-0.mp1.Chicago1.Level3.net [209.247.10.161]

 12   60 ms   70 ms   70 ms  so-6-0-0.edge1.Chicago1.Level3.net [209.244.8.10]

 13   61 ms   70 ms   70 ms  POS1-2.BR1.CHI13.ALTERNET [209.0.225.42]
 14   60 ms   80 ms   60 ms  0.so-5-0-0.XL2.CHI13.ALTERNET [152.63.73.21]
 15   90 ms   90 ms   90 ms  0.so-3-0-0.XL2.CHI4.ALTERNET [152.63.2.50]
 16   90 ms   90 ms   90 ms  0.so-4-0-0.XR2.CHI4.ALTERNET [152.63.2.58]
 17   90 ms   90 ms   90 ms  290.ATM6-0.XR2.CHI6.ALTERNET [152.63.65.106]
 18   90 ms   90 ms   90 ms  500.at-7-3-0.CL2.CHI6.ALTERNET [152.63.64.33]
 19   91 ms   90 ms   90 ms  0.so-7-0-0.GW8.CHI6.ALTERNET [152.63.64.25]
```

TTL 22

```
 20   90 ms   91 ms   90 ms  hostway-gw.customer.alter.net [157.130.122.174]
 21   90 ms   91 ms   90 ms  lfw100.siteprotect.com [66.113.129.251]
 22   90 ms   90 ms   91 ms  lsh148.siteprotect.com [66.113.130.206]
```

3 packets sent to obtain average delay

Exhibit 8. Sample Traceroute

The 8 bits of the protocol field in the IP header describe what the header that follows the IP header is going to be. Combined with the Internet header length field, the receiving host now knows how many total bits are included in the IP header and when those bits end, and what the next group of bits should be interpreted as. There are 95 defined protocol values that can be found here; the most common are listed in Exhibit 9. While the list in Exhibit 9 is by no means all-inclusive, it does represent the most common values that would be found in a secure environment, especially one that is using IPSec. If you should happen to see protocol values that include anything different, then it would be worth your time to investigate what is creating them and where they are going. If you have a requirement for a

Exhibit 9. Common IP Packet Types

Protocol	Decimal Value	Hex Value
ICMP	1	0x01
IGMP	2	0x02
TCP	6	0x06
UDP	17	0x11
RSVP (end-to-end QoS reservations)	46	0x2E
GRE (tunneling protocol commonly used with VPNs)	47	0x2F
ESP (IPSec encrypted packets)	50	0x32
AH (IPSec authentication header)	51	0x33
IGRP (routing)	88	0x58
OSPF (routing)	89	0x59

more complete listing, the most recent port assignments can always be found at http://www.iana.org.

The checksum field of the IP header is simply a mechanism used to ensure that data in the IP header itself is not corrupted in transit. Because certain fields in the IP header such as the TTL need to be changed at each hop, the checksum likewise needs to be calculated at each hop. The normal behavior for a host that determines that the checksum is corrupt is to discard the packet. It would be very difficult to manipulate this field into an effective attack.

The final two fields in the IP header are fairly self-explanatory. They contain the values of the source and destination of the packet. One thing that is not often clear and is worth pointing out is that most routers will only act upon the destination of the packet. The source of the packet is irrelevant until it comes time to return the packet to the sender. It is therefore a simple matter to send IP packets with spoofed source addresses. The routers along the path generally do not pay attention to the source. This also means that technologies such as network address translation (NAT), discussed Chapter 8, are not required to *send* packets over the Internet. NAT just makes sure that the packet has a valid source so that the data can be returned.

Finally, the last field of the IP packet header is the options field. This field is appended to the IP packet header in 32-byte increments if additional options are added to the IP packet. While there are a number of options available, we will only discuss the one that deals most directly with security — source routing — and then explain why IP options are rarely used.

Of the 25 or so defined IP options, from a security perspective, the most interesting options are those that define source routing. Source routing comes in two flavors: loose and strict. Both options include IP addresses that the sender of the packet wishes to send the IP packet through, as it is en route to its final destination. As the name suggests, loose source routing defines a single hop. This option in effect says to routers along the path, "I don't care which path you take to get me to my final destination, but make sure you send me through the network node with this IP address in it." Strict source routing, instead of offering a single hop, defines the entire path along which the packet should be sent. Strict source routing says to routers, "When sending me to the final destination, make sure that you send me through each node in this list of IP addresses."

Source routing used to be a popular and effective tool for network troubleshooting. It allowed network administrators to remotely test various parts and paths of a network, regardless of how the routing protocols preferred to route data. Unfortunately, this functionality is rarely used anymore because this same technique can also be used by attackers to route packets through networks of their choosing. This is an effective way to get packets onto private networks, for example. Attackers on the Internet may wish to send a packet to a server located at a private address on a target LAN. Normally, they could never send a packet directly to this server; but using source routing, they can define the path right up to the company access routers and manage to inject the packet onto the otherwise unreachable private address space. Thus, most routers now filter source routing to reduce the risk of this option.

IP options, in general, are rarely used. The reason is that IP options tend to negatively affect router performance. IP-based routers, in order to forward packets at very high speeds, perform the forwarding logic in hardware. The registers that hold the IP header information are very specific and work well when the fields are very well defined, such as a standard IP header. IP options, however, can be any number of values. Like fragmentation, this means that the forwarding for the packets must be popped out of the hardware logic and processed by software — a process that is considerably slower than hardware forwarding.

3.2.2 Address Resolution Protocol (ARP)

IP routing needs the assistance of other protocols to be fully functional. ARP (Address Resolution Protocol) is just one of those protocols. While the TCP/IP suite finds other computers using a globally unique IP address, the actual data transmission has to occur over some type of data-link layer. This is commonly known as layer 2 forwarding in deference to the OSI Model.

Multi-access data-link layers such as Ethernet or Token Ring on the other hand may have hundreds of hosts on any network segment. There needs to be a way to uniquely identify these hosts for the transmissions of frames at the data link. The address used by these protocols is known as a

MAC address (i.e., Media Access Control address). Every network interface card sold for Ethernet networks, whether they are used in routers, workstations, or firewalls, come with a factory-set MAC address that is globally unique.

When a local host has a packet to send, it will encapsulate that IP information in a data-link frame and that frame will contain the MAC address of the sending host in the data-link frame. To obtain the MAC address of the destination of the packet, the sending host will first use the ARP process to query the local network. A broadcast LAN frame is sent out saying, "Any host out there on the network with the IP address 200.20.15.5 please respond to this broadcast with your MAC address!" (Of course, substitute the IP address given above with whichever one is being queried.)

Each data-link layer has its own method of addressing. Some protocols such as Frame Relay use a data-link connection identifier (DLCI) that takes a value from 15 to 1024; and others such as as PPP or HDLC have nominal addressing because they are only used on point-to-point links. In the case of point-to-point connections, if a host receives a frame, it is not difficult to figure out where it came from; and more importantly, there is not a lot of thinking that needs to occur when attempting to send the packet.

The results of the ARP queries let hosts know where to find each other at the IP layer. For example, Host A will learn that the IP address of Host B can be reached by sending frames with a destination MAC address of 00-40-05-DF-20-9C[7] and that the IP address of Host C can be reached by sending a frame with the destination MAC address of 00-10-A4-0A-4C-4F. As far as Host A is concerned, the MAC address in its database *is* the identity of the remote host.

This has interesting implications from a security point of view. An attacker can quickly masquerade as any given IP address by simply listening to the network and responding to ARP requests. At the very least, the location of active hosts can be ascertained, because an ARP request is broadcast and forwarded by all switches.

Switches listen to ARP broadcasts, responses, and data frames to learn the network topology. As each ARP request passes through the switch's interfaces, it records the MAC address source of the frame containing the ARP and associates that MAC address with a port on the switch. When future frames are sent, the switch knows to forward a frame appropriately out a given port and thus create the appearance of a private circuit between two communicating hosts and improving overall network performance and privacy.

As previously discussed, one advantage to employing a switch was that it became more difficult to sniff passwords and other sensitive information off the network because the switch would only forward traffic between the two hosts involved. By understanding the operation of ARP, this privacy can be circumvented. By occasionally responding to ARPs for important network resources, the attacker can make it appear to the switch that the location of the network resource has changed ports for a time. The switch, believing the new information to be correct, will forward frames to the port of the attacker, allowing them to observe information for some period of time. If it happens to be the period of time that a user is sending their log-in information, then the effort may be worth it for the attacker.

3.2.3   *Internet Control Messaging Protocol (ICMP)*

The second major protocol that is generally considered part of the Internet layer is the Internet Control Messaging Protocol (ICMP). To understand the utility of ICMP, consider this: most of the time IP itself is either passing incoming data up to the TCP/UDP transport layer, or passing outgoing data down to the network interface layer. What if there was an important message to deliver *to* the Internet layer itself? Examples might be messages such as: "The host (IP address) you are sending packets to does not exist," or "The time to live of the packet that you sent has expired and it was discarded en route to its destination." To deliver messages such as these and others, the ICMP is used. One of the most useful applications for network troubleshooting is the Ping application. Ping generally uses a special ICMP packet that sends an echo-request that asks, "Are you there?", to which the remote host (assuming it is there) replies with an echo-response saying, "I am here."

There are a total of 11 ICMP message types, each of which applies to Internet-layer-to-Internet-layer communications. Some ICMP messages such as "source quench" are rarely used, due to a lack of need. Source quench was designed to have one host tell another to slow down the transmission rate of information that is being sent. For the most part, that applications that require such service have built in their own flow control algorithms. Even if a receiving host sends a source quench, there is no assurance that the sender is going to slow down anyway.

Other ICMP message types are used with caution as they can be used to cause Denial of Service attacks. This option refers to the "redirect" ICMP message (see Exhibit 10). Commonly, ICMP redirect messages are used on network segments with multiple gateways. Each host is configured with a default gateway, but if the gateway itself receives a packet and determines that another locally attached gateway would better serve in the routing of that packet, a redirect will be sent to the original sending host of the packet telling it to forward packets directly to the secondary gateway in the future. This application of the redirect function makes the gateways operate more efficiently and improves performance for the sending host. The ICMP redirects can also be used to denial of service a network as well. By

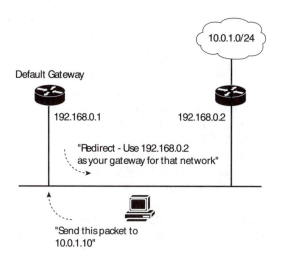

Exhibit 10. ICMP Redirect Example

sending redirect packets to a host that look like they came from a gateway, the host will then begin to forward packets to a nonexistent gateway.

ICMP, like IP itself, is a connectionless protocol. This means that packets are sent and there is no means of keeping track of what has been sent, what order they have been sent in, or flow control. The ICMP packet itself does contain an identifier field that may or may not be used on a per-packet basis. Its use is determined by the type of ICMP packet being sent, as described below.

The "spray and pray" connectionless nature of ICMP makes it an excellent tool for flooding a network with packets in DoS attacks. It is also a commonly used transport for fragmentation-based attacks such as the Ping of Death and other variants.

ICMP presents a particular problem when configuring stateful packet filters and receiving ICMP packets. Consider the following example. Host A wants to ensure that Host B is "alive," so it sends echo request packets using ICMP. Because ICMP is connectionless, the Internet layer itself makes no effort to associate outbound packets with any type of state information. When Host B receives a number of ICMP packets and returns the echo reply, how does Host A know which reply was in response to which packet it sent out? Or, what if Host A was simply trying to connect to a Web page and was sending a TCP SYN packet to a remote host? At this point, Host A is expecting a TCP SYN ACK in reply; but if the remote host is not available, Host A may receive an ICMP "host unreachable" message from an intervening router. In this second case, Host A is not even expecting an ICMP packet and between the connection attempt and the response may have sent out dozens of packets. How does it know to associate the host unreachable packet with that single failed TCP connection?

To provide information to the receiver of the ICMP packet, ICMP responses include the first 64 octets of data from the packet that generated the error condition. In the case of echoes, this allows the ICMP echo-request information and the identification field of the echo-request field to be included. In the case of the failed TCP connection, the data returned is the IP header and the TCP header, which would include source address and port information. In each case, by providing extra information, the sender of the first packet is able to piece together what has occurred. If multiple echo requests have been sent, the sender is able to associate each response with a request. If dozens of TCP connection requests have been made, the originator of the requests is able to determine which request has failed due to the ICMP information returned in the error message.

This behavior by ICMP makes it particularly suitable for use in covert channels. A covert channel is a communications pathway that is not clearly a communications path. By manipulating the value of bits in unused or seldom used fields, information can be relayed. It may not be very high bandwidth, but the information can be hidden and passed through a firewall. Because ICMP has a comparatively large number of bits in the identification field that are only used rarely, this field is ideal for hiding information.

Here is an example using ICMP as a covert channel for controlling a remote application. You have somehow managed to convince someone internal to the network that you wanted to attack, to install a Trojan program on a host. Perhaps you e-mailed it to them or got them to download it from a Web site. To control the Trojan, you need to communicate with it, so you have it configured to send ICMP echo-request packets to a remote site when the host is turned on. Because most firewall policies allow echo-request through for troubleshooting purposes, this packet makes it to your remote command center. To communicate your intentions back to the Trojan, you simply send back an echo-reply. Inside the ICMP header, encoded in just a few bits, are your instructions for the Trojan. The popular denial-of service-tools based on Tribe Flood Network (TFN) operate in this very manner.

ICMP can be a double-edged sword in the world of network protocols. On the one hand, it is incredibly useful when trying to troubleshoot a remote network or otherwise deal with connectivity issues. Any network troubleshooter of any skill will first start with the PING application to quickly zero in on the problem. Either the remote host is not working properly or the network is not working properly. PING and ICMP allow a trouble-shooter to quickly establish where to concentrate their efforts.

The information available from ICMP, while valuable for troubleshooting and reporting, is also dangerous when used against your network. An attacker can determine the approximate layout of your network in a matter of seconds using ICMP and PING sweepers — programs that send out a number of PING packets to a range of IP addresses rather quickly. Firewalls and other network access controls need to be carefully configured to allow only the proper ICMP message through.

Commonly, packet filters will be used to deny all ICMP traffic inbound to the network except ICMP echo-reply packets. The theory is that if someone on the inside of the network sent an ICMP echo-request packet as part of the PING application, the only legitimate response should be an echo-reply. Other solutions include configuring a single server with full ICMP access. When troubleshooting through the firewall, network technicians will source traffic from this single host.

3.2.4   IP Options

IP also supports the inclusion of multiple options. The most commonly encountered options are those related to source routing. For reasons of security and performance, options at the IP layer are commonly disabled, not used, or not allowed on certain networks.

As previously discussed, source routing is the ability to define in an IP packet the path that the IP packet should take en route to its final destination. Due to the potential for abuse, both options are typically disallowed on routers and through firewalls. Imagine the scenario where an attacker instructs two hosts to communicate with each other yet routes the packets through his or her remote network.

As discussed with fragmentation, the use of options also degrades the overall performance of routers. Because the options can take many different values, they must be individually examined by the software routing process instead of letting the much more efficient caching of routes forward the packets.

3.2.5   IP-Related Issues

Along with the construction of the IP header, there are numerous other technologies that security-conscious professionals need to be aware of. This section discusses the operation and security implications of technologies such as Dynamic Host Configuration Protocol (DHCP), private addresses, network address translation (NAT), and the various routing protocols that can be used on a network and how to employ them in a secure manner.

3.2.5.1   Dynamic Host Configuration Protocol. The first topic of discussion is the DHCP. Odds are that you may have changed the IP address on your computer at one point in time. The process of changing an IP address, for any given computer, takes anywhere from one to five minutes. This of course does not include the time it takes to walk to the computer, talk to the user for a couple of minutes, get them to save their work, etc. For any single device, the process is not that onerous. Multiply that by 100 or 500 and IP address management becomes a job that most network administrators dread. It should come as no surprise that we enlisted the help of computers to make this process easier on us. After all, that is why we use them so much, is it not? Instead of managing IP addresses on single computers, we create a small server that has a pool of IP addresses. When a computer powers up first thing in the morning, the first thing it does, network-wise, is to send out a broadcast packet requesting an IP address from any local DHCP server. The DHCP server will then select an IP address from its pool of available addresses and loan it to the requesting client.

From a security point of view, this should be the first concern. Because the computer that is booting does not yet have an IP address to use, or any type of IP configuration for that matter, it cannot send a request to a specific DHCP server. Instead, it broadcasts the packet, and the first DHCP server that answers the broadcast is the one that the booting host accepts. A rogue DHCP server could potentially provide configuration parameters to requesting clients a good portion of the time if it were able to respond to client requests before the valid DHCP server were to.

To examine the level of vulnerability to false DHCP configuration requests, let us first examine what else that DHCP can be used for. The primary purpose — the assigning of an IP address — we have already covered. An IP address, however, is not all that a computer needs to be able to utilize network resources. At a minimum, any IP address requires a subnet mask to be relevant. This is not a book on subnetting, but to put it briefly, a subnet mask is a way of letting a computer know how the IP network has been broken up. Instead of having one big network with 500 computers in it, each using a single IP address, you can have two (or more) smaller networks, each with only 250 hosts in it. A host computer understands the way you have broken up the network based upon the information in the subnet mask.

With an IP address and a subnet mask, a computer has everything that it needs to be able to communicate, using IP, with other computers on its directly attached network. This means that if all the computers are attached to the same hub or switch, they can communicate. For modern networks, which we expect to communicate with networks all over the world, we do not have enough information yet. We also need to tell the computer where to send packets that are destined for other networks. Because we cannot reasonably assume that each desktop, laptop, or server on a network knows the location of every single other of the

500 million hosts attached to the Internet, we simply give our hosts a single instruction: "When you have a packet destined for somewhere not on your network, send it to the default gateway and let the gateway figure out what to do with the packet." All we need to do on the host to make this process work is tell it the location of the default gateway. Default gateways are also known as default routers in some applications, so do not be concerned if you see different terminology. The "default" is the clue that will explain the function.

You would think that we have everything we need by this point — and we do. We have everything that we need on the host to get it to forward IP packets properly. All you need to know now is the IP address of the remote resource and the protocols take care of the rest. If I were to give you a quick quiz and asked you the IP address of your company's Web server, unless you were the administrator of the e-mail server on your network, you would either have to think for a moment or just plain look it up. Imagine if I were to ask you to browse to the fark.com Web site. Quick! What is the IP address?

Of course we poor humans cannot remember such details for all the possible network resources we want to use, so we use the domain name system (DNS) to do this lookup for us. For a host computer to be able to perform such a lookup, it needs to be configured with the IP address of one or more DNS servers. This is another common element that DHCP will configure for our hosts.

IP address, subnet mask, default gateway, and DNS servers — these are the four minimal configuration options for Internet connectivity. There are others types of servers and information that DHCP can provide for hosts but they are specific to the operating environment. From these four alone, however, three risks immediately present themselves.

3.2.5.2 DHCP Security Concerns. A rogue DHCP server assigning either a bad IP address or subnet mask would effectively create a denial-of-service (DoS) for the network host. Likewise, assigning incorrect DNS servers or default gateways would do the same. Incorrect information in any one of these fields would prevent hosts from accessing network resources, as many network administrators have discovered from their own legitimate DHCP configurations. While an annoyance, such attacks are easily discovered. Because something was not working, the first thing a network administrator would typically do is examine the IP-related information that was assigned to that host. Even a casual examination would show that incorrect information has been assigned and the hunt would be on for the cause. A double-check of the legitimate DHCP server would show it to be working and, in short order, the rogue DHCP server would be discovered. Imagine, however, an attack that is much more insidious and shows no outward indications of breaking anything. If, for example, an incorrect default gateway is assigned, all traffic leaving the network could be sent to a particular host and then back out onto the network. The user notices nothing, but all the while the host acting as the default gateway is able to examine each packet as it is sent. This form of packet sniffing would defeat even a switch. Because most users do not habitually check their IP address information obtained through DHCP (if they even understand what they are looking at), this attack can go undetected for some time.

Another attack along those same lines is simply to change the location of the DNS servers. Instead of using the company DNS server, name/address resolution requests could be sent to a DNS server with custom entries for certain sites such as the company's mail server, Web pages, and SQL server. The location of the rogue DNS server and modified network resources are irrelevant as the helpful network ensures that packets are being forwarded correctly. With a bit of doctoring, each of these fake resources could be made to appear as the actual resource. This is especially effective when log-ins are required. At some point, the process would break down, but by then a great deal of damage could have already been done.

Lest you believe such events to be unlikely on your network, consider that custom mini PCs with built-in networking cards are easily created, built from scratch, or built from game consoles (Sony Playstations, for example) that can contain the DHCP server, sniffer, DNS server, and false server resources all at once. These devices are then configured to periodically "phone home" to deposit any information that they have learned. Inconspicuously dropped into a vacant network port and kicked under a desk, these devices can be very difficult to find and require only a moment of physical access to the network and in most cases are small enough to fit in a briefcase or knapsack.

While a rogue DHCP server can be difficult to find, the effects of one can be greatly minimized by following sound security principles. Restrict physical access to the network to only those who require it. Encrypt traffic in transit so that it cannot be sniffed. Use server authentication in the form of public keys to prevent other devices from masquerading as important resources. Each of these options for reducing these threats will be discussed in the following sections and chapters.

3.2.5.3 Private IP Addresses. IPv4 addresses are rumored to be in short supply. Around the mid-1990s, there was such a worry that the growing Internet would utilize all 4.2 billion available IP addresses that a flurry of activity was undertaken to find solutions to this problem. In addition to utilization, there were a number of other problems with IP addresses related to the scalability of our current addressing plans. One of the most clear-cut solutions to all of the problems of IP addressing was IP version 6

(IPv6). This increases the number of available IP addresses into the trillions and at the same time solves a number of other scalability problems, including security. The security solution introduced with IPv6 is the IPSec suite of protocols that we now use to secure our networks. As far as the rest of the IPv6 protocol, it became clear that the work required to migrate a global Internet to a new network layer protocol would take years, if not decades, to accomplish. In the short term, a number of other solutions were introduced at the same time as IPv6. These solutions include variable-length subnet masking (VLSM) and classless interdomain routing (CIDR). These two solutions together are used to solve many of the scaling problems of IPv4. They do not, however, directly affect the number of available IP addresses that we can use with IPv4. The value of these solutions is that they allow us to more efficiently utilize our existing IPv4 addresses.

The primary shortage of IP addresses and IPv4 is a result of the requirement that each Internet host use a unique address. Each IP address and each IP network number can only be used once. This means that the network number your ISP has assigned you for your network can never be used on another network without causing confusion on Internet routing tables. To many, this seemed inefficient. What we needed was some way to reuse the same network numbers.

To help overcome this shortage, the IETF (Internet Engineering Task Force) combined an existing address allocation scheme known as private addressing with a new technology, network address translation (NAT). For some time, there had been the requirement that private IP networks not connected to the Internet have a reserved address space. The goal of this was to avoid any confusion should a network ever connect to the Internet and to spare companies without Internet access the task of applying for IP address blocks from the IETF. The IETF took a look at the current IP address allocations (*circa* mid-1990s) and found large chunks of the old class A, B, and C address space that were unallocated. The IETF then decreed that these network spaces would be able to be reused by anyone on their private networks. There was, of course, one caveat. If you were going to connect to the Internet, you could not advertise these private addresses to the rest of the world. That is, they could only be used to get information from point A to point B inside your own network, not across the Internet.

The addresses designated as private appear below:

10.0.0.0/8 (255.0.0.0) — 16,777,216 addresses

172.16.0.0/12 (255.248.0.0) — 1,048,576 addresses

192.168.0.0/16 (255.255.0.0) — 65,536 addresses

NETWORK PERIMETER SECURITY: BUILDING DEFENSE IN-DEPTH

Clearly, such large address spaces are meant to be subnetted into smaller networks, allowing companies quite a bit of flexibility with complicated internal network topologies.

When working with customers and training, I commonly hear the association that "private addresses are not routable." This is not accurate. Private addresses are just as routable and functional as normal public IP addresses. Any one of the private network numbers can be used to create private routed networks that are quite large, all with no special network configuration required. Private networks and packets destined to private addresses are not exchanged over the Internet because ISPs will filter private networks from their routing tables. This is important to remember when considering network security. Unless configured otherwise, a router or other network host will treat a private address just like any other address. We revisit this concept when discussing router security and route filtering.

3.2.5.4 Network Address Translation. The ability to reuse the same network space by separate unconnected organizations through private addressing was a great boon to the temporary shortage of IPv4 addresses. Clearly, however, at some point network administrators with private addresses would want to connect to the Internet. If this is going to happen, there needs to be some way to translate the private reusable addresses into something unique. This is the role of network address translation (NAT) and it is the second technology that has allowed us to conserve the IP address space by allowing network administrators to connect privately addressed networks to the Internet. NAT is a service that resides on a gateway device, be it a firewall or a router. The best way to understand the operation of NAT is with a quick tutorial. In Exhibit 11, Host A is sending a packet to Host B on the Internet. When Host A sends the packet, the source of the packet is Host A's private IP address and the destination is Host B's public IP address. When the packet passes through the firewall, the firewall changes the source of Host A's packet to make it look like the source is a public IP address that is part of a pool[8] of public addresses reserved on the firewall. In this specific example, the public address pool is the same as the address assigned to the firewall public interface. At the same time the address is changed, other options in the IP and TCP header are changed as well to reflect the new source address. When Host B receives the packet and returns its own packet, the source of the packet is now Host B's public IP address, and the destination is the public IP address that the firewall inserted into the packet.When the firewall receives the packet, it consults its NAT table, which is simply a table that indicates that it changed the source of a packet from Host A to Host B. When the return packet is seen, the firewall performs a reverse translation and changes the destination IP address of the packet from the public address to the private IP address of Host A.

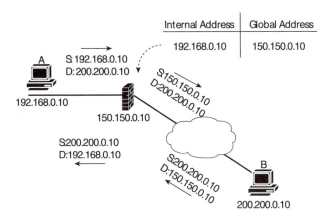

Internal Address	Global Address
192.168.0.10	150.150.0.10

Exhibit 11. NAT Example

Internal to the private network, the packet is routed to Host A, which receives the packet none the wiser that any translation has occurred.

It is a common misconception that NAT is needed to *send* packets onto the Internet. From the example above, we see that Host A sends a packet that is entirely able to make it to Host B as the *destination* of the packet is correct. Without NAT, however, when Host B tries to *return* the packet to Host A, the routing of the packet will fail because now there will be a private address in the destination. Because backbone routers and most access routers are specifically configured to filter packets to private addresses, the return of the packet to Host A will fail.

To perform a translation, the NAT device needs to be configured with at least one public IP address to use in translations. In the early days of NAT, this led to a NAT device only being able to concurrently translate addresses on a one public:one private basis. For example, if a NAT device were configured with six public addresses, then at most, six devices internal to the network could access the Internet at a time. This was the only way that the NAT device could keep packets straight in its NAT table. If you had a network of 200 users and could expect concurrent Internet sessions from all of them, you would need 200 public addresses for the NAT device. This is hardly an address saving technique!

Allowing more internal hosts configured with private addresses to share public IP addresses requires additional information to allow the NAT device to properly associate return traffic from the Internet with the proper internal host. In addition to IP addresses, transport layer and other protocol headers provide enough unique information to allow return traffic to multiple internal hosts to be reverse translated from a single IP address. By expanding the NAT translation tables to include both IP addresses and transport layer ports, network address translation expanded to include port address translation (PAT). Today, PAT is so common that when NAT is mentioned, it is commonly assumed to include PAT.

For some time, NAT has been touted as a network firewalling technique. It is commonly employed as part of a firewall, but should never be considered a stand-alone security solution for your company. We now discuss the relative security offered by NAT. First, the pro-firewall logic will be examined.

"NAT protects your internal network because unless there is a currently active connection, someone scanning your network from the outside cannot reach your internal hosts. This makes it more difficult for people to map your network and make connections to internal hosts."

This is true. The way that NAT works is that the NAT table creates a temporary entry when dynamic NAT is used. Dynamic NAT simply means that every time a client passes through the NAT device, there is no assurance that it will receive the same translation as it did the last time. In the case of a large NAT pool, Host A will appear to the Internet to be a different IP address each time it connects to Internet resources. When the connection has completed, the old entry in the NAT table is removed, allowing other hosts to use the address/port combination for outbound traffic.

NAT fails as a stand-alone security technique in several respects. The first is that dynamic NAT is not the only way to employ NAT. Let us assume that internal to your private network you have some resources that you want remote sites to be able to access, such as SMTP and POP3 servers. Because internal to your network they are configured with private addresses, you will need to translate packets sent from them or to them at the NAT gateway. To ensure reachability from outside the firewall, you will have to make sure that the NAT is the same IP address and port all the time. That is, you will have to create static NAT entries. From the point of view of someone on the Internet, some of your most interesting resources (servers) look like they have public IP addresses. That NAT is being transparently employed between you and the attacker has no effect on the attack. Packets sent from the attacker are translated with the same facility that legitimate packets are sent. Thus, no protection is provided for Internet resources through the use of NAT.

When attacking other internal hosts, there are many easier ways to attack a network host other than actively scanning a NAT device and guessing at active translations. Perhaps the easiest way to attack a computer on a privately addressed network is to simply convince the user to connect to you or otherwise download your attack to their computer themselves. This is true regardless of the presence or absence of NAT. For example, you could send them an e-mail with a suggestive subject line and a plausible-looking attachment. Despite this being one of the most common transmission methods for viruses and worms, it still works. Once a program is installed on a computer with private addressing, it can connect or "phone home" right through the NAT device just as any other application on the computer would. There are a number of attack vectors that are not related to scanning that NAT does nothing to protect against.

What does NAT do for us? It allows the use of private addresses internal to our network to ensure that traffic sent from our network can return properly. Does it provide some security? Yes, but NAT alone should never be considered adequate protection from network attacks. If you go through the process of creating a security policy and properly evaluating threats and vulnerabilities, you would find that only defense in depth will ever protect your network properly.

3.2.6   Routing Protocols

This section discusses the operation of common routing protocols, how they affect the security of your network, and the steps that can be taken to help the routing protocols operate in a more secure manner.

3.2.6.1   LAN Routing Protocols. A router forwards packets. A router forwards packets according to the information in its routing table. It is the cardinal rule of routing that if there is not an entry in the routing table instructing the router what to do with the packet, then the packet is dropped. Clearly, the routing tables are important to the overall functioning of our networks. The question is, how does network information get into the routing tables to begin with? There are basically two ways to accomplish this. As a network administrator, you could sit down with a diagram of your network, log on to each router, and specifically tell it where to send packets to reach all parts of your network. This manual entry of routing information is known as *static routing*. While you create a very complex network using nothing but static routing, only the most masochistic network administrator would attempt such a thing. When static routing is used, the routers will use the information entered by the administrator, regardless of the state of the network. Thus, if there were a failure or addition to the network, the only way to ensure reachability to all portions of the network would be to log back into all of your routers and update the static routes. In the meantime, your network users are in the parking lot racing office chairs because no network-based work can occur.

Indeed, instead of relying on static routes, we looked for some way to have each router inform all other routers in the network of what networks it is attached to. This process of automatic communication between the routers is known as a *routing protocol*. As with most things in technology, there are multiple ways and opinions as to the best way to do things and routing protocols are no exception. There are a number of routing protocols

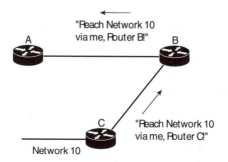

Exhibit 12. Distance Vector Routing

that can be used on your own network and all enable each router to learn the relative position of each network to itself.

Production routing protocols come in two major flavors known as distance vector and link state. Simply put, a distance vector routing protocol exchanges routing information directly with its neighbor. As Exhibit 12 shows, Router A learns about Network 10 from Router B. Router C tells Router B, and Router B then tells Router A. There are three distance vector routing protocols in common use and they go by the names of Routing Information Protocol versions 1 (RIP) and 2 (RIPv2), Interior Gateway Routing Protocol (IGRP), and the Enhanced Interior Gateway Routing Protocol (EIGRP).[9] The other major family of routing protocols likely to be found on internal networks is the family of link state routing protocols. Using multicast packets, link state routers communicate with all other routers in the network. Thus, in Exhibit 12, Router A hears about Network C through a multicast packet sent directly from C. Link state routers use this information to create something known as a link state database. This link state database is essentially a snapshot of the network. From the link state database, the routing tables are created. The most common link state routing protocol found in commercial environments today is the Open Shortest Path First (OSPF) protocol. The Intermediate System to Intermediate System (IS-IS) protocol is also used, although with less frequency and typically on larger, older ISP backbones. Functionally, the two protocols are similar; and if one is employed, there are few compelling reasons to change to the other.

3.2.6.2 The Border Gateway Protocol. All the routing protocols mentioned thus far are known collectively as Interior Gateway Protocols (IGPs). This means that they are all meant to be used internally to an autonomous system (AS). An autonomous system is nothing other than a routing domain that is under the administrative control of a single entity. Therefore, the largest enterprise network is a single AS and my test network within my office is a single AS. Size is not important with regard to the definition of an AS, but who controls the network is. By this definition, we can see that when most people talk about their network or their company LAN/WAN, they are technically speaking of their AS. Inside your AS, the IGP that you use is totally up to you. You will make a decision about which routing protocol to use based on the size of your network, the amount of changes and growth you expect your network to have, the amount of control you want over your network traffic, and, of course, the security required for your routing protocols. You can use either link state or distance vector routing protocols. While many networks converge on a single routing protocol, it is not unusual to find link state and distance vector protocols coexisting on the same network. When you send traffic to another network, you will typically have one of two choices: either static routes or the exterior gateway protocol known as the Border Gateway Protocol version 4 (BGPv4 or just BGP).

BGP is known as a path vector routing protocol, so it is not quite a distance vector routing protocol and it is most certainly not a link state routing protocol. Rather, it is in a class of its own. BGP is the routing protocol that allows the packets on your LAN to reach a Web server on the other side of the world, and its use is mandatory if you wish to be a major network presence on the Internet. As a routing protocol, BGP simply creates a routing table such as RIP or OSPF; but because it needs to control enormous numbers of routes from networks around the world, it is quite a bit more powerful, flexible, and configurable. As such, we will see that the security considerations of routers running this protocol need to be taken into consideration because anyone able to control BGP is able to inflict serious damage not only to your network but also the Internet as a whole.

With that cursory introduction to routing protocols out of the way, let us examine how the choice of routing protocols can affect the security of your network. In the above discussion, we saw that routing protocols can roughly be divided into two categories: (1)those that are used inside your network, the interior gateway protocols (IGPs), and (2) those that are used between your network and someone else's, the exterior gateway protocols (EGPs). Of the EGP family, there is only one routing protocol that is used, the Border Gateway Protocol version 4 (BGP). There is also a special type of routing table entry, the static route that can be used inside and between networks. Each of these will be addressed in turn.

IGPs control where the traffic inside your network is sent. The vast majority of small office/corporate office networks only have one or two routers at most. In this case there will not be much redundancy in the network and, as such, the routing protocols will be sharing limited information. In the rest of corporate or ISP networks that have quite a few routers and are large networks, there may be hundreds of routers sharing a common routing protocol and building local routing tables on each router. It is these routing tables that allow all areas internal to your network to be reached and direct traffic off your network as appropriate. The manipulation of these routing protocols can have disastrous effects on your company. A brief example illustrates this.

The operation of the routing protocol RIP is to broadcast packets to any host that will listen to the state of that particular router's routing table. Other RIP routers listen for those packets and then update their own routing tables according to what they hear. The ability to capture a routing table, while not the type of information you would normally want available, pales in comparison to what else someone with malicious intent could do while taking advantage of RIP operation. Because RIP is configured to listen to any packet that looks like a RIP packet, it is a simple procedure to create a fake RIP packet with routing information that suits the attacker's goals. This can have several effects. One effect would be to funnel all routed packets through a particular machine for reading. Because the routing tables can be manipulated on a per-subnet basis, this can also affect traffic destined to only a particular subnet — such as the server farm. Less sophisticated manipulation can simply route all packets to incorrect subnets, effectively creating a denial-of-service situation.

This type of problem is caused because routing protocols, by default, do not perform any authentication of the information they receive. Whether it is RIP, EIGRP, or OSPF, packets that look right are assumed to be valid. The solution to this problem is to configure authentication as part of the routing protocols. A password/key for each router interface can be assigned as part of the routing protocol configuration. The key is hashed[10] using MD5 or SHA-1 and then sent as part of the routing protocol updates in each packet. Routers that receive the updates will hash their own password/key and compare the result to that included in the packet. If they are the same, the routing update is considered to be from a valid source. Replay attacks are prevented through the use of incrementing sequence numbers that are also protected by hashing.

There are a couple of things to be aware of with this solution. The first is that not all routing protocols support authentication. RIP is a notable example of a routing protocol that does not allow authentication and is very commonly implemented. If authentication is required, then RIPv2 should be used instead. It should be noted, however, that the IETF considers RIP itself a historical protocol and advocates the use of OSPF in future installations. The second major consideration regarding authentication is that none of these routing protocols support the actual encryption. Anyone with the ability to capture data would still be able to read your routing tables. That said, there are other ways to figure out a network topology without reading the routing tables, but it certainly does make things easier for a would-be attacker.

The final consideration of authentication is that someone on your network can easily end up inadvertently negatively affecting network reachability. If you change or otherwise carelessly modify the authentication key on one interface, that router will immediately stop accepting updates from its neighbors, effectively cutting itself off from the rest of the network. This creates an additional amount of maintenance, administration, and configuration overhead that must be considered when determining if the authentication scheme should be used.

For routing between ASs, such as your network and that of a business partner or an upstream ISP, either static routes or BGP will be used. Typically, if a network is only single-homed — that is, it has only one data connection to another network — static routes will be used. If a network is multi-homed, having more than one data link to one or more remote networks, BGP will most commonly be the routing protocol in use although it is not unheard of to use static routes in this instance as well.

BGP is unique among routing protocols in that it is designed with flexibility and control at the forefront. Other routing protocols can be manipulated to control what routing information they accept, but that is really a secondary function for them. BGP, on the other hand, must be configured with this control to work. It is easy to demonstrate the reason. When you control the routing information, you control where information is sent and what information is sent to you. By controlling what you send other networks, you affect who is able to reach your network. By controlling what you receive from other networks, you control your ability to reach Internet destinations. From a security and routing efficiency point of view, these are things that we would expect from any protocol that allows you to directly peer with another network.

The configuration of BGP requires that you manually configure your peer relationships. This means that between you and your service provider, you will enter a command in the BGP configuration that says, "Only accept network updates from this particular peer router." Because your upstream connection is typically a point-to-point serial link of some sort, the ability of someone to interject false information between you and your service provider is limited. Inside your own network, you will also create BGP peering sessions with other routers. To preserve the integrity of routing information exchanged via BGP peer routers, BGP allows the configuration of authentication much like the IGPs allow.

The far greater risk associated with BGP, however, is the insertion of inconsistent or bogus routing information from networks that you do not peer with. Remember that the entire Internet is simply a bunch of networks connected at various points and share routing information via BGP. So, the entire networking world is a mesh of BGP peers sharing routing information. Neither you nor your neighbor may be originating bad information, but someone in another country could be sending bad information, which could eventually find its way back to you. If this is the case, your network would be only one of thousands that would suffer from a wide-scale threat. To prevent this, ISPs and other responsible organizations will configure their own BGP to double-check the information they are sending and, more importantly, receiving from others. You will need to ensure that your BGP configuration does the same.

The actual process of configuring BGP is complicated and is best left to those who specialize in configuring BGP. Therefore, I will not offer specific advice in this text on the configuration of the protocol. Entire texts have been written only for this purpose. Importantly, however, there is a difference between configuring BGP for optimal routing and configuring BGP in a secure manner. In practice, optimal routing and security can be achieved. This discussion provides information you need to work with your routing expert to ensure that BGP is being applied in a secure manner. It should be noted that most service providers, recognizing the importance of BGP to the overall health of the Internet, apply the same general rules to their own BGP configurations.

Filtering routes with BGP is very specific to the vendor you are using, yet a few rules can be generalized. First, the Internet routing tables, when summarized, account for 108,000 to 120,000 routes. From time to time as someone else misconfigures their BGP, the number of routes may jump by 50,000 to 60,000 routes. This spike will adversely affect the performance of your router. Most BGP implementations allow you to limit the total number of BGP routes being accepted from your peers. Placing a conservative number of 125,000 routes should be acceptable for legitimate routes and still protect against leaks in the routing table.

Every time a route is added or removed from the BGP tables, that update must be propagated through the Internet. On the scale of over a 100,000 routes, these changes alone create quite a bit of traffic and consume processing as each router readjusts its own routing tables to reflect the new change. By purposely causing a number of routes to go up and down (such as pulling the connector on the access-link), instability can ripple across the Internet. To help protect against this, a technique known as *route flap dampening* can be applied to the BGP process. Route flap dampening simply means that if the state of a route changes a configurable number of times within a certain time frame, then the route will be suppressed (removed) from the routing table. Typically, the dampening period will be three times in 15 minutes with a suppression of 45 minutes. Even with route flap dampening configured, the number of changes on the Internet routing tables is on the order of one to two updates per second.

When possible, BGP should be configured to accept and send only those routes that you specifically want the rest of the world to gain access to. For example, assume that you have two major network numbers in your internal network. These networks are each divided into ten subnets. One of the networks is an internal network that you do not want to be advertised. If you do not advertise it out over your Internet connection, nobody will ever be able to send packets to that network. You have taken several other precautions, such as firewalling and packet filtering traffic from that network, but the extra layer of information to consider is ensuring that the private network is not advertised at all using BGP. Control routing tables and you control traffic. Do not tell anyone about the private network and no traffic will be sent to it.

Likewise, there is no need to advertise the ten separate subnets of your public network to the rest of the world. Most ISPs will not accept all of the subnet entries because it would cause their routing tables to grow too quickly. To ensure the efficiency of the Internet routing tables and shield specific information about your network as much as possible, you should only advertise the network block summarized as a single network and not the specific subnets.

The other common method of configuring routing, especially to upstream peers, is through the use of static routes. Due to the amount of processing power required to process BGP information and the fact that if you have only one access link to the rest of the Internet, a simple static default route saying, "Send any traffic not part of my network upstream," is sufficient. After all, knowing 100,000 routes only makes sense if you have a choice as to which way to send packets, hence the application of BGP to multi-homed networks.

From a security perspective, static routes have advantages. Because they are configured on each router and do not depend on information from another source, they are difficult to change or influence without access to the router itself. On the other hand, they can be an administrative nightmare because they do not reflect changing network conditions. For a simple single-homed network, however, static routes are preferred. Indeed, unless you are multi-homed, many ISPs will insist that you use static routes when peering with them.

3.2.7 *Transmission Control Protocol (TCP)*

3.2.7.1 Transmission Control Protocol Basics. Of the most common protocol headers, the Transmission Control Protocol (TCP) header (see Exhibit 13) contains the most detail and is the most complicated. While the

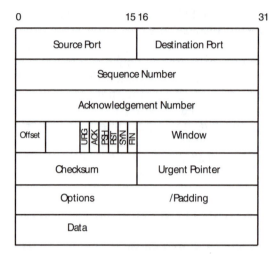

TCP Header Format

Exhibit 13. Transmission Control Protocol Header Format

combination of fields and options may seem overwhelming, understanding this protocol is critical to the understanding of network-based security.

The first two fields — source and destination ports — apply to the software addresses used by the transport layer processes to pass data to application layer processes. It is the information in the port fields that allows a computer to run multiple client and server applications at once. If a server is acting as a Web server, mail server, and DNS server, when it receives a packet to its single IP address, how does the TCP/IP stack know which application the packet is ultimately destined for? When initialized, each server process listed above will begin to listen for information on a port listed in its configuration file. Each client process will use a random source port for its communication to the server.

In a simplified example, Host A wishes to view a Web page at Host B. Host A sends a TCP packet with a destination port of 80, which is the standard port for an HTTP server. The source port of that packet will be a random port,[11] generally higher than 1023. For this example, assume that it uses port 5440. When the Web server at Host B receives the request, it reverses the source and destination ports and sends the reply to port 5440 with a source of 80.

A port can be any number between 0 and 65535. With such a range, the Internet community has come to the consensus that certain popular services, such as relaying e-mail, Web servers, file servers, and the like, will be run on certain "well-known" port numbers. This ensures that a user in Europe can connect to a Web server in the United States without having to first call the company she is interested in to learn of the port that the TCP connection should be initiated to.

A complete list of the well-known ports and a number of other ports commonly used for services can be found online at http://www.iana.org. Note that this list is considered the standard and obsoletes an older RFC 1700 that defined the well-known ports.

Other than the well-known port numbers, which are ports in the range of 0 to 1023, there is also a range of "Registered" ports. These ports can be used for application servers that do not fall into the traditional well-known range. The Registered ports are in the range of 1024 to 49151. Above that range, the ports are considered "private" and can be used freely within an organization.

Just because a certain port is listed as a certain service does not mean that if you notice that port 80 is running on a host device that it is necessarily running a Web server. Ports are easily configurable within an application. To try to confuse would-be attackers, some network administrators run their network services on non-standard ports. This technique does not work for long because port scanning will show that *something* is listening on an open port. It is generally just a matter of connecting to the port once you notice it is listening to determine the service running.

Running services on non-standard ports is also a way to circumvent firewall rules. "Legitimate" Internet services such as the World Wide Web are often found on port 80. Chat servers or media streaming servers are configured to listen on port 80 with the assumption that most firewalls allow users to surf Web pages. This knowledge can also be used by attackers and is commonly how spyware operates. If an attacker manages to install a Trojan on a host computer, that host computer can generally be assured Internet access through port 80 on the firewall. Spyware, which monitors user's Internet activities for sale to marketing services, will also phone home on port 80 with the assumption that traffic through the firewall is generally allowed.

The combination of TCP port information and the IP addresses used in the connection is known as a "socket" and is used to uniquely identify connections between TCP hosts. The common representation of a socket is [IP address]:[local port]. As an example, an HTTP connection between a client and a server would be represented as 200.1.1.1:2053 as the socket for the client and 200.1.1.100:80 as the socket for the server.

The next field in the TCP header is that of the sequence numbers. This 32-bit number is how TCP processes on hosts keep track of what has been sent and received. When initiating a connection, the TCP stack sends an initial sequence number to the remote host. This number essentially tells the host, "When I send you data, I'm going to start counting at 1,657,145,002."

Each *octet of data* that the sending host then sends will increment the sequence number by a value of one.

Because it would be very wasteful of network bandwidth to send a single octet (8 bits) of data per packet, TCP sends a group of packets all at once.

The receiving TCP host acknowledges what it has received from the sender by using the Acknowledgement field. This 32-bit field is where the receiver indicates that "The next sequence number I expect from you is: 1,768,145,953." Upon receiving the acknowledgement number, the sender will then determine if the receiver has received everything that has been sent. If there is a discrepancy between the sequence number that the sender has counted to and the acknowledgement number that the receiver has, then the sender will know exactly what data is missing and resend it.

The data offset field in the TCP header serves the same function that the Internet header length (IHL) field in an IP packet. It describes to the receiving host how many 32-bit words are in the TCP header. At a minimum, this value will be 5; but because options are more commonly used in TCP than in IP, it can greater than 5.

There are 6 bits reserved in the TCP header. According to the official specifications, these reserved bits need to be zeros. They can, however, be used for covert data channels although this use is more commonly found using an ICMP packet along with popular Trojans.

There are six control bits in the TCP header. Using these bits, the TCP connection is created, controlled, and torn down at the end of a transmission or due to errors. Understanding these bits is critical to the proper implementation of a packet filter firewall. In order, the bits are named URG (urgent), ACK (acknowledgement), PSH (push), RST (reset), SYN (synchronize), and FIN (finish). A short discussion of the significance of each follows.

The URG bit indicates to a receiving TCP process that some of the data in the data field is considered "urgent" and demands immediate attention. What qualifies as urgent is up to the application developer. To tell the TCP receiver where the urgent data is, another field in the TCP header known as the Urgent Pointer indicates where in the bitstream the urgent data starts.

The ACK bit is set every time a packet acknowledges the receipt of data from a remote sender. TCP is a protocol that operates in full duplex. That is to say, that while Host A is sending data to Host B over a virtual connection, Host B can send data to Host A over the same connection. There is no need to establish a separate channel for return data. It also means that at the same time Host B sends data to Host A, it acknowledges what it has received from Host A up to that point. Under normal circumstances, for established connections, the ACK bit can be set in every packet. This is so typical that to determine the difference between a previously established connection and a new connection, a packet filtering firewall looks for the presence of an ACK bit alone or in conjunction with a SYN bit in TCP traffic to determine if it should filter the packet.

Under normal circumstances, a receiving TCP host will buffer a certain amount of data and reassemble it into application layer data before passing up to the application layer itself for use. This introduces a small amount of delay that might be noticeable in interactive applications. When the PSH bit is set, this informs the receiver to pass the information up to the application layer without first buffering it. The most common applications of the PSH bit are in the use of HTTP applications. Imagine that an entire Web page is 150K in size. As the receiving host, my Web browser could buffer the entire 150K until the transmission is complete and then display the page in its entirety. The alternative is to display the data as it arrives. From the point of view of the network, it takes the same amount of time to transmit the data in either case. From the point of view of the user, however, the second option seems to be the more responsive Web site because visual feedback is provided as the page loads on the Web browser.

If there is an error in the communications that one host cannot recover from, a packet is sent with the RST bit set. This is a notification that the connection is going to terminate — immediately. Attackers trying to determine the presence of a host, even if ICMP is disabled, can use this behavior to their advantage. By sending a packet with the ACK bit set to make it look like part of an established connection, a remote host will send an RST packet in response. From the point of view of the host sending the RST, the original packet that was part of a scan was just a packet "out of the blue." Assuming that there must be some sort of error in the connection, the host helpfully responds with the RST in hopes of alerting the scanning machine of the error condition.

Because TCP sequence numbers do not start from zero, at the initiation of every TCP connection, the sequence numbers must be synchronized. This is an indication that a new connection is being requested and the synchronization of sequence numbers occurring is signified through the SYN bit in a TCP header. Under normal circumstances, this bit will only be set twice in a TCP communication. The first SYN is set in the initial connection request packet along with the initial sequence number. The second SYN seen in the transaction is sent in reply to the first packet. This indicates that the second host is willing to accept the connection request and synchronize its own sequence numbers with the initiator.

If TCP sequence numbers started at zero, then the synchronization process would not be necessary. There is a design reason for not starting the sequence numbers at zero. Assume that Host A connects to Host B and starts transmitting data. For the sake of this example, the sequence numbers have started at zero. At some point in the connection, the socket between Host A and Host B is broken. Host A reconnects and creates a new virtual circuit to continue the data transmission and starts the sequence numbers at zero again. From some other point in the network, a few packets from the first connection show up at Host B. Because the sequence number space for the two connections overlaps, Host B has no way of knowing if the packets are from the first connection or the second connection. No matter the decision that Host B makes about the packets — to keep them or discard them — there is a significant chance of the second connection becoming corrupted.

For this reason, the sequence numbers must increment periodically to make sure that in the event of new connections, the sequence numbers between the two connections are unique. This also translates into a security mechanism. If the sequence numbers would be easy to predict, which they would be if the session started from zero, an attacker would be able to guess what window the remote host were accepting and insert packets into the stream, hijack the connection altogether, or replay previous packets in an attempt to disrupt the integrity of the transmitted data.

For the proper synchronization of sequence numbers at the start of a TCP connection, three packets are required. Host A sends a packet with the initial sequence number (ISN) and the SYN bit set, indicating that it would like the remote host to acknowledge the ISN and synchronize its own sequence numbers. The remote host, Host B, responds with a SYN of its own and its ISN. To acknowledge to Host A that its sequence numbers were properly received, Host B also sets the ACK bit. At this point, both sides now know the sequence numbers that the remote is going to use when the transfer of user data begins. One more packet is required, however. Host A sends back an ACK of its own to indicate to Host B that it has received the SYN from Host B. This TCP connection setup process is known as the "three-way handshake."

The final control bit, aptly named the FIN bit, is used by hosts to indicate that they are ready to take down an established TCP connection. While a three-way handshake is used to set up TCP connections, two, two-packet exchanges are used to take down the connection. Host A will send Host B a packet with the FIN bit set, indicating that it is ready to tear down the connection. Host B will respond with an ACK of the FIN. Because TCP is a full-duplex connection, Host B may still have data to transmit. To indicate that Host B is finished sending data, Host B will send its own FIN packet and receive the ACK packet from Host A to finally tear down the connection.

3.2.7.2 TCP Operation. We examine a typical TCP connection below; but after our discussion of the control bits of the TCP header, you might start to get the idea that, under normal circumstances, there are only certain combinations of controls bits that should ever be set at any point in time. For example, it really only makes sense for the SYN bit to be seen either alone or with the ACK bit as part of a TCP connection setup. It would be atypical to see the SYN and FIN bit together, however. The earlier programmers of TCP/IP applications took logical control bit combinations into account. Often, the TCP process was programmed only to understand what to do when the obvious logical combinations were presented to it. Attackers took advantage of this type of programming to create a number of threats that exploit the TCP stack. By creating packets that contained control bit combinations that do not make sense, attackers soon realized that a number of TCP stacks on various operating systems could be crashed. Two of the most well-known variations are the "Christmas tree" packet and the null-packet. In the Christmas tree packet, all the control bits are set at the same time. This would typically end up crashing the host recipient of such a packet, as it simply does not have a place in normal TCP communications. The null-packet, on the other hand, has none of the control bits set. This is just as surprising to a receiving host as careful examination of the data exchange process shows that, at the very least, either the SYN or ACK bit is normally set.

All of these combinations have been tried, crashed a lot of systems, and then patched. While we hope that current protocol programmers will account for non-valid data as much as they do valid data, it is helpful to know that a crucial element of overall network security is the secure development of applications. Sadly, constant examples of new attacks using malformed packets show that the overall network community is still learning that all data must be checked before being processed.

To control the amount of data sent between hosts at any given time, the window field is used. This is a 16-bit field that indicates how many octets the sender of the packet is willing to accept. Through this mechanism, a slower TCP host can establish some sort of flow control with a faster TCP host. The size of the window is related to the buffer space that the receiver of the TCP segments has available. With each ACK that a host transmits during a connection, the window size will be set in a packet that indicates how much buffer space in octets of data is available. The host that is transmitting data, upon receipt of the information in the window field, then knows how much to send before it expects an ACK for the information. This amount of information may represent a single packet's worth of data or multiple packets of data.

The proper behavior of the TCP, based on the information in the window field, is crucial to the scaling and performance of TCP on the Internet and in your own networks. Because TCP is connection oriented, when data is lost, it must be retransmitted. Data in a TCP connection can be lost in one of two places: it is lost in the network, or the receiver has run out of sufficient buffer space to hold the packets. Either case will result in resending the TCP data that was lost. If the sending host does not honor the window size information, then packets may be continually dropped as the remote host constantly fills up its buffers and is forced to discard packets. These packets end up being retransmitted and contribute to further congestion in the network.

The window field is also used to slow down a TCP host when packets are successfully transmitted and make sure that packets transmitted are not dropped. If packets are lost in the network, the sending host will assume that the network was congested and reduce the window size, effectively reducing the amount of information that is sent at one time.

The relationship between the window size and TCP behavior during network congestion has a couple of interesting ramifications. The first is that certain programmers have created TCP stacks that behave just the opposite of normal TCP when congestion (packet loss) occurs. Because these programmers know that if there is network congestion, everyone else's TCP connections will automatically slow down, they create their stack to speed up, thus taking advantage of the newly freed up bandwidth (to the detriment of all other network users). While an interesting application of TCP behavior, other ways of exploiting normal TCP behavior are more damaging to your network.

The flow control that TCP exerts on its own connections makes it a well-behaved protocol. Other protocols, such as UDP (User Datagram Protocol) and ICMP, have no concept of flow control. If packets are lost in a UDP stream, there is not even a mechanism for either the sending or the receiving host to notice the loss. Well-behaved traffic like TCP can be muscled off a network by protocols such as UDP. As the network traffic increases, the TCP application slows down and UDP will fill in the remaining bandwidth. This is one reason that UDP and ICMP are popular protocols to utilize in network bandwidth-based denial-of-service attacks. The only real way to prevent this from occurring is to artificially flow control UDP and other connectionless traffic through the use of network QoS (quality-of-service) mechanisms. In this case, proper network design and quality of service become effective countermeasures for the risk of denial-of-service.

Similar to IP, TCP makes use of a one's complement checksum algorithm. Unlike IP, the TCP checksum is based on the information in the TCP header itself and the "pseudo header." The pseudo header includes the source and destination IP address from the IP field, the protocol type field, and the TCP header and data length. The inclusion of the pseudo header in the checksum helps prevent the inclusion of misrouted segments as part of a valid TCP connection.

TCP has the ability to include options. Unlike IP, TCP options are more commonly used. Some of the most common options are discussed below.

The most often seen TCP option is the selective-acknowledgement. It would be an inefficient use of network resources if a receiving host sent back an ACK packet for every single TCP packet it received. It would be inefficient from the sending hosts perspective because for each packet that was sent, it would have to wait for the packet to get to the remote host and for an ACK to be sent back. On a network that operated at high speeds or one with latency due to the distances involved — or both, this wasted time would add up to a considerable decrease in the overall transmission of data. Instead, the sending host will send a number of TCP segments up to the advertised window size and then wait for an ACK for the last packet that was sent. Remember that the receiver of these segments is counting the octets of data that it receives and only needs to send an ACK for the next sequence number that it expects, implicitly acknowledging the receipt of all data up to that point.

In the event of a network error, one or more packets of the series that was sent to the host may be lost. Normal operation of TCP is to resend all segments starting with the last one the receiver acknowledges receiving. If the third out of eight packets is the only one to be lost, this would mean that the third, fourth, fifth, sixth, seventh, and eighth packets would be resent. Clearly, this is a waste of network resources. The selective-acknowledgment (SACK) option allows the two hosts to specifically communicate which segments were lost and only resend those segments.

The maximum segment size (MSS) is used to indicate to the remote host what the MTU for the data should be. This is determined through the use of IP don't fragment bits in the initial packets to the remote host. Preventing the fragmentation of packets by sending data that is properly sized to the data-link layer improves overall network performance and security of the network, as discussed in Chapter 3.2.1.

TCP was a protocol developed for fairly low-speed networks with high delays. The overall performance of TCP is not based simply upon the bandwidth of the link. Because TCP is connection oriented and expects acknowledgment of the data that has been sent, the performance of TCP is related to both the bandwidth of the network, the end-to-end delay of the network, and the number of packets lost during a TCP transmission. Impacting any one of these will affect the overall performance of the TCP session. To understand this, remember that the maximum window size of a TCP segment is only 64 KB. This means that the most data that can be sent at any time is only 64 KB before an ACK is required.

Modern networks can be high-bandwidth in the case of fiber-optic and gigabit networks, and high-delay as in the case of satellite network connections. In the case of a high-bandwidth cross-country link with 30 ms of delay, 64 KB of data can be sent in multiple packets in much less than 30 ms. For the remainder of the 30 ms for the sent data to arrive and the 30 ms required for the ACK to return, the sender is idle. From the point of view of the user, the expensive high-speed link they are paying for is not operating at full capacity.

Instead of trashing TCP however, two options appeared that allow TCP to take advantage of higher-speed networks. The first of these options is the window scale option. This allows the window size to be increased beyond 64 KB by indicating in the options field a "multiplier" of the header window field that can be used to communicate the true window size.

The second option is the use of the Timestamp option. Normally, TCP will wait around for as much as 120 s before determining that a packet it is expecting to arrive has been lost in the network. This is because during the early years of TCP, there was not a mechanism available that could be used to accurately compute the mean round-trip time of a packet. The round-trip time is the average time that it would take a packet to travel to a remote host and the response to find its way back to the original sender. On high-speed networks, 120 s is far too much time, yet TCP still has a need to estimate how long it should wait before declaring an expected packet missing in action. The inclusion of a timestamp in the TCP options field allows for communicating TCP hosts to accurately estimate how long the average round-trip time for their particular connection is and thus timeout and retransmit missing packets more rapidly.

3.2.7.3 TCP Vulnerabilities. The preceding discussion was a brief introduction into the operation of TCP, yet there is much more to know. From the security point of view, the major points have been hit. Next, we examine the operation of the protocol in its entirety. This will provide a complete context in which to place the earlier TCP discussion. Once again, our hypothetical Host A and Host B will create a TCP connection, share a small amount of data, and then tear down the connection. Exhibit 14 shows this transaction in process. The previous discussion and illustration suggest one more way to take advantage of normal TCP behavior to exploit remote systems. If we assume that Host A is a client and Host B is a server, we see that the server commits some of its resources to maintain its side of the connection before the connection itself is fully established. Imagine now that the remote client sends a dozen connection requests and the server responds to each of these connection requests with a SYN ACK and a small commitment of resources while the server waits for the final ACK from the client. If the server does not receive the final ACK from the client immediately, there is no way for the server to

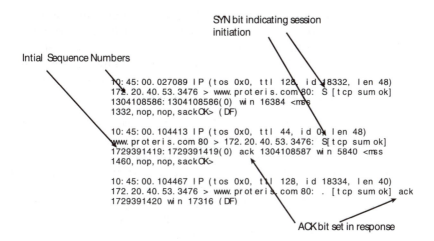

SYN bit indicating session initiation

Intial Sequence Numbers

```
10: 45: 00. 027089 IP (tos 0x0, ttl 128, id 18332, len 48)
172. 20. 40. 53. 3476 > www. proteris. com 80: S [tcp sum ok]
1304108586: 1304108586(0) win 16384 <mss
1332, nop, nop, sackOK> (DF)

10: 45: 00. 104413 IP (tos 0x0, ttl 44, id 0, len 48)
www. proteris. com 80 > 172. 20. 40. 53. 3476: S[tcp sum ok]
1729391419: 1729391419(0) ack 1304108587 win 5840 <mss
1460, nop, nop, sackOK>

10: 45: 00. 104467 IP (tos 0x0, ttl 128, id 18334, len 40)
172. 20. 40. 53. 3476 > www. proteris. com 80: . [tcp sum ok] ack
1729391420 win 17316 (DF)
```

ACK bit set in response

Exhibit 14. TCP Three-Way Handshake

know if the ACK packet from the client has been lost or delayed in transit or if the client is simply not going to respond. With no way to know, the server is committed to wait a standard time out period for the packet. At this point, the server TCP connections are said to be in a "half-open" state.

For a dozen connections, the effects on the server are insignificant. If the client or a group of clients coordinating an attack were to increase the number of connections requests to hundreds or thousands per minute, then the server could conceivably use up all of its resources on half-open connections. This is the trademark characteristic of a SYN attack, a form of denial-of-service attack.

Unless the attacks are coming from a single source, it is generally not possible to simply filter SYN packets as this would prevent legitimate traffic from connection — in effect causing the same behavior as the denial-of-service we were trying to avoid. In this case, the vulnerability is that the normal behavior of TCP is to wait a certain period of time for the final connection request. To solve this, the behavior of TCP needs to be altered. While it is possible to do this on a per-server basis, it is generally much more efficient to do this on a firewall. Typically known as SYN filtering, TCP intercept, or some similar sounding term, a firewall will intercept incoming TCP connections and reply to the connection on behalf of the servers. When the final client ACK arrives back at the firewall, the firewall will then forward the connection request to the appropriate server.

The advantage to this approach is that the TCP timeouts can be greatly reduced. Therefore, bogus connection requests are detected and dropped at a faster rate. This same firewall functionality can also dynamically adjust the TCP timeout period based on the number of incoming connection requests. This means that during normal circumstances, the TCP connection timeouts are quite generous. As the traffic increases, for example during a SYN attack, the connection wait period will decrease to compensate for the increased traffic. Another advantage to performing SYN filtering on a single device such as a router is that network administrators can avoid needing to adjust TCP variables on individual hosts.

3.2.7.4 TCP Sliding Windows. TCP is a complicated layer of the networking model. It needs to provide flow control and error checking over links of an unpredictable nature between parties of unknown capabilities. To do this, TCP employs a number of congestion avoidance and flow control algorithms. One mechanism that is particularly noteworthy in terms of security is that of the sliding window. While the sliding window is primarily a flow control technique, understanding it will also make security discussions clearer. Between two TCP hosts, information is sent within the packet that indicates the allowable window size. At the same time, acknowledgments are sent indicating the highest octet of data that has been received. If Host A sends a window of 1000 octets to Host B and acknowledges sequence number 100,000, then it stands to reason that any data that Host B sends back to Host A should be in the range of 100,001 to 101,000. If Host A should receive anything outside this window, then there has either been a problem on the network, the sending host, or someone is trying to send information to Host A, making it look like it came from Host B but they guessed wrong.

3.2.8 The User Datagram Protocol (UDP)

Compared to the TCP header, the User Datagram Protocol (UDP) is much more straightforward. As can be seen from the protocol header itself (Exhibit 15), UDP provides only the basics required by a remote host to associate a packet with a connection.The source and destination port of UDP operate in exactly the same fashion as the TCP. When reviewing the assigned numbers, you will notice that for many of the well-known TCP ports, there is a corresponding UDP port.

The one small exception to the UDP port fields is that because UDP is connectionless, there may not be a reply expected to a stream of data. The standards themselves allow the setting of the source port in UDP to be zero. In practice, UDP commonly expects some sort of reply to the packets that it sends and so the source port is set to facilitate return traffic.

The length field is simply an indicator of the overall length of the user datagram, including the UDP header, and is used in the same manner as the TCP length field. Likewise, the checksum is the same as the TCP header in that covers the pseudo header of the IP field, the UDP header itself, and the data.

```
0                    15 16                    31
┌──────────────────────┬──────────────────────┐
│                      │                      │
│     Source Port      │   Destination Port   │
│                      │                      │
├──────────────────────┼──────────────────────┤
│                      │                      │
│       Length         │      Checksum        │
│                      │                      │
├──────────────────────┴──────────────────────┤
│                                             │
│              Options                        │
│                                             │
│                        ─────────────────────┤
│                                             │
│                Data                         │
│                                             │
└─────────────────────────────────────────────┘
```

UDP Header Structure

Exhibit 15. User Datagram Protocol Header Format

What stands out the most about the UDP header is what it does not contain. There are no control fields, sequence numbers, acknowledgements, or windowing. UDP does not have the ability to keep track of the data that has been sent or received. If this function is important to the data that UDP is transporting, then the application layer itself must make provisions for the accounting of data. Furthermore, UDP has no concept of flow control. Because senders and receivers do not know when data has been lost, it continues to transmit at a given rate regardless of the network conditions. As with the accounting for data, if flow control is required as it commonly is in VPN or VoIP connections, the application layer must establish a method of providing this for the data.

3.2.8.1 UDP Security Concerns. The lack of a built-in flow control mechanism in a UDP stream means that it is also an effective denial of service tool capable of easily using up all the available network bandwidth. In the design of networks or access-links, it would not be uncommon to restrict the amount of UDP data that can utilize network bandwidth to prevent just this use of UDP. These types of attacks can be reduced in severity through the use of bandwidth throttling. This technique is also known as creating a committed access rate. Essentially, a router or other firewall device is configured to only allow a certain amount of a particular traffic type through over a period of time. For example, a 1.544-Mbps T-1 line could be configured to never allow more than 128 Kbps of ICMP traffic and 512 Kbps of UDP traffic.

The type of bandwidth flooding that UDP packets are capable of is most likely to affect the fairly low bandwidth WAN links. Unfortunately, the most accessible place for most companies to configure this type of filtering is on the ingress interface of the router that connects to their upstream ISP. This means that the traffic leaving the ISP router interface is congesting the ISP router WAN interface to the customer. Filtering this traffic overload on the customer router does little to alleviate the denial-of-service. To be effective, committed access rates must be configured on the ISP routers before the traffic is sent down the low-bandwidth WAN link to the customer site. How likely this is to happen is solely a factor of how easy it is to work with your ISP. Will the ISP configure these for you prior to activating the link to protect you from the beginning? If you decide to apply this filtering during an attack, how easy is it for you to get in touch with the engineers who can actually apply these filters? If these bandwidth starvation attacks are a consideration for your company during the risk analysis phase, it is essential to determine the answer to these questions prior to implementing the security policy.

3.3   Servers and Hosts

This section concentrates on some of the issues relating to server and hosts on the network. To say that servers and hosts are vulnerable to lapses in organizational security is an understatement. Even the most technologically green computer user, when faced with questions regarding the importance of system security, will reply with something along the lines of, "Well, it's important because someone can get into our computer and do stuff."

To prevent this, we typically will employ network security services. This means that we employ a firewall at the perimeter of our network and perhaps a VPN access point for remote users. Anti-virus software is used to prevent infections from damaging computer code and servers may be kept separate from the rest of the organization. With these steps in place, many network administrators feel that their servers and hosts — and therefore their network — are now secure.

This is commonly the approach taken when a company lacks a coherent security policy. It is lacking in several respects. In a thorough risk analysis, security experts and management will see that user resources are at risk from a number of threats and vulnerabilities. Hosts are vulnerable to threats from the network — and a fairly robust defense plan will reduce the severity of the majority of these attacks. Hosts are also vulnerable to threats that sit at the keyboard. Network security is not much help against these.

Yes, I am implying that an important threat to consider when doing a risk analysis is the user of the network. I commonly bring this up in consulting meetings, only to be met with stares of shock and disbelief. "That may be true elsewhere, but our users would never do anything like that!" is the common reply.

I agree that most users do not "attack" the network out of malicious intent — although research consistently shows that the majority of network security incidents occur from the inside. Most internal threats are well-intentioned users who either make a mistake in the course of their daily business activities or are circumventing secure computing practices to make their jobs easier and more productive. Expensive applications that protect your network against packet-based attacks will do nothing to protect the most likely source of security incidents in your company. Subsequent chapters discuss what can be done to protect hosts against this type of intentional or accidental misuse; but for now, the major point is that the most expensive firewall in the world is not going to help your network when someone sits down at a computer and is able to circumvent its local security safeguards.

Servers are a special point of concern for most organizations. After all, this is where the most expensive data is stored. Many of the same considerations that apply to hosts also apply to servers. Due to their sensitive nature, physical access must always be denied to unauthorized users. Access to the servers themselves from other network administrators must also be closely monitored. What can a company do to protect a server against the intentional or accidental misconfiguration by a network administrator? This is simply another example, that no matter how much we discuss technical controls in this text, it is really a variety of controls applied in depth that provide the best reduction of risk for all systems.

When discussing network hosts and servers, there are a couple of common terms that must also be defined when discussing network security vocabulary. As the *lingua franca* of networking, these terms will allow you to clearly discuss with vendors and security professionals your specific needs and solutions.

3.3.1 Bastion Hosts

The term "bastion host" is used to describe a host operating system that has had all unnecessary programs and kernel components removed. It is commonly said that a bastion host has been *hardened*, that it is has been specially configured with security as the primary focus. Bastion hosts often serve as the base operating system for firewalls, VPNs, or IDS devices.

The theory behind a bastion host is that any program, application, or process can contain vulnerabilities that can be potentially exploited by a knowledgeable threat — a theory that has until now seen little reason to be disputed. By removing every element of the operating system not used in actual application of the host computer, the risk is reduced accordingly.

I have heard various arguments as to where the bastion host concept should be applied. Commonly, bastion hosts are specifically configured on systems that will almost certainly face threats — firewalls, DMZ hosts, VPN servers, etc. Some network administrators who apply the bastion host concept to all hosts in the organization use that same argument. If there is no need for the users of host system to use a media player, then the media player applications are removed. Ultimately, where to apply bastion hosts is going to be a function of your final security policy.

3.3.2   The Network Demilitarized Zone (DMZ)

Various sources use different definitions for the DMZ. The strictest definition is the same applied to the border between North and South Korea; a "no man's land" where the land is a buffer and not clearly under the control of either party. A network DMZ is a section of network that acts as a buffer between the external Internet and the internal trusted network (see Exhibit 16). Other definitions of the DMZ include a separate network that contains company Internet servers such as Web servers, external DNS servers, file servers, mail relay, etc. In this case, the network clearly is part of the parent company and under its control but the terminology of the DMZ is often applied in this instance as well.

It would also not be uncommon for a company to have a number of DMZ zones that employ both of the above definitions.

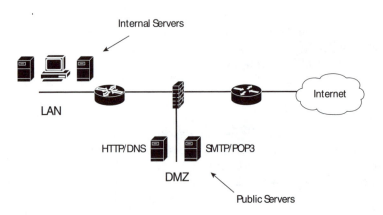

Exhibit 16. The Demilitarized Zone

Regardless of its application, the DMZ term has evolved into a term that means a section of the network that has access restrictions that are different from the company internal network.

Notes

1. For connection-oriented protocols such as TCP (to be discussed shortly), error rates have a significant impact on how much of that transmission potential can actually be used to transfer data.
2. That said, the maximum bandwidth for common LAN usage is still 1 Gbps — a transmission rate more than adequate for Web surfing and checking e-mail.
3. ATM, strictly speaking, is an entire protocol stack much like the TCP/IP suite with standards for addressing and path finding. As commonly seen from the point of view of IP, however, ATM simply serves as a layer 2 technology.
4. IPv5 was never released as a production protocol. It was developed for a real-time stream protocol that was never widely adopted.
5. That is 3.4 followed by 68 zeros.
6. To improve performance, many routers will cache routes or use some sort of "express forwarding" mechanism that allows packets to bypass the normal software-based routing table and use an interface-based forwarding table. This is not the same as keeping count of individual packets, however.
7. While IP addresses are represented in decimal for human consumption, MAC addresses are traditionally represented in hexadecimal. Thus, each character of a MAC address represents four binary bits.
8. In NAT terms, a pool can be a range of public IP addresses, or a single IP address.
9. While Cisco sometimes markets EIGRP as a routing protocol with link state characteristics, it is fundamentally a distance vector routing protocol. For those still skeptical, I offer the following exercise: create a small test network using EIGRP and OSPF. Attempt to filter outbound route updates within your autonomous system (EIGRP) or area (OSPF) as appropriate. Note your findings.
10. We will discuss hashing in a bit. For now, consider it a form of one-way encryption.
11. In theory, the ports are random. In practice, some vendors increment the sequence numbers by one for each new connection. So the first source port for packets will be 1024, the second 1025, etc.

Chapter 4

Cryptography and VPN Terminology

Crucial to the configuration and discussion of network security is an understanding of cryptographic terms. This vocabulary is essential when evaluating any type of encryption technology, be it files encryption or the encryption of packets in transit (as through a VPN). While we will not include enough detail on the algorithms to write your own implementations, we will discuss the most important terms and algorithms to allow you to better compare countermeasures.

The first terms to discuss are *plaintext* and *ciphertext*. Plaintext is what you are reading now; that is, normal unencrypted text. Ciphertext is thaw uoy era gnidaer won.[1] The process of converting plaintext to ciphertext is known as encryption, and the process of taking a section of ciphertext and producing plaintext is known as decryption.

When discussing plaintext and ciphertext, it is easy to visualize this if you are looking at a page of text versus a page of code. One of them you can read because it is in English and the other does not make any sense. It is important to realize, however, that the idea of plaintext and ciphertext are to some degree abstractions. That is, typically in a VPN (virtual private network) scenario, normal *bits* that make sense to a computer are also plaintext and *bits* that another computer can make no sense of are ciphertext. To you and I, there is no difference between the unencrypted start of the UDP header "00000110" and the same encrypted header "01001000"; but when a receiving host tries to sort out the bits, the bits of the first header fall into values that are expected while the bits of the second header do not. When we are talking about encrypting and decrypting computer data, this is typically what we are discussing. There is generally no problem in reading the stream of bits, but making sense of them is the problem.

In the above example, there are 256 ways that the second string of bits can be interpreted. Which one of them is correct? The only way to figure this out without knowing the way in which they were encrypted would be to try each combination and see if it makes any sense in the context we are expecting. Of course, a computer could do this in far less than a second, but by adding a single bit to the above patterns, we suddenly do not have

256 combinations; rather, we have 512 combinations that need to be tried. In fact, each bit that we add to the encrypted block doubles the amount of choices that we have to sort through to find the right information.

To decipher our earlier example, eight encrypted bits, we use an eight-bit key. To decrypt the encrypted string of bits above (01001000), we would need a key that says something like "The key is 11100111. Compare that to the ciphertext and XOR the two. The result is the correct text."[2] As noted, this would not take long for a computer to do. To increase the complexity, we increase the key length. For each bit we add to the key length, the problem becomes twice as difficult to solve. If you are thinking to yourself, "yes, but a computer should be able to work through that pretty fast, even with long keys," Then try this experiment. Grab a chessboard and the biggest bag of rice you can get from your local supermarket. Put one grain on the first square; and then on each successive square, double the grains of rice. That means two grains on the second, four on the third, and eight on the fourth, etc. When you are done, take all the rice that you have used and donate it to a charity. You should have enough rice to feed the world for quite a while.[3] The number of grains you have on the last square would be equivalent to a 64-bit key. While computers can operate very quickly, the number of possible combinations confounds even the most powerful computers. Any key can be cracked eventually in this manner, but with the common 128-bit, 160-bit, and 256-bit keys used to encrypt information over VPNs today — as long as the algorithm is secure (more on that later), it is likely that any computer today able to crack such keys would report its success to a barren and cold Earth long after the sun has passed through its red giant phase. That is, nobody is going to be around to care.

This is not to say that longer keys are always secure. Furthermore, computers now exist that can break 56-bit keys, regardless of the algorithm used. They are just fast enough to try all the combinations. The beauty of our encryption algorithms, however, is that by simply adding another bit to the key, the message is suddenly twice as difficult to decipher.

4.1 Keys

One of the most common terms heard when discussing cryptography is the term "key." A key is nothing more than a special type of password. If you and I agreed that our code (algorithm) used in the encryption of notes between the two of us would be an alphabetic shift, our key would be the number of letters we shift. For example, normally we can assume "A, B, C, etc." to mean A and B and C. But if we agreed that our shift is one to the right, then "A" really means B and "B" really means C, etc. The "shift 1 to the right" is the key that I would use to convert my plaintext to ciphertext. The same key would be the one that you would use to convert my ciphertext to plaintext to be able to ready my original message. This type of key is known as a *symmetric* key. You and I both need to know what the key is in order to encrypt and decrypt messages to each other. If anyone else knows what the key is, they would be able to read what our messages are, so it is important that we keep this key secret. It should be no surprise then that this type of key is also known as a *secret* key.

The problem with a secret key is as noted above; if someone else were to have access to the key, our code is broken. The question then becomes: how do we make sure that nobody knows what that key is? Between you and me, we could agree to meet at a public café and surreptitiously exchange briefcases under the table. In the briefcase I give you is the key. We could then run back to our secret bases and begin encoding messages to our hearts' content. Or I could just call you up and tell you the key over the phone and hope that nobody is listening in on the conversation. In either case, the ability to exchange the secret key securely is crucial.

Meeting in person, this is not that difficult. When we attempt to do this over the Internet, however, we have a chicken-and-egg-type problem. I have to assume that someone is listening to our packet conversation. Otherwise, why would I go through the trouble of encrypting the data? But if someone is listening, how do I get the secret key to you without them knowing about it so I can then start encrypting data?

To work around this quandary, *public* key cryptography was introduced. The idea of public key cryptography is that anyone can know one of the keys (called the *public key*). As long as they knew the public key, they could encrypt messages but the other participant in the conversations would need the other key to be able to decrypt messages. Because there are two different keys in use here, public key cryptography is also known as *asymmetric* cryptography. One of the two keys is known as the *public* key, which anyone is allowed to know; and the other key is known as the *private* key, which is used to decrypt messages. It is important that the private key be kept just that — private.

To better understand how public key cryptography is used to enable the secure transfer of secret keys, the following analogy is commonly used.

I want to send you a letter (the metaphor for the secret key) but I cannot trust the post office or anyone else to not read the letter between you and me. To make sure nobody can open the letter, I am going to put my letter in a box and padlock it shut. I have the only key to the padlock. The box with the letter inside is then shipped to you. Once you get it, you of course cannot open the box without the key I have. Instead of shipping the key separately (after all, someone could hold on to the box and then wait for me to ship the key or just pretend to be you and ask for the key), you will then take your own padlock and key and put your padlock on the box. Now the box has two locks on it. Yours and mine. Because you cannot open the box with my lock on it, you ship the box back to me and I remove my lock with my key. Now there is only one lock on the box — yours. I ship the box back to you and you use your key to open the box. You can then read the letter I sent about our luncheon plans for last Tuesday.

Clearly, if I were going to send a number of letters to you, we could shorten the back and forth process quite a bit if you just shipped me a bunch of extra locks. That way, whenever I wanted to send you a letter, I could just grab one of your locks, lock the box and send it. Because it is your lock, once I fasten that lock, even I cannot open the box to change the letter I just placed in there. If you had so much fun with this and liked getting secure letters, you could get big crates full of your padlocks and just leave them lying around. That way anyone who wanted to send you a secure letter could just pick up a lock at the gas station or the post office. In fact, it does not matter who picks up your lock because the only thing they could do with the lock is secure a letter to you.

Above, the lock you left lying around was the public key. The key to that lock that you safeguarded on a chain around your neck was the private key. The letter that I was sending you was the secret key.

You may be wondering at this point why introduce two types of keys — symmetric and asymmetric? After all, why not just use the public key (asymmetric) technology to send encrypted information? If you can use it to send a secret key, why not use it for all data? That is a good question and it really comes down to security and performance.

We have already established that, in general, the longer a key is, the more secure it is. To ensure that our asymmetric keys are as secure as possible, they are normally quite long (in the range of 1024 to 4096 bits long). The price of longer keys, however, is speed. Encrypting and decrypting data with keys that long is cumbersome and slow. To compensate, we will use short secret keys on the order of 128 bits to 256 bits that we will use for a single communication session and send them encrypted with the larger key space of the public key. These shorter keys are designed not only for security, but also for the ability of hardware and software to operate on them quickly. The rationale is that all keys can be broken in time. Because public keys can be used for periods of a year or more, they need to be long to increase the difficulty in breaking them. And because the secret keys are used only for relatively short communications, their length is sufficient for the need. Do not forget, however, that 128 bits is still a big, secure key.

Before going any further, let us do a quick review.

- Secret key cryptography = symmetric key = both sides use the same key to encrypt and decrypt data. Commonly used for the actual encryption of data.

- Public key cryptography = asymmetric keys = one key used to encrypt, another used to decrypt. Commonly used to send secret keys.

4.2 Certificates

The process of creating an encrypted session using modern technologies is trivial. Most of us use them every day without knowing it, while checking our investment portfolios, banking, and online shopping. The real problem is knowing to whom you have just created an encrypted session. While public key cryptography was a great advancement in the field of cryptography, it still lacks from the ability to prove the other side is who they say they are. Knowing my name, you could create a public/private key pair that *looks* like it came from Cliff Riggs. If you sent it to someone who had never met me, they would have no way of knowing otherwise. The same problem can be applied to online commerce. Just because your browser has a little lock symbol in the corner, indicating that the session to the Web server is encrypted, how are you to know that you are actually encrypting information to your banker and not to a rogue Web server that is just masquerading as your banker?

To eliminate this uncertainty and provide some assurances, we need to introduce another technology, known broadly as certificates. We use certificates all the time. When I board an airplane, I establish my identity to the ticket agent, the pre-security security checkpoint, the security guard, the airline representative who checks my tickets before I board, the person who meets me on the concourse to check my ticket, the person who greets me getting on the plane, and the occasional random person who seems to be in some way associated with airport security through the use of my picture driver's license. This certificate is used to establish that the holder of the ticket is indeed none other than Cliff Riggs. This small army of people who check my ID do not know me personally, but they had sufficient faith that the state of Vermont had taken the appropriate steps to ensure my identity. These airline representatives may not trust me, but they do trust the entity that provided the certificate. In this case, the state of Vermont was acting as a *certification authority* (CA). When we apply this concept to cryptographic keys, we have the digital equivalent of a photo ID.

4.3 Hashing

Take a volume of reasonable size such as a dictionary. You have a need to send that dictionary to me in electronic form and at the same time ensure that nobody has captured the dictionary and changed even a space in the text. One way we could do this is to laboriously sit and compare what you had sent with what I received. To make things a bit easier, we could have a computer compare the two copies. While effective, these solutions are not optimal. At the very least, this would be a time-consuming operation, poring through thousands of pages of text. Furthermore, what if we did not have two copies to compare? After all, if you sent me another copy, how do we know that will not be changed either? Or, if we were just storing the file on a computer and we wanted to make sure that nobody had changed the file since the last time you or I looked at it?

What we need is some way to mathematically represent the text of the dictionary in a shorter form than the original. At the same time, we would want to make sure that the mathematical representation of the dictionary would change even if the smallest change were made to our original file. It would be even more helpful if you cannot take the mathematical representation and work backward. That is, you cannot reverse the process upon our hash value and come up with the contents of the dictionary! If we could figure this out we would have a very handy formula to keep around. Not only would it let us know if *anything* in the file had changed, it would not allow someone who had captured the mathematical representation to know what the original was.

Before we spend lots of time trying to figure out how to make such a formula, however, someone would surely note to us that just such a set of algorithms has already been created. Known as hash algorithms, these formulas are used to condense data into what are known as *message digests*. To see how they operate, let us try a test.

To illustrate the usefulness of a hash, I have created a text file that reads:

```
"Security is now our number one priority."
```

Saved, I ran an MD5 hash utility on the file. The following is the output:

```
07338ca773ad441b465e60ce3f461e98
```

I then changed the text to:

```
"Security is now our number one priority.  "
```

Notice the difference? There is not much of one other than the insertion of a single space. Saving the file and running the same MD5 hash algorithm produces the following result:

```
d1b9c4d605306d4e0cf80f41317fcd8f
```

Even with the insertion of a single space, the hash not only changes, but it changes dramatically. In fact, one of the goals of a good hash algorithm is its ability to produce dramatic and obviously different hash outputs after any change to the document. If only the fifteenth character were to change from a "1" to a "2," then determining the change in value between hash outputs becomes less obvious and less helpful.

A more practical example would be a legal contract. Anyone who was sent a legal contract along with the hash value would immediately know that the contents of the contract had changed simply by comparing the hash value. The fact that the hash value has changed is proof enough that the contents of the text had changed.

Note that the hash values given above do not indicate *where* the change has occurred, only that it has changed. For many applications, this is enough however.

Now imagine the applications of this technology. First, we can make sure that the contracts that you and I agree upon have not changed. When dealing with electronic documents, it would be easy enough to change a contract by adding a couple of extra zeros to the left of a decimal point, right? You and I can both use a hash like this to electronically verify that the document we have agreed upon is identical. So much as an extra carriage return at the end of the document would change the value of the hash.

If you were to ever receive an e-mail from me, you would notice that each of my e-mails ends with a signed hash much like the following:

```
— — -BEGIN PGP SIGNATURE — — -

Version: PGP 7.0.4

iQA/AwUBPIkgAy1iZLqbmZBAEQIvGgCeInyJLt8avLwYzcVIBjC2uO
br0i4AoNsN

DC1jB0TuhfD15tvo9X9S8AKE

= JWjq
— — -END PGP SIGNATURE — — -
```

I use my private key to digitally sign a hash of the e-mail that I have sent. Not only can you make sure that the e-mail was actually from me, but that no changes were made to the e-mail after I had sent it.[4] In other words, my digital signature also provides *non-repudiation* services. I cannot deny the sending of that -mail if it was signed with my digital signature.

We can also use hashing to make sure that files on our hard drives do not change. We know that attackers commonly like to install Trojan versions of the software that we use on our systems. Detecting such software can be very difficult. If we were to run a hash value over every executable on our servers, any change to the program itself would generate an entirely different hash when we run the hashing program again. This would immediately tip us off as to what program has changed. While we may not know what has changed, we know enough to start investigating further.

The same concept can be applied to data that we send. We will see in our discussion of VPNs that IPSec uses hash values on entire packets to ensure that the packet that was sent is the same as the packet that is received at the other side.

In short, for every instance in which there is a need for integrity of data, hashing is the technology of choice.

4.4 Digital Signatures

When describing some of the applications of hashing above, one example was the process of digitally signing a document. Careful examination would reveal that there must be more to the process than just using a hash algorithm on a document. Using just a hash would provide the same value for anyone. You or I or the guy sitting next to you on the bus could all run a hash algorithm on a copy of this book and create the same value. That is the point of the hash. The three of us could quickly establish that we have all received the exact same copy of this book.

Another example will further explain this. You and I have negotiated a contract via e-mail. We both have two primary goals. The first is that we have actually agreed upon the same contract. That is no problem; we have hash values to do this for us. The second issue, however, is more complicated. Because you and I have never met each other face to face, you do not know if you have actually agreed to the contract with Cliff Riggs (me) or someone claiming to be me. When I do not hold up my end of the bargain, you come looking for me. I naturally say that I have never seen that contract before in my life and because this is all digital documentation, you must have made up the whole thing. Whether I have actually reneged on the contract or someone else had been negotiating in my place is immaterial.

You are naturally feeling wary about future dealings over the Internet and thus start to think of a solution to this problem. Being of above-average intelligence, you quickly realize that we can take existing cryptographic technologies and solve this problem. What do we use to make sure the data has not changed? Hash values. What technology do we have that could prove that someone is who they say they are? Certificates and public key encryption. In future negotiations, you could require me to run a hash value against the contract, then sign the hash value with my private key. You could then use my public key as verified by a certificate authority that not only has the document not changed, but that I have reviewed the document myself. You have established something important to cryptography. You have established *non-repudiation*. I cannot easily deny that I have not seen the document. After all, the entire point of the private key is that I am the only one who knows of it. This combination of technologies used to digitally sign documents is known as a *digital signature*.

4.5 Common Encryption Algorithms

This section describes some of the most common encryption and hashing algorithms that you will come across in evaluating security products. While it is not extensive, it does provide a good basis of comparison for discussing and comparing features.

4.5.1 Symmetric/Secret Key Algorithms

Algorithms in this category are used in the actual encryption of bulk data, whether it is data stored on a hard drive or data sent over a VPN. They all have in common fairly short key lengths compared to public key algorithms, but for most applications, the keys should be secure for years to come.

4.5.1.1 Data Encryption Standard (DES). One of the first public key algorithms available for general use, DES was a derivative of an encryption algorithm that IBM had been circulating known as Lucifer. DES is a block cipher, meaning that it breaks up the data into blocks of 64 bits and then encrypts each block separately. DES can operate in several modes, with each mode treating the blocks of data to be encrypted differently. For example, the cipher block-chaining (CBC) mode of DES creates a master key that is applied to the first block of data. The key itself is modified in a defined way and then applied to the second block of data. In a sense, each prior block serves as a randomizing agent for the key that is used on the next block of encryption. This method of operation makes it more difficult for someone to analyze the ciphertext and look for patterns that could reveal the key. It also means, however, that if a single block of data is corrupted, the rest of the data cannot be recovered, even if the initial key is known.

In contrast, the electronic code book (ECB) mode of DES operation treats each block of 64 bits as a separate entity. Thus, block 2 is not dependent on block 1 for keying material. A lost block will not render the rest of the data unrecoverable. This is the fastest form of DES; but because it makes it easier for someone to capture and analyze ciphertext, it is considered the least secure.

DES uses keys that are 64 bits long; but because eight of those bits are only parity bits and used to ensure that the key itself does not contain undiscovered errors, the effective length of the key is only 56 bits. While DES is fast, it has been broken using commercial-grade computers in a "reasonable" period of time that can be as short as three days. As computing power increased, it became clear that DES was less secure than it once was. To respond to this vulnerability, a new encryption algorithm known as Triple DES (3DES) was developed.

Despite having been cracked through a brute-force attack, DES is still found quite often in implementations. Manufacturers in the United States are prohibited from exporting strong encryption technology and thus, by default, do not include 3DES in all products. DES, on the other hand, can be considered the common denominator of encryption. It is widespread and can be found in all cryptographic implementations.

4.5.1.2 Triple Data Encryption Standard (3DES). Due to DES having lost some of its strength as computers have become more powerful, there was a movement afoot to find stronger encryption algorithms. In this regard, there were two lines of thought. The first was to simply create new algorithms. The other was to use the intellectual investment in DES to create a stronger version of DES. The result of that second effort was Triple DES. As the name suggests, 3DES is simply DES applied three times with three keys to a single block of data. Any increase in processing time was offset by the greatly increased processing power in our encryption devices since the first implementation of DES. In this case, the effective key length of 3DES is 168 bits (56 bits $\times$ 3). Like DES, 3DES is very widespread and any device claiming to support "strong" encryption will most likely support 3DES as the default option. Because it does classify as strong encryption under U.S. law, U.S. companies are not automatically allowed to export this technology. In some cases, products are sold with DES encryption only and 3DES must be added on after completing a short form promising that you will not export this technology to enemies of the United States.

4.5.1.3 International Data Encryption Algorithm (IDEA). 3DES was not the only suggested replacement for the DES algorithm. As can be imagined, there were any number of candidates vying for this position. IDEA is one of the more popular of the suggested replacements for DES. Like DES, IDEA encrypts data in block lengths of 64 bits. IDEA, however, uses 128-bit keys. IDEA also employs techniques to "confuse and diffuse" encrypted information. While the implementation of these techniques is interesting in of itself, it also provides a good background to introduce some of the problems that cryptographers run into when creating an encryption algorithm.

There are essentially three ways to break an encryption algorithm. The first is to simply try all the possible keys. This is countered by making the key space sufficiently large. The second possibility is to discover some sort of flaw in the encryption algorithm itself that allows it to be calculated more easily than through use of a brute-force attack. This is why peer-reviewed algorithms are always much more secure than "secret" encryption algorithms. If you have made a mistake in your new "SuperSecure" algorithm, someone will point it out and allow you to fix it. Finally, the third possibility is that an attacker can attempt to determine the key used to encrypt data by performing a cryptanalysis of the ciphertext.

There are several different forms of cryptanalysis. Some attempt to look for repeating patterns in the encrypted information. For example, if you were encrypting TCP information, you would at least know the organization of the headers and could take a good guess at the information in the headers. Other attacks have the cryptanalyst encrypt a known piece of plaintext and view the encrypted output. Knowing what to look for may provide clues as to how to decipher everything else that has been encrypted. There are more variations but the key to all of them depends on the statistical relationship between the ciphertext and the plaintext. That relationship of course is the key.

To prevent this, the IDEA cipher attempts to "confuse" by using three separate encryption mechanisms on the same data. The goal is to scramble the original data enough so that it is difficult to even determine *what* the original was. IDEA attempts to "diffuse" by ensuring that each bit of ciphertext is influenced by the preceding plaintext. Thus, a single bit of plaintext influences more than just a single bit of ciphertext in the same way that the previous block of DES would influence the encryption of the following blocks. Any structure to the plaintext that would aid a cryptanalyst would hopefully be eliminated through this mechanism.

IDEA is a popular algorithm for no other reason than it was included in the PGP product that many use to encrypt e-mail correspondence and personal files. While generally supported, it is not as widespread as DES and 3DES. In other words, you cannot count on finding it as part of an encryption solution.

4.5.1.4 Blowfish. You will not be a student of cryptography or information security for long before the works of this algorithm's author become very familiar. Bruce Schneier wrote Blowfish with the intent of creating a secure, compact, and fast encryption algorithm. Due to its fairly small code base, Blowfish is easy to review and to this point has not been compromised. Blowfish has several characteristics going for it. To start, the goal of creating Blowfish to be small and fast seems to have been successful. Blowfish can run in only 5K of memory and operates with few clock cycles on 32-bit processors, thus making it ideal for software implementations. To future-proof the algorithm, Blowfish also supports a variable-length key of up to 448 bits.

While most hardware encryption chips use either DES or 3DES, Blowfish is ideal for software-based encryption implementations. SSH as an example is an encrypted version of the Telnet protocol. This often is configured with Blowfish because it is an application that provides its own encryption services. I know of more than one software-based VPN that uses the Linux FreeS/WAN VPN server to create an efficient and powerful VPN based on the Blowfish algorithm.

4.5.1.5 Advanced Encryption Standard (AES). When the U.S. Government decided that it was time for a new encryption algorithm to be used by government facilities, a contest was held. From four finalists, the winning algorithm, known as "Rijndael,"[5] was selected. In determining the winning algorithm, the National Institute for Standards and Technology (NIST) judged finalists on their suitability for both hardware and software implementations, memory requirements, performance, and, of course, security. AES is a block cipher as are most symmetric algorithms in common use; but unlike the algorithms discussed thus far, AES operates on blocks of 128 bits. To accommodate varying security/performance considerations, AES offers key lengths of 128, 192, and 256 bits in strength.

Due to its acceptance by the U.S. Government as part of its Federal Information Processing Standards (FIPS), AES is guaranteed to be a very popular encryption algorithm. Many non-government and non-U.S. governments will also adopt AES, simply due to the review of the algorithm by the NIST.

When considering a new VPN implementation based on hardware encryption, AES is generally considered the go-forward algorithm of choice. Care must be exercised, however, because the relative newness of AES means that support cannot be assured in all encryption products. Support considerations are especially relevant if integration with legacy equipment must be considered.

4.5.2 Asymmetric/Public Key Algorithms

Unlike the symmetric key algorithms, asymmetric algorithms use a considerably larger key space. As described above, their primary purpose is for authentication and the encryption of symmetric keys.

4.5.2.1 Diffie–Hellman. It would not be a stretch to say that the field of cryptography and the Internet boom that followed were based on the principle of secure communication and would have otherwise languished were it not for the work of the researchers Whitfield Diffie and Martin Hellman.

Consider this scenario. You and I are in a crowded room and we wish to begin speaking in code. To do this we have to verbally agree on the key that we will use to encode and decode information. Because we are limited to verbal communication, however, there is the chance that anyone in the room could hear our key exchange and thus know our code. What we need is some way to exchange keys while everyone listens.

The algorithm discovered by Diffie and Hellman accomplishes just this feat. Using algebraic equations that your average ninth grader could understand, Diffie–Hellman provides a way to exchange keys while assuming that anyone else may be listening.

You do not need to know how this is accomplished to make a decision regarding Diffie–Hellman as a countermeasure; but because it is so simple, so elegant, and so important to the science of cryptography, it is worth briefly examining the protocol.

The operation of the protocol is based on modular mathematics. Anyone who remembers learning division and learning that 16/6 equals 2 with a remainder of 4 knows what modulo arithmetic is. In this case, the remainder is the modulus. So 16 = 4 mod 6 is an equivalent statement. It essentially says that 6 goes into 16 X number of times with a remainder of 4. What X is, is irrelevant to the solving of the problem. The interesting thing about the modulus is that there are an infinite number of problems that will all return an answer of 4, so knowing this is not going to help you figure out what numbers were used to generate it. For example, 29 = 4 mod 5 and 6148 = 4 mod 1024 as well.

Essentially, the two computers are sending a remainder to each other and deducing the same secret key from this. To use this technique to create a secret key, two computers will publicly agree on a value p and a value q. There are some rules to the values of these numbers. For example, p needs to be a very large prime number and q must be a value lower than that of p. One of the two computers will then privately choose a value x and the other will privately choose a value y. The only requirement for x and y is that they are less than p. With the private number in hand, the two computers will then compute an equation based upon the p, q, and the x or y value, respectively. They will then send the *answer* to that equation to each other over a public network. From the answer, they will then create a shared secret key. Although everyone may find out what the answer to the equation is and know the p and q values, they will have a very difficult time (read, thousands of years) figuring out what the secret key is because only the computer that generated either the x or y value will have the information needed to solve this problem. Because these values are never shared, the secret keys are secure. Remember: with modular arithmetic, there are many different ways to come up with the same remainder.

Exhibit 1 shows this operation using sample numbers. To keep the problem simple, I am going to use really small numbers. If a computer was doing this, rather than myself with a calculator, the numbers would be 768, 1024, or 1536 bits long, on average. Those are really big numbers. In modern implementations, Diffie–Hellman is widespread. It is commonly used in key exchanges and for transferring authentication information. This is important to note. Diffie–Hellman alone has no mechanism for authenticating the remote host and because of this, the protocol is susceptible to man-in-the-middle-style attacks if an attacker can fool a user into relaying his connection through the attacker's computer. The user creates an encrypted channel to the attacker and the attacker creates a connection

Alice   Bob

$x = g^a \bmod p$ $y = g^b \bmod p$

Alice and Bob publicly agree that $p = 839$ and $g = 3$

Alice picks a Secret $a = 56$ Bob picks a secret $b = 23$

Alice calculates her public key x from the secret: $x = 3^{56} \bmod 839 = 602$ and sends that result to Bob.

Bob calculates his public key x from the secret: $x = 3^{23} \bmod 839 = 661$ and sends that result to Alice.

Alice uses her secret x and the public p value along with Bob's public key to determine the shared secret.

$(661)^{56} \bmod 839 = 30$

Bob uses his secret x and the public p value along with Alices's public key to determine the shared secret.

$(602)^{23} \bmod 839 = 30$

Alice and Bob now both know the secret to be shared and no one is the wiser!

Exhibit 1. A "Simple" Diffie–Hellman Example

---

to the remote host on behalf of the user. Everything that the user sends is then decrypted, read, and then retransmitted by the attacker in the middle of the connection.

While Diffie–Hellman forms the basis of asymmetric cryptography, it is commonly only implemented in Diffie–Hellman situations that have other protocols available for authentication. The most well-known use of Diffie–Hellman is in the use of the IKE key exchange protocol used to set up IPSec sessions. Authentication is provided in a number of ways, all discussed in the IPSec section of this text. Suffice it to say that Diffie–Hellman is used to encrypt the information used for authentication. Another popular use is in the SSL protocol. This is the protocol used to secure Web sessions and other transport layer connections between hosts. In this case, Diffie–Hellman is used to encrypt the transfer or RSA or DSS signatures to verify the remote party's identity.

As noted, common Diffie–Hellman exchanges are based on 768-, 1024-, or 1536-bit keys. Longer keys are, of course, more secure, but also consume more processing power. Because most Diffie–Hellman exchanges are only used for short authentication sessions, their duration is short and the key strength is currently adequate, given the computing power likely to be brought against the algorithm.

4.5.2.2 Rivest–Shamir–Adleman (RSA). Building on the possibilities of the Diffie–Hellman algorithm, researchers Ron Rivest, Adi Shamir, and Len Adleman created the RSA algorithm that has since become the most commonly implemented generic approach to public key encryption. Because it is so common, the "generic" description of public key applications that I described above is also the generic description of the RSA algorithm and its applications.

Some of the biggest news concerning RSA has been the licensing of the algorithm. As the *de facto* standard for public key encryption, RSA was entitled to charge licensing fees to the thousands of companies that used their technology. In 2000, a week earlier than expected, the RSA algorithm was released to the world in the public domain. Some felt that the control that RSA had over data encryption slowed down innovation and adoption of encryption technology. Others noted that the restrictions placed upon RSA actually spurred the creation of new technologies that could be more widely implemented.

Regardless, RSA has been around since 1978 and continues to be a widely implemented and trusted encryption algorithm for public key applications. More likely than not, your public key solutions are going to include RSA in some way.

Like Diffie–Hellman, the actual math behind RSA is not that complicated. The key to the security of the algorithm is the difficulty in factoring large numbers. Two large prime numbers represented as p and q are chosen. They are multiplied together to create another number represented, as n. "n" then becomes the modulus that is transported as part of the key. Recall from our discussion of Diffie–Hellman that knowing the mod value does not really help you find out what equation was used to create the modulus.

From n we also create two values, e and d. E becomes our public key and d becomes the private key. If you wanted to send something using RSA encryption to me, I would send you both e (the public key) and n. You would use those values to encrypt information to me. Because you do not know what d value I have, you cannot decrypt any information that has been encrypted only with e (the public key).

Of course, saying that the algorithm is not that complicated and then throwing letters out like that does not make the argument very convincing. Suffice it to say that these cryptographic keys are nothing more than some very big numbers with certain characteristics.

Due in part to its popularity, RSA has been the focus of several dedicated attempts at cracking the encryption. Unlike secret key encryption, the most straightforward way of cracking RSA is to attempt to factor the prime numbers that have generated the keys. Because we know that RSA is not created from random numbers, but from random prime numbers, it narrows the search quite a bit. The keys are still very difficult to break, but given enough time and computing power, the prime numbers that have created our keys can be determined. Such attacks generally require specialized algorithms and distributed processing. Because the algorithms are constantly being tweaked and improved, and as computer power becomes cheaper and more common, the strength of RSA keys is slowly eroding.

This is not to suggest that RSA is "insecure." Although researchers have published ways to quickly factor 1024-bit keys, these solutions are still unproven. They also cost more than most companies (but not governments) would be willing to spend, at around $1 billon per "RSA breaker." Even at this rate, 2048- and 4096-bit keys are quite secure for the foreseeable future. Weaker keys should be avoided in implementation.

4.6 Split Tunneling

Common to VPN discussions is the term "split tunneling." This refers to the routing of information with a VPN tunnel present. A common scenario is a remote client from a SOHO network creating a VPN tunnel to a corporate gateway. The remote client has two options for sending data. When split tunneling is used, only information destined for the network internal to the VPN gateway is sent encrypted down the VPN tunnel. Packets destined for other remote sites are sent normally. When split tunneling is disabled, all packets are sent through the VPN tunnel, no matter the destination.

While the definition of split tunneling is simple enough, the consequence of allowing or disallowing split tunneling should be considered when planning the implementation of a security policy.

Allowing split tunneling for VPN clients improves the performance of both the client Internet connection and the corporate Internet connection. Referring to Exhibit 2, on the left we see a client sending packets to the corporate network encrypted over the VPN. When the client is sending to an Internet site that is not part of the VPN, however, packets are routed normally over the Internet. Compare this to the illustration on the right, which shows a network with split tunneling disabled. All traffic from the client PC

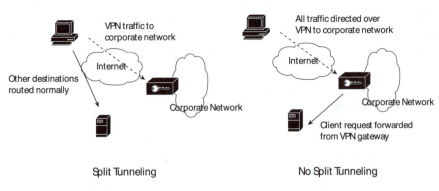

Exhibit 2. Split Tunneling

is sent over the VPN. That means, for general Internet traffic, the packet must first be encrypted, sent over the VPN, routed on the remote company network, and then sent over the Internet to the ultimate destination. Return traffic follows the same process in reverse. This not only adds delay to the user experience, but it also increases the bandwidth usage of the corporate network. The advantage of not allowing split tunneling with VPN clients is that all traffic must pass through the company network. This means that remote user traffic must conform to the same security policy that users on the LAN must follow. It also makes it more difficult for the company to be threatened by compromising remote clients and launching an attack from that compromised client into the corporate network. If split tunneling is allowed, it is possible for a remote attacker to take control of the user computer over the Internet and then use the client PC's VPN connection for a tunnel directly into a company LAN.

Most VPN solutions allow administrators to choose whether to enable split tunneling. This can be configured on the VPN gateway and pushed to all clients. Generally, split tunneling is prohibited while the VPN is active and enabled when the VPN is inactive. This means that while the VPN is connected, all user traffic is encrypted and sent over the company LAN.

Split tunneling also has some applications for wireless network security. For companies that have needed secure wireless connectivity on short notice, it has been possible to create a VPN over the wireless network to a VPN device. By prohibiting split tunneling over this VPN connection, only encrypted traffic is ever sent over the wireless network.

Notes

1. Ciphertext is what you are reading now. Notice the advanced algorithm in use.
2. This example was chosen only for the sake of simplicity. It does not mean to imply that all keys have to be the same length as the message they are encrypting.
3. On the last square alone, you will have 18,446,744,073,709,551,616 grains of rice. That does not include the 9,223,372,036,854,775,808 grains on the second to last square, and so on. That is a lot of rice!
4. This fact has also been used against me in certain circumstances where I would write and send faster than I would think.
5. Pronounced alternately as "rain doll" or "Reign Dahl."

Chapter 5
Application Security Needs

The security of your organization is going to live or die according to the security of your applications. This is true regardless of whether your application is a firewall, VPN gateway, file server, or network printer. Due to the enormous variety of applications and security configurations, this is not a book that can offer configurations on all possible configurations, but we can hit on some of the highest risk areas.

Many times when lecturing or consulting, I am asked the question, "What is the single greatest step I can make in securing my network?" This invariably launches me into a ten-minute discussion that good network security is never a single action, but a combination of actions. There is no single technology that will make your network more secure. Once that explanation is clear, I am then invariably asked the familiar question, "What is the single greatest step I can make in securing my network?" Depending upon my mood at that point, one of the most accurate answers I provide is to, "Keep up to date on your security patches."

It is sad to say, but the majority of network administrators are lax in their attention and application of security patches. Network administrators have a number of good reasons to behave this way. First, few administrators have the luxury of being full-time network security professionals. They have any number of things on their plates on a daily basis, from fixing the loose RJ-45 jack on Nate's computer to explaining to the CEO how to check e-mail while they are in a hotel room. Wading through security bulletins and picking out the patches that are critical to their systems can be time consuming.

Many system administrators have also been burned applying a security fix. Most experienced administrators can relate a story of a simple "fix" that ended up breaking a mission-critical application. Nobody likes spending the weekend fixing something that should be working in the first place. Even worse, nobody likes spending a workday fixing something that was working last night while their supportive user base offers one helpful hint after another. Instead, it is often easier to not install a fix when it is released but, instead, schedule some downtime on a semi-periodic basis and apply many fixes at once. An even better solution is to create a test network where the patches can be installed and assessed for impact prior to applying the fix to a production network.

Still other system administrators just do not know how or feel comfortable working with vendors' patches. Many times, instructions can be cryptic and difficult to understand if you are not working with the program on a daily basis. Most system administrators have so many responsibilities that they are rarely experts in any one element of their network. It is easy for individuals who are slightly uncomfortable with a procedure to put it off. If you do not believe me, think about the last time you had to go to the doctor.

Unfortunately, not taking the time to apply security patches is one of the number-one vulnerabilities that a network will face. Applying security fixes to a working configuration is usually a matter of understanding the basics of network security, reading the documentation of a product, and checking the right options on a configuration screen specific for your organization. The very nature of a patch means that something that you thought was working correctly is not. Thus, a network administrator may initially start with a network configured to meet the needs of their security policy, but as time passes and new vulnerabilities are discovered in the hundreds of applications and services that the average network runs (many of which users and administrators do not even know are running), the network moves further and further away from the goal of the security policy. All of this happens without the network administrator changing a thing on the network.

The shameful result is that most networks are compromised by attacks for which prevention already exists. From time to time, information security reports will reveal a totally unknown, new attack that has compromised a large number of systems or caused other havoc, but most attacks take advantage of the fact that hackers are more efficient in utilizing old vulnerabilities than administrators are in patching them.

A simple example of this is that as I write this chapter, the SQL Sapphire/Slammer worm is attacking large portions of the Internet. While the attack itself is interesting in the aggressive nature that the worm takes in spreading itself, the vulnerability that has allowed this worm to spread has been known for about six months. Furthermore, Microsoft had released a patch to prevent exactly this type of event. Nevertheless, large portions of the Internet are being rendered unusable due to the number of systems that have been affected and the IP traffic that the worm generates. Just to illustrate the difficulty in keeping up-to-date with patches, it turns out that Microsoft itself has been hit with the worm.

5.1 The Network Time Protocol

One often-overlooked service on a network is the Network Time Protocol (NTP). NTP is a protocol that allows networked devices to synchronize their internal clocks and is amazingly accurate in its operation. NTP clients receiving clocking information from a central server will automatically attempt to compensate for the estimated delay of the informational packets as they travel over the network. This intelligence results in devices over a large geographic area synchronized to within a few microseconds of each other. For the normal operation of a computer network, this is normally not a critical function. Most computers contain their own chronometer that sets the time quite well. When considering the security of your network, however, NTP should be considered an essential protocol to include as part of the implementation of an information security policy.

NTP clocking should not be confused with the term "clocking," which is commonly used to represent the speed of a computer. The CPU chip, most likely Intel or AMD, which sits in your desktop computer, was most likely marketed to you by using the Hz speed of the processor. We have been trained to understand that a 2.2-GHz CPU is faster and better than a 2.0-GHz CPU. A small quartz crystal vibrates at a certain speed and determines the CPU speed along with other components of your average computer system. NTP has nothing to do with how fast your computer operates. NTP is a way of setting the clock on you computer in the same way you would set your wristwatch or kitchen wall clock. The benefit of NTP is that it is like setting your clocks all at once for daylight savings and at the same time making sure that your kitchen clock is not five minutes faster than your VCR clock.

NTP, like most TCP/IP protocols, is client/server in nature. This implies that there is a central server that keeps the master clock information. Other devices around the network, acting as clients, periodically check with the NTP server to ensure that their clocks are current and synchronized. An NTP server itself can be configured to query another server at a different location and synchronize to the remote server. This allows a hierarchy of NTP servers, providing accurate timing information on a global basis.

Those really interested in time know that not all clocks are created equal. Some are more accurate than others. Currently, the best clocks we know of are the so-called "atomic clocks" that measure their ticks according to the vibrations of certain atoms. These top-tier, highly accurate clocks are known as stratum one clocks. Because not everyone can afford their own atomic clock, but can afford a "pretty darn good" clock, there are also a number of stratum two clocks that synchronize themselves to the stratum one clocks on a regular basis. Below stratum two clocks are stratum three, stratum four, etc., all the way down to stratum sixteen clocks. In theory, each clock higher on the stratum hierarchy is more accurate and reliable than the one below it. When considering NTP, we do not need to worry about what stratum our desktop computers and servers are; we only need to know that NTP servers follow this stratum hierarchy. A stratum three clock always trusts the time of a stratum two clock but not a stratum four clock.

A typical network using NTP will have one or two clocks that act as time servers for the rest of the network. If two NTP servers are configured, they will synchronize with each and normally synchronize with a public stratum two NTP server. Lists of public NTP servers are readily available on the Internet. Internal to the network, everything else will act as a client and synchronize their clocks to the same as the local NTP servers. This is particularly relevant from the perspective of network security. Many networks will have more than one source of logging information; each one of these log sources will mark their logs with the local time configured on the server. When these logs are collected and examined, unless the timestamps on the logs are precisely synchronized, determining the order of events — a critical element of forensic analysis and auditing — will be next to impossible. It is for this reason, the facilitation of network logging information for event auditing, that NTP is critical.

Some time has been spent discussing NTP and if you were not familiar with the protocol you may think that this is another expensive server or, worse yet, two expensive servers that you need to install and maintain along with purchasing the NTP server software itself. Not so. NTP is a small, efficient protocol and server application that is readily available for free or as part of a bundled OS. The application can easily run in conjunction with any other applications as part of a single server or on separate low-end computers. The power of the host computer is not an issue for the NTP application. All the needed information is obtained from a much more expensive and accurate computer out on the Internet.

Even synchronizing with stratum two clocks on the Internet is optional. What is more important is that your network is synchronized to itself. In most cases, it does not matter that your network NTP differs from the "actual" time by two seconds. What matters is that every device that your NTP server provides time for, agrees on the time down to the millisecond. Internal consistency for your logging information is the goal — not external synchronization with the rest of the world. That said, it is so easy to connect to public stratum two servers that most NTP implementations go through the minor effort to ensure their time is globally accurate as well. Stratum one clocks are available, but public access to their highly accurate timing is not normally allowed. This is not a flaw; stratum two clocks are more than accurate for all but the most demanding of timing applications, such as satellite navigation or signaling for public telephone network circuits.

5.2 Domain Name System Servers

To a computer, an IP address is simply a string of 32 ones and zeros. We humans, however, have a difficult time remembering when someone tells us to PING the IP address 11000000101101000000000000000001. Instead, to keep our sanity, we represent this string of ones and zeros in 8-bit chunks and then translate each of those 8-bit chunks into decimal numbers, with which we are more familiar. It is much easier to PING 192.168.0.1.

Even this abstraction is not workable in the long run, however. It simply would not do to remember that Proteris had servers in the IP address range of 200.0.0.5–30, except for the mail server, which was hosted at another location and had its IP address of 134.0.100.10. In an effort to further simplify the usability of network resources, it did not take network engineers long to create something known as an *alias*. In its purest form, an alias is simply a text string that is associated with an IP address. For example, I used a text file on my home office network called hosts.txt. Each machine had an identical copy of this file and it was used to provide a mnemonic shortcut to IP addresses. This text file has a number of entries in it that look like:

```
192.168.10.10      Calvin
192.168.10.11      Hobbes
192.168.10.12      Bart
192.168.10.13      Lisa, etc.
```

When testing network configurations and rapidly moving from host to host over the network, I do not need to trouble myself with the IP addresses of each host. I simply type "SSH Calvin" or "SSH Bart." The source host examines the host.txt file and automatically translates my query into an IP address. While this is a very simple system, each time I added a new machine to the network, this file would have to be updated on all other hosts to ensure that the host.txt file remained consistent. As the network grew to over 20 devices, this system became unwieldy. Instead, it was simpler to maintain a single database at a central location and configure all devices to query that single device for a name to address resolution. The server that I installed to serve as the central database was, of course, a DNS server.

Much of the early Internet used a system very similar to this for access to networked hosts. Host files were stored locally to each networked device and updated on a regular basis. As the number of networked devices grew, network engineers discovered long ago the same thing I discovered in my own office — keeping multiple database files up-to-date was an unmanageable task. The issue was further complicated by the fact that multiple government and educational facilities were trying to manage their own domains. Because the entire host file was essentially a flat database, a change to one network meant that all other network administrators had to update their own host files.

The domain name system was developed in an effort to decentralize the management of name to address translation tables. Ideally, nobody really would need to know that State U had changed the IP address of the Web server www.stateu.edu from 145.15.9.10 to 145.15.9.11, especially if others never had the need or desire to connect to the Web server.

The DNS is what is known as a distributed hierarchical database. Starting from a central point, the "root," the domain space is broken into several top-level domains. Each of these top-level domains is, in turn, broken into domains, which are in turn broken into sub-domains or hosts. In the example shown in Exhibit 1, we see a logical representation of this structure. As an example, there is a "Proteris" domain as part of the .com and .net top-level domains. Each Proteris domain, in turn, may be further subdivided into sub-domains or include hosts in the Proteris domain itself. We see in Exhibit 1 that each Proteris domain contains a Web server with the host name "www." To unambiguously differentiate between the two occurrences of Proteris Web server, DNS names are always referred to using the full domain structure, as in www.proteris.com and www.proteris.org. This format of identifying hosts through the use of sub-domains (if present),

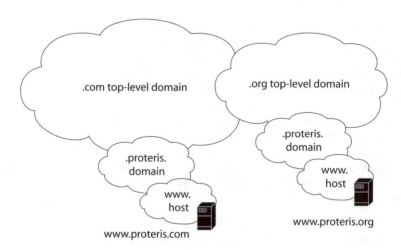

Exhibit 1. The Logical Structure of the DNS Name Space

domains, and top-level domains is known as a fully qualified domain name (FQDN).

A DNS server is an application service that runs on a host. The DNS process refers to a number of text files. There are a number of files that allow a DNS server to provide full functionality, but the two most important ones are the zone file and the in.addr file. The zone file contains host names such as www, mail, server_1, etc. Each host in the zone file is associated with an IP address. Each time a request for a host that is part of a domain (such as proteris.com) is sent to the DNS server, this file is consulted to find the requested host name and return the appropriate IP address in response to the query. The in.addr file performs just the opposite function. It contains IP addresses and the associated host name. When a request is sent to the DNS server to ensure that a particular IP address is really part of a given domain, this file is checked. The structure of these files can be seen in Exhibit 2.

At the top of the DNS hierarchy is a set of servers known as root servers. These are the servers that contain information on how to get to all other DNS servers in the world. The root DNS servers then have no information about host names or sub-domains. They simply know where to find the authoritative server for each domain. If, for example, you want to browse to www.proteris.com, your Web browser would make a request for a name to address resolution to your local DNS server. Assuming your local DNS server did not have such a mapping in place, it would then make a request to a root server that could be paraphrased as, "Do you know where the DNS server that has information about the proteris.com domain can be found?" The root would respond back with the IP address of the proteris.com DNS server. Your DNS server would then send a request to the proteris.com DNS server that could be paraphrased as, "I'm looking for the host named www. Do you have any host that matches that name in your zone file?" The zone file would be referenced and the proper IP address would be returned to your DNS server to be forwarded to your host to complete the browsing process.

There are currently 13 root servers in the world today. Some of these 13 root servers are not single servers, but actually clusters of servers. They are built to handle a fantastic number of requests per second and are located at some of the major hubs of the Internet. Even this hardware, however, cannot always keep up with demand. In an effort to make the DNS resolution process described in the preceding paragraph more efficient, DNS servers often cache name-to-address mappings in case anyone else wishes to make a similar request. Thus, if one of your co-workers wished to visit www.proteris.com, your local DNS server would already have the IP address cached from your earlier request. Many times, an upstream cache is utilized as well. This means that if your local DNS server did not have an

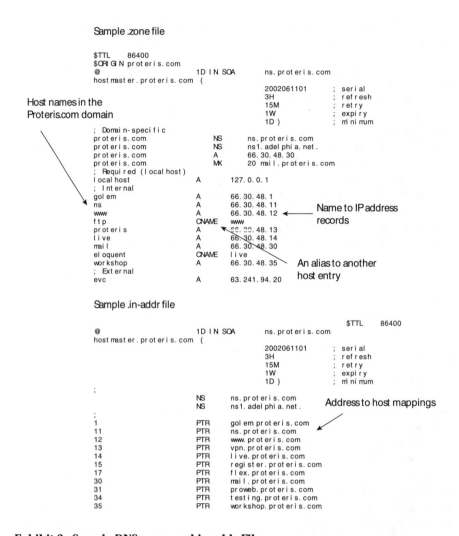

Exhibit 2. Sample DNS .zone and in.addr Files

available translation for your initial request, then instead of immediately forwarding a request to the root server, it may query another DNS server, typically one maintained by your service provider. The logic of this is that because the service provider theoretically answers requests for a larger number of hosts than your company, odds are that someone from another location has already made a request for the same name-to-address resolution you are making.

5.2.1 DNS Security Concerns

The primary role of DNS is simply the name-to-address translation and address-to-name translation that it provides. This simple role, however, has major security implications. From what we now know of the DNS process, we can easily identify some points of concern.

The first is simply the entering of incorrect information into the system. Using the example of my test network, if someone were able to hack into the network and change the address resolution of the host Calvin, I could go on using the alias Calvin without knowing that I was actually being diverted to another host. Apply this on a larger scale and we have problems. If, for example, you were diverted to another Web site that looked exactly like the first one (a trivial process), you may be tempted to try to log in using a username and password. You may even be tempted to shop for a product and enter credit card information. DNS has been the victim of some spectacular vulnerabilities that have made these types of attacks possible. While patches are released to patch the latest vulnerability, odds are that there are going to be new ones in the future.

The zone file that is part of every DNS implementation is also an attractive target for someone simply seeking to learn information about a target company. To ensure availability of the DNS, DNS servers have a built-in ability to transfer the entire zone file to another host. Many times, however, this transfer is not restricted to only a designated backup host. Instead, anyone making a request for the zone transfer can receive it. This file, having a mapping of all host names, aliases, and the IP address of hosts on the network is a fantastic resource for anyone seeking information for a later attack on the network.

Cached DNS entries are also vulnerable to attack. Many DNS servers will simply cache a name to address resolution packet when they receive it — even if they had never made a request for that name in the first place. This means that an attacker can send a crafted DNS query response to a caching DNS server and point a popular network resource to an alternate host. Anyone downstream of the cache will then be redirected to the cached, illegitimate address instead of the legitimate destination. This process, known as cache poisoning, allows an attacker to give the appearance of your site having been hacked without ever having to have actually compromised your network.

Finally, although DNS is not required for Internet connectivity in a strictly technical sense, it is essential for humans to be able to make productive use of network resources. Being able to take a DNS server offline is normally just as effective as launching a denial-of-service attack on a site, as is flooding the targets access-link with traffic. If the normal end user cannot receive proper name resolution for the destination, it is unlikely that they will ever be able to visit your site.

Due to the critical nature of DNS and the multiple avenues that can be used to compromise either a DNS server or the service they provide, special care must be taken when considering the implementation of a DNS

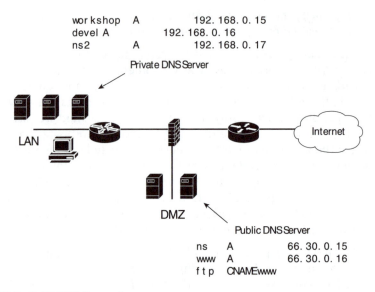

Exhibit 3. Split DNS Example

server. One common solution attempting to reduce this risk is the implementation of a split DNS configuration. Split DNS, as the name suggests, is the configuration of multiple DNS servers to serve a network. One DNS server is placed on the internal network or as part of the local LAN server farm and the second DNS server is placed in the DMZ as illustrated in Exhibit 3. The internal DNS server operates as a normal DNS server and LAN hosts are configured to query this DNS server for name-to-address resolutions. The zone files on the LAN are complete and have name-to-address information for all hosts. The DMZ DNS server, on the other hand, has only zone information for hosts that would normally be accessible to the public. Even if the DMZ DNS server were compromised, the attacker has discovered no information that could not already be easily found.

It is important to configure two DNS servers. I have found that some network administrators attempt to outsmart themselves by setting up either two separate zone files on a single DNS server or running two DNS processes on a single server. Separation in this case can be achieved by installing two network interface cards on a single device. While this may make financial and logical sense, it suffers from two critical flaws. The first is that the entire point of a DMZ is the assumption that despite your best efforts, hosts in the DMZ will be compromised. Once this has been accomplished, you cannot guarantee the integrity of either your internal or external DNS databases. The second problem is that once this host is compromised, due to the multiple network interface cards, you have created a backdoor past your firewall into your internal network. It seems silly, but I have seen this configuration in practice. Do not do it.

Chapter 6
Access Control

Perhaps the most important element of your information security system is controlling how people access the network resources. The goal of access control is typically described by the abbreviation AAA or "Triple A," short for authentication, authorization, and accounting.

Authentication, the first goal of access control, is to ensure that users are who they claim to be. Authentication of users can be established in one of three ways:

- *Something the user knows.* This is normally an intangible that only the authorized user should know. Common examples include a password or a personal identification number. Other examples, while not unique to the individual user, can also be used, such as mother's maiden name or other mnemonic trick. The primary advantage of using password-type authentication is that it is well-established in both the psyche of users and the design of network components. It is easy to implement and easy to manage. The primary disadvantage is that users tend to pick something easy to remember. "Easy to remember" is often shorthand for insecure. The problem is compounded when an organization relies on different passwords for multiple systems.
- *Something the user has.* The second most common method of access control is by assuming that only the authorized user will be in possession of a physical object that will prove his or her identity. A common object is a token or magnetically striped card. The primary problem with this solution alone is that the physical object itself can be lost or stolen. Consider the example of a common object that utilizes something you have as the authentication method — automobiles. The key to the automobile serves as the physical token with the assumption that only the authorized driver of the car will be in possession of the key itself. This, of course, is not always true.
- *Something the user is.* This third category of authentication relies on some individually unique personal characteristic of a person to establish identity. Arguably, this is the same as something the user has; but because in this case we are referring to a biological identifier, a separate authentication category is typically assigned to it. From our DNA to our fingerprints, humans have a number of unique

characteristics that can be used to establish identity with a very high degree of probability. While biological identifiers are generally considered the last word in authentication, they suffer from several implementation problems. Most notably, accuracy, user acceptance, and cost are issues that limit the widespread adoption of this form of authentication.

Any system of authentication that employs only one of the above listed methods of authentication is known as single-factor authentication. Systems that employ two of the above methods of authentication are similarly known as two-factor authentication systems and are generally preferable to single-factor authentication systems. Two-factor authentication is also fairly simple to implement, assuming that the network infrastructure has been created to support it. Consider the two-factor authentication that we use every day with automatic teller machine (ATM) cards. First, we must be in possession of the ATM card itself — something we have. In conjunction with the card, however, we must also know the PIN (personal identification number) assigned to that account — something we know.

Two-factor authentication significantly improves the confidence we have in our authentication systems. Consider the ATM and PIN example. From a security point of view, the use of a four-digit PIN as access control would be unacceptable. With only 10,000 available values in a PIN, a PIN is less secure than even a password selected right from the dictionary. Combined with the requirement for a physical token, however, the level of security the PIN provides becomes adequate for the application.

Three-factor authentication is not unheard of, just less widely deployed. While a biometric (something you *are*) is commonly applied with something you have or know, the increase in security versus the increase in cost in complexity for three-factor authentication must be carefully evaluated.

Once user identity has been authenticated, authorization is the next step. The access rights that a user has on the network must then be established. This is typically done via associating a username with an access control list that applies rules dictating what a user can access and what a user is specifically prohibited from accessing.

From a network management perspective, methods of authorization can be divided into three primary models: discretionary, mandatory, and nondiscretionary access control.

Discretionary access control (DAC) allows the owner of a resource to create access rules defining access to the resource. If I create a spreadsheet on the network, then as the owner of the spreadsheet, I am allowed to define who has access to that spreadsheet. Using the discretionary model, users are able to define the access rights for the resources they create. Thus, you, being part of the project, may have full read access to the spreadsheet but Jim down the hall is not allowed to read our important information.

Discretionary access control is ideal in a decentralized environment, but can be difficult to manage. Because network administrators are not involved in assigning rights to resources created by the users, it can be difficult to ensure that all resources have the appropriate level of rights assigned to them. For example, as the average user, I may have inadvertently provided more access to the spreadsheet I had created than is allowed considering the sensitive nature of information on the spreadsheet. If this were the case, a network security officer would be unlikely to know about my intentional or unintentional security configuration until it was too late.

The response to a discretionary access control model is mandatory access control (MAC). Using the MAC model, users and objects are assigned security labels. When a user attempts to access an object, the security labels for the user and the object are compared. If the user's security level is higher than that of the object, access is allowed. Any fan of spy thrillers will recognize this model. An agent with "top secret" clearance can access files of a "confidential" nature because "top secret" is a security label assigned to a user that has a security value higher than the value of "confidential."

For mandatory access control to operate properly, each object or resource in a system must be assigned a security label. These labels follow a strict hierarchy, with each label on the hierarchy more trusted than those below it. The security label hierarchy can be repeated among different categories in the organization. Thus, a company may have a research and development (R&D) category and an accounting category. Both R&D and accounting may have several security labels, such as confidential, proprietary, corporate, and sensitive. To access an object in the accounting department that has a security label of corporate, a user would have to be classified as part of the accounting category and have a clearance of corporate or sensitive to be able to access that object.

Mandatory access controls are beneficial for large organizations with centralized management. The creator of the file can still determine what level of security his document requires, but it is the operating system itself that determines the users who have access to the file and who can override the owner of the file regarding security permissions. If you were to assign a security label of "proprietary" to a spreadsheet, anyone who is in the same category of your organization (e.g., accounting) with a security clearance of confidential or higher would be able to access your document and possibly change or reassign the security label to a higher level.

The most common implementation of mandatory access controls is found in the military. There, the security levels from lowest to highest are unclassified, sensitive but unclassified, confidential, secret, and top secret. In a business environment, when strictly implemented, mandatory access control security labels from lowest to highest are public, sensitive, private, and confidential.

Purely discretionary and mandatory access controls suffer from a management problem in that users are assigned permissions on an individual basis. For large organizations, this becomes a cumbersome chore, making sure that each user has the appropriate rights for any given network resource. Imagine for a small company of even 500 employees with 10 network servers, 25 printers, and hundreds of files and folders, each requiring different levels of access permissions to utilize them. Network administrators for this company would spend much of their time assigning rights to new employees and troubleshooting rights that they have already assigned ("I can't use the printer down the hall for some reason, but I can use the one on the third floor. Can you fix this for me, please?"). Such complexity also puts the information security policies of the organization at risk because misconfiguration or excessive privileges may go unnoticed until it is too late.

When implementing any security policy, a hallmark of a good implementation is to provide rights to users that are exactly appropriate to their job function, a philosophy known as "least privilege." Least privilege means that as a user on the second floor of the engineering department, I have access to network printers on the second floor of the engineering department but not those printers in the executive suite. I have network access that allows me to share resources on the engineering department file servers but have no access whatsoever to the accounting department file servers. These permissions serve to protect the company against myself should I decide to initiate malicious actions against the company, but it also protects the company and myself should someone illegitimately gain access to my accounts.

A common risk associated with privileges is something known as "privilege creep." Privilege creep is the slow accumulation of rights that an individual acquires as they change roles in the company. A person may be transferred from one department to another or promoted from one position to another yet retain the permissions associated with their previous position along with acquiring the permissions of their new position. Of course, this is the exact opposite of least required privilege in that the user now has network permissions that exceed his required job function.

To address the issue of management and privilege creep, the nondiscretionary access control model is often implemented. Also known as role based access control (RBAC), users are assigned roles within a company.

The roles are then assigned the proper permissions. As an example, John is a new hire in the engineering department and working on the secret project to power fuel cells by methane in the hopes of greatly increasing the fuel efficiency of 18-wheelers by harnessing to this point untapped power of the truck drivers themselves. The role name of this project is "Buy Beans." The network administrator has taken the time to set up the permissions for the "Buy Beans" role to access only those resources critical to the success of the project and no others. That means that members of the Buy Beans group cannot even access other ongoing engineering projects. As can be imagined, in this company, the complexity of this task could have taken the network administrators a couple of hours to ensure that permissions were correctly assigned. When John signs on, instead of duplicating the work for John in assigning permissions, John is simply assigned the role of "Buy Beans." His permissions then take on exactly that of the Buy Beans role.

Should John transfer to another project, one more appealing to his sense of smell, the network administrator could simply assign John a new role. When assigned to the new role, John then has permissions only to objects defined by the new role. The benefit of nondiscretionary access controls then includes both ease of management and improved security. By assigning users to roles, management is eased because users do not need to be individually assigned rights to network objects. Security is increased through the use of roles by ensuring that rights assigned to roles are exactly those required by the role. When changing roles, the rights of the users are then changed, helping to prevent privilege creep.

For those familiar with network administration, a number of popular operating systems where users are put into groups and then groups assigned rights will immediately spring to mind. This is very similar to role-based access control with only one minor difference. In role-based access control, users have only those rights assigned to the roles. In systems that employ groups, the user is generally allowed to assign privileges on an individual basis as well. Furthermore, users may be generally placed in multiple groups. Thus, most popular operating systems allow the flexibility of discretionary access controls with the management capabilities of nondiscretionary access controls.

While flexible, this combination of access control authorization models does have its drawbacks. The most significant is that it is difficult to determine a user's effective permission to any given object. If users are allowed only read access to a network object in one group but are allowed read and write access in another group, what permission do they have when actually accessing the objects? Most operating systems default to the most restrictive rule in this regard. This overlap of rules can make administration of the system confusing, and confusion is always poor security. The best way to avoid this is to create your groups as if you were creating roles for your users. That is, create your permissions and groups based on defined roles in your organization. Done properly, you will be able to assign users to a role-based group to accomplish their required tasks, instead of assigning users to a number of groups to be able to accomplish their daily functions.

The third and final component of access control is accounting. No information security system can be considered complete until proper accounting is configured (and reviewed on a regular basis, but that is a different story altogether). It is unlikely that all computer attacks are going to be discovered in real-time. Even if the effect of an attack is noticed, by the time a human decides to intervene, most of the time the damage has already been done. The best we can do, short of using computers themselves to respond to attacks in a reactive manner, is to review the evidence of an attack and make an assessment as to whether or not the attack was successful. One of the most important elements in this regard is thorough accounting.

As the name suggests, accounting is the ability to associate a user account with a series of actions and the time they occurred. It is the ability to know who did what and when they did it. The ability to accurately and completely log user information leads to a number of questions that must be considered when comparing countermeasures.

The first element for consideration is the ability to do logging at all. Most access control applications allow some sort of logging, but this may be little more than knowing that user *jdoe* logged in at 8:45 Monday, December 16, 2002, and stayed logged in to the network for eight hours. More advanced reporting will also be able to inventory what *jdoe* did while logged in.

It may be natural to assume that the more information that can be gathered, the better; this is not necessarily the case. The auditing of information is only important if someone is going to actually review the logged information. Even in a small network, assuming that this function takes place on a regular basis, the amount of information that can be collected about users can quickly become overwhelming. Too much information is just as bad as not enough information. This is for two reasons. The first is that information overload will discourage the review of the accounting information in the first place. The second is that actual misuse can be lost in the mountains of accumulated data.

Instead of simply looking for the amount of information to be collected, a more accurate comparison of access control countermeasures would be to examine *what* information they collect and how configurable the accounting rules can be. For example, you may not wish to audit every single failed log-on attempt. Instead, you would want to only record log-on attempts that fail a certain number of times. Most users will, from time to time, mistype their passwords. If they mistype it more than three times, however, that may be an indication of a problem. Or you may wish to only log network log-ons that occur outside normal working hours so that you can concentrate your efforts on specific events. If you have reason to suspect misuse of network resources by a particular user, it would be helpful to be able to audit everything that this particular user does, yet leave the rest of the network users at the default logging level.

The process of being able to specify logging only after a certain number of events occur, such as failed network log-ons, is known as being able to establish a *clipping level*. Clipping levels are essential in reducing the amount of accounting information that a reviewer is presented with by removing events that alone may not be significant, but in a group may be very significant. Note, however, that clipping levels normally have a decay period associated with the clipping level. That means that three failed log-ons in ten minutes may be recorded, but three failed log-ons in 30 minutes may have caused the clipping level timers to reset and thus not be logged. Good attackers are very patient.

The ability to manipulate accounting data is also very important. While a single, long text file is technically an accounting log, woe to the person that needs to peer through that log to decipher usage patterns. Instead, the ability to manipulate data is important. While I would rather manage my servers using a command-line interface, I cannot dispute the advantage of humans using graphical interfaces to be able to interpret aggregate data.

Mechanisms used to store information in access control accounting are very important. If the accounting of a network of any size is being performed, then a good deal of data is going to be recorded. This logged data is going to be important if anyone on the network is suspected of misuse or an actual attack has occurred through a user account. It may be important enough to have to serve as legal evidence. To ensure the longevity, integrity, and even admissibility of the accounting data in court, be sure to examine backup mechanisms, timestamping, and the cryptographic signing of data through the use of either the access control accounting software itself or a third-party solution. Speaking of timestamping, it may also be a good time to note that most networks do not adequately ensure the consistency of time settings between their systems. Even having a 60-second difference between the settings of multiple hosts will make conclusive reconstruction of events from the accounting log impossible. Ensure that your network time protocol server is functioning properly and hosts are configured to synchronize their system clocks on a regular basis.

Common methods of securing accounting data include rather straightforward methods of recording data to a removable disk or writeable CD-ROM. Once full, the removable media can be replaced and stored in a safe location. In either case, cryptographically secure timestamping and hashing of the information should be performed as soon as possible; in some cases, each entry is timestamped and hashed as it occurs. This provides reasonable assurance that the information has not been tampered with after the fact. In certain instances where the integrity of data must be ensured, network administrators have even gone through the effort of printing out hard copies of accounting information as they occur. This procedure tends to generate quite a bit of paper, but ensures that any information logged cannot be easily altered or deleted from a network-based attack.

In medium to large networks, there may be multiple systems that perform the access control function. This can make the examination of accounting data troublesome if the logging information is likewise distributed among a number of authentication and authorization services. No matter the diversity of access control systems in use, make it a point to ensure that the logging can be collected from a central location.

An experienced attacker will make the accounting system one of his first targets once the network has been compromised. To make the attacker's work more difficult, it is imperative that the server hosting the log files be especially secure by configuring it as a bastion host as all network devices should be and protecting the logging file with a firewall. Disabling remote management of the accounting information server altogether would not be a bad idea either.

For most attackers, circumventing access controls is the goal of the intelligence-gathering phase of their attacks. Once allowed access to network resources in any form, an attacker will then attempt to use clues available within the network infrastructure itself to elevate their privileges and eventually obtain the information they are seeking or gain control of the network itself. The most significant step that can be taken to prevent this is to make it difficult for attackers to access your network.

As previously discussed, access control is more than simply ensuring that users pick a good password for logging in to the network. The bulk of our security controls implemented by our firewalls, VPN devices, and intrusion detection systems are an effort to ensure that access is only granted at points where it is appropriate. This logical control of the network can be extended to physical access controls as well. While there are any number of risks associated with network access attempts, these pale in comparison to the damage that someone with physical access to your information infrastructure could cause. Most host computers can be compromised with a simple floppy disk at a user workstation. A denial-of-service attack that comprises the simple step of physically removing (stealing) your servers would clearly be hard to recover from.

6.1 Passwords

The Achilles heel of most networks is their reliance on passwords. There are alternatives to passwords, such as one-time passwords and biometrics, but these solutions may not always make sense in all environments, especially when a risk analysis determines that the extra cost involved with these solutions is not justified by the security required of the application.

Passwords, on the other hand, are virtually universal in application. Regardless of the security required or purchased for your installation, it is a sure bet that, at a minimum, passwords are provided as a security mechanism. The reliance on passwords makes them especially important to the security of information but, unfortunately, poorly chosen passwords and poor password security are the single biggest risk that most organizations face.

Organizations that rely on passwords for authentication face a number of associated risks associated. The first is that people tend to choose weak passwords. A survey performed by a British ISP revealed that 47 percent of people choose passwords based on family names or significant dates in the family. After all, who would ever guess that your password was your youngest daughter's name with a couple of numbers after it? Another 32 percent had passwords that were based on sports stars or other celebrities. Thus, nobody would ever make an association between your Simpson's screen saver and your log-on password. A full 11 percent of users reported passwords that were in some way representative of an alter fantasy ego of the user, such as "stud," "sexy," "goddess," etc. Only 9 percent of users reported using passwords that were considered cryptographically strong; that is, comprised of random characters with upper and lower case characters combined. With just a bit of knowledge about a person, a hacker could, within a short time, compromise 91 percent of all user accounts.

Why do people choose such poor passwords? Most users are not trying to lessen the information security policy of the organization on purpose. They are simply trying to pick a password that they are likely to remember. The problem is compounded by requiring users to have multiple passwords for different services on the network and by requiring that users change their passwords on a regular basis. If we force users to create truly random passwords, then they end up writing them down. In other words, users choose poor passwords because they do not have the memory capabilities of a computer.

Network security has progressed to the point were most applications — Telnet, POP3, and FTP excluded— do not send plaintext passwords over the network. Furthermore, passwords are not generally stored in plaintext on an application server. The risk of someone gaining access to the password file and learning everyone's passwords is too great. Thus, anyone obtaining a password file must still go through the task of determining what that password was. Passwords are generally not encrypted as we might do in a VPN; instead, passwords are hashed using common hashing algorithms such as MD5 or SHA-1.

Using hashes as a way to store and transmit passwords ensures that someone cannot simply look at the hash and determine what the password is. It does not, however, render the passwords immune to attack. If, for example, our passwords only have four characters, there are a finite number of combinations on a keyboard that those four characters could be. It would be a small matter for a computer to simply generate random combinations of four characters, hash them, and examine the output. If the hash output from the randomly generated characters matches the captured hashed password, then we can conclude what the password is. The more characters included in a password, the longer this process can take; but given enough time, any captured password can be discovered in this manner.

This process can be significantly speeded up with an understanding of user psychology. Knowing that users will use terms that are related to family, sports, television, and fantasy images of themselves, of all the trillions of combinations that a password could be, we simply try the most popular hundred thousand variations of family names and sports stars. Entire dictionaries can also be included in our hash files, allowing us to break most passwords based on common choices in virtually no time. It is only those 9 percent of cryptographically strong passwords that cause a password-cracking program any trouble.

Based on this information, we cannot trust users to create their own passwords without some guidance. Instead, we must offer assistance in the creation of secure passwords. One alternative is for network administrators to generate passwords on the behalf of users and trust the network administrator to choose secure options for the users. This is not ideal for three reasons. The first is that it creates an unnecessary amount of overhead on the part of the network administration staff. The second reason is that a user could reasonably argue that the use of a password for identification is flawed from the beginning in that at least one other person knows the password. Ideally, network administrators can reset password for users or create an initial password, but user passwords should be encrypted even from the knowledge of the network administrators. Finally, users do not do well remembering passwords that are not of their own creation. A cryptographically ideal password generated by a network administrator will simply end up being written on a post-it note and stuck under the keyboard or, worse yet, on the side of the computer monitor.

Software does exist to allow users to evaluate or create their own secure passwords. The first class of software can be broadly categorized as a password creator. While better than allowing a network administrator to create the password, this creates the same problem — the user has no ownership of the password and will again be forced to take steps to remember the password. The second class of password software is known as a password checker. This software runs in the background or as part of the password creation/changing software interface and gives users an indication of the relative strength of their password. Thus, if a user were to pick a password such as "Patriots03!," the password checker would recognize that the majority of the password was based on a common name and warn the user that he had chosen a weak password. Because the user is still allowed to create the password, there is a better chance that he will come up with a secure password that can be easily remembered. When evaluating an operating system or other access control mechanism, the existence of password checking software would be advantageous.

The question still remains, however, if an organization is forced to rely on passwords for authentication, how can users easily remember to choose a good password that seems random? The most helpful technique I have found in this regard is to teach users how to create mnemonic-based passwords. Instead of using a password, users create a *passphrase* that they then condense into a password. For example, if a user is familiar with Lincoln's Gettysburg address, the following phrase may be familiar to them, "Four score and seven years ago our forefathers...." Clearly, nobody wants to type this in each morning as they log on, but by borrowing the first letter from each word, the password "fsasyaof" Is generated. Clearly, that is not a dictionary word. Mixing up lower case and upper case characters can make a password more complex for systems that recognize the difference between the two, such as "FSaSyaoF." This password can be made more complex by including numbers instead of letters in some parts of the password, such as "420a7yaof." The inclusion of special characters also greatly increases the security of a password. While not all access control mechanisms support special characters, if they did, the following password would be easy enough to remember: "4@)a7yaoF." In this case, some of the numbers were replaced with the special characters accessed via the shift key on most keyboards. To someone unfamiliar with the phrase that generated this password, this would be a difficult password to guess. Instructing users in this method of password generation and allowing them some time to create some in a group setting to ensure that the method has sunk in can create fairly strong passwords created on a regular basis using any key phrase relevant to the user.

Regardless of the method used for creating passwords, passwords can be sniffed as they pass over the network medium. As mentioned, most security-conscious applications will at least go through the effort of hashing the passwords using MD5 or SHA-1 hashing. Using a mnemonic password is not going to prevent someone from using a password hacker on an encrypted password and eventually breaking the password — a good password will, however, greatly increase the time required to break it. Just for comparison, almost any password that is based on any common dictionary word, name, or sports team will be revealed by password cracking software in well under ten seconds. Passwords such as 4@)a7yaoF can take weeks to months to break, depending on the hardware on which the password cracking software is running.

Before passwords are exchanged between client and server, if there is the opportunity, any form of IP encryption available should be used. This ensures that even the password hash that is being sent is itself encrypted. Someone capturing a password encrypted using SSL will first have to crack the SSL secret key used to encrypt the password and then start working on the hashed password itself. This process would take long enough to convince all but the most determined attacker that it was not worth the effort.

It should also be noted that some applications do not encrypt or hash passwords at all. Notorious in this regard are common applications such as POP3, Telnet, and FTP. As such, these applications should always use unique passwords that are unlike any passwords used elsewhere by the user. In each of these instances, established protocols such as SSL, SSH, and SCP for the three protocols, respectively, can all be used to encrypt the sessions themselves before the passwords are sent. Most client software such as e-mail, terminal, and file transfer software support these more secure protocol versions as a configuration option on the server and as part of the client.

Eventually, even the most cryptic password can be compromised. For this reason, it is standard operating procedure to mandate that passwords be changed on a regular basis. The timeframe used for changing passwords is one that is often troubling for those implementing a security policy. Making the timeframe too long increases the chance that bad passwords will be discovered and used. Making the timeframe too short annoys users and encourages them to simply re-enter the same old password as the new password. Keeping a password history in the access control system that prevents users from reusing any of the last four, eight, ten, or any number of configurable previous passwords can prevent this behavior. Users quickly figure this out and will then rapidly change their password a number of times in order to cycle back to the original password. This behavior can be prevented by implementing a hold-down timer in the access control system that prevents users from changing passwords more than once in any given time period. For example, users can be prevented from changing their passwords more than once a day. Users will then circumvent this by choosing passwords such as "password01," "password02," "password03," etc. Each password is then only slightly different from the previous one — a dubious increase in security. Because the ability of users to confound even the most well-intentioned security policy can never be underestimated, it is always more productive for security personnel and network administrators to work with the human factor and establish fair time intervals for the mandatory changing of passwords.

The best guideline for the changing passwords depends on the sensitivity of the user role. Normal network users may be fine only changing passwords on a three- to six-month basis. Users with administrative rights on the network should be changing their passwords on a two- to three-month basis. Note that the goal of changing the administrative password is to prevent anyone who has somehow discovered administrative passwords from continuing to use them on the network. Simply changing the password, however, is not sufficient to ensure the security of servers. Unless user behavior has changed as well, it is a good bet that whoever learned the password the first time will simply learn it again. Furthermore, any competent attacker will promptly install a backdoor to access a server that does not rely on administrator access at all.

6.1.1   One-Time Passwords

While steps can be taken to ensure that a password is difficult to guess or discover using specialized password cracking software, the fact remains that the longer a password is valid, the greater the chance that someone will discover what that password is. Ideally, we would like to use passwords that are only good for a single access. We have seen, however, that user resistance to having to create a new, cryptographically strong password each day would simply be unacceptable.

One-time passwords (OTP) is an authentication system that attempts to implement our desire for short-lived passwords but at the same time be fairly user friendly. In its most pristine form, one-time passwords can simply be a printout of a number of passwords. Users simply work down the list when logging on. The first time they log on, they enter the first password. The second time they log on, they cross off the first password and use the second password. Whatever service is authenticating the user has a similar list and performs the same procedure as the user, incrementing the valid password to the next one on the list each time the user logs on.

This simple form of one-time passwords is clearly no better than normal passwords. Should the password list be lost or photocopied, an attacker would still have the same access to user information if the user simply posted his password on his computer monitor. Instead, OTP is implemented using some sort of electronic card or token. The card itself contains a microchip and a quartz clock that maintains synchronization with the server. The microchip and the server both contain a program that will ensure that the card and the server generate the same password as long as the clocks are synchronized. By synchronizing the card or token with the server, both the card and the server will periodically create a new password on a 30- or 60-second basis. The system can be visualized by imagining that you and I had agreed on a simple code, and each hour we would change our secret code in a predetermined manner.

As there is still a risk of the smart card itself being lost or stolen, most one-time password systems employ two-factor authentication, utilizing a PIN to establish proper ownership of the card and using the card generated password for authentication to the access control system. While more secure than passwords alone, OTPs do suffer from the disadvantage of requiring additional hardware and software to support this function. Additionally, the cards occasionally lose synchronization with the server, thus requiring administrative intervention or additional software support to resynchronize the devices. Are they worth the extra effort? Your risk analysis should tell you that.

6.2 Biometrics

Biometrics, once the domain of the James Bond style spy novel, is quickly gaining acceptance as an attractive addition to access control systems. Just recently, a report of a United Kingdom school employing iris scanning to account for student lunch purchases has come to light. If a public school in any country can afford and employ biometric authentication, we know that this technology has come of age.

As the earlier discussion of access control and passwords illustrates, it is difficult to attain reasonable authentication through the use of passwords alone. Good passwords are difficult for users to remember. Passwords that are difficult for users to remember are written down and compromised. Ideally, we would like an authentication system that is impossible to forge, steal, or give away to another user, but at the same time recognize user needs for quick and efficient access. Coincidentally, everyone carries with them a vehicle for such identification — their own bodies. Biometrics is an attempt to use an individual's own measurable and uniquely individual characteristics to authenticate their identity to a network. The most common example is the fingerprint used by police investigators to identify criminals and other individuals.

Virtually any element of a person's body or behavior can be used to facilitate biometric authentication as long as it is measurable, unique to the individual, and difficult to forge. Weight and height, for example, are not good biometric indicators because there could be tens of thousands of individuals around that are 6 ft 5 in. and 280 pounds. Worse still, someone willing to wear some platform shoes and lead weights in their pockets could fake such measurable characteristics.

Instead, we would like something like signature dynamics that identifies individuals by the way that they sign their own names. While it might be easy to replicate a signature, replicating the *way* that a person signs his own name is much more difficult. The speed and pressure of the pen measured during the process of signing a signature can be measured, so the measurable criteria is fulfilled; finding someone who signs the same signature in the same way when subjected to the exacting measurements of a computer is also difficult, satisfying the other two criteria of unique and difficult to forge.

No matter what a sales brochure states, biometric systems are not perfect. Biometrics can fail in one of two ways. They may, for example, reject someone who is authorized to use the system based upon a biometric identifier. When a biometric system rejects an authorized individual, that is known as a *Type I* error. When a biometric system accepts an *un*authorized individual, that is known as a *Type II* error. Adjusting the sensitivity of the biometric reading device can modify Type I and Type II errors.

The tuning of biometric identification systems strives for a low CER (crossover error rate). This is a point where the number of Type I errors (false rejections) equals the the number of type II errors (false acceptances) and is generally considered the most important element in determining the accuracy of a biometric system. A biometric system with a CER of 4 is better than another biometric system with a CER of 5, for example.

Tuning a biometric system by either reducing or increasing the sensitivity of the device is the perfect example of the conflicting needs of security and usability. If the Type I errors are too high, users become frustrated and administrative overhead increases. The security, however, errs on the conservative side and the number of false acceptances is lessened. Tuning the biometric system to not be so precise decreases the number of problems that legitimate users face by decreasing Type I errors, but increases Type II errors and the chance that someone who is unauthorized will gain access to the system. As a compromise, most biometric systems will also enlist two-factor authentication, which would require a PIN along with the biometric reading. Requiring a PIN and a not so exacting thumbprint decreases the chances that an unauthorized user will gain access to network resources.

Biometric techniques vary and not all have equivalent crossover error rates. The list below identifies and describes some of the most common biometric methods in descending order of average accuracy.

- *Palm scans*. It may not be intuitive that this is the most effective method of authentication, but the palm contains many unique identifiers for an individual. This includes the ridges, creases, and grooves on the palm. This also includes fingerprints for each finger. Based on this fact alone, it should be clear that a fingerprint for each finger, along with all of the other information that the palm contains makes it more accurate (lower CER) than the fingerprint alone.

- *Hand geometry.* Unlike the palm scan, hand geometry refers only to the length and width of a person's hand and fingers.
- *Iris scan.* Also one of the most socially acceptable methods of biometric identification, the iris scan is concerned only with the colored portion of a person's eye. The colors, rings, furrows, and corneas all create a unique identifier for each person. This is also popular because it requires only that people look at a camera, which can be located some distance away.
- *Retina scan.* The retina is the back of a person's eye and matches information based on the blood vessels in the person's eyeball. To be able to access the back of a person's eye, the individual must place their eye against a specialized camera. This involves putting your eye right up to the same place where many others place their eyes. Thus, while it has a fairly low CER (which is good), it is also the least socially acceptable method of biometric authentication.
- *Fingerprint.* Just like in the movies or in criminal forensics, the fingerprint is a unique identifier that identifies individuals based on the patterns, ridges, and crests of a person's fingerprint.
- *Voice verification.* The pattern of a person's speech and other measurable differences in their voice allows individual identification based on speech.
- *Facial recognition.* Ironically, one of the least accurate methods of individual identification is emerging as the way that we identify criminals and terrorists at airports and sporting events. This biometric control takes into account bone structure, nose shape, eyes, forehead sizes, and chin shapes.
- *Signature dynamics.* This is more than just comparing a person's signature in a database. A static signature is fairly easy to copy. What is much more difficult is *how* a person signs his name. Signature dynamics records electrical signals on a sensor pad as a person signs his name, which is subsequently compared to a stored signature dynamic.
- *Keystroke dynamics.* The encryption program SSH, when generating a person's private key, looks for some type of truly random input. To create this random input, a person is asked to type on their keyboard. As with signature dynamics, the way a person types is fairly difficult to mimic — even if the typed text is known in advance, it is difficult to replicate the timing of another person.

In addition to the accuracy of a biometric solution, user resistance must also be taken into consideration. Users generally avoid any solution they find particularly uncomfortable or intrusive. A common example is the retina scan. The actual execution of a retina scan requires users to place their forehead against a device to enable the reading of the retina information. Some systems require a small puff of air to be blown into the eye. Looking around the office now, you no doubt can think of a few people that you do not want your forehead sharing the same space with day after day.

Users will naturally prefer to use biometric authentication systems that are as least intrusive as possible. For example, an iris scan, while still involving the eye, can be performed from several meters away and only require the user to look in the direction of the camera. Most of the time, this can occur without significant effort on the part of the user. Palm geometry testing, while requiring contact with a surface shared with others, is generally considered more acceptable than sharing a surface with other parts of the general public's anatomy.

Naturally, if biometric access controls are deemed necessary, you will be interested in a solution that combines a low error rate with high user acceptance. As mentioned, iris scanning, due to its very low intrusiveness, is considered the most acceptable by most users. Following this, keystroke dynamics and signature dynamics are the next most popular solutions for the simple reason that they both involve user characteristics that users are comfortable with sharing. Voice and facial recognition follow on the list of user acceptance, again due to the fact that a user's "space" is not invaded in order to take a measurement. Both of these solutions require a remote reading device that may be either a camera or a microphone. Not surprisingly, the lowest on the list of user accepted biometric readers are those that require actual physical contact. Unfortunately, these are also some of the most accurate methods of biometric identification other than the iris scan. Of the "shared physical space" solutions, the fingerprint and palm scan are the most accepted by users, followed by a hand geometry scan. The least accepted biometric identifier is the retina scan.

Ultimately, the choice of biometric identification is going to be a combination of not only accuracy and acceptance, but also price and availability. The above discussion serves only to guide you as you compare the products available for your situation.

6.3   RADIUS/TACACS+

A discussion of access controls would be remiss without some discussion of one of the most popular access control systems of all time, the Remote Authentication Dial-In User Service (RADIUS), and its close cousin, Terminal Access Controller Access Control System (fortunately, commonly referred to as just TACACS+[1]). Each of these is a centralized access control mechanism.

You do not need to have a very large network to understand the advantages of centralized access control. Imagine the following scenario, which may be common on even a small network. You have access control as part of the network operating system that controls users' ability to access network resources while locally logged on to the network. You also maintain a small modem bank and a remote access server that manages user connections over the modem bank. Finally, in an effort to reduce the costs associated with the modem bank and toll-free telephone calls, you have a separate remote access server that manages VPN connections incoming from your wide area network. Each of these three devices can require a separate user database along with associated permissions for network access. This implies that each user addition, removal, or change must be replicated in at least three locations. Not only is this a pain from an administrative point of view, but it is also detrimental to the overall security of a network. Complexity leads to mistakes and oversights on the part of network administrators. These mistakes may provide the vulnerability that a threat can utilize to gain access to your network.

Instead, the preferred solution is to centralize the access control mechanisms. RADIUS and TACACS+ are two systems that will accomplish just this for your network and they are both available as free services for your network or as bundled services in other operating systems or remote access controls. While commonly referred to as a service, RADIUS and TACACS+ are technically protocols that provide for the authentication, authorization, and various levels of accounting for users logging on to the network. Because the protocols are very similar, the remainder of this discussion will focus primarily on RADIUS, with attention paid to TACACS+ when it differs significantly from the RADIUS standard.

RADIUS was originally developed by Livingston labs and has since moved into the realm of free software. Many free implementations of RADIUS are available for downloading. TACACS+ started out as the TACACS protocol and was extended by Cisco to the current version. Originally tightly controlled by Cisco, TACACS+ implementations are also available free of charge. The historical difference between RADIUS and TACACS+ ownership and cost is what caused many ISPs to implement RADIUS as the access control mechanism of choice and, to date, RADIUS maintains its position as the more often deployed protocol of the two.

Like most TCP/IP protocols, RADIUS is a client/server protocol with the exception that RADIUS protocol is not found on user hosts. Instead, it is a protocol that operates between a remote access server (RAS) and a RADIUS server. Exhibit 1 shows the common implementation of RADIUS into the network.When a user attempts to log in to the network via a remote access server, the RAS sends a RADIUS packet to the RADIUS server with the username and the encrypted user password. The fact that only the

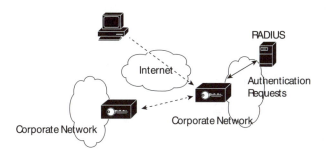

Exhibit 1. Sample RADIUS Implementation

password is encrypted is a concern to some. While the password is certainly the most important element of the packet, there is a great deal of other interesting information available to someone who manages to capture the packet over the network. Most significantly is the username itself. Because so many users tend to pick poor passwords, knowing the username allows someone to start making educated guesses about the password itself. This information is only ever transmitted between the remote access server and the RADIUS server. Whether or not this is a significant threat depends on your security needs.

TACACS+ addresses the issue of unencrypted data of a RADIUS exchanges by encrypting the entire packet. Thus, someone capturing a TACACS+ packet will only see that a TACACS+ transaction has occurred, not who has logged in.

The primary advantage of centralized AAA servers such as RADIUS and TACACS+ is that user management is centralized. Instead of having to maintain user databases and access permissions on multiple RAS devices and other authentication points, network administrators are able to maintain that information in a single location and configure all other devices that perform authentication to query that central user database. With RADIUS and TACACS+, network administrators can maintain this user database on their own LAN and authenticate users company wide.

Note

1. There are actually three versions of TACACS. The most recent and commonly employed is TACACS "Plus," thus the "+" symbol after the acronym. The versions are not compatible with each other.

Chapter 7
The Public Key Infrastructure

The purpose of this section is to describe the need for the public key infrastructure (PKI) and then walk the reader through the process of creating a PKI that meets their specific needs. The PKI is a term that is constantly bandied about as being something that is "essential" and "necessary" to the long-term growth of the Internet and electronic information processing. Many people, however, would be hard-pressed to walk into a network and say, "this is part of the public key infrastructure" while pointing at a piece of hardware on a rack of equipment.

The reason for that is twofold. First, although the need for a PKI is often discussed, the definition of the PKI is difficult to nail down. The second reason is related to the first; a PKI is not a device, or even a single technology. The PKI is just as its name implies, an *infrastructure*. It is the combination of a number of technologies that enables us to effectively utilize public key technologies.

While the math may be somewhat obscure to the non-mathematicians among us, the actual process of encrypting data using public key and secret key algorithms is quite straightforward. The chances are very good that you, in your normal Internet activities, have used encryption without ever even realizing it. The problem is not the actual encryption of data in a secure manner. Rather, the problem is *knowing to whom you are encrypting the data.* In our day-to-day lives, you know that you are speaking with your mother because the identity of your mother has been imprinted upon you for quite some time. You know her by sight and you know the sound of her voice. On the Internet we do not have the benefit of feedback from our own direct experience to identify someone, even if it is our mother. What we need is an electronic way of identifying a remote party — even if we have never met them prior to our first encounter.

The way we do this is through *certificates*. Certificates are simply public keys that have been publicly associated with a particular individual. Because it is unlikely that any one of us would have the chance to meet all the parties we would be interested in conducting business with on the Internet, we rely on a third party to verify that "Jane Doe" is, in fact, the Jane Doe that lives at 123 Highpoint Terrace, in the city of Winooski, Vermont, and not the Jane Doe living at 345 Oak St. in the same city — and most importantly, that it is not Sam Spade pretending to be Jane Doe. The organizations that we rely on to verify that there is a relationship between a public key and a user (or an Internet host) are known as *certification authorities* (CA).

For our purposes, the trust of the CA is going to be implied. That is, it does not matter which organization performs the function of the CA as long as we as the user of the certificate trust that the CA has done due diligence in establishing the identity of certificate holder. It could be the state or federal government, a hospital, our employers, the remote party's employer, or a separate corporation that has no other function than the verification of certificates.

Just having a trusted third party to perform the verification of individuals is not enough. How do I find Jane Doe's certificate if I need to contact her? What happens if Jane Doe suspects someone compromised her private key? What if Jane Doe changes jobs and her CA no longer chooses to stand behind her credentials? How does Jane Doe assure herself that the communication was indeed with me? What types of operations are Jane Doe's certificates valid for? Can I use her certificate to send her secure e-mail, or is the certificate only permitted when Jane Doe wants to connect to her company's VPN server?

To answer these questions, we need to create an infrastructure that supports the creation, dissemination, and termination of certificates. These functions and more are the realm of the public key infrastructure. PKI is not a single technology or even a piece of hardware. It is an abstraction created from many component parts that together answer the essential questions posed in the previous paragraph.

If PKI is an enabling technology, then what exactly does it enable other than the integration and management of certificates and public keys in our organization? After all, what can we accomplish with those two things? Quite a bit, as it turns out.

The most obvious application of PKI is in the assistance of secure communications. As discussed in the cryptography section of this text, public keys and certificates are not used to actually encrypt information. That is the role of secret key algorithms. Instead, public keys signed as a certificate are used to authenticate the remote party in a secure exchange and to encrypt the secret key itself as it is passed from one party to another. By maintaining an infrastructure that allows the easy access and control of public key certificates, encrypted sessions to any member of that PKI are trivial.

The PKI will also play a key role in the emergence of digital documents as legally binding entities. We have discussed that cryptography can also allow us to digitally sign documents. This can be the basis for a legally binding contract or can be used as the basis of a non-repudiation system, or even for notarization purposes. If you and I agree on a contract and I digitally sign it using my private key, then I cannot refute the fact that I have indeed seen and actually signed the contract. The use of certificates means that a third party has taken the steps to ensure that the key-pair I used to sign the document actually belonged to me. Thus, I cannot even argue that someone borrowed my identity to sign a document in my name. The only way that we can have confidence in the identity of digital signatures is if there exists an easy way to ensure that the signature in question is conclusively associated with a given individual. As an example, a government CA could sign the keys of individuals who were to act as notaries. While you or I may not understand the significance of a digital signature, the signature of the notary could be verified to the approval of the court system based upon the trust and verification of the government. The PKI, through the use of certificates and trust, provides this assurance.

Of particular importance to companies is the use of the PKI in privilege management. Capable of including more than just keying information, certificates can also contain extensions that describe user privileges. This can become the basis of a single sign-on system for a company, eliminating the need for multiple sign-on in the use of a heterogeneous operating environment. This is a particular benefit to the security of a company because password proliferation tends to encourage people to make a number of easy-to-remember passwords and then write them down to keep them straight. We know that passwords alone can be insufficient in ensuring the identity of a user. It is advantageous to provide users with a system that allows the use of a single password for all resources and then to instruct users in the selection of a single secure password. Certificates can also operate with smart card systems, in which case the single secure password is a one-time password generated by the smart card reader in association with a short PIN required of the user. The certificate of the PKI, by design, supports the integrity of the key that is signed by the certificate authority. Combine this with the verification of identity provided by the certificate authority and we can see that a PKI provides several major services along the way of authenticating users.

A final benefit of the PKI is the ability to provide timestamping services. Secure timestamping is not one of those things that immediately springs to mind when considering information security, but timestamping is an essential element of almost all security services. What use is notarization or privilege management if there is not also a secure way of ensuring when the documents were examined or any time limits on user privileges provided? Timestamping is also a critical function of logging. As a system administrator, I may not care if my logs were digitally timestamped when troubleshooting a problem on the network. As a forensics investigator investigating or assisting in the prosecution of computer crimes, however, I am very interested in assuring legal authorities that the logs are intact and could not have been altered without detection. A digital timestamp, providing protection of the log contents as well as verification of the time recorded, is another element of network security that the PKI can provide through the use of keys and certificates.

In a business environment, these technologies can be used to provide secure communications and log-ins for business partners, and local and remote users. This means VPNs can be established between branch offices and remote users, ensuring that cryptographic information is transferred securely and mutually authenticating both parties in a single action. Through the use of timestamping technologies and user certificates, extensive auditing capabilities are now available to a corporation.

Databases and other file systems can be secured so that the contents of the drive themselves are encrypted and only allow access to users with the proper certificates. This alone is a significant advantage in that most methods of secure communication only protect data in transit. Secure communications do not protect any stored data. It is a generally accepted fact that few are going to waste their time trying to decrypt an IPSec session. It is usually far easier to simply attack the machines at either end of the connection and hope to access the transmitted data in unencrypted form on one of the host systems. Encrypting file systems provides an effective countermeasure to this behavior.

The process of encrypting sensitive documents on a hard drive also underscores another advantage of the PKI. It is not enough simply to sign and distribute certificates. For the technology to be useful in a business environment, the PKI must also be an effective management tool. If a key employee were to become injured or leave the company, any data he or she has encrypted would become unavailable under normal circumstances. PKIs used in a corporate environment should always have the ability to back up or escrow key components. That ensures that keying material is not simply lost through the destruction of a hard drive, or the death or departure of an employee. It also serves as a certain safeguard to ensure that employees are not using encryption technologies in a manner that might cause harm to other people or the company itself.

In a comprehensive PKI, a device known as the certification authority (CA) is the cornerstone of the system. The CA provides all of the essential key management functions required for an enterprise. It is through the CA that users register their keys. It is the CA that provides the signing key for the organization and it is the CA that distributes signed keys to those that request them. The CA is also responsible for maintaining key histories and any backup or escrow functions that may be desired. Finally, the CA is the arbiter of revoked keys and provides revocation information if required.

The functions of a CA may be offloaded to another device known as a registration authority (RA). Due to the sensitive nature of the CA, it may be advantageous to provide many key management functions on a separate device and reserve the CA for the act of issuing and assigning new keys. In a busy environment, this provides more efficient operation and allows better isolation of the CA.

The security requirements of the CA cannot be understated. Commercial organizations that provide CA services for individuals and other companies spend a good amount of marketing budget describing the security steps they have taken to protect the signing keys. Their caution is warranted. The foundation of the PKI is the trust that the users have in the system. If the signing keys for a CA are compromised, then the entire infrastructure that relies on these keys is in jeopardy. That includes VPN communications, encrypted data, personnel authorization, logging, accounting and auditing functions, and any data that may have been digitally signed after the time of compromise. Imagine walking into work on a Monday morning and having to sort out all that. Thus, when considering the total expense of a PKI, steps taken to secure the CA itself must be considered. In many ways, it is akin to performing another risk analysis specifically for the CA. This may mean creating a separate secure subnet with the associated dedicated firewalls, increased logging and monitoring of CA activity, and building a physically secure storage area for the CA independent of the security of other network hardware and services. Of course, the final expense for this system will also be based on the total cost of the information protected versus the cost of the countermeasure.

As an enabling technology, the PKI can add quite a bit to your network. Because the capabilities are so extensive, rarely do you see a PKI that provides all the possible services that the PKI is capable of. Instead, you find the components that directly apply to the information security needs of your network. If this is the case, then we must first discuss the capabilities of the PKI and then determine what needs we have that can be addressed by a PKI.

A PKI can address any of the following needs:

- *Confidentiality.* Public key and secret key technologies can be used to encrypt data, either on a VPN or as files to be transported.
- *Integrity.* Through the use of digital signatures, we can ensure that information has not been modified from the original without detection.
- *Authentication.* Certificates can be used in conjunction with private keys to authenticate users.
- *Key management.* Keys must be generated, distributed, backed up, recovered in the event of loss, and occasionally revoked. A combination of software and protocol functions enables this in the PKI.

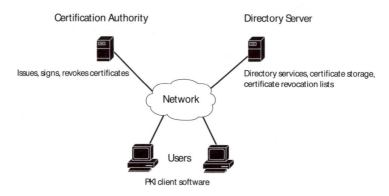

Exhibit 1. Logical PKI Implementation

- *Certificate management.* Like key management, there are a number of functions that must be performed here, such as the issuance of certificates, storage, backup, revocation, certification of keys, and distribution of certificates to requesting entities.
- *Notarization and non-repudiation.* This includes digital timestamping and is applicable when the PKI is asked to support legal documentation.
- *Policy and privilege management.* The PKI can also be enabled to serve as a sign-on system for network resources. This is especially valuable in single sign-on situations as it can increase the security of a system while enabling users to sign on once to access network resources.
- *Client software.* Depending on the installation, client software may be included as part of the application that is requesting PKI services or included as a separate program that all applications requesting PKI services may access.

Together, the elements of PKI combine to create a system similar to the diagram in Exhibit 1.

While Exhibit 1 is dense with information, it represents the various parts that combine to create a public key infrastructure. Not all of them may be employed in any given PKI environment.

The single most important element of a PKI is the concept of trust. When designing a PKI, some effort should be spent understanding the trust model that is applied to your particular PKI solution. To place the issue in context, consider the following common example of trust structures.

When I go to the liquor store to purchase some beverages, due to my boyish good looks I am constantly asked by the clerks to show proof of age. To furnish such proof, I provide picture identification in the form of a driver's license. My state government signs this license with its official state seal. While the clerk at the liquor store does not know me personally and does not know the person at the state government who signed my picture ID, he does have some faith that the state government has taken steps to ensure that the name on the license with the attached birth date does indeed match the picture on the license. The ability to use a picture ID then relies upon the trust that the liquor store clerk has in the state government. In this case, the state government is acting as a certification authority for its citizens.

I could issue my own ID card that I created on a computer and laminate that. Should I attempt to present it to a clerk, however, no matter how official looking I make it seem, the clerk will most likely be unimpressed with the certificate that I have presented. This is because the clerk does not have the requisite element of trust that I am an unbiased third party capable in the issuance of my certificate. In this instance, the element of trust in the certification authority is missing.

Were I travel out of state and attempt to purchase a bottle of wine in another state, I will be asked to provide picture ID there as well — again because of my boyish features. Although I am using an out-of-state ID card to prove my identity, the clerk in this out-of-state store trusts another state's certifications because, presumably, their own state recognizes my state as a valid issuer of identity cards. Were this not the case, I would have to apply to the new state government for a locally issued identity card in order to purchase a bottle of wine. To finish the analogy, the ability for independent certification authorities to trust each other allows the PKI to scale much larger than it would otherwise be able to do.

As can be imagined, the issue of trust is relative. For example, your employer may act as a CA for your corporation. This enables you to ensure that Jane in accounting is really Jane from accounting although you have never met, or that the company intranet Web server is really the company intranet Web server although you have never actually seen the machine to which you are connecting. Within your domain of trust, it is reasonable for your company's CA to certify the public key of the Web server because the users of that device are within the same domain of trust. I, on the other hand, may have no faith in your CA because I am not affiliated with the company. If you wish to have me perform online transactions on your Web server, you will need to have a third party certify the key of your Web server so that I can trust the device.

As with any important issue, trust relationships can be represented in a number of ways within the PKI. Some of the most common trust models are described in the following paragraphs.

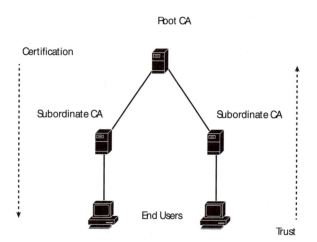

Exhibit 2. PKI Hierarchical Trust Model

A hierarchical trust model is conceptualized in Exhibit 2. We see that there is a single root CA that all subordinate CAs trust. The subordinate CAs generally provide services to the end users, although the root CA may perform this same service. In all instances, the trust model is very linear. Each device trusts the devices upstream from it, but not the devices downstream. Thus, a subordinate CA would trust a certificate signed by the root CA, but the root CA would not necessarily trust a certificate signed by an end user. Furthermore, subordinate CAs trust each other only because they share the same common root CA that has signed the keys of each of the subordinate CAs. While a strict hierarchical trust model is ideal for single organizations, it is unlikely that all entities that need to trust each other will share the same root CA. This is especially true as the PKI grows and it becomes more common to check certificates before communicating with remote parties. To accommodate the scalability requirements of a truly global PKI, a distributed trust model is more common.

In a distributed model, illustrated in Exhibit 3, root CAs will sign each other's certificates. This is similar to the manner in which state governments trust each other's identification cards. This allows a user from one trust domain to trust a user in another trust domain because the root CA from the remote domain is now trusted. Following this distributed model, the PKI can scale quite large. In comparison, some of the largest databases used on the Internet — the domain name system — are distributed systems. Each CA becomes responsible for only its own end users. As long as the trust relationship between the root CAs remains intact, the system can accommodate tens of millions of users. The distributed and hierarchical models are ideal for corporate environments where an IT staff is there to support users and users themselves can be expected to have some sort of

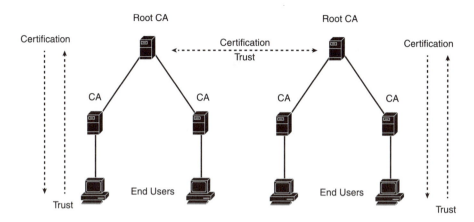

Exhibit 3. PKI Distributed Trust Model

training regarding trust and the use of the PKI. For some applications, however, the full services of a PKI and the CA are either unnecessary or impractical to implement, considering the user base. In these instances, other trust models may be required. A good example of this is the use of trust on the Internet in Web browsing and online shopping.

The particular requirements of online shopping have led to another form of trust model, deemed the "Web-based" trust model. Before describing the trust model itself, let us consider the requirements of such a model. For the Internet public at large, it would be unreasonable (and unlikely) for them to fully understand the issues of trust in creating secure communications. At the same time, for online business to evolve, nontechnical users are going to have to trust the infrastructure that has been created — without knowing how it works. This leads to a requirement of a certain amount of transparency in the trust models used for Web commerce.

In the Web-based trust model, it is most important that users trust the sites they are visiting. While it would be helpful in reducing fraud for Internet users to fully authenticate themselves to Web sites with signed digital certificates, it is unlikely that the average Internet user is going to be able to secure their private key and adequately maintain a personal certificate with a CA. Thus, authentication of the user identity is typically not enforced using certificates. Simpler measures such as passwords and credit cards are used when this authentication is important.

For users to trust the sites they visit, the sites have their certificates signed by a third-party CA that is in the business of establishing the identity of the Web server. When a user browses to a Web site and establishes a secure communications channel with the Web site, the Web server sends the browser its certificate. All popular browsers are bundled with the

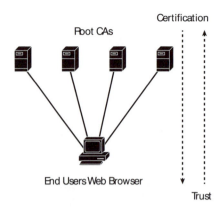

Exhibit 4. PKI Web-Based Trust Model

public key and certificate of most of the popular CAs. To keep users from having to worry about certificate expirations, most CAs include multiple keys and certificates in Web browser software. This is to reduce traffic to the CA itself by distributing the load among many, and because the CA that an online business uses may vary from business to business.

In the Web-based model then, there is a very linear relationship between the user and the CA. Instead of one root CA representing many users, as in a strictly hierarchical model, a single user may refer to multiple root CAs in the course of normal browsing. While this is not ideal from an infrastructure perspective, it represents the realities of employing the PKI in a mass-market environment. This Web-based trust relationship is illustrated in Exhibit 4.

The final common trust model is known as the user-centric trust model. The most famous implementation of this trust model is through the personal privacy and encryption software known as Pretty Good Privacy (PGP). The user-centric trust model essentially enables each individual user to operate as an independent CA (see Exhibit 5). Alice knows Bob and has personally verified Bob's public key, usually by verifying the contents of the key over the phone or in person. Alice then signs Bob's key with her own key. Thus, anyone who trusts Alice should also trust that Bob's key is legitimate. As users meet and exchange keys, this web of trust grows larger and more encompassing. While the user-centric model is intriguing, in practice it has scaling problems. Businesses have avoided such trust models because they eliminate the control that the root CA of the business has over the PKI. It can also require a good deal of responsibility on the part of the end user. I work in two major elements of the information economy: network design and security. It is sometimes difficult for my colleagues on the design side of the network to fully grasp the workings of the PGP user-centric model although these colleagues are extremely literate in technology. Much of the confusion centers on the issue of trust and trust relationships

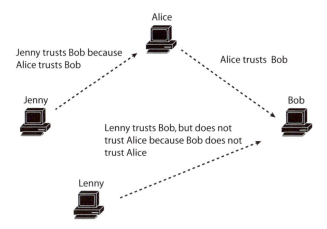

Exhibit 5. PKI User-Centric Trust Model

within the user-centric models. While trust is just as important in other models, the actual implementation of trust is more transparent to the end user than the user-centric model. Ultimately, user-centric models are ideal for technologically and security literate folks who wish to create secure relationships between diverse groups of users without the interference of centralized control.

7.1 PKI Protocols

Like any suite, PKI has a number of technologies that together create the PKI. Some of the most important protocols and standards you will examine when creating your own PKI are listed below. This list is not all-inclusive, but covers the technologies that are most related to PKI installations.

7.1.1 X.509

The process of certification is the most essential element of the entire PKI concept. Accordingly then, the X.509 certificate format is one of the most important standards associated with the PKI. X.509v2 and, more commonly, the X.509v3 certificate format are the most widely recognized certificate formats enabling the interoperation of PKIs on a global scale.

The X.509v3 certificate structure is outlined in Exhibit 6, along with a brief description of the relevant fields. Interested readers can also follow along using their own Web browsers. As mentioned, most commercial Web browsers include a number of certificates for root CAs that are used to verify the certificates of online merchants. Although the path to locate them will be different for each application, in Internet Explorer follow the path of Tools | Internet Options | Content | Certificates to find certificates locally stored on your PC. Odds are you will have to scroll to the right to find the root certificates. In Netscape or Mozilla, you may find the installed

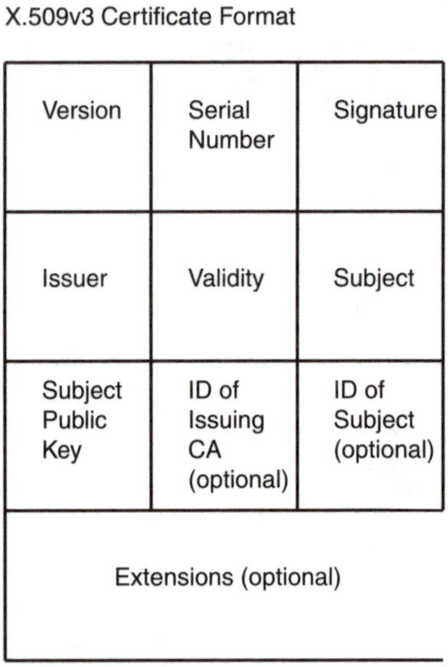

X.509v3 Certificate Format

Version	Serial Number	Signature
Issuer	Validity	Subject
Subject Public Key	ID of Issuing CA (optional)	ID of Subject (optional)
Extensions (optional)		

Exhibit 6. X.509v3 Certificate Format

certificates by following the path of Edit l Preferences l Privacy & Security l Certificates l Manage Certificates. As with Internet Explorer, you may have to select the "Authorities" tab to view installed certificates. The version number in this case will be version 3; however, version 2 certificates are still found. As we will discuss shortly, version 3 has quickly become the accepted standard due to the use of optional extensions that allow certificate holders and signers to include important attributes with the certificate.

Following the certificate number, a serial number is used to ensure that the certificate is unique for the certificate issuer. This serial number is assigned by the issuer. The algorithm, which should be familiar to those who have read the cryptography material of this text, is listed next.

The issuer field follows the signature algorithm. This must be a distinguished name (DN) for the certificate issuer. A distinguished name is a particular naming structure that is similar in operation to the domain name system (DNS). The major difference is that a DN naming structure is more flexible and has more layers of hierarchy than that used with DNS. As with domain names, there is a particular problem in a global infrastructure of ensuring that the name of any entity is globally unique. Using the DN convention from the X.500 standard with unique organizational identifiers assures this and also ensures that certificate signers can be uniquely identified.

Of particular interest is the validity date imprinted in the certificate. As the name suggests, this is the period of time for which the certificate is valid. Such a simple requirement causes no small complication in the management of certificates. The longer a certificate is valid the greater the chance that someone will be able to compromise the certificate by compromising the keys that were used to sign it. Configuring the validity period of the certificate to be too short adds administrative overhead to the PKI, as retired certificates must be replaced with valid ones. Just to gauge the difficulty of this task, imagine that the certificate you may be viewing in your Web browser were to expire. How would that certificate be replaced for the millions of users, most of them uneducated concerning certificates in the first place?

The subject field of the certificate follows the same DN format of the issuer, as described above.

The heart of a certificate, the part that makes it trustworthy, is the subject public key information in the certificate itself. This is the public key of the entity that the certificate is certifying. The entire point of this certificate and the PKI itself is to ensure users like ourselves that this public key really belongs to the organization in question. The organization that has signed the certificate is vouching for the authenticity of this key. This key will then be used to transmit a secret key between the remote host and the server, and it is the secret key that actually encrypts the data. In another scenario, the public key is the basis for authenticating the user and the certificate includes permissions of the user for the given application.

The issuer and subject ID fields are optional; they are not used in practice and are not recommended by the relevant RFCs for the Internet environment.[1]

In addition to the key itself, the extensions field is the portion of the certificate that makes X.509v3 relevant to modern PKIs. Both private extensions and optional standard extensions may be included in this field. This field enables the X.509v3 certificates to provide the necessary functions for a given application. Some common extensions include information that describes the permitted use of the certificate, information about revocation lists that may contain information about the certificate, and the ability to associate a certificate with more than a distinguished name, such as an e-mail address or other identifier.

While the X.509 standard does not specify the use of IP networks for certificate management functions, in most cases, IP is going to be the underlying network protocol responsible for communication between end entities and certification authorities in the PKI environment. To this end, the IETF (Internet Engineering Task Force) created the PKIX working group to define the required and optional extensions that may be found in X.509

certificates specific to the IP and IETF environment. The PKIX working group also defines the protocols that are used to manage certificates and perform other operational duties. The PKIX working group has been responsible for a number of RFCs that detail the different elements of IP/X.509 interaction. At the time of this writing, there were at least eight different RFCs with a number of the original eight already having been rendered obsolete and updated. Due to the work of the PKIX, the certificate format of X.509 has the ability to communicate among diverse portions of the Internet.

7.1.2   Lightweight Directory Access Protocol (LDAP)

The X.509 certificate format was based on work done for the ISO/ITU-T X.500 series. Together, the X.500 series defines a robust directory structure with a great deal of flexibility and power. The PKI and X.509 certificates were created to assist with access control to the X.500 directories. With this standard, however, came functionality and complexity that was not required in most implementations. In response to the need for a less complicated directory access protocol, the IETF created LDAP. LDAP devices are integral to a PKI in that they can contain both certificate information about directory subjects and include certificate revocation lists for the PKI.

7.1.3   Online Certificate Status Protocol (OSCP)

Critical to the functioning of a PKI is knowing that a certificate is valid, and just as important is knowing when a certificate should no longer be trusted. The OSCP is a straightforward protocol that queries a URL if provided in an extension to the X.509 certificate to check the certificate against a certificate revocation list (CRL), which is a list maintained by CAs to assist in the detection of revoked certificates. Likely responses from the CRL server are "good," "revoked," or "unknown."

Those with a suspicious mindset will immediately think, "How do I know that the CRL list that is being checked is valid?" After all, if someone were attempting to forge a certificate, why not point the certificate toward a CRL server that would respond that the CRL is valid? Fortunately, this has been considered as well, and OSCP responses from the servers use the same public key certificates that we use to ensure the trust of other Internet resources. However, it is useful to point out that OSCP does not determine if the certificate is valid or not. The certification and signing processes determine that. OSCP only determines if the certificate has been revoked — an important distinction!

7.1.4   Secure Multipurpose Internet Mail Extensions (S/MIME)

Due to the fact that SMTP was only developed to send plaintext e-mail, the Multipurpose Internet Mail Extensions (MIME) standards were proposed. MIME allows the encoding of a variety of information through the encoding of information in ASCII (plaintext) format. Based on the MIME specifications, RSA Security and other security vendors created S/MIME, which allows e-mail clients to encrypt mail using the MIME format. Due to industry acceptance of S/MIME, the specifications were adopted by the IETF into a series of RFCs detailing S/MIME's integration with IP, SMTP, and the PKI. Unlike IPSec, which encrypts the packets used to transfer e-mail, S/MIME encrypts the message itself. Therefore, when it is received, S/MIME messages need to be decrypted by the remote host.

S/MIME was constructed with an eye toward integration with the PKI. As such, S/MIME allows the use of certificates for both signing and encrypting e-mail, along with integration with certificate revocation lists and cryptographically signed return receipts.

The other program commonly used to encrypt e-mail and files is Pretty Good Privacy (PGP), created by Phil Zimmerman. PGP, as described in the trust models section above, utilizes a user-centric trust model. S/MIME, on the other hand, integrates with whatever trust model is being employed by the organization. Thus, S/MIME is suitable for both personal and business use. This, as well as the integration into an organizational PKI, makes S/MIME the more commonly found personal encryption client on corporate networks.

7.1.5   IP Security (IPSec)

Like the PKI, IPSec is a suite of enabling technologies that span a number of RFCs. Most commonly implemented in VPNs and other instances of secure communication exchange, a portion of IPSec responsible for the authentication and exchange of keys used in the creation of encrypted sessions can be configured to operate using the PKI. Known as Internet Key Exchange (IKE), this protocol is widely used in the establishment of all IPSec sessions. More information on IPSec and IKE can be found in the VPN section of this book (see Chapter 10).

7.1.6   Public Key Cryptography Standards (PKCS)

PKCS are a series of standards developed by RSA laboratories that define the operation of cryptographic operations with the PKI. Currently, there are 15 PKCS standards that cover some of the most common PKI operations. You will most likely run into these standards when you evaluate PKI solutions, as each vendor will note which PKCS they are compliant with. A brief listing of the standards can be found below. More information, along with the actual standards documents, can be found at the RSA Web site.[2]

- *PKCS #1: RSA Cryptography Standard.* This is the original document that defines the implementation of public key cryptography using the RSA algorithm. PKCS #2 and #4 have been combined with PKCS #1.
- PKCS #3: Defines the operation of the Diffie–Hellman algorithm, but you know how that works now.
- PKCS #5: Password-Based Cryptography Standard. Defines key creation, encryption, and message authentication based on passwords.
- *PKCS #6: Extended certificate-Based Syntax.* As our discussion of X.509v3 above describes, this standard defines the way in which an extendable certificate can be used to certify information in a certificate above and beyond the public key itself.
- *PKCS #7: Cryptographic Message Syntax Standard.* Defines the application of cryptography to data such as digital signatures.
- *PKCS #8: Private Key Information Syntax Standard.* Describes the syntax of private keys and their attributes.
- *PKCS #9: Attributes.* This standard defines the acceptable attributes used with PKCS #6, #7, #8, and #10.
- *PKCS #10: Certification Request Syntax.* Defines the proper way to ask for a certificate, distinguished name, and the associated attributes.
- *PKCS #11: Cryptographic Token Interface.* Expands the use of PKI to provide an application interface for the integration of tokens.
- *PKCS #12: Personal Information Exchange Syntax.* Defines acceptable methods of storing and transporting user private keys and certificates.
- *PKCS #13: Elliptical Curve Cryptography Standard.* This is a standard still under development. It is widely believed that elliptical curves that are computed over a group of points defined by a solution to an elliptical curve algorithm will yield smaller keys that are equivalent in security to the larger keys more typically used. Elliptical curve algorithms are used more commonly with Diffie–Hellman algorithms and the future of this standard is uncertain.
- *PKCS #14: Pseudo-random Number Generation.* Currently in development, this standard attempts to describe the process of creating suitably random numbers using binary processors. Although it may be surprising, most computers have a really difficult time coming up with truly random numbers. They may appear random to humans, but generally there is a pattern that can be detected if steps are not taken to generate truly random input as a seed for the random numbers. More than one security scheme has been broken by those who have figured out how the "random" numbers have been generated.

- *PKCS #15: Cryptographic Token Information Format.* This standard expands upon PKCS #11 and attempts to ensure compatibility between all token devices and cryptographic applications. This type of compatibility will be essential if the ability to use a single "ID" card for multiple reasons will be realized.

7.1.7 Transport Layer Security (TLS)

Transport layer security is better known as the Secure Session Layer, or SSL. Introduced by Netscape Corporation with its browser product, SSL was instrumental in the success of secure Web browsing. Using encryption techniques much like IPSec does at the network layer, SSL creates encrypted application layer sessions between hosts. As with S/MIME, the success of the SSL protocol made it the *de facto* standard for encryption for both the transfer of Web pages, e-mail, and other applications. This success led to adoption by the IETF, which created the TLS specification from SSL. Reflecting their combined histories, this standard is often referred to as TLS/SSLv3.

The PKI is instrumental to the operation of TLS. To create an encrypted session to a Web server, the server sends the client a certificate signed by a CA to guarantee the authenticity of the server. The client encrypts a secret key to be used to establish a secure session with the Web server based on the public key part of the certificate. Encryption can take place without the certificate, but it is the certificate that provides the trust for the transaction to continue.

7.2 PKI Implementation

As discussed, not every application will have all the requirements of a fully implemented PKI. As an example, let us consider the application of the PKI to the Internet. The most common model used, of a browser client connecting to a remote Web server, only needs to utilize specific portions of the PKI. The required elements include:

- *Certificate management.* Here, the only essential requirement is that of the certificate authority to sign the public keys of Web servers. More advanced features are not required because either users cannot be expected to take advantage of them (for example, checking for expired or revoked certificates is rarely performed), or they are unnecessary (as in maintaining a revocation server since they are rarely utilized). This limited functionality is because the major need of Web transactions is to authenticate Web servers. Encryption keys are generated between the client and the Web server.

- *Confidentiality.* This is expected through the use of the Transport Layer Security (SSLv3.0) standard.
- *Integrity.* This is also addressed in the TLS standard.
- *Authentication.* Web servers use certificates signed by a CA and checked against the CA public key installed on a Web browser to ensure that the Web server is the party that the user expects it to be.

Note how the functions differ if we were to use the PKI to enable the secure exchange of e-mail between those in our own business:

- *Certificate management.* Because we will be using certificates that will affect our ability to access data in the future, our certificate management needs to be much more robust and able to effectively manage keys across the entire life cycle of the certificate. This includes acting as a repository for certificates of those we would wish to e-mail, along with a directory service to find those individuals, maintaining certificate revocation lists, and signing services for new certificates.
- *Key management.* As with certificate management, we need to ensure that our private keys are not lost due to computer theft, job termination, or hardware destruction. To minimize the impact on users, automatic key updates are also helpful to ensure an efficient work environment for users. Furthermore, it is advantageous to maintain a history of public keys to ensure that encrypted documents are always available to authorized users.
- *Client software.* Client software is normally bundled with the e-mail client that is used to encrypt the e-mail. In some cases, it may be a separate application that is bundled with the e-mail client.
- *Confidentiality and integrity.* The use of secret keys transported via public key hash algorithms signed by private keys ensures the confidentiality and integrity of transmitted messages.
- *Authentication.* The confidentiality and integrity functions depend on the authentication that is provided by the actual certificate.

While this list is more extensive, it is still simply a sub-set of the entire PKI capability set. For each instance that we could conceivably wish to implement a PKI, such as for VPN sessions or single sign-on authentication, there is a set of PKI elements that is applicable. The first challenge then is to determine the needs of our environment. For the sake of discussion, let us assume a common network scenario and examine the relevance of a PKI to it.

In our hypothetical business environment, we have a policy that requires us to securely authenticate remote VPN users, support TLS sessions with our Web server, and encrypt sensitive documents, including e-mail correspondence. This is a pretty typical set of what public key cryptography can be expected to support. Once we have defined the needs according to policy, we need to examine what elements of the PKI we require.

7.2.1 Certificate and Key Management Functions

Given keying material, we need to have the ability to sign keys created by our end users. In most cases, we will need to sign and manage multiple keys to reflect the fact that the keys we use to encrypt data are generally different than the keys that we use to sign data. Encryption keys will need to be centrally backed up to ensure accessibility to data. A third party should never back up signing keys, used for non-repudiation purposes, lest their integrity be called into question. Because the user population can be assumed to be somewhat dynamic, we will also need the ability to revoke keys and perhaps escrow keys to ensure access to encrypted information after an employee leaves. The state of all keys should be reflected in up-to-date revocation lists. We also need to ensure that certificate information is easily available and trustworthy, even to employees who communicate with each other but have never met face to face.

We may also have the need to have a higher CA certify our own CA. This is most likely the case of for our Web server certificate. While acting as our own CA for employee mail will be sufficient, remote users of Web services are not necessarily familiar with our company and will require third-party verification of our server before trusting our certificates. We will want our CA function to also manage trust relationships for this application.

7.2.2 Client Software

Client software will be a consideration. Because we are enabling client applications to perform at least three different functions, will there be any interaction on the client platform regarding certificates? Most likely, the Web browser, e-mail client, and VPN client will all use separate client certificate software. This may require the management of even more keys, one for each application per client.

7.2.3 Authentication

Authentication will be provided through the use of certificates in each case. The certificates distributed by the PKI will provide authentication for remote VPN clients and local users performing single sign-on for network resources and ensure that e-mail users are communicating with the desired remote party. Server certificates can also be used to perform two-way authentication to ensure that the services our users are connecting to are legitimate and not spoofed sites.

7.2.4   Confidentiality

The actual encryption of data will occur after the authentication process.

7.2.5   Integrity

The keys that have been signed by the CA will be used to sign cryptographic hashes to ensure the integrity of data both stored and transmitted.

7.2.6   Policy and Privilege Management

To enable our PKI to integrate with network resources, we need to ensure that policy and privilege tokens can be assigned to the user certificates.

With a clear idea of what we need from our PKI, we can then begin the process of deployment. The next step occurs in two parts. First, we must examine the cost and effectiveness of implementing the PKI ourselves versus the cost and effectiveness of having a third party provide a PKI solution for us. In evaluating our own solution and that of a PKI vendor, there are several important questions to consider.

- *Support.* Do our proposed vendors provide adequate support? Is the support available when needed, and is it helpful? If we are providing the service in house, can our IT staff be expected to provide an adequate level of support given their other responsibilities? How easy is the PKI to administer?
- *Standards.* To ensure interoperability with business partners as the functions of the PKI expand, we must ensure that our solutions are standards based. Furthermore, even standards-based implementations may not interoperate with the standards-based implementation of other vendors. This must also be evaluated.
- *Security.* Have any independent third parties examined the security of the solution? Have the products been evaluated and given a Common Criteria rating to provide assurances that the products provide the security that they claim?
- *Reputation.* Whether using products in house or a third party, what is the reputation of the vendor? Are they well-established and likely to be around months from now? If the vendor were to shut its doors, would your encrypted data, certificates, and keys still be valid?
- *Facility requirements.* The security of the CA is paramount to the trust that we have in the certificates that it signs. Should the CA and CA private key be compromised, the attacker could issue certificates at will. In short, the validity of the entire PKI comes into question. Can a local solution be adequately logically and physically secured? What security steps will a third party take?
- *Personnel requirements.* A PKI will require several roles to operate properly. A security officer should be assigned to enforce security

policy. A PKI operator will have the responsibilities of installing and maintaining the PKI systems. A PKI administrator will be required to perform daily functions such as user and privilege management.

- *Disaster planning.* What would happen to encrypted data if keys were lost or compromised? How does your solution handle key backups, restoration, and revocations? Can you secure the backup media as well as the CA itself?
- *Control.* How willing is your company to lose control over the PKI process? This would mean that both keys and certificates, the heart of a PKI, would be out of your direct control. Is this an acceptable security risk?
- *Cost.* Once the above criteria for our own in-house or third-party PKI have been examined, how do our solutions compare in cost? A PKI only makes good financial sense if the cost of the PKI is less than the cost of the information it is trying to protect.

Answering these questions based on our PKI needs will help us determine if the PKI is most likely something that our company should implement itself or if it is best left to third-party solutions. There is even the possibility that, based on our current security needs, the cost of implementing a PKI is not justified.

Like all information security systems, a PKI should be implemented only in response to a detailed risk analysis and adoption of a comprehensive security policy. Because a PKI is a modular structure by design, it is imperative that the needs to be fulfilled by the PKI are first defined. Before the purchasing of products begins, the question "How will this PKI achieve the goals of my security policy?" must first be answered.

The price and technical details for implementation must be carefully considered if the PKI is going to be a truly effective countermeasure. Although a PKI is not terribly difficult to implement with proper preparation, many institutions tend to outsource the implementation and perhaps even the management of their PKI in the hopes of leveraging the economies of scale that a dedicated PKI provider can achieve.

Notes

1. RFC 3280, Internet X.509 Public Key Infrastructure Certificate and Certificate Revocation List (CRL) Profile contains the relevant information regarding recommended X.509 fields in an Internet environment.
2. The PKCS standards can be found on the RSA Web site at http://www.rsasecurity.com.

Chapter 8
Firewalls

While strictly an extension of the network elements section, firewalls are divergent enough to warrant their own discussion. The first thing to establish is that a firewall is more of an idea than it is a single device. Many network administrators, when asked to display their firewall, will proudly point to a box of some sort with a bunch of network interfaces on it and say, "That there is our firewall." It would be more accurate to say, "That there is a box that is part of our firewall." Being more than a semantic issue, a firewall is the sum total of devices that are used to protect an inside network from an outside network. Most companies have at least two pieces of hardware that serve as their firewall — an access router and a hardened bastion host that acts as a filter of some sort upon data. A company could also include a proxy server or mail relay/attachment scanning station as part of its firewall. In the end, the firewall is everything that a company uses to protect the "inside" from the "outside." This distinction drives the configuration options of most firewalls, as rules can be independently configured for both traffic passing from the inside to the outside and vice versa.

8.1 Types of Firewalls

While entire books have been written about the different types of firewalls, components that can be used in creating firewalls, and their configuration options, they can be broadly summarized as follows.

8.1.1 Packet Filters

Packet filters are often referred to as "first-generation" firewalls in that they are straightforward and somewhat unsophisticated compared to more-modern firewall technologies. This is not to say that they are obsolete, only that they employ a fairly simple logic that is fast, easy to configure, found in any firewall application, and reasonably simple for a determined attacker to get around.

Packet filtering firewalls make forwarding decisions based on the contents of the IP header or the TCP header. Applied to interfaces, either "inbound" or "outbound" packet filters use a list of rules to examine packets as they enter or leave the network interface. In most packet filtering implementations, these rule sets can be applied differently to each interface on a firewall device.

A set of common packet filtering rules may read something like the following:

- Allow any inbound traffic as long is it is part of an established TCP connection.
- Allow inbound connections from any source as long as it is destined to our Web server application on this host.
- Allow return DNS traffic in reply to UDP DNS queries.
- Allow zone transfers for DNS zone files only between our primary internal DNS server and a defined remote DNS server.
- Allow inbound e-mail traffic to the mail server.
- Allow remote POP3 clients to check their e-mail on the POP3 server.

Of course, the actual rules will vary, depending on the security policy chosen by the company, but the above represent a pretty typical rule set for a company that hosts its own Web site, DNS servers, and mail services. The above is also only an inbound list. An equivalent set of rules must be established to control outbound traffic as well. We will discuss the creation of firewall rules in accordance with our security policy a bit later. For now, we are interested in examining how a packet filter would act upon the above rules.

To enforce the above rule set, a packet filter firewall inspects information that is in the packet headers. The IP header provides information about the source and destination IP addresses and the fragmentation status of the packet. The TCP header contains information about the connection status of a TCP circuit and the source and destination ports of the TCP segment. This information is used to determine which application the data is to be forwarded to on the receiving host. Our rule set will have a series of statements in them that will:

1. Look for the connection status of TCP segments. If the connection status indicates that the packet is part of an established connection, let it through. Otherwise, check the next rule.
2. Look at the destination IP address of the packet. If its destination is the company Web server IP address, then look at the port of the packet. If the TCP destination port is port 80, allow the packet through. Otherwise, check the next rule.
3. Look at the source port of a UDP packet. If that source port is equal to 53 (the DNS port), allow the UDP packet into the network. Otherwise, check the next rule.
4. Look at the source IP address and destination IP address of the packet. If the source is the remote secondary DNS server and the destination of the packet is the local primary DNS server, then check the TCP port. If the port number is 53, used to DNS zone transfers, then let the packet through. Otherwise, check the next rule.

5. Check the destination of the IP packet; if the destination of the IP packet is that of our mail server and the TCP port is equal to the one that our mail server runs on (port 25 by default), then allow the packet through. Otherwise, check the next rule.
6. Check the destination of the IP packet; if the destination of the IP packet is that of our POP3 server and the TCP port is equal to the default POP3 port of 110, then allow that packet through.
7. Deny any packet, regardless of the information in the packet.

The last rule is usually not configured, but it is important to know that firewalls frequently add this rule. The default "deny all" that is the end of rule set means that any traffic that is not specifically permitted in the preceding rules is dropped. When discussing firewall theory in an academic situation, there are two generally accepted modes of configuring network-based access controls. The first method is to only block that traffic which you do not want to enter or leave your network. Given the ease with which most applications can change ports, however, this is a futile gesture. Of the 65,536 ports available in TCP and UDP, blocking ten ports because they are used for prohibited applications is like putting a steel pole in the middle of a soccer field and hoping that the intruders happen to hit the pole as they run across the field. So, while it is useful in discussing packet filtering academically, practically speaking, the converse rule is more useful and is normally applied — that which is not specifically allowed is denied. The default deny all rule at the end of every firewall enforces this concept.

You will notice a great emphasis on mentioning that if a particular rule is matched, then the packet is processed. If there is no match, then the packet is checked against the next rule. This is one of the most fundamental issues of firewall design. The order of the rules is very important. As an example, let us add another rule. We do not want any packets from the outside that have a source of our networks IP address into our network — a process known as *spoofing*. Clearly, if a packet coming from the Internet has the source IP address of our internal network, something is afoot. Creating a filter to protect against this is known as configuring *anti-spoofing* rules.

Where we place that rule into the above rule set is vitally important if we want the security policy to be enforced. If the rule is applied at the end of the policy, then there are a number of opportunities to get around it. For example, Rule 5 only checks the destination of the IP address and matches to that of the internal mail server. If someone on the Internet were to send a packet to that IP address with a spoofed source, the packet filter would allow it through the firewall. In this case, the rule needs to be placed at the top of the list. In this way, any packet is first checked against the anti-spoofing rule and discarded before any other rules are processed.

The primary advantages of packet filters are that they are fast and fairly straightforward to configure. They are fast because, comparatively speaking, packet filters do not have much work to do on each packet. They simply examine them and make a forward or drop decision. No extra effort is spent interpreting what the information in the packet means and no "state" or memory is kept in the firewall device to associate one group of packets with another. Each vendor does have its own particular syntax to use in creating the rules, but generally the pattern is very similar and is based on defining protocols and IP addresses. Packet filters also enjoy broad support due to their low overhead. Indeed, it would be difficult to find a general-purpose firewall device that did not support at least packet filtering.

For all of these advantages, packet filters are not ideal firewalls on their own, although they play an important part in a more complete firewall configuration. For example, Rule 1 above examines inbound packets to see if they are part of existing connections. Examining the TCP header and looking for the ACK bit, which is a response to a packet that has already been sent, do this. The logic is that if the ACK bit is sent, then something on the inside must have sent out a packet in the first place. This simple logic is easy to defeat by those with malicious intent. It is a trivial exercise to set the ACK bit on any TCP packet and then just send it through the firewall. A straightforward packet generator will allow any attacker access through the firewall by fabricating a packet complying with Rule 1. Granted, the attacker could not establish a new connection, but there is plenty of harm that an attacker could do just by getting packets to the device in the first place. At the very least, it allows an attacker to map out the internal network by launching a network scan.

Setting the TCP ACK bit works because the packet filter does not have any context to work with inasmuch as it does not keep any state information about the packets that it forwards. The packet filtering firewall, for example, does not know that for the past two hours there has been no TCP traffic headed to the internal host at 200.200.1.10. When a packet arrives from the outside destined for this host, as long as the ACK bit is set, the firewall assumes that it is legitimate traffic.

This problem is compounded when trying to allow UDP applications through the firewall. Unlike TCP, UDP has no method of maintaining the state of the connection between two hosts. Indeed, the entire concept of a "connection" using UDP is foreign to the protocol. In this case, the network administrator has a tough decision to make. The administrator must either allow UDP traffic based only on port information — in which case traffic can be sent at any time or disallow access for UDP traffic altogether. One decision will increase the security on the network, but will not make the users who depend on those UDP applications to get their jobs done very happy.

Because many popular applications use UDP traffic, network administrators are often forced to allow the protocol through the packet filtering firewall. To further complicate things, many of the applications that depend on UDP traffic, such as video, voice, and real-time media, tend to use a wide range of UDP ports. The network administrator can only narrowly reduce the numbers of ports that these applications use and thus must open wide ranges of UDP port space on the packet filtering firewall. Because there is no state, or remembrance of what has been sent and what should be arriving back on the packet filter, these ports end up accepting traffic at all times.

While packet filters were a great security concept when first introduced — and they still serve an important function in an overall firewall configuration— they are only the first step. What we are really interested in is more functionality. Enter the stateful packet filter.

8.1.2 Stateful Packet Filters

When we give a packet filter "memory" and some understanding of normal protocol behavior, we have created a stateful packet filter. This is a firewall device that understands that it should not receive an ACK packet inbound to a given host, because the host in question has not recently established a connection to the source of the packet. The net result is to make the network more secure and easier to configure. As you may recall, one of the characteristics of a good countermeasure is ease of configuration, so this is not an insignificant consideration.

To understand how the stateful packet filter operates, let us look at Rule 1 in our sample inbound firewall rule set:

"1. Allow any inbound traffic as long is it is part of an established TCP connection."

A stateful packet filter would alter this rule just a bit to say:

"1. Monitor any new outbound connections from the inside network. Only allow return traffic back into the network if it matches the IP addresses and port numbers used in a recorded outbound connection."

Thus far, all we have done is add overhead to the packet filter. Now it must maintain connection information between hosts based on the traffic it monitors. The effect, however, is to increase the security on our network. No longer will tricks such as setting the ACK bit work. Furthermore, the concept of an "established" connection is unique to TCP. Other protocols, such as UDP and IP, do not have the established concept to work from. With a stateful packet filter, however, the state mechanism can be configured to logically associate connections. For example, if a DNS query is sent from the inside network to an outside server, the stateful packet filter notes the source and destination of the IP packet and the source and destination UDP port numbers. If a UDP packet returns with source and destination values reversed, then the stateful packet filter can safely assume that the return packet is associated with the packet that was just sent. To prevent misuse of this feature, most stateful packet filters allow a network administrator to configure a timeout value for connectionless protocols. Therefore, the stateful packet filter can keep the UDP connection information active for 60 seconds. If no packets are observed for a period of 60 seconds, the connection information is removed.

We see that this allows us to shorten even our simplified rule set by at least one entry. We no longer need to specifically allow return DNS traffic back into the network. If other UDP protocols need to be used by users of the network, then this also does not require additional configuration to the filter list. In a more complex environment, the rule set would most likely be able to eliminate even more distinct rule set entries. Shorter rules are less complex and easier to manage. Shorter rules are less likely to be misconfigured because they are easier to follow. Shorter rules have less overhead for the firewall device. Shorter rule sets are better!

For all of their advantages over traditional packet filters, stateful packet filters are not without their shortcomings. First, they do have additional overhead associated with the process of keeping track of connections. While this was more of a problem in the past, computing power has so outpaced the speed of the average company Internet access line that this is not really a pressing issue in more recent configurations. This means that even a fairly low powered and very inexpensive hardware platform would be sufficient to keep up with the average T-1 access rates that most companies use for WAN access.

The real problem with stateful packet filters is that they still only have limited intelligence when working with packets. The problem might best be explained through the use of a couple of examples. The default installation of Windows 2000 IIS 5.0, a popular Web server for Microsoft Windows networks, has a security flaw that allows an attacker to send a specially constructed URL, such as

www.proteris.com/scripts/..%c1%c1../ winnt/system32/cmd.exe?/
    c+copy+c:\winnt\system32\cmd.exe+c:\winnt\system32\root.exe

that allows remote users to move between directories on the IIS server and change files to suit their goals. This means that a Web user can enter a specially constructed URL similar to that above and read the contents of almost any drive. Depending on the permissions given to the Web server, the user is also allowed to create, delete, and otherwise manipulate server files. This clearly can be considered a serious vulnerability.

When the above attack is in progress, the stateful packet filter, following our rule set, would allow traffic to the Web server and keep track of the connection information. After all, to the stateful packet filter, the packet simply looks like an IP packet with source and destination IP addresses that match our rules and the destination TCP port is allowed as well. In this case, however, the packet itself is legitimate but the instructions contained in the packet constitute the real risk.

The concept works the same in the reverse direction, when users connect to the Internet. Like many companies, we will assume that our outbound filters have a rule similar to the following:

1. Allow users internal to our network to view normal and secure Web pages.

This would translate into two rules that would monitor outgoing IP packets for the following information:

1. Allow packets with a source IP address of our network and any destination IP address that have a TCP destination port of 80 for normal Web traffic. Otherwise, check the next rule.
2. Allow packets with a source IP address of our network and any destination IP address that have a TCP destination port of 443 for secure Web traffic. Otherwise, check the next rule.

The stateful packet filter will duly note the establishment of a new connection that matches the above rules and allow the return traffic back into the network. This is where the functionality of the stateful packet filter will stop, however. The traffic is in no way monitored to see what the user is accessing via this connection, be it work-related information, stock quotes, pornography, or downloading viruses via HTTP. Even the URL itself may be dangerous to the health of the connecting computer, as recent operating system security reports have shown us. The stateful packet filtering any more than the traditional packet filter cannot prevent this activity.

What is required is some way to be able to interpret the user data and make forwarding decisions based on the information inside the packet. The simple way to do this is through a proxy server.

8.1.3 Proxies

Over the course of several years, I have had reason to designate my wife as a proxy in certain circumstances. Generally, this is due the need to travel on business during important personal legal exchanges. When acting as a proxy, my wife is authorized to do things on my behalf. In the networking world, proxies operate with the same concept. A proxy will act on the behalf of another host in the network. While not strictly a firewall

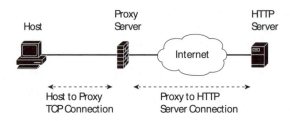

Exhibit 1. TCP Proxy Example

technology, proxy servers are often used as part of an overall firewall solution. An example is in order to explain the proxy concept.

A host internal to the network creates a connection to a Web page in the outside world. The Web browser has been configured with the IP address or host name of the proxy server (see Exhibit 1). Instead of sending the request to the Web page itself, the host browser application sends the request to the proxy server. The proxy will then make a decision based on its configuration to either deny the request or make a connection to the requested Web page on behalf of the internal host. The host itself does not make outside connections; the proxy does. The primary advantage of this approach in a corporate setting is that the proxy can be configured to allow or deny access to certain types of resources. For example, a list of allowed or prohibited Web sites can be configured into the proxy. When a user request is made, the proxy checks its lists and forwards or drops traffic according to its configuration. A proxy can also be configured to make this decision based upon the username or group permissions used to access the proxy itself.

Proxy servers have two main classifications. The first is that of the *application proxy*. The application proxy is, as the name suggests, specific to a single application. You may have a server on your network that will operate as an HTTP or FTP proxy. To further confuse the issue, proxy servers are readily available that combine a number of application proxy servers. This means a single server may operate as both an HTTP and FTP proxy. The second class of proxies is known as a *circuit-level proxy*. This proxy differs from the application-level proxy in that it will proxy all TCP/IP traffic. Instead of operating only for a single application layer protocol, circuit-level proxies act as intermediaries for all transport layer traffic.

For most application layer proxies, there is a secondary performance benefit that makes the use of a proxy advantageous to network users as well. If a second host inside the company wished to access the same Web page as the earlier host, the proxy could be configured to cache, or store, the Web page locally. For the second and subsequent requests, the proxy need not make a connection to the remote site but can serve the page

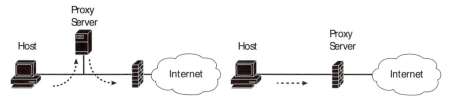

Exhibit 2. Proxy Implementation Considerations

locally. This improves performance for the network users and reduces bandwidth consumption on the WAN link.

Proxies can also serve an important role in the auditing of Web traffic patterns. Most proxy applications will also record the Web sites that users access, allowing a convenient way to track individual usage patterns on company time.

The placement of a proxy is an important consideration as to the amount of security and monitoring of network traffic they can provide (see Exhibit 2). If the network configuration is not designed so that egress traffic must use the proxy, an enterprising user can simply choose to bypass it. This is because most proxy configuration is done as part of the configuration for the application itself. For example, if I were to configure the Mozilla Web browser to use a proxy server, I would enter the appropriate IP address or proxy name in the "Proxy" preferences dialog box. Each HTTP request sent from the Mozilla Web browser would then be directed to the configured proxy. If I open up the Internet Explorer Web browser without a proxy configuration, my requests are sent directly to the remote Web site, bypassing the proxy. From this, it becomes clear that the protections offered by an application proxy may require a willing public. There are several ways around this issue. The first is that if your operating system allows it, configure the user profiles so that they cannot change the settings on the Web browser. This may be effective for those who access the Web through a host on your network, but does little to control those who connect via other programs or rogue hosts. The second option is to configure what is known as a transparent or in-line proxy server. In examining Exhibit 2, the configuration on the left is a typical proxy configuration where users are allowed to connect to the Internet via the proxy or without the proxy. The configuration on the right, on the other hand, has the proxy server inline with outbound requests. The only option for Internet connections in this case is through the proxy server.

There are other options to prevent users from directly accessing the Internet without the mediation of a proxy. One mechanism is to configure any firewalls to only allow outbound application traffic sourced from the proxy server. In this way, users who do not use the proxy are blocked by the firewall, but proxy connections are allowed through. Another option is that some firewall products will transparently redirect traffic to a specified proxy server. In this case, all traffic to be proxied is redirected, regardless of the wishes of the user.

The final option is to configure a circuit-level gateway that proxies all incoming connections. The advantage of this approach is that it can intercept all connections without end users being aware of or having to configure their hosts at all. For those who travel frequently and stay in hotel rooms equipped with high-speed Internet service, you may have noticed that some service providers allow you to connect to the Internet without changing any IP information on your computer. Assuming that people with all sorts of host configurations are connecting to the hotel network, how is that possible? By placing a circuit-level gateway into the network, the hotel gateway is able to accept connections from any IP configuration and proxy it to a consistent configuration in the same manner as network address translation.

Disadvantages of an application-based proxy server are that they require client software that is aware of and can interact with the proxy server itself. For the most common applications, such as HTTP, HTTPS (SSL), and FTP, this is not a problem and most Web browsers and other client software are preconfigured to support proxy servers. Newer or less commonly used protocols, however, may not have proxy support built into them. When a new application is developed, there is commonly a lag time between the time that the protocol becomes popular and the time that the proxies are developed to support secure and controlled usage of the protocols. This can leave network administrators in a difficult spot in the meantime.

By necessity, proxy servers can also slow network response times. Each time user traffic is redirected to the proxy server, there is a short delay as the proxy checks its cache for a local copy of the resource the user is requesting. If it is in the cache, then user performance is greatly improved. If it is not in the cache, however, the proxy must then initiate the outbound connection. While the delay is not great, depending on the size of the proxy, the speed of the hard drives, and the number of requests per second, the proxy can increase delays in a busy network. For the sake of comparison, depending on the usage patterns of users, most proxy administrators feel that they are getting high marks if their proxy can locally service 30 percent of network requests. If the caching feature of proxy servers is not utilized, then the delay that is introduced is minimal; however, there still may be overhead associated with maintaining the logical network connections for a great number of hosts. It should be noted that for the 30 percent of network requests that the proxy can serve locally, the performance for those users is excellent and bandwidth utilization on the company access link is likewise reduced.

While proxies can be an improvement in the amount of control over network traffic, what is really required is an application that can dig into the user data and make judgments as to what should be in the data itself. These devices are known as application layer firewalls.

8.1.4 Application Layer Firewalls

While packet filters are primarily interested in the IP, TCP, and UDP information that is in a packet, application layer firewalls are interested in the application layer data found within these headers.

For the sake of example, let us recall the protection that a packet filter would provide our internal Web server from the outside world. Data entering the network would be controlled through the examination of the packet IP address — the destination IP address of traffic entering the network must match that of our Web server. Furthermore, the TCP port must match that of the process on the Web server, typically port 80. Once those two elements have matched the access-list, the packet is forwarded to the Web server, regardless of the data that the packet actually contained.

In this specific example, there is really only a fairly small set of valid requests that the client application should be sending to the Web server. An application layer firewall could check the data of the packet against a database of attack patterns and a database of allowed and normal page requests. If the packet is found to be valid, it would then continue to the Web server. If not, it would be rejected.

The application layer firewall has an understanding of the normal structure of data used by a particular application. It can check the data of a received packet against a database of what is "good" or "bad" and make independent decisions based upon the packet.

Application layer firewalls offer a great deal of control and protection for our network traffic. As usual, however, we cannot have it all. Based on their operation, application layer firewalls are very specific to a particular type of application. While the most popular application services are supported, they may not all be supported on one device. For example, you would need a separate program to check your e-mail for attachments and viruses, a different one to monitor user Web traffic for downloads and harmful applets, and yet another to protect your own Web server against attacks from the Internet. Not all applications are supported either. As with proxy servers, there is a market lag between the development of a protocol and the ability to application firewall it.

8.1.5 *Network Address Translation*

While we commonly refer to a firewall as a device on a network by point-ing to it with a stubby finger and saying, "That is our firewall," the reality of it is that a firewall is a service more than a device. Likewise, a firewall is the entirety of protections that we put into place on our networks to protect the inside from the outside, and vice versa. Based on this, our definition of a firewall must include network address translation (NAT). The advantages and disadvantages of network address translation were discussed in an earlier chapter, but it is fair to include NAT as part of an overall firewall solution, regardless of any IP addressing issues that may exist.

8.2 Decisions, Decisions

So which type of firewall is best for your network? The easy answer to that is that it depends on your security policy. What assets are you trying to protect? What level of protection do your assets require, and are there other countermeasures that sufficiently reduce the risk and are more cost effective? For example, would it be more cost effective in the long run to employ the concept of least privilege for all users on their own hosts, instead of setting up an expensive application layer firewall to screen inbound Web traffic? Can a proxy be configured to reject questionable sites instead for less cost as there are a number of free, robust proxy servers available?

To put things into perspective, however, we will look beyond the needs of our security policy a bit and think logically about the utility of the fire-wall on our network. It would be helpful to discuss what a firewall *cannot* do to protect your network.

A firewall will not protect your network against traffic that does not go through it. That seems obvious when printed on the page, but is a fact that is often overlooked in network design. Unless the forwarding behavior of your network can be controlled to an extent that you know where all traffic is being sent, a firewall will only provide a false sense of security. Users who are allowed to connect modems to their desktops are effectively cir-cumventing the security policy by circumventing the firewall put into place to enforce it. Multi-homed networks are another consideration. Care should be taken to ensure that all egress and entry points to the network are configured appropriately. You may believe that the secondary link is only being used in an emergency, but depending upon your routing poli-cies, traffic may indeed be using the link. Furthermore, what would happen if an emergency were to strike? Would users be able to continue their daily operations using the secondary link, or would differing firewall polices prevent this?

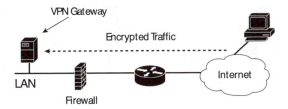

Exhibit 3. Firewalls Cannot Check Encrypted Traffic

A firewall also cannot protect your data if it cannot understand it (see Exhibit 3). Many companies create holes in their firewalls to allow VPN traffic through the firewall. Unless there is additional checking being done in the encrypted traffic elsewhere in the network, this is a bad idea. A VPN only encrypts data — ensuring confidentiality; it does nothing to ensure that the data being encrypted is good for the health of your network. Because a firewall cannot read encrypted data, companies may be creating an avenue of attack right through their own firewall.Firewalls are a collection of hardware and software that must work together to enforce a security policy. Like any other computer program, there may be flaws in the program that runs the firewall. These flaws need to be patched. Therefore, the firewall itself needs to be maintained. This maintenance also implies regular inspection of the rules. More than once I have visited a customer site to find a firewall that was several patches behind and had a rule set that had slowly changed over the years as new requirements were made of the network. Instead of removing old rules, the network administrators were so afraid of breaking things that they just added rules onto the end. The effective security of the firewalls as they were configured in this state was very low. Old rules that were not removed were allowing access to inappropriate internal hosts and the firewall operating system itself was several patch levels behind, thus increasing the risk of remote compromise.

In my role as an educator and consultant, I am often asked the question, "Which firewall do you think is best? Brand X, Brand Y, or Brand Z?" The response is always the same. "Which are you most comfortable using?" is the reply.

This brings me to a final point about the effectiveness of a firewall solution. I am sure that any firewall vendor will be happy to report the pros of their devices compared to those of their competitors, but the most effective firewall is going to be one that users are comfortable using. If the network administrator is not comfortable reviewing the logs, changing the rule sets, and installing patches, then the firewall is going to be an ineffective panacea at best.

The deployment of a firewall is an important issue, especially where other security technologies are included. For the relevant technologies, such as VPN integration, the information will be included in those sections. For now, we will only discuss the firewall alone.

As previously discussed, it is common to point to a box and say "That there is my firewall." From a security point of view, however, it is more accurate to say, "My firewall is created from these technologies."

Every firewall has the idea of the "inside" and the "outside," which allows the network administrator to control the flow of traffic from one side of the firewall to the other. What is the inside and outside, however, may vary, depending on the placement of the firewall. For example, there is no rule that states that firewalls can only be placed on the edge of the network. Internal resources and server farms can also be protected from internal malicious and unintentional damage through the use of a firewall. Your security policy will dictate if this is a requirement.

Many organizations use multiple firewall devices. Sometimes, these are configured in parallel and other times in series. The parallel configuration is the ideal solution to address network availability. This is particularly helpful in multi-homed environments where there are multiple WAN links and availability has a high priority.

When considering the firewall as a group of devices, typically the first device that a packet hits when it enters the network is the access router at the edge of the customer network. Modern routers sport fairly robust processors, memory, and operating systems. Many can operate as stateful packet filters or even higher layer firewalls in their own right. Because every organization needs a router to connect to the Internet in the first place, this is an excellent place to begin your perimeter security.

As a packet travels into the network, it will typically hit another firewall. This is a firewall that complements the packet filtering that is going on in the router and may include the higher layer functions such as proxy services and application layer filtering. The hardware that supports this second line of defense may have a number of network interfaces, with some network interfaces supporting the internal network and others supporting DMZs. The DMZ area may host a number of application layer firewalls; these will typically be mail relays that can be configured to scan for attachments and viruses.

In situations that require high security, internal firewalls may also separate sections of the network. For the sake of performance, this can be as simple as stateful packet filtering, limiting access to protected hosts by port number (see Exhibit 4). Configuring firewalls in series increases the security of the network by creating multiple hops that the network attacker must jump through to access the network. If you are considering

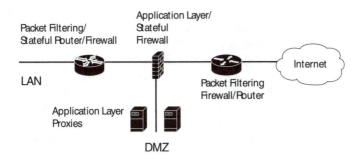

Exhibit 4. Together, These Devices Operate as a "Firewall"

this solution, consider at least two different firewall vendor products for placement in series. If you go through the expense of purchasing and maintaining two firewalls, it would be a shame to have them both felled by a single, previously unknown exploit that bypasses their security features. By using the products of two different vendors, this chance is reduced. Be aware that employing firewalls in a series will also add additional delay to any packet transmissions that are sent through the firewall. In practice, this is only a concern if real-time communications are employed, such as Voice-over-IP (VoIP), which has one-way tolerances of 150 ms.

I do not discuss specific firewall products because the technology and vendor offerings change rapidly enough to render the information in such a section obsolete. When considering which firewall to purchase, refer to the information in previous chapters on evaluating countermeasures. Armed with that information and a complete security policy, you will have all the information you need to ask the right questions. Yes, a firewall can be an expensive product, but there is more than one robust firewall solution that can run as open source software requiring only the hardware to support the product.

8.3   Router Security Considerations

Routers are an often-overlooked part of a network security plan. Many companies that fall into the small- to medium-sized range with a single access router and limited routing expertise tend to hope that whatever configuration options are available on the router are good enough to secure it. I have often found that service providers that install the routers are not diligent about either mentioning the need for a secure router configuration or configuring it securely for customers when installing a new circuit.

The most common response that I receive when inquiring about the security of a router is, "What does it matter? The firewall will pick it up anyway." This is a flawed argument in at least two respects. The first is that a firewall will only inspect packets that flow through the firewall. Because the router is generally the network device prior to the firewall from the point of view of the Internet, it is possible to attack the router without ever involving the firewall. Of the two misconceptions, however, this is a minor one. The second major fallacy is that a firewall is a single device on the network. Any device that can increase the security of your network or assist in the implementation of your security policy should be employed as such. The secret of good network security is not complicated — defense in depth. Use as many resources as you can to protect your network against threats.

For many companies, the router is *the* firewall for their network as well. The common adage used to be, "Let the routers route, get another box for a firewall." This is something that I generally agree with, with some exceptions. Routers are best at routing and because you can "roll your own" firewall for very little cost in hardware or software, I find it difficult to justify not having at least two packet filtering devices on the network. The router does some simple packet filtering and the firewall does the more complex work. This, however, is not the best solution for all companies. Many companies, after performing a cost/benefit analysis for their network are looking for a way to provide the maximum protection with either minimal investment or with equipment they already have. In these circumstances, a router can act as a fairly robust firewall.

Advancements in processing and computing power have also rendered the old firewall/router adage somewhat obsolete. Today, it is difficult to tell the difference between the two. Routers are created with firewall feature sets that rival the most sophisticated firewalls and multi-homed firewalls can forward traffic at acceptable rates between subnets and speak all of the most common routing protocols. The functionality of the two devices is becoming one and the same, with the only difference being which vendor logo appears on the box.

For companies in this position, this section offers some advice on how to configure a router to operate as a firewall. Because these functions are also found in stand-alone firewalls, it will also be a good case study as to the implementation of the concepts discussed previously in this chapter. Finally, making a slight digression from the rest of this text, we will be speaking primarily about Cisco routers here. There are many fine and innovative router vendors out there and some that compete quite well with Cisco in specific markets; but for the market that we are discussing, where a router is likely to be used as a security device, Cisco dominates. When speaking of server operating systems, it is difficult to be specific without alienating a large portion of the market or including sections in your book for Microsoft Windows 2000, XP, various Linux flavors, and other UNIX-style operating systems — not to mention the numerous

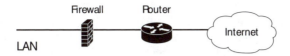

Exhibit 5. Simple Network Diagram and Firewall Placement

vendors that supply VPN products, authentication servers, and intrusion detection devices. Cisco routers however, primarily dominate access-routers and thus, playing to the demographics, we focus on that platform in this section.

Cisco or not, any commercial router that is likely to be found at the edge of a company network will allow you to do simple packet filtering. If the router is not your only firewall, you are going to be interested in filtering packets. Now that we have discussed what packet filtering is in the preceding text, we can now discuss what you would likely want to filter.

8.3.1 Packet Filtering Router and Firewall Together

Exhibit 5 illustrates a typical network set up with an access-router and a stand-alone firewall server. This section examines some of the more important implementation considerations that should take place in such a configuration. In this case, we know that the firewall is going to be doing the heavy lifting. Our goal with the router is to filter packets that we know are just plain wrong and let the firewall deal with packets that have the appearance of legitimacy. So what constitutes a packet that is "just plain wrong"?

With a little thought we can quickly come up with a list of things we do not think we should ever see on our network; these include:

- We should never accept a packet from the Internet with a source of our own network number. This is called "spoofing."
- We should never accept a packet from the Internet with a source address that is in the private address ranges of 10.0.0.0/8, 172.16.0.0/12, or 192.168.0.0/16. This is most likely some form of attack, but may just be a misconfigured NAT device from a legitimate source. Regardless, the packet will never make it back to whomever sent it, so drop it at your router. These are also called "Martian addresses."
- We should never accept packets with a multicast source address. Multicast addresses are found in the range of 224.0.0.0 to 239.255.255.255.
- We should never accept packets with a source address from class E "experimental" addresses in the range of 240.0.0.0 to 255.255.255.254.

- We should never accept packets that are sourced with an address assigned to the auto-DHCP range of 169.254.0.0/16.
- We should never accept packets from the Internet with a source of all 0s or all 1s (0.0.0.0 and 255.255.255.255). These are illegal for use as source addresses and are most likely some form of attack.

Because these are all packets with addresses that should not be seen arriving from the Internet, we can safely discard them at our router and not burden the firewall with additional processing. While these rules are clear, there are others that fall into a grey area. Some of these and the considerations that surround them are as follows.

8.3.1.1 We should never accept packets from network numbers that are currently unassigned. These addresses are called "bogons." While there is a great deal of discussion about IP addresses being used up, there are still quite a number of IP network ranges that are unassigned. Because nobody legitimately can be using these addresses, why would we be getting packets from them? Knowing that private addresses and clearly bogus addresses, as discussed above, are commonly dropped at the edge of a network, network-based attackers will commonly disguise their attacks by choosing addresses that look real, but are unassigned. Of course it makes sense not to accept these packets, but implementing this rule is another matter altogether. The assigned addresses are constantly changing. This prohibits router manufacturers from making a simple command that says, "filter bogons." Instead, the list needs to be manually created. Furthermore, these lists change and, if your network manager does not keep up with the changes, legitimate traffic from the newly assigned network blocks will be dropped. Finally, there is nothing stopping a network-based attacker from simply changing the source IP address of an attack to someone else, in effect stealing a legitimate user's IP address.

The decision to filter "bogons" is one that is going to have to be based on your security policy. This filter does indeed provide more security than not having it; however, the cost of maintaining it must be weighed against the incremental increase in security.

8.3.1.2 Never accept packets from the outside that are destined to the router itself. This rule simply states that packets from the Internet that are destined for one of the router interfaces should be discarded. Packets going through the router are unaffected; only packets with a destination of one of the routers IP address are filtered. Other than a bandwidth-based denial-of-service attack, any attack on the router itself is going to have to be sent to the router. It then stands to reason that denying traffic of this sort further increases the safeguards you have installed on your router. While effective, this configuration can also lead to problems in

206

troubleshooting your network. Normally, there is no reason for someone on the Internet to be connecting to your router, unless it is the technical support of your service provider. If your ISP is managing your router, it is doubtful that this configuration will ever be included because your ISP cannot then connect to the router to make changes to it. If you get in a bind while managing your own router, then this configuration can make troubleshooting from the outside more difficult.

If outside management is an issue, there are several ways to incorporate this into your network. The ideal solution is to never allow outside connections to your router and configure the router via a dial-up modem attached to a router auxiliary port. The high-tech solution to protecting the modem against war dialing[1] is to use a modem that supports user databases, hardware encryption, and authentication. The low-tech way is to keep the modem unplugged unless it is required and then someone local to the router plugs it in for use.

If the modem is not an option, then the router should be configured to accept only SSH connections. SSH, or Secure SHell, is an encrypted version of Telnet that encrypts all information sent, including usernames and passwords. This prevents someone from sniffing the log-in password but does not stop someone from guessing what that username and password are. SSH has occasionally been cracked on its own, meaning that if your router were running a vulnerable version of SSH, it could be compromised regardless of your other protection mechanisms.

Many protocols allow the configuration of a router but the commands and information are sent in cleartext and have weak authentication schemes. The least acceptable remote configuration protocols for routers are SNMPv2,[2] HTTP, or Telnet. HTTP servers on routers have been known to have security holes. A general rule of security is to run only essential services on computer equipment. In this case, HTTP is not essential and only increases the chance that someone will successfully attack your router.

As we can see, the strategy has been to simply filter packets that are clearly invalid. While the filtering capabilities of a router can be implemented in a much more complex manner, limiting our access-lists to this allows the router to perform at optimum efficiency while ensuring that our firewall only spends processing power on packets that are legitimately destined for our internal network. With this summary comes a brief editorial. It is a fact that access-lists do impede the performance of a router. That said, for your average T-1 connection, as long as they are constructed in a logical manner, your access-lists could be quite lengthy without impacting performance to the point where anyone notices.

8.4   The Router as the Firewall

This section describes two separate options for the configuration of a router as an actual firewall. The first is configuring the router as the only firewall on your network, and the second is the configuration of a router as a second firewall on your network. In each case, the configuration would be the same; only the implementation philosophy differs.

Before explaining how a router alone could operate as a fairly robust firewall, we will spend some time re-examining why you would not want to do this if you could get away with it. Note that this entire argument is based on the conclusions of your risk analysis. We are assuming that the need for security at this point outweighs the additional cost of a separate firewall.

As has been mentioned several times in this text, effective countermeasures are layered. Defense in depth is the best approach to implementing a security policy. If one device or countermeasure should fail or be circumvented, both of which are circumstances you should count on, we need to have other countermeasures to continue providing protection. If your router is your only firewall, and if it is incorrectly configured, your defenses are not as robust as you think. In fact, unless you take the time to carefully audit your configuration, you may simply have a false sense of security.

By using a firewall in addition to a filtering router, you have provided additional protection to your network. If your router is compromised, your internal network at least remains secure. Some implementations take this philosophy to the point of placing multiple firewalls in series. This configuration ensures that if one firewall should be compromised or misconfigured, a second one is there to continue the protection. In this configuration, firewalls from different vendors are often employed to ensure that an undiscovered vulnerability affecting one device does not affect the second. In a real sense, by configuring your router as a firewall along with a separate firewall, you will have implemented just this philosophy.

Performance has often been cited as a reason to not configure a router as a complex firewall. In days of yore, that was the case. Routers were not powerful enough to rapidly forward packets and enforce access-list rules at the same time. Times have changed and the phenomenal increases we have seen in computing power and architectures apply to routers as well. No longer are routers simply a "poor man's firewall;" rather, they are robust and configurable combination routers/firewalls in their own right. There are only two situations in which this argument should be a consideration for your implementation. The first is when you are committed to making the most of existing (and somewhat dated) hardware. The second is if you are processing packets at high speeds for optical (OC) type Internet connections. Remember that, for the most part, the speed of your LAN and the firewall is not going to be the limiting element for network performance.

The speed of the WAN link is going to be the bottleneck; and $50,000 for a high-speed firewall is not going to change that.

The primary argument against using a router as your single firewall device is the lack of redundancy. In security terms, this could affect all the things we are trying to ensure: confidentiality, integrity, and especially availability.

For the configuration of a router as a firewall, we will want to include all of the rules we configured when implementing a router to work as a screen for another firewall. That means no obviously invalid packets and control access to the router itself. We also need to consider the rest of the security policy.

As with the rest of security, the actual configuration of the firewall is one of the last steps to take when implementing a firewall. There are several steps that precede the implementation of rules. The first is examining the security policy and determining what rules need to be implemented. Do not give into the temptation to skip the security policy step and survey the network to learn what applications are being used and simply configure the firewall around them. Doing this creates a reactive configuration that only reflects the current state of the network without evaluating the security of the applications you are allowing through the firewall. In effect, you are simply making sure that insecure applications have access through the firewall if you follow this approach.

Instead, create your firewall rules based on your security policy. While there are a number of ways to create configuration rules from policy, standards, and procedures, I prefer a decidedly low-tech approach using a piece of notepaper. I create a box on a blank sheet of paper that represents the firewall. I then make one side of the box "inside" and the other side of the box "outside." If part of the deployment, I will also include another section of the box that is labeled "DMZ." This serves to remind me of the firewall's view of the world. From the point of view of the firewall, there is only traffic entering its interfaces and traffic leaving its interfaces. All rules must be written to reflect this somewhat egocentric point of view.

Once I am reminded how the firewall looks at things, I then start combining the standards and procedures document, looking for rules that the firewall must enforce. Because a security policy is a high-level document, it should not contain configuration statements such as "allow traffic from any source on the Internet to access the SMTP mail server at 200.1.1.100 on port 25 only." Instead, a security policy standards document might include statements such as:

- "Our perimeter will allow Internet access to our DMZ only, which will contain the following essential application servers: DNS, SMTP, POP, HTTP, an HTTP/FTP proxy, and FTP server.

- Access to the Internet from the internal network will be limited to application traffic not easily proxied and will be limited to connections initiated from our clients only. Essential applications are Telnet for VTY100 terminal emulation and ICMP traffic."

Of course, there are many more statements of principle that might be found in a security policy, but the above should be enough to give us a chance to practice our firewall logic. We will find that even from such simple statements, there are number of lessons we can learn about the router/firewall and the configuration of firewalls in general.

From this point, it is simply a matter of assigning ports and addresses and diagramming their directionality on the notepaper. Once this has been completed, you may want to type up your rule set into something presentable because most management types or clients do not like to see scribbled notes as part of your final documentation.

- Let us see how this would work based on our current rule set. We will assume, for sake of simplicity, that the hosts on our network have the following IP addresses in the DMZ:DNS: 200.1.1.10
- SMTP: 200.1.1.20
- POP3: 200.1.1.30
- HTTP: 200.1.1.40
- HTTP/FTP Proxy: 200.1.1.50
- FTP: 200.1.1.60
- LAN network is 200.1.2.0/24

Using our notepaper, we can easily diagram the allowed traffic:

- Allow DNS, UDP destination port 53, from "outside" to "DMZ" 200.1.1.10. Outside to inside tells us that traffic from the Internet is allowed in to the server.
- Allow SMTP, TCP destination port 25, from "outside" to "DMZ" 200.1.1.20. The rule allows the receipt of e-mail from our mail server.
- Allow SMTP, TCP destination port 25, to "outside" from "DMZ" 200.1.1.20. This allows the sending of e-mail from our mail server.
- Allow POP3, TCP destination port 110, from "outside" to "DMZ" 200.1.1.30. This rule allows remote user clients to check their e-mail on our POP3 server.
- Allow HTTP, TCP destination port 80, from "outside" to "DMZ" 200.1.1.40. This rule allows Internet hosts to access our Web server.
- Allow HTTP traffic from the "inside" network to "DMZ" 200.1.1.50, TCP destination ports 8080 (our proxy server port number). Allow clients from the LAN to connect to the proxy.
- Allow HTTP traffic from the proxy on "DMZ" 200.1.1.50, to access the Internet. Because Web sites can theoretically run on any number of ports, we will only restrict this traffic according to IP addresses instead of ports.

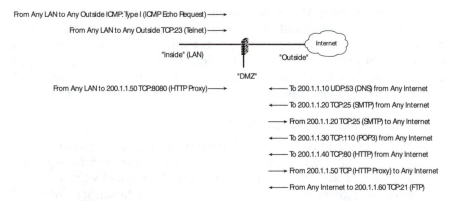

From Any LAN to Any Outside ICMP: Type I (ICMP Echo Request) ⟶

From Any LAN to Any Outside TCP:23 (Telnet) ⟶

"Inside" (LAN) | "Outside" Internet

"DMZ"

From Any LAN to 200.1.1.50 TCP:8080 (HTTP Proxy) ⟶

⟵ To 200.1.1.10 UDP:53 (DNS) from Any Internet

⟵ To 200.1.1.20 TCP:25 (SMTP) from Any Internet

⟶ From 200.1.1.20 TCP:25 (SMTP) to Any Internet

⟵ To 200.1.1.30 TCP:110 (POP3) from Any Internet

⟵ To 200.1.1.40 TCP:80 (HTTP) from Any Internet

⟶ From 200.1.1.50 TCP (HTTP Proxy) to Any Internet

⟵ From Any Internet to 200.1.1.60 TCP:21 (FTP)

Exhibit 6. Initial Notes for Firewall Rules

- Allow FTP, TCP destination port 21, from "outside" network to "DMZ" 200.1.1.60.
- Allow Telnet traffic, TCP destination port 23, from "inside" network to the "outside."
- Allow ICMP traffic, IP protocol type 1, from "inside" network to the "outside."

Just following our rule set gives us a notepaper that looks like the diagram in Exhibit 6. If we were to implement this rule set, however, we would find that our functionality is severely limited because there is much that must also be considered for even these simple rules. Consider the simple scenario where a user on the inside tries to create a Telnet session to tel-net.testservers.com. First, the client must perform a domain lookup. Assuming the we also have a split DNS, the client PC will query the LAN DNS server, which will forward the packets to the DMZ DNS server when it fails to provide a local name resolution. But our current rules will not allow this. We need to allow DNS traffic from the "inside" to the DMZ and then allow the return traffic. So we add another line to our diagram:

- Allow DNS queries, destination port 53, from the "inside" network to the "DMZ" DNS server at 200.1.1.10.
- Allow DNS reply traffic, source port 53, from the "DMZ" DNS server 200.1.1.10 to the "inside" network.

We can pause at this point and discuss several items that our rule set has also suggested.

8.4.1 Firewalls Define Themselves According to Their Interfaces

Our firewall has three interfaces, each labeled as "inside," "outside," or "DMZ." Any rule on the router simply tells the router/firewall if it is allowed to forward traffic to a specific port or drop the traffic that is not allowed.

Firewall filtering rules should always be defined from the point of view of the firewall. If you have trouble visualizing packets entering and leaving the router, imagine that you are sitting at the interface of the router with a checklist that represents your rule set. In a sense, you are the door guard of the router. You are checking packets as they enter the interfaces and, from your point of view, "in" and "out" are from the interface itself.

8.4.2   All Traffic Must Be Explicitly Defined

Virtually any field that is available for reading in either a network or transport layer packet header defines traffic. Common filtering fields include source and destination IP addresses, IP protocol values, IP fragmentation, IP packet length, source ports, destination ports, and TCP option bits. To properly filter traffic, this information needs to be defined. Note that from our above rules, not all of the listed fields must be defined, only those that are relevant to the filtering process. Depending on the protocol, the most difficult element of creating firewall rules is simply ensuring that all of the protocols that work together to enable an application are properly defined. Some firewall products have sophisticated default rule sets that allow you to simply say, "Allow all traffic associated with SIP, the protocol commonly used for VoIP."[3] In this case, the firewall vendor has predefined the associated protocols and port values — a great timesaver and aid in reducing security-affecting misconfigurations. Someone with experience can easily create these rules manually; but if you do not have experienced firewall staff on hand, they are a convenient resource.

8.4.3   Return Traffic May Not Be Automatically Assumed by Firewall Rules

It only makes sense that if you want to allow users to access HTTP sites on the Internet, then the return traffic, the packets with the actual text and graphics that show up in the users' Web browser, should be allowed back into the network. Firewalls, by design, are very conservative and do not necessarily allow this return traffic. Therefore, instead of simply stating, "Allow clients to access HTTP sites on the Internet," you need to explicitly state, "Allow traffic from clients to access HTTP sites, and allow the return traffic from HTTP sites to return to the clients." Just as with Rule 8.4.2, however, there are a number of firewall products that will automatically configure these rules for you through the use of preconfigured rule sets. Regardless of the user interface, however, the implementation on the firewall needs to explicitly allow this traffic.

There are more rules, but right now lets just apply these three to our existing firewall notes. Thus far, we have included DNS, but other rules that need to be included to make our network operate as we would expect.

- Allow our "DMZ" DNS server at 200.1.1.10 to make queries to other DNS servers on the Internet. These packets will have a destination UDP port of 53.
- Allow LAN clients to access the POP3 server as well; TCP destination port 110 from "inside" to "DMZ" 200.1.1.30.
- Allow HTTP traffic, TCP source port 80, from "DMZ" 200.1.1.40 to "outside." This allows HTTP traffic from our Web sever to return to Internet hosts that request content.
- Allow HTTP proxy traffic to return to the LAN by allowing "DMZ" 200.1.1.50 to send packets with a TCP source port of 8080 to "inside."
- Allow Telnet traffic from the Internet to return to the "inside" hosts by allowing traffic with a TCP source port 23 to return to the "inside" network.
- Allow ICMP traffic to return to the "inside" network by allowing the IP protocol 1 from the "outside" network to the "inside" network.

By the time we have included all these new rules, our firewall notepaper looks like the diagram in Exhibit 7. As we can see, manually defining return traffic for all our services is complicated and prone to error. In fact, it is so complicated and prone to error that we are going to look for another way to complete the same task in a much simpler fashion. Let us first state our goal so that we can then redefine it. Our intent is to make our network secure by only allowing traffic that is defined by our security policy. This includes limiting inbound and outbound traffic to specified ports and networks.

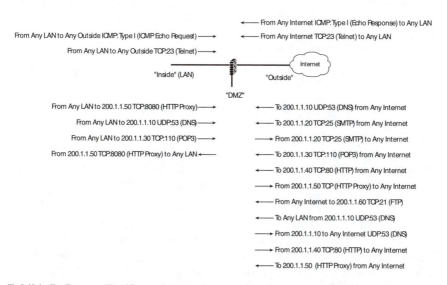

Exhibit 7. Return Traffic and Essential Protocols Added to Firewall Notes

But our rules are not perfect. While we want to allow return traffic, we really only want to allow return traffic that is part of an existing connection. Right? In other words, the rule above, "Allow Telnet traffic from the Internet to return to the "inside" hosts by allowing traffic with a TCP source port 23 to return to the "inside" network," does not really do just that if we closely examine its operation. This rule allows any packet with a TCP source port of 23 access to our internal network when we really only want packets associated with an established user Telnet session. So how can we control this traffic and make the configuration of our access rules simpler and therefore more secure? Here is a hint: refer back to the TCP materials and take a look at the TCP header. Are there any options in the header that would help us filter based on only established connections?

There is! We see from the TCP three-way handshake that the first three packets of a TCP connection are used for setting up a TCP session. The client sends a TCP packet to the appropriate IP address and port with the SYN (synchronize) bit set, and the server responds back with both the SYN and ACK (acknowledgement) bits set. Finally, the remote client sends a final ACK to acknowledge the receipt of the server's packet and the transfer of data begins. During the actual transfer of data, we may see bits such as the ACK, RST (reset), URG (urgent), PSH (push), and FIN (finish) bits set, but we never see the SYN bit set again. In fact, the only time we should see a SYN bit alone in a packet is during the initial setup of a session.

Voila! We now have a way to filter based upon the state of the connection. We can simply tell our router/firewall that if it sees any packets from the "outside" that are destined for the "inside" or the "DMZ" that if they *do not* have the SYN bit in the TCP header, then assume that they are part of an established connection and allow the traffic back in. This can be done for all our services with a single statement:

- Allow packets that are part of an established connection from "outside" to "inside" and "DMZ."

Notice the change this single rule has on our firewall notes, shown in Exhibit 8.

While this single line serves to simplify our firewall rules slightly, there are a number of problems with it as it stands. We will discuss these shortcomings and offer solutions. For now, we want to continue with the basic firewall configuration.

There is one more troublesome entry in our firewall that we must examine. As it stands, we are allowing all ICMP traffic in both directions from the Internet to our LAN. Presumably, our security policy specified that internal hosts be allowed to use ICMP traffic as it assists in error reporting and troubleshooting. Programs such as PING and traceroute make extensive use of ICMP, and other error messages such as "host not found," "network not

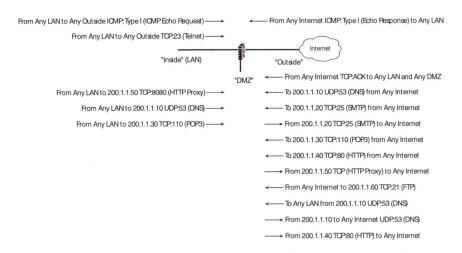

From Any LAN to Any Outside ICMP: Type I (ICMP Echo Request) ⟶   ⟵ From Any Internet ICMP: Type I (Echo Response) to Any LAN

From Any LAN to Any Outside TCP:23 (Telnet) ⟶

"Inside" (LAN)   "Outside"   Internet

"DMZ"   ⟵ From Any Internet TCP:ACK to Any LAN and Any DMZ

From Any LAN to 200.1.1.50 TCP:8080 (HTTP Proxy) ⟶   ⟵ To 200.1.1.10 UDP:53 (DNS) from Any Internet

From Any LAN to 200.1.1.10 UDP:53 (DNS) ⟶   ⟵ To 200.1.1.20 TCP:25 (SMTP) from Any Internet

From Any LAN to 200.1.1.30 TCP:110 (POP3) ⟶   ⟶ From 200.1.1.20 TCP:25 (SMTP) to Any Internet

⟵ To 200.1.1.30 TCP:110 (POP3) from Any Internet

⟵ To 200.1.1.40 TCP:80 (HTTP) from Any Internet

⟶ From 200.1.1.50 TCP (HTTP Proxy) to Any Internet

⟵ From Any Internet to 200.1.1.60 TCP:21 (FTP)

⟵ To Any LAN from 200.1.1.10 UDP:53 (DNS)

⟶ From 200.1.1.10 to Any Internet UDP:53 (DNS)

⟶ From 200.1.1.40 TCP:80 (HTTP) to Any Internet

Exhibit 8. Allowing Return Traffic Looking for ACK Bits

found," and "Time to live expired" are all essential to the normal operation of our host computers.

At the same time, ICMP can be used for nefarious purposes. The clearest example of this is to use ICMP echoes, the types of packets used by the PING program, to map a network. As our rule stands, although we have a router firewall with a DMZ and fairly strict rules in place, an attacker from the Internet could use echo packets to map our entire LAN network and learn the number of hosts and subnets on the network.

These same ICMP packets could be used to try to crash our host computers through the use of illegal options. Although this technique is becoming rarer as protocol stacks become tighter, it is good policy to also guard against unknown vulnerabilities. The best way to do that is to only use the functions that are essential to your business operations.

A more realistic rule is to examine ICMP and note those packets that are most likely to be used in normal network operations. If one of your users used PING and sent an ICMP "echo" packet to troubleshoot a network connection, you would reasonably expect an ICMP "echo-reply" in return. So echo-reply is an ICMP packet we would want to allow back into the network. On the other hand, if someone were to map your network using PING,[4] he or she would be sending ICMP "echo" packets to your network. These inbound packets from the "outside" would be something that would not be allowed.

Another ICMP packet type that is commonly seen coming back to our network is the ICMP "destination unreachable." Unlike echo traffic, destination unreachable packets are returned during normal IP traffic operation. A user might send a normal TCP connection request to a remote network, only to find that they have entered the address incorrectly or the host is no longer available. In this case, allowing ICMP destination unreachable traffic back into your network would allow users to more quickly realize that there is a problem with the connection instead of sitting around for a couple of minutes waiting for the connection to timeout because the router/firewall is discarding the error messages. We might then consider allowing ICMP "destination unreachable" packets back into our network as well.

Based on our understanding of ICMP operation, we are ready to modify our firewall notes a bit more. Instead of blindly allowing ICMP traffic in and out of our network, we allow only certain useful ICMP traffic. In this case, we allow all ICMP traffic out of our network, and allow only two types back in — namely, echo-replies and destination unreachable messages. Our rule set is modified to reflect these changes:

- Allow all ICMP traffic, IP protocol 1, from the "inside" network to the "outside."
- Allow all ICMP traffic, IP protocol 1, from the "DMZ" network to the "outside."
- Allow only ICMP "echo-reply" and "destination unreachable" traffic from the "outside" to the "inside" network.
- Allow only ICMP "echo-reply" and "destination unreachable" traffic from the "outside" to the "DMZ."

Note that separate rules were required for the DMZ and inside networks, as they represent different interfaces on the router/firewall. For now, we are keeping them logically distinct on our firewall diagram to ensure that they are properly implemented. When actually writing the rules, we will look for a chance to combine the inside and DMZ networks to shorten our overall rule set and increase efficiency.

Note also that we have made a conscious decision to allow all ICMP traffic from the inside network to the rest of the world. This is something that should be carefully considered as you write your security policy and implement the rules into your firewall. Many organizations will rightfully control outbound traffic as much as they would control inbound traffic. Others will allow most types of outbound traffic and tightly control only inbound traffic.

There are pros and cons to each decision. When you control outbound traffic, you control what applications users can access on the Internet. This is certainly useful, given the number of productivity-wasting sites that can be found out there. If users are using chat programs, the programs can be effectively blocked by only allowing applications with destination ports that match commonly used legitimate services such as HTTP (TCP port 80), FTP (TCP port 21), Telnet (TCP port 23), DNS (UDP port 53), etc.

When you control outbound traffic, you may also be reducing the risk of Trojanized programs or worms on your network. Many of these programs are configured to "phone home" periodically. The intent is that because many organizations do not restrict outbound traffic, firewall rules can effectively be circumvented if the program on the inside of the network initiates the connection to the attacker's location. Because return traffic that is part of an existing connection is typically only lightly filtered, if at all, this is a very effective technique.

Controlling outbound traffic also helps your organization behave like a good Internet citizen. By carefully controlling what traffic your network produces, you reduce the risk that someone or a program is going to use your network as a launching ground for attacks on other Internet sites. Not only is this good Internet etiquette, but it may also reduce your legal liability for such attacks.

Controlling outbound traffic is not without its drawbacks. The first is that it may increase the overhead and maintenance on the part of your IT and information security staff. Invariably, someone will discover a program or application that is a "must-have" and require that the firewall be reconfigured to allow this traffic inbound and outbound. Of course, proper planning for the security policy would hopefully eliminate these types of situations.

It may happen, however, that legitimate services are being run on alternate ports. There is no Internet law that states that Web servers need to operate on port 80. It is just a common convenience. Because most people access Web sites through links and not by entering in the full URL, it is a simple matter to redirect users to alternate ports without their knowledge. From the user's point of view, legitimate resources are not available. From the network security staff's point of view, because services can be run on any port, the additional overhead to open outbound ports here and there turns into a situation where you might just as well open them all.

Others argue correctly that most Trojan makers understand that certain ports will almost always be open to outbound traffic. It is a pretty good bet that a company that filters outbound traffic will allow outbound TCP port 80 through the firewall because this is popular for Web servers. Just as there is no law stating that you must run your Web server on port 80, there is no law stating that a service running on port 80 must be a Web server. Many companies that surreptitiously install spyware on computers make use of this fact to allow their software to phone home to a data collection center through home and corporate firewalls. Other gray-area programs such as chat programs and peer-to-peer file sharing programs can also be configured to send traffic on port 80 to allow their usage in a firewall environment. It would seem, then, that from one point of view, the effort to control outbound Internet traffic only adds complexity to the firewall configuration and provides little real benefit because of the ease with which IP services are reconfigured.

Another point of view, however, understands that controlling outbound traffic will have only a limited effect on network security, but limited effect is what network security is all about. If we were to wait until the "magic bullet" of network security is invented that solved every conceivable problem before implementing our own security policy, then we would be waiting a long time. Information security, and the firewall itself, is about the combination of countermeasures, each one incrementally reducing the risk on our networks. If controlling outbound traffic is a limited protection, and can be provided with the same hardware and administration that we are already paying for to control inbound traffic, then it seems logical to go through the effort to deploy it as part of our security policy implementation.

At this point we have the basis for our firewall implementation included on our notepaper. We are ready to start the configuration. Before we do, however, there are two essential rules of firewalls that we must first discuss. The first is, no matter the vendor, firewall rules are applied to packets in the order in which they are written. That means that as a packet is checked against a firewall rule set, Rule 1 is checked first. If the packet matches that rule, then it is processed according to the rule. If the packet does not match Rule 1, it is checked against Rule 2, and so on. The implication of this is that you can sabotage your rule set if you do not ensure that your rules are applied to the firewall in the proper order. Let us examine a simple example. Consider the two rules below:

- Allow any traffic to our HTTP server at 200.1.1.30 when it has the TCP destination port 80.
- Deny any traffic that has a source IP address from the Internet that is part of the private address ranges of 10.0.0.0/8, 172.16.0.0.12, and 192.168.0.0.16.

If applied in this order, we can see that a packet with an invalid source IP address but with a destination to our HTTP server on the proper port will be allowed through the firewall. This is certainly not our intent. Instead, the rules should be applied in the following order:

- Deny any traffic that has a source IP address from the Internet that is part of the private address ranges of 10.0.0.0/8, 172.16.0.0.12, and 192.168.0.0.16.
- Allow any traffic to our HTTP server at 200.1.1.30 when it has the TCP destination port 80.

Now the proper security will be enforced.

Because we know that packets will be checked against our rule set, it is also good practice to place the most commonly matched rules toward the top of the rule set. There is no sense in making a router/firewall check through 50 rules for 80 percent of packets. The difficult matter to resolve is how to implement the most commonly used rules with the checking of rule sets in order. In summary, you cannot always make it work. Consider our modified rule set from the preceding paragraph. Unless we are the victims of some serious troublemakers from the Internet, HTTP traffic will easily match more often than spoofed source packets. From our previous discussion, we see that we cannot easily place the rule to allow HTTP traffic prior to the rule that prohibits private addresses.

You may have a question as to which traffic is going to match particular firewall rules the most. Many times, this can be guesstimated through knowledge of your networking environment. If the majority of your Internet-bound traffic originates as user traffic, then it makes sense that the rule that matches established sessions is going to be the most commonly matched rule. If you host your own Web server and that server sees very high volumes of traffic, then the rule matching traffic to your Web server is going to be the rule with the most matches.

Many times, you can tune a firewall by examining the logs. Most firewall implementations have a logging option that will display the total matches for each rule in the firewall rule set. Simply configure the rule set in the manner that makes the most sense to you at the time, and then tune it after some period of "normal" network activity. Worrying that one rule getting 500 more hits is checked after another rule is not really worth the effort, but the general concept is simply to place commonly matched rules at the top of the list as long as overall security is not affected.

The second essential rule of firewall operation is the implicit "deny all" at the end of every filter list. This means that any traffic that is not explicitly permitted in the preceding filter statements is automatically denied. Many times, knowledge of this rule is assumed and the "deny all" statement does not actually appear in the rule set, but it is there.

In academic settings, the origin of the "deny all" rule is linked to the gradual evolution of firewall and information security philosophies. Some of the earliest security philosophies were defined as "permissive." That is another way of saying that only traffic that was explicitly denied would be blocked. All other traffic would be permitted. In practice, this shows up as an implementation rule that an application like Instant Messaging would be blocked to prevent lost worker productivity and all other traffic would be allowed. We know that there are 65,536 TCP ports that can run applications. Changing the server port the forbidden applications were running on could easily circumvent blocking one port.

In a very short time, it became clear that a restrictive security policy was the only real way to provide network security. All traffic would be blocked in each direction unless it was explicitly allowed. This should be your *only* option for configuring filters.

Now that our simple rule set has been established, we can put it into action. We will first want to include our filters for packets that should just never show up on our network.

- Deny any packet from the "outside" with a source that matches our "inside" network.
- Deny any packet from the "outside" with a source IP address in the private range of 10.0.0.0/8.
- Deny any packet from the "outside" with a source IP address in the private range of 172.16.0.0/12.
- Deny any packet from the "outside" with a source IP address in the private range of 192.168.0.0/16.
- Deny any packet from the "outside" with a source IP address of 0.0.0.0/32 (an all 0s source address).
- Deny any packet from the "outside" with a source IP address of 255.255.255.255 (an all 1s broadcast address).

Our risk assessment has convinced us that, for our needs, maintaining a "bogon" filter, which is dozens of separate entries in our filter list for unallocated source networks, is going to cost more in management than it will provide in security. Thus, we will forego the configuration of a "bogon" filter list.

We now add the rules that permit our network traffic.

- Allow packets that are part of an established connection from "outside" to "inside" and "DMZ."
- Allow DNS, UDP destination port 53, from "outside" to "DMZ" 200.1.1.10.
- Allow DNS, UDP destination port 53, from "inside" to "DMZ" 200.1.1.10
- Allow DNS, UDP source port 53, from "DMZ" 200.1.1.10 to "inside." Allow the DMZ DNS server to respond to queries by the "inside" hosts.
- Allow DNS, UDP source port 53, from "outside" to "DMZ" DNS server. This rule allows query responses to be returned to the DMZ DNS server from Internet DNS servers.
- Allow SMTP, TCP destination port 25, from "outside" to "DMZ" 200.1.1.20. This rule allows the receipt of e-mail from our mail server.
- Allow SMTP, TCP destination port 25, to "outside" from "DMZ" 200.1.1.20. This allows the sending of e-mail from our mail server.

- Allow POP3, TCP destination port 110, from "outside" to "DMZ" 200.1.1.30. This rule allows remote user clients to check their e-mail on our POP3 server.
- Allow HTTP, TCP destination port 80, from "outside" to "DMZ" 200.1.1.40. Allows Internet hosts to access our web server.
- Allow HTTP traffic from the "inside" network to "DMZ" 200.1.1.50, TCP destination ports 8080 (our proxy server port number). Allow clients from the LAN to connect to the proxy.
- Allow HTTP traffic from the proxy on "DMZ" 200.1.1.50 to access the Internet. Becauses Web sites can theoretically be run on any number of ports, we will only restrict this traffic according to IP addresses instead of ports.

Allow Telnet traffic, TCP destination port 23, from "inside" network to the "outside."

- Allow ICMP echo packets from the "inside" network to the "outside."
- Allow ICMP echo packets from the "DMZ" network to the "outside."

8.4.4 Testing Our Filtering

Now that the router/firewall has been configured, the process of auditing our work needs to occur. Initially, this work can be done by ourselves as the network administrator. At some point we will want to have another party audit our network. We humans are funny in that we often allow ourselves to look with rose-tinted glasses at our own work. We do our best the best way we know how. Naturally, our own auditing of our rules will match our own expectations. As a friend of mine is prone to saying, "We don't know what we don't know."

To overcome this shortcoming, it is essential to have another party examine your work. Creating a bullet-proof packet filter is very difficult to accomplish the first time through, and there is no reason to fear someone else pointing out what you have done wrong. When configuring network security, you should err on being correct in your configuration over being proud.

At this stage, auditing will take two different forms. The first is ensuring that user applications are operating correctly. Ideally, you are applying your firewall rules at night or on the weekend and you have a chance to test the most commonly used applications on your firewall. If you do not do your testing either prior to implementation or during an off-peak period, you will find that users are very helpful in pointing out your misconfiguration through a continual stream of calls, pages, and frenzied visits to your office. You will, of course, share their excitement and then risk further misconfiguration in an attempt to appease them. Test your rule set before imposing it on the users trying to do their jobs.

Common problems in this area are generally related to an incomplete understanding of the protocols that users employ on a daily basis. Even simple protocols such as FTP use a combination of ports for normal operation and have multiple "default" configurations, depending on the client software in operation. Multimedia and voice applications are even less forgiving, in that entire ranges of ports need to be configured for proper operation. Many tunneling protocols used by VPNs have different ports used for session management and data transfer.

Many times, return traffic is not sufficiently accounted for. Traffic is allowed out of the network and not back in. If you have a complicated subnetting scheme due to remote branch offices, make sure that when you define the "inside" network, you are including the remote IP subnets in your definition of "inside." Otherwise, your local LAN will operate correctly with regard to user traffic, but applications on the remote LAN will not.

The other type of auditing is sometimes called "penetration testing" or "ethical hacking." This is testing your own defenses against threats by attacking your own network. There are a number of tools available on the Internet to perform these attacks, so I will just outline the general concept here and provide more details in Chapter 12, "Network Penetration Testing."

As you deploy your perimeter security to match your security policy, you should constantly monitor your progress. A computer that is isolated from your network should be used to perform a number of attacks and scans on your network. A laptop is ideal for this purpose because you can scan from a number of locations. You can download tools separately and run each one against your network — or you can utilize the free programs Nmap and Nessus. In combination, Nmap will scan your network and firewall looking for open ports and servers listening through the firewall. Nessus will then compare your services and firewall against a fairly up-to-date attack database that will catalog your network services, vulnerabilities, and suggested fixes. While it is not a good idea to rely on a single tool, or a pair of tools, for network auditing, these two tools in combination are a perfect way to fairly quickly gauge your progress and check for any glaring errors.[5]

8.5 Improving Your Security beyond Basic Packet Filtering

At this point, your audit may turn up some surprising results, especially if you use Nmap and Nessus to scan your network from the outside. You may even find that despite your allowing only established sessions and limiting ICMP traffic, Nmap is able to scan quite a bit of your network, including your LAN. This is because the type of firewalling we are doing right now is simple packet filtering. From the point of view of the firewall, each packet is an independent entity and no relationship is made between one packet and the next. Therefore, your firewall lacks the logic to associate a packet forged to look like part of an established session with the fact that no outbound traffic was sent outbound to establish a session in the first place. Decisions are made based solely on the settings of the bits in the packet headers.

If we were to try to make our network rules more complex, we would also notice other failings with our firewall rule set as it is. We know now that we can infer if a TCP header is part of an established session through the use of the control bits. What if we had an application that used UDP? How would we know if the UDP packet incoming from the Internet is in response to a UDP packet being sent out from our LAN or a UDP packet being sent into our network for some nefarious purpose? Because UDP has no way of establishing a session, the fact is that we cannot determine the nature of that incoming UDP packet. So, for UDP, we are stuck with manually configuring ranges of ports to allow traffic in and out of our network just as we had to do with TCP. Even worse for our network security, UDP is commonly used for interactive multimedia applications and these applications use enormous ranges of UDP ports. For example, some VoIP implementations use a range of thousands of UDP ports during normal operation. For these applications to operate properly on our firewall, we would have to allow unrestricted inbound and outbound access on those UDP ports. This is clearly at odds with our restrictive philosophy of firewall configuration.

What we need in our firewall is some logic that keeps track of outbound UDP packets and only allows UDP packets back into the network if they correspond to the IP addresses and ports used by the outgoing UDP traffic. This, of course, is exactly what a stateful packet filter accomplishes for us.

By enabling stateful packet filtering on our router/firewall, we can reduce the complexity of our rule set while at the same time increasing the overall security. These benefits are realized because we no longer need to establish complex rules to allow return traffic and the firewall is able to track traffic other than TCP. With stateful packet filtering, if someone were to generate fake packets in an attempt to circumvent our established connection filter, the process has just gotten a lot more difficult.

Applying stateful packet filtering to our current rule set allows us to eliminate the rule used to watch for established connections. To provide an example of how this occurs in our current rule set, let us consider the example in which a host on the internal network initiates a Telnet session to an Internet host using DNS to resolve the host name.

Our host is configured to forward requests to the internal DNS server using our split DNS configuration. This internal DNS server is then configured to forward requests to the DMZ DNS server, which then forwards the request upstream to either another DNS server run by an ISP or to one of the root DNS servers. With normal packet filtering, we would have to specifically allow UDP DNS responses back into our network segments, because we could not rely on any connection information in the packet header to alert us that this is a response to a recent request. Configuring the router as a stateful firewall, we can simply ask the router to watch for any DNS request from the inside to the DMZ and create a dynamic rule in the rule set that temporarily allows responses from the DMZ DNS server to the inside DNS server.

To ensure that the dynamic access rule is as secure as possible, the stateful filter will remember the IP address and source and destination UDP ports seen in the packet traveling from the inside to the DMZ. Only packets from the DMZ to the inside that match the IP addresses and ports will be allowed through the stateful firewall. The same process is used when the DMZ DNS server makes a request from the upstream DNS server. Only UDP packets that match the IP addresses and the UDP ports used to send traffic outbound will be allowed back into the network.

Depending on the vendor, this process may be hidden from view, but a stateful packet filter essentially has the ability to create temporary, very specific rules. One rule is created for each packet flow initiated from the inside heading out. To prevent rules from utilizing too many resources on the router/firewall, the stateful packet filter is configured to remove these rules when a TCP session is torn down. If UDP, ICMP, or other protocols are being evaluated, then the stateful session simply keeps track of the last time a packet was passed that matched a given rule. After a reasonable time period, say 60 seconds, if no further packets are observed, the rule will be automatically removed from the firewall rule set.

After configuring our firewall to accept stateful filtering, our rule set then becomes:

- Watch for new Telnet and ICMP sessions outbound from the LAN. Record the source and destination IP address, protocol, and any ports that are being used, and create a rule allowing return traffic back into the network.
- Watch for HTTP proxy traffic from the LAN to the DMZ and create a dynamic rule to allow return traffic from the HTTP proxy server to the DMZ.
- Watch for IP traffic sourced from the DMZ. Record the source and destination IP address, protocol, and any ports that are being used to create a rule allowing return traffic back into the network.
- Deny any packet from the "outside" with a source that matches our "inside" network.
- Deny any packet from the "outside" with a source IP address in the private range of 10.0.0.0/8.

- Deny any packet from the "outside" with a source IP address in the private range of 172.16.0.0/12.
- Deny any packet from the "outside" with a source IP address in the private range of 192.168.0.0/16.
- Deny any packet from the "outside" with a source IP address of 0.0.0.0/32 (an all 0s source address).
- Deny any packet from the "outside" with a source IP address of 255.255.255.255 (an all 1s broadcast address).
- Allow DNS, UDP destination port 53, from "outside" to "DMZ" 200.1.1.10. Outside to inside tells us that traffic from the Internet is allowed into the server.
- Allow SMTP, TCP destination port 25, from "outside" to "DMZ" 200.1.1.20. The rule allows the receipt of e-mail from our mail server.
- Allow SMTP, TCP destination port 25, to "outside" from "DMZ" 200.1.1.20. This allows the sending of e-mail from our mail server.
- Allow POP3, TCP destination port 110, from "outside" to "DMZ" 200.1.1.30. This rule allows remote user clients to check their e-mail on our POP3 server.
- Allow HTTP, TCP destination port 80, from "outside" to "DMZ" 200.1.1.40. Allows Internet hosts to access our Web server.
- Allow HTTP traffic from the "inside" network to "DMZ" 200.1.1.50, TCP destination ports 8080 (our proxy server port number). Allow clients from the LAN to connect to the proxy.
- Allow HTTP traffic from the proxy on "DMZ" 200.1.1.50, to access the Internet. Because Web sites can theoretically be run on any number of ports, we will only restrict this traffic according to IP addresses instead of ports.
- Allow FTP, TCP destination port 21, from "outside" network to "DMZ" 200.1.1.60.

We see at this point a slight reduction in the amount of rules, most notably in the rules surrounding DNS and ICMP access in and out of the network. For connectionless protocols such as UDP and ICMP, stateful firewalling is a great convenience. If we were to complicate our rule set by adding multimedia and voice applications, we would be especially grateful for the services provided by stateful firewalling.

Because we host servers on our DMZ, stateful firewalling did not reduce the number of TCP rules a great deal beyond what connection tracking did by looking at SYN bits. We have, however, increased the security of our network, as another audit would show.

Stateful firewalling used to be the realm of the most expensive and advanced firewall platforms; but like most things in computing, the technology has trickled down quite a bit. Today, even personal firewalls and free operating systems such as Linux can be configured with stateful packet filtering and is enabled on most routers with or those without a "firewall feature set." In short, there is really no reason to consider using a regular packet filter when these tools are available to you.

8.6 Application Layer Filtering

At this point in our configuration, our stateful filtering firewall is fairly robust and may at this point meet the requirements of our security policy. As previously noted in this chapter, however, stateful packet filters still suffer from some significant weaknesses compared to the number of threats they face in normal operation. Each one of these threats is able to take advantage of the fact that a stateful packet filter still only makes filtering decisions upon the information in the network or transport layer headers. What we need to fully protect our information is something that is able to look deeper into the packet and make a determination as to the legitimacy of the packet itself. This, of course, is the domain of the application layer firewall.

Configuring a router to operate as an application layer firewall used to be unheard of. To some extent that is still true, in that the most complex application layer filtering is still the province of dedicated hardware and software, but a surprising amount of functionality can be found on most modern routers, functionality that is advanced enough to keep up with the emerging virus, worm, and Trojan threats.

Unlike the transition from a packet filter to a stateful packet filter, adding application layer filtering is not going to significantly change our existing packet filters. Instead, application layer filtering is going to complement our stateful packet filtering.

An example of the usefulness of an application layer filter would be in the detection of a Nimda, Code Red, or Klez infection. A router, sitting at the edge of the network, would be a logical place to drop HTTP or SMTP headers with information specific to the virus, preventing the attacks from reaching your network altogether. Of course, this may be a poor example as these two worms can only successfully attack unpatched systems and everyone's systems have been patched long ago. Have they not?

8.7 Specific Protocol Considerations

Some protocols, for one reason or another, are particularly difficult to operate with firewalls. This section examines the most common problem protocols and explains how to work around these problems. Where appropriate, configuration tips are offered. You will want to understand that some firewall vendors fix these problems by offering preconfigured sets of rules that implement the solutions that we describe below.

8.7.1   File Transfer Protocol (FTP)

One of the most common problematic protocols to firewall is FTP (File Transfer Protocol). The normal operation of FTP does not lend itself to firewalls protecting remote clients due to its manner of operation.

Historically, FTP client/server relationships operated in what was known as *normal mode*. The method of operation is as follows. A remote client sends a connection request to the FTP server on a remote network on TCP port 21; this is also known as the control connection. With this connection, you can browse directories and see the contents of files. When you attempt to download something, however, the remote FTP server will then send your client computer a packet that says the server is about to send you data on a random high-order port with a source port of 20. That is, the client makes the first connection and the server makes the *second* connection *back* to the client. This separate connection is called the data connection because it is the one that actually transfers the files you are requesting.

The problem is the configuration of the firewall that is protecting the client PC. It is easy to configure the firewall to allow outbound TCP port 21 connections. The problem is that the data connection is initiated by the remote server and instructs the client to listen on a random port. From the point of view of the local PC firewall, this is unacceptable. The only way to allow the transfer of data is to accept inbound connections on all TCP ports higher than 1024 (see Exhibit 9).

Before revealing the solutions available, it is worthwhile to note that this two-connection behavior is one of the reasons that FTP scales so well. Through the use of multiple sessions, FTP using normal mode can be configured to have a single FTP server control any number of other FTP servers that contain the actual data to be transferred. It is a shame that this elegance interferes with our desire for information security on the client side.

The primary way to overcome this problem is through the use of passive-mode FTP. This is a configuration option that simply tells the server to wait until the client initiates the data connection rather than having the

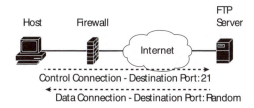

Exhibit 9. Normal Mode FTP Operation

server perform this function. This simple concept has profound implications for our client-side firewall.

As in the previous example, the client PC connects to an FTP server through port 21. Using the control connection, the user can log in and browse directory contents. When the time to download data is at hand, in passive mode, the client then asks the server what ports will be used for the connection and initiates the outbound connection. From the point of view of the firewall, these outbound connections are preferable because the ports used for incoming traffic can now be correlated with outbound client connections.

All commercial FTP servers offer the option to operate in both normal mode and passive mode concurrently. Thus, the decision to use passive mode is a client-side request. Fortunately, most client programs, including Web browsers that support FTP allow themselves to be configured for passive-mode FTP.

Understanding the operation of these two modes of FTP is also helpful in troubleshooting a firewall installation. If you are allowed to browse FTP directories but not download files, this is typically an indication of conflicts between the client-side firewall wall and normal/passive settings on client software.

8.8 Additional Router Firewall Features

Whether used as a stand-alone firewall or in combination with dedicated hardware, a router is capable of providing security features beyond that of simple traffic filtering. This section discusses some of the other security features that can be included on routers to protect both your perimeter and the Internet as a whole.

8.8.1 Limiting Denial-of-Service Attacks

When an attacker is frustrated with your overall network security and has no other recourse, a denial-of-service (DoS) attack will be his or her avenue of attack. While DoS attacks generally do not damage your information, they certainly do affect the availability of information to authorized parties. DoS attacks can take a number of forms, but are generally sorted into two categories:

1. *Bandwidth-based attacks.* These attacks simply try to send more packets over your network than your network can handle. Because the access link is generally the lowest-speed link in your network, this is where the attack effects are felt. The goal is to send enough traffic into your network over this link so that the routers start discarding packets that build up in the interface service queues. When the upstream router begins discarding packets, legitimate

traffic is also discarded. Likewise, packets that do make it to the remote side of the network will generally create an error condition of some sort, requiring return traffic to be sent back over the link, and congesting your outbound access-router queues as well.

2. *Operating system attacks.* Instead of flooding your network with so many packets that the network collapses, a better approach is to send a single packet that simply crashes or restarts your server. This is just as effective in rendering the target unavailable as a bandwidth-based attack. Common examples of this attack include the historic PING of Death. Many programmers built their networking stacks to accept the normally encountered packets. By sending purposefully malformed packets, these systems would collapse.

There are a two common ways to reduce the risk of a DoS attack. We will see that neither is foolproof, yet each contributes to the overall defense in depth to assure the availability of our network resources.

The most common way of dealing with these attacks is to configure bandwidth throttling on a router. Let us assume that your HTTP server is the subject of a bandwidth-based DoS attack from a single source. The easiest solution is to contact your ISP and have it configure an access-list preventing traffic from that source from being forwarded on to your network. The most difficult part of this solution is actually being able to contact the correct person at the ISP who can sit down and configure the access-list in a reasonable timeframe. The actual creation of the list is trivial.

The problem, however, becomes more complicated when the attacker launches an attack from multiple sources or modifies the source address of the attack point to make it look like entire networks of random sources are attacking your network. How do you know which requests from the Internet are parts of the DoS and which requests are from legitimate users? There is no easy way to create a blanket access-list covering all possible sources of attacks without affecting legitimate users of the networked resources. The two techniques discussed below are an attempt to respond to DoS attacks while still providing the maximum availability for legitimate users or other networked services.

8.8.1.1 Committed Access Rate. Bandwidth-based attacks are successful when the attacker has more bandwidth available than you do. Difficult to accomplish when the majority of Internet access was dial-up links, these attacks are made much easier due to distributed denial-of-service (DoS) clients that enlist thousands of cable, DSL, and dial-up connections to attack sites with high-bandwidth access-links. Instead of needing a government or university link to attack another organization using a bandwidth-based DoS attack, millions of residential users can unwittingly participate to saturate even the highest bandwidth links. A common method of protecting your network against such attacks is a technology that is commonly applied to quality-of-service issues. This technology is known as committed access rate (CAR). Committed access rate attempts to slow down certain types of traffic to a given bandwidth by selectively processing traffic. Rate limits can be "hard" or "soft." Hard limits will discard certain types of traffic over a given threshold. Soft limits will allow rate limited traffic to burst above its CAR, thus allowing more flexibility in controlling competing traffic types. When applied to reducing the impact of DoS attacks, we are interested in the hard limits imposed by CAR.

To explain the operation of CAR, let us use an example. A company has an HTTP server, an SMTP/POP server, and a DNS server hosted at its site via a T-1 connection at 1.544 Mbps. The HTTP server becomes the target of a DoS attack. In response to the attack, the network administrator of the company asks its upstream ISP to configure CAR for HTTP traffic at 512 Kbps. Noticing the attack in progress and agreeing, the ISP makes the requested configuration and suddenly any HTTP traffic over 512 Kbps destined for the customer HTTP server is dropped. The result for the customer is that DNS and SMTP traffic can still pass from the ISP to the customer over the T-1. The customer still suffers from an HTTP DoS but the other network applications that they rely upon are still available for legitimate use.

This solution is predicated on an important assumption. You must have an ISP that is willing to work with you in this manner. It has been difficult to either convince ISPs to configure this or find someone qualified to do so. This is changing as the adoption of the process is gaining recognition and support in the networking community. CAR is commonly configured as part of a network quality-of-service plan and when CAR is used to mitigate DoS attacks; it is generally applied in a temporary manner. This means that users interested in security will not always have CAR configured, while those that take quality-of-service seriously generally will.

While you are welcome to configure your own CAR on your access router for traffic flowing from the ISP, the best effect of this technique is for the ISP to police traffic heading to your network. To understand this, we must take a slight detour into the realm of quality-of-service (QoS).

Most QoS, no matter the name, is simply the attempt to manage an output queue on a device. You have two packets in a queue for the same interface. How do you determine which one goes first? The device must be configured with some way of marking the packets just as it would for an access list that filters traffic for our routers. Congestion and thus a denial-of-service is simply more traffic entering an outbound queue than the router can process.

Note the emphasis on the outbound queue. Many people will incorrectly note that my "link is congested." This is not entirely accurate. A "link" can never be congested. A T-1 line will always process 1.54 million bits per second. It never tries to cram 1.6 million bits per second onto the link. The congestion is actually occurring on the interface that sends information over that link. The router interface may have 1.6 million bits to process in a given second, but the T-1 will only support 1.544 million bits in that same timeframe. Thus, the router is forced to store the extra information in a queue, hoping that the next time increment will provide space for the extra bits; but if information is entering the router faster than 1.54 Mbps, eventually the queue will fill up and the router has no choice but to drop the excess traffic. This is the principle of a DoS attack.

Based on this information, we can see that configuring CAR at your router to affect traffic it receives from the ISP has limited effect. The damage has already been done as the high-bandwidth backbone links of the ISP are suddenly throttled into the 1.54 Mbps of your T-1. The policing of the output queues that CAR allows needs to be configured where the congestion is.

8.8.1.2 TCP Interception. While the PING of Death and other attacks based on operating system flaws are characterized by programming that does not take into account all possible invalid responses, some attacks take advantage of the normal operation of a protocol. The best example of this is the TCP SYN attack. Knowing that a TCP session is initiated with a three-way handshake, an attacker making a TCP SYN attack simply sends a connection request to a server. The server dutifully sends the second SYN ACK packet as an acknowledgement of the request. At this point, the connection is known as "half-open," in that the server is keeping the connection information in its memory, waiting for the third and final packet from the client to fully establish the TCP session. The client, of course, never sends the last packet, but instead sends a barrage of additional TCP connection requests to the same server. Within a short period of time, the available memory on the TCP server is used up with half-open connections and legitimate connection requests have to be refused. The problem is solved because the TCP server is programmed to wait a period of seconds for TCP requests to finish. In the early days of the Internet, it would not be uncommon for a packet to be delayed up to 120 seconds before reaching its final destination. Thus, TCP stacks were configured to wait out this period in hopes that the final packet would eventually show up.

The first way of reducing the effect of one of these attacks is to employ load-balancing hardware to distribute the load from a single server to multiple servers. This countermeasure is effective but expensive and simply raises the stakes. The hope is that your network will have more memory available for connections than the attack will have to make connection requests. The danger with this reasoning is that the war of resources simply escalates. As with distributed bandwidth-based DoS attacks, the potential is there to employ thousands of hosts making TCP SYN attacks, forcing you to respond with more servers and more load balancing.

The effects of this type of attack can be mitigated with the help of a router or firewall through the use of a TCP intercept configuration. This is a simple configuration that configures the router to act as a proxy for all incoming TCP requests to the servers it protects. When the router detects a new connection attempt to an internal server, it responds to the request as if it were the server. Internal servers can be defined individually, allowing a single router to protect multiple servers or only those that are most likely to be subject to an attack such as an HTTP server. If the request is legitimate and the final packet in the connection request is received, then the router completes the connection request to the TCP server on behalf of the remote client. If the connection is an attempted TCP SYN attack, then the router waits a much shorter timeout period than the server and discards the connection information, saving the server from having to spend its resources maintaining illegitimate connection requests.

When a full-scale TCP SYN attack is launched on a site, with thousands of TCP requests per second, the router will then enter an aggressive mode where TCP connections are discarded after just a few seconds if the connection is not finalized by the remote client, thus further reducing the impact of TCP SYN attacks on the local TCP server. When traffic has returned to more normal levels (that you define), the aggressive mode behavior will end and TCP interception will operate as normal.

You have no doubt surmised that the TCP intercept feature of routers is not bullet-proof protection against TCP SYN attacks. Eventually, enough requests will overrun the available bandwidth and turn the SYN attack into a bandwidth-based DoS. Nevertheless, as a countermeasure to increase the security of your network, it is difficult to argue against a feature that is built into most routers for sites that have average hosting needs. For very high volume sites, load balancing hardware, redundant servers, and high-bandwidth connections will remain the primary protection mechanism for the near future.

8.8.2 Reverse Path Forwarding

This section addresses good citizenship. The Internet would be much more secure for the rest of us if every network administrator would take the time to properly implement good information security practices. The fact that network security has recently gained a lot of momentum and consideration by vendors, management, and government is a good sign that good information security is being taken more seriously. *Reverse path*

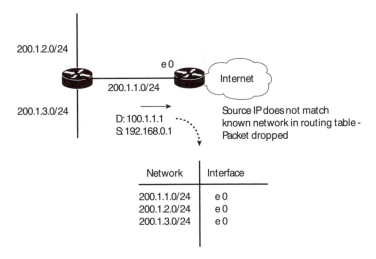

Exhibit 10. Source Routing Operation

forwarding (RPF) is a process that attempts to eliminate spoofed traffic from originating from your network.

Assume that your Internal LAN network uses the network block 200.1.1.0/28. If this were the case, it would be a simple matter to create an access-list on your access router that only allowed traffic from this network block to exit your router to the Internet. It becomes more complicated, however, when you have 15 network blocks that you are responsible for over multiple far-flung subnets. If you use an access-list, the list must be updated to reflect any changes in the network topology; otherwise, legitimate traffic may be blocked from leaving the network.

A much simpler and robust solution would be to examine the routers' routing table. Referring back to our 15 hypothetical network blocks, if the source network of a packet entering the LAN interface of a router is not listed in the routing table as being located on the same LAN interface, the router will assume that the packet has been spoofed and drop the packet.

We see in Exhibit 10 that our access router has a routing table showing three networks on the LAN side of the router. When a packet from a host enters the LAN interface of the access router, it is checked against the routing table. If the source of the packet does not match what interface it should be received upon from the point of view of the router, the packet will be dropped. RPF is superior to access lists in preventing spoofed traffic from leaving the LAN for two reasons. First, as noted above, it is easier to configure and maintain. Instead of relying on the network administrator to get the configuration of the access-list correct,[6] we let the routing protocols already in use on the router maintain the proper network filtering.

The second primary advantage is that the RPF function performs better than access-lists. This is because RPF uses a router cache table, instead of an access-list, to match packets. Explaining this requires just a little bit of knowledge of how routers forward information. It used to be that a router would consult a routing table for each packet it forwarded. This software process was inherently slow from a processing point of view. To enable routers to forward packets at astounding rates, the forwarding logic has been moved to the hardware on the router interfaces. Routers now create a forwarding table based on the routing table, with each interface knowing only what networks are reachable through it. RPF takes advantage of this information that already exists in the cache and, because it is implemented in the hardware itself, is able to operate much more quickly.

Despite the advantages, RPF is not ideal for all situations. Some older routers, for example, do not have the ability to create express forwarding tables on the interface. These routers then would be unable to support the RPF function.

Furthermore, RPF is not suitable for routers that are in the core of a network. The reason for this is that it is not uncommon for IP packets to take one route to a destination and another route on the return path. With complex network topologies, RPF may end up incorrectly discarding packets. Because RPF only examines the local forwarding tables, this will result in information that is inconsistent with the packets that the router is receiving and cause the router to incorrectly drop packets. Thus, RPF is best configured only on access-links for traffic leaving the LAN because the traffic flows are generally tightly constrained on these routers.

8.8.3 Null Interface Routing

As an additional courtesy to the Internet as a whole, packets that clearly have invalid destinations should be dropped. The use of a null interface instead of access-lists is a minor trick that is sometimes useful when filtering traffic. The idea is to route invalid packet destinations to the null interface.

A null interface is simply a virtual trash bin on a router. Although the router treats a null interface as a normal interface, it does not really exist and any packets to be forwarded over that interface are discarded. If you were to enter this command on a router — "Forward all packets destined for the 10.0.0.0/8, 172.16.0.0/12, and 192.168.0.0/16 networks to the null interface." — then these packets would effectively be discarded. The addresses do not need to be destined to private networks but can be used for any network destination that you wish to block.

Although this accomplishes the same thing as an access-list, the process is much more efficient for a router because the router does not need to take

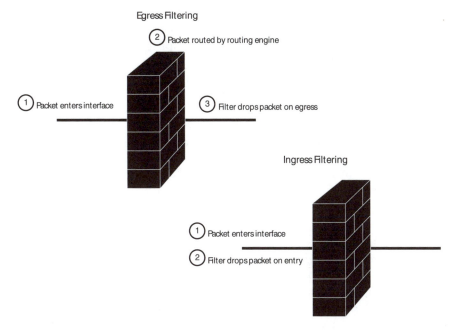

Egress Filtering

(2) Packet routed by routing engine

(1) Packet enters interface

(3) Filter drops packet on egress

Ingress Filtering

(1) Packet enters interface

(2) Filter drops packet on entry

Exhibit 11. Where to Place Firewall Filters?

the time to consult the access-filter, but instead follows its normal, high-speed routing procedures.

8.8.4 Source Routing

A technique sometimes used in conjunction with routing to the null interface is the use of source routing. Most routing decisions are based on the destination of a packet only. As the name implies, source routing also allows you to create custom forwarding tables based on the source of a packet. Instead of forwarding packets with a destination IP address of a private network as we did above, we could also create forwarding tables that route all packets with sources of the private address space (or any other network block you wish to discard) to the null interface.

Once created, access-lists need to be applied to an interface for them to be effective (see Exhibit 11). Packets can be checked relative to the interface itself. That means that a packet can be checked as it *enters* an interface or a packet can be checked as it *exits* an interface. Note that this is per interface and not per firewall. Unless there is a specific need otherwise, packets should generally be checked as they *enter* an interface. To understand why this is, refer to Exhibit 11. In the first example (egress filtering), the firewall device accepts the packet, routes it by determining which interface the packet should be forwarded out of, and then filters it as it exits the interface. Assume that the rule that matches the packet as it is filtered causes it to be dropped. We have wasted queue and processor resources to drop a packet. In the second example (ingress filtering), we filter the same packet as it enters the interface of the firewall. Because our matching rule causes us to drop the packet, the packet is discarded without utilizing resources on the outbound interface or the processor in routing the packet. There may be exceptions to this rule but they are generally minor and are to meet the requirements of specific implementations. For example, if a firewall has more than two interfaces such as a DMZ or another LAN or WAN segment, then outbound rules on an interface may be required to ensure secure operation. In general, the most efficient operation is to filter and drop packets as they enter a firewall interface as much as possible.

8.9   Writing and Applying Filters

In many vendor firewall implementations, the question of which interface to apply access-lists to is taken care of for the network administrator by the firewall software itself. Thus, the question of whether to filter traffic as it enters or leaves the network interface is taken care of transparently. In this section, we examine the logic of access-list placement and apply it to manual firewall configuration and at the same time shed some light on the operation of all firewall products.

Thus far we have discussed quite a bit about packet filters and stateful packet filters, but we have not discussed how to write them or where to apply them. How to write them is generally well documented on the vendor's Web site or in the documentation that has been included with the product. Although the syntax from product to product will vary, the effect and operators of the filtering statements have several characteristics in common no matter what the product.

8.9.1   There Is Some Method of Ordering the Rules

This may be as simple as having rule numbers or creating a list that is read from top to bottom. The important thing to remember is that all firewalls process rules in order.

8.9.2   There Is a Way of Defining the Source and Destination of the Packet

This is the most common filtering option and allows the network administrator to define what to apply the rules to. Sometimes, the network definition can be very large, as in "all IP networks;" narrower in scope, "My LAN only;" or very specific, "The HTTP server only."

Source and destination addresses are also relevant to the directionality of rules. Thus, you can apply different rules to packets from the "inside" destined to the "outside" than packets from the "outside" destined to the "inside." Each source and destination pair may also have different operations performed in each rule. So you may have multiple lines defining how packets from the "outside" to the "inside" are to be filtered. Each line has a different action to check or perform on the packets.

8.9.3 *There Is a Way of Defining the Protocol to Be Checked*

Firewalls can make filtering decisions based on virtually any field in the network and transport layer headers. One of the very important characteristics of a packet and a protocol is which transport layer protocol is being used. Typically, values here will include IP, UDP, TCP, and ICMP. TCP, UDP, and ICMP, however, are not the only protocols that have their own IP protocol value. Other protocols that may be commonly checked are some routing protocols and IPSec protocols.

Unlike IP addresses or ports, which may have a different source or destination values in normal operation, there is generally only a single protocol in use per session.

8.9.4 *There Is a Way of Defining Which Port to Check For*

If TCP or UDP is checked by the filter list, we must also define which port to check for, as ports are the way that application layer processes are identified in an IP packet. Generally, only the well-known ports are checked for as part of the destination of a packet. This is because when a client creates a connection to a remote host, the source port of the packet sent from the client to a remote host is a random port above 1024. Because port selection is essentially random, it is difficult to filter or identify which ports a client will pick.

8.9.5 *Other Protocol Options May Be Present*

Most firewalls will also have syntax to filter based upon other network or transport layer information. For example, there is generally a syntax that will allow the firewall to check for fragmented packets. Another common option is the option bits of a TCP session.

8.9.6 *What to Do with the Packet Is Part of the Configuration*

It is presumed that you are creating a firewall rule because you either want to permit the traffic, drop (deny) it, or forward it to some other location. It then stands to reason that there must be some way to define what to do with the packet in the rule. Generally, access-lists start with a rule that defines what traffic to always drop, such as clearly invalid traffic, then have a bunch of permit statements that define what traffic to allow through, then everything else is denied by the default "deny all" that is assumed at the bottom of every access-list.

8.9.7 An Option to Log Rule Matches Is Included on a Rule-by-Rule Basis

After finally creating a rule, you will then have the option to log matches to the rule. This is not the same as logging the contents of the packet; this is simply a way to tally the rules that are being matched the most. This can serve as a warning system if many deny packets are being matched or assist in the tuning of the firewall by placing the most often matched rules at the top of the list.

Based on these common features in all firewall rule configurations, we can now analyze a rule set enforcing the same policy from each vendor and describe the syntax used to implement the policy.

Below there are three rule sets for the same rule. Each of these pairs of rules allows clients on the internal network of 192.168.1.0/24 to access HTTP and HTTPS servers on the Internet. The first example is from the IPchains firewall software that is included by default on most Linux distributions. The second example is the same rule set created using a Cisco access-list and then applied to an interface. The third set is the same rule set included from a Check Point firewall. Relevant details from each rule set will be included following the example.

Linux IPchains example.

```
ipchains -A output -p tcp -s 192.168.1.0/24 1024:65535
 — destination-port 80 -j ACCEPT

ipchains -A output -p tcp -s 192.168.1.0/24 1024:65535
 — destination-port 443 -j ACCEPT
```

Rules for IPchains are added one at a time to a rule set through the command line. The program used to do this is unsurprisingly called "ipchains;" thus, each rule above begins with a call to the ipchains program. The "-A" adds the rule to the rule set named "output." If you wish to delete or insert rules, a different argument would be included at this point. Once this framework is established, the rule set seems pretty straightforward; the protocol (-p) to examine is TCP and the source of the packet (-s) is matched at anything from the 192.168.1.0/24 network with a source port in the unprivileged range of 1024 through 65535. As the syntax of the statement indicates, another element of the TCP header is checked, and that is the destination port of the packet. It must match either the well-known HTTP server port of 80 or the well-known HTTPS server port of 443. While there is nothing prohibiting a Web site from running on port 81 or 82, the rules we are examining now would not allow traffic from our site to connect to them. Finally, the statement ends with the "-j" argument that informs us of which action the firewall is to accept when a packet matches a rule. In this case, the rule is clearly marked as accepting the packet. Other common options may be to deny the packet, redirect it, or address translate the packet, a term the Linux community describes as "masquerading" the packet.

Defining the source port for these rules is optional, but does reflect a long-held tradition that client processes, such as a request from a Web browser should only have source ports in the "unprivileged range," so called from the other long-standing tradition of server processes such as HTTP, SMTP, FTP, and others listening on ports lower than 1024. With the number of services available on the Internet today, the rule of server ports always being less than 1024 has long been abandoned, but clients still generally make requests with the higher order ports. In the Cisco example below, the source ports can also be defined but generally are not.

The example above would be what was entered from the command prompt to include these rules in a live server. The problem, of course, would be that if the server were power cycled, the rules would have to be reentered. In almost all instances, our rule set is going to be much more complicated than that above and thus the reentering of the rules from the command line is clearly an unacceptable option. In response, all Linux firewall operators instead create scripts that are run when the server is restarted that automatically re-add the firewalling rules each time the server is restarted.

The next list to examine is the same rule set as implemented on a Cisco router:

```
access-list extended INPUT-LAN

permit tcp 192.168.1.0 0.0.0.255 any eq 80

permit tcp 192.168.1.0 0.0.0.255 any eq 443

interface eth0

description LAN side interface

access-group INPUT-LAN in
```

Just as in the IPchains example, we create a list that will serve as the reference point for our rules. In this case, our first statement creates an extended access-list named "INPUT-LAN" to remind us that we are going to place this list on our LAN interface to filter traffic as it enters the interface from the LAN. The list could be called anything we wish, but descriptive names are much more helpful in avoiding configuration errors on the part of memory-challenged humans.

Cisco routers support many types of access-lists for many types of protocols. In fact, if a layer 2 or layer 3 protocol can be sent across a Cisco router, there is most likely an access-list of some sort that can be configured for it. For IP protocols, the most common access-list types are standard or extended protocols. Of the two, the extended access-list is the most common. Standard access-lists only let you match IP packets according to the source of the packet. These are useful when configuring routing tables, but of only limited use for network security. Extended access-lists, on the other hand, allow you to match almost any IP or transport layer protocol and header information you would reasonably want to. This, of course, explains their usefulness in the configuration of filter lists.

The second line of the access-list defines that it will permit TCP traffic with a source of the 192.168.1.0/24 network to any destination address with a destination port of 80. This is the only section where those new to the Cisco way of thinking get confused. How does "192.168.1.0 0.0.0.255" relate to 192.168.1.0/24? In a Cisco extended access-list, the source and destination addresses must always be listed. Normally, when describing an address to be relevant, we must also include the subnet mask that defines the actual network. This is not the case in the Cisco operating system. Instead, we will define what is known as an "inverse mask," which is just the opposite of a subnet mask when written in decimal notation. So if a/24 subnet in decimal notation is known as 255.255.255.0, we will just turn all the 1s in that subnet mask to 0s and all the 0s to 1s and we will be left with the inverse mask of 0.0.0.255.

The third line applies the same rules, but this time to destination ports of 443, the HTTPS well-known port.

To understand the logic of an inverse mask, we must remember how a host uses a subnet mask. Normally, the 1s of a subnet mask are used by a host to do a logical "AND" to reveal what the network portion of an IP address is. This is used to determine if the destination of the packet is on a local or remote network from the perspective of the sending host. The same process is used in a Cisco access list, but this time we are interested in the hosts, not the networks. So to check the hosts for a particular network, we must place the 1s of the inverse mask to match the location of the host bits in a network mask.

The example here is known as a "named access-list," so called because an access-list called "INPUT-LAN" has been created. This replaces and is much easier to work with than the traditional way of creating an access-list on Cisco devices — that is, using numbered access-lists.

A numbered access-list that reflects the above rules would read as:

```
access-list 101 permit tcp 192.168.1.0 0.0.0.255 any eq 80

access-list 101 permit tcp 192.168.1.0 0.0.0.255 any eq 443
```

Notice that the name has been removed, along with the identifier that the list is an "extended" access-list and replaced with the number 101. The list number 101 identifies the list as extended instead, as does any list between the numbers 100 and 199. After entering the number, the actual rules are included. While both named and numbered access-lists are equivalent in operation from the point of view of router software, it is generally easier to work with named access-lists.

Consider the following scenario: you have a router with 16 interfaces, each of which requires different rules applicable to the downstream networks. If you have an inbound and outbound list for each interface, you will have at least 32 access-lists to keep track of. While it can be done, it generally requires quite a bit of knowledge about the network environment or extensive note-keeping. You are looking at interface 0/1/4 and you see that access-list 186 has been applied to it. You scroll through the configuration, past the first 86 access-list entries and finally get to 186. What was it you were looking for again? It is so much easier to be able to scan through a router configuration and see a descriptive name applied to an interface or the list itself. In very large installations, it is also worthwhile noting that named access-lists are not limited to 100 per router as are numbered extended access-lists.

Cisco access-list rules are applied during normal router configuration and are automatically applied when the router restarts. Technically speaking, the actual application of the rules is much the same as the Linux IPchains (The Cisco IOS and Linux share the same UNIX roots), but the process is hidden from the user. From the point of view of the network administrator, the rules are written, applied to the appropriate network interface, and then automatically applied each time the router is restarted.

The screenshot in Exhibit 12 is a very simple configuration for the Check Point firewall that was created using the Check Point policy editor and matches the rules we have created above for the Linux and Cisco operating systems. The policy editor is the Check Point GUI that allows users to easily create rules and apply them to the firewall application. The major difference

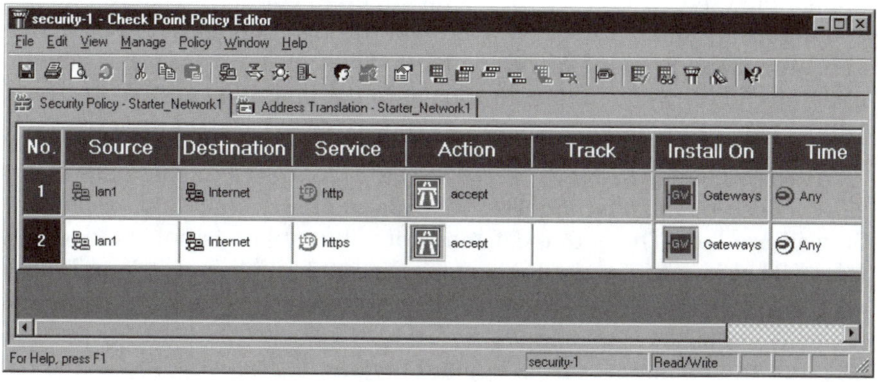

Exhibit 12. Check Point Policy Editor

between the Check Point and the other examples we have seen is that Check Point allows users to create objects such as "lan1," "Internet," and "http" that describe the elements that we are configuring. Thus, in our example, "lan1" has been configured to represent the IP address range 192.168.0.0/24 while "http" has been configured to represent the TCP port 80. Once these objects have been defined, it is a straightforward matter to create rules using these objects.

One of the primary advantages of using Check Point is that a great number of objects are predefined for the advantage of users. Check Point can also determine the likely network objects, such as the address range of the LAN network. While this example does not show it, these objects are particularly handy for complicated protocol groups such as those that are used to firewall multimedia and real-time protocols.

For instructional purposes, Check Point further reinforces the basic concepts of firewall operation. The "from" and "to" networks are defined, along with the protocol service. From here a decision must be made to accept or drop the packet and options are provided to log it.

In Exhibit 12, note that there is also an "Install On" option. This is another particularly useful feature of Check Point (although this functionality is found on many firewall products). The firewall administrator can define and manage multiple rule sets for distributed firewalls and update them from a single location. While the Check Point, Linux IPTables, and Cisco methods of packet filtering are very similar between vendors, it is the additional features that ease configuration and management that make dedicated firewall products, like Check Point and others, the more popular option for large deployments.

8.10 Maintaining Firewalls

Like any network device, firewalls require regular maintenance to remain effective. A firewall that is an effective countermeasure one day could become an attack vector overnight through the discovery of vulnerabilities in the firewall software itself. Thus, it is critical that regular updates and critical updates be applied to the operating system in a regular manner.

When evaluating firewalls, it is a good idea to examine some of the security-focused mailing list archives for vulnerabilities that may exist in the firewall product. The actual existence of vulnerability is not the deciding factor. That is, you are not looking for the total number of vulnerabilities exclusively (although it should be an important factor); just as important is the attitude that the vendor takes in working with the security community and the release of operating system patches to address discovered vulnerabilities.

The relationship between those interested in security and those that sell security in their products is an interesting one. The issue of disclosure is the point of the most contention. We can illustrate this with a short example.

Assume that the fictitious firewall vendor "Strong Security" creates and markets the product "StrongWall" as a firewall product. Being a drop-in solution with support for VPNs, various authentication schemes, good logging, friendly user interface, and, best of all, a very affordable price, the StrongWall product becomes very popular. With this popularity comes the attention of the security researchers, the "white hats," and the security threats, the "black hats." The black hats, knowing that a large number of their targets may be running the StrongWall product, begin looking for weaknesses in the product themselves. This may even mean purchasing or stealing a few copies of StrongWall so that they can put it through its paces in a lab setting without attracting much attention. At the same time, the white hats are doing something very similar, but in this case the goal is to assure the world at large that the StrongWall product provides the security that it claims.

At some point, the white hats discover vulnerabilities in the StrongWall product. This is not unusual. Virtually every software product (and even hardware) will fail if subjected to enough scrutiny. While there are some mistakes that experienced, security-minded programmers should never make, it is difficult to thoroughly test every conceivable combination of events that a product will see in a production environment and still price a competitive product within a target market. So compromises are made in the development and quality assurance portion of development, simply in acquiescence to business needs.

When the vulnerability is discovered, the question then becomes what to do with the information. Should it be released to the world at large to alert them to the vulnerability? If the black hat community has already discovered the same information, then a great number of StrongWall installations could be at risk and users of the product should know that they are vulnerable. On the other hand, if knowledge of the vulnerability is not at this point widely known, alerting the security community and users of the StrongWall product would also inform the black-hat community of the same vulnerability. In the time-frame between the public release of the knowledge and Strong Security's release of the patch, attackers could easily create and distribute exploit code, leaving the users of the StrongWall product in a difficult predicament.

The better solution, and the most commonly followed one, is to privately contact the firewall vendor and work with them in examining and resolving the vulnerability. In this case, the vendor reaction to this forewarning is what to pay attention to. Many vendors will work with researchers who discover legitimate security flaws and create a patch that will be released to the public at the same time the vulnerability is revealed. This provides the researchers with some acknowledgment of their contribution to the security community, allows the vendor to market its response to security vulnerabilities, and allows users of the StrongWall product to patch their systems and immediately address the threat the vulnerability presents.

The process breaks down when the firewall vendor, in this case Strong Security, refuses to work with the security researcher. It may be that Strong Security wants to protect its public image of secure firewall products and hopes to avoid drawing attention to itself. Strong Security may even go so far as to threaten the security researcher or any institution assisting the that security researcher in disseminating information about the vulnerability with legal action. Strong Security may also simply, and legitimately, feel that what the security researcher terms a vulnerability is simply not the case. For example, if a security researcher "discovered" that someone with a boot disk could override the security settings of the firewall if they were able to manually boot the server from the boot disk itself — well, that is a vulnerability, but it is a vulnerability that every product has and is not easily solved through software in the firewall application itself. In this case, Strong Security may simply decide that the vulnerability is either outside its area of control or that the discovered vulnerability simply does not warrant an update to the software.

In either case, the security researcher may feel that either Strong Security does not take their information seriously or is moving too slow on the information. In this situation, the information may be released to the rest of the security world along with the attending consequences. Strong Security would typically respond to customer concerns by then developing and releasing some sort of patch for the vulnerability if it is possible or issue a statement describing why the discovered flaw is not really a flaw at all.

Based on this fairy tale, we see that a vendor relationship with the security community is in many ways more important than the number of vulnerabilities that have been discovered in a given product. As a consumer of the product, you want to know that patches will be released in a timely manner when vulnerabilities have been discovered. You are also hopeful that when vulnerabilities are discovered, security researchers are confident that vendors will work with them to provide the fix at the same time the vulnerability is released so as to not leave you in the lurch and your network in a risky situation.

Another important issue in maintaining firewalls is the patching procedure supplied by the vendor and patching procedures supplied by any operating system that the firewall runs on. For example, the Check Point firewall is an application that can be run on several operating systems, including Microsoft Windows and UNIX platforms. When evaluating firewall platforms, you must also ensure that the people who will be responsible for the maintenance of the firewall are comfortable working on such a platform. It will do you no good if Check Point is easy to patch yet the system administrator is unsure how to install, secure, or patch the UNIX OS hosting the software. If this is the case, you may lean toward a firewall appliance, meaning that the firewall and OS are bundled as a single drop-in product.

Finally, when considering the maintenance and care of a firewall, there is the rule set and any application layer filters that must be maintained. Application layer filters are filters that may include virus scanning. Because new viruses are released all the time, it stands to reason that these application layer filters need constant updating. Examine your proposed vendor's track record in responding to new Internet threats. When a threat is released, are their configuration servers unavailable for downloading due to the huge demand for the update?

Changes to your rule set may occur from time to time. Ideally, these should only occur when the security policy as a whole is examined or new applications are required for your business and some thought has been devoted to understanding the impact of this new application on information security. Remember that the security policy is what drives the implementation rules on the firewall; the firewall configuration does *not* drive the security policy. There should never be an issue of making changes to the firewall because someone comes running to the desk of the network administrator demanding, begging, or bribing the firewall administrator to open a port for whatever reason.

That said, when changes do occur, how friendly is the firewall in supporting changes? I have worked with more than one customer who has never made changes to the firewall because the person who made the rule set had left the company and nobody was really sure which rule was doing what. As part of the documentation process that occurs with the implementation of the firewall, an annotated copy of the rules should be kept as a backup. This way, someone picking up firewall administration duties can easily pick up the logic of the current rule set and make changes, confident that he or she is not affecting any other parts of the security policy.

8.11 NAT, Firewalls, VPNs, and the DMZ

Network address translation (NAT), as previously discussed, is best defined as a supporting firewall technology. In this role, NAT is commonly found as part of a firewall product. The purpose of this section is to describe the integration with NAT and packet filtering. Depending on the firewall vendor, this section may be entirely of an informative nature. For some vendor's NAT implementations, the configuration decisions we are about to discuss are configured with a single checkbox during firewall

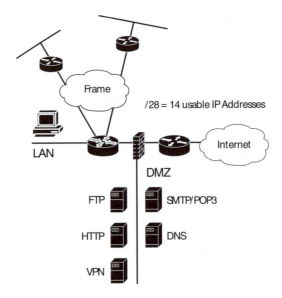

Exhibit 13. NAT and the Firewall: Setting the Scene

setup. Other times, NAT must be properly configured and this section describes the issues surrounding NAT.

The discussion in this section assumes an average mid-sized network. As illustrated in Exhibit 13, the network has a single Internet connection, two Frame Relay links to remote offices, and a single DMZ housed off the firewall. On the DMZ, the company has the most common services available, such as a POP3/SMTP relay, a public HTTP server, a public DNS, and a public FTP server. Although the subject has not yet been discussed in depth in this text, we are also going to include a VPN server on the DMZ. The contract signed with the service provider allocates a /28 address space for the 200 local hosts on the company LAN. A /28 network will provide a maximum of 14 usable IP addresses, assuming that the network is not further subnetted. Clearly, NAT is going to be an important technology to allow full Internet connectivity for the internal hosts and the DMZ hosts.The only tricky part about this network diagram is to remember to include the subnet between the access router and the firewall during the NAT design. This segment is an Ethernet segment but will only include two devices on it.[7] Nevertheless, it requires a full subnet for proper routing. Many are confused as to whether the addresses for this subnet need to be private or public. The answer, of course, depends on how you configure your NAT. We will find, however, that it permissible to have the DMZ be a public network while still keeping this intermediate subnet in the private range.

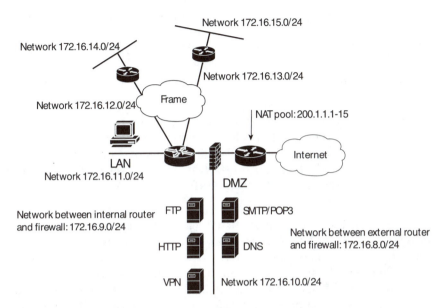

Exhibit 14. Using NAT on the Screening Router

Based on this topology, there is more than one way to configure NAT to effectively utilize the available address space. The first is to configure the access router with NAT for the entire /28 address space and be done with it. This would allow you to configure the entire network using a private address space. This means that the DMZ would be configured with private addresses, the subnet between the firewall and the router would be in the private address space, and the LAN would be a subnet from the private address space. Access to the each of these networks would be through NAT performed on the router itself. Logically speaking, the network would look like that in Exhibit 14.

For sake of discussion, let us assume that we are using the 172.16.0.0/12 range as the private address range and 200.1.1.0/28 as the public range. This provides a usable address space of 200.1.1.1 through 200.1.1.15 for NAT translations on the access router.

To allow the DMZ services to be reachable from the outside world, you would have to perform static mapping on the access router to map a public IP address to the private address of the device on the DMZ. Thus, the DMZ POP/SMTP relay might have a private address of 172.16.10.10/24. You will advertise the relay in DNS as 200.1.1.10. Thus, when a host wishes to send mail to the mail.proteris.com server, it will send a packet addressed to 200.1.1.10. The access router will have a configuration statement that states that every packet destined to 200.1.1.10 should be translated to

172.16.10.10. Each additional service will also include an identical configuration statement on the access-router with a different public and private address pair. Thus, the HTTP server might be 172.16.10.11 internally and advertised as 200.1.1.11 publicly. The VPN server might be 172.16.10.12 internally and advertised as 200.1.1.12 publicly and so on for each additional service.

Any public addresses not allocated for the one-to-one relationship between a DMZ server and LAN clients connecting to Internet resources will use the remaining nine public IP addresses as part of a pool. Because there are 200 internal LAN hosts, to allow more than nine internal hosts to access the Internet at a single time, NAT with port address translation (PAT) will be utilized.

It is worth noting that in this particular case, there is no need to have the entire /28. A single public IP address would also suffice. Assuming the single public IP address was 200.1.1.1,you would allow the LAN hosts to access the Internet using PAT. The publicly available servers would statically map to the public IP address of 200.1.1.1 *and* a port. For example, the HTTP server is listening on port 80. You would advertise www.proteris.com as 200.1.1.1. The access router would be configured to translate any packet sent to 200.1.1.1 with a TCP destination port of 80 to translate into 172.16.10.11:80. The SMTP gateway, which listens on port 25, would be advertised as 200.1.1.1 as well, but packets sent to the access router with a TCP destination port of 25 would be translated into a private address of 172.16.10.13:25 instead. This process would be repeated for each internal service running. As long as the destination port for each server is different, there would be no confusion on the part of the access router. Where this system would not work would be if there are *two* Web servers, each listening on port 80 on the DMZ. In this situation, the access router would not know to translate a packet destined to 200.1.1.1:80 to the first Web server or the second Web server.

While this solution is feasible (and commonly implemented), there are a couple of disadvantages to the current configuration. The first is efficiency. Packets that are NAT'ed naturally have more overhead than an untranslated packet. There is a slight delay in the actual translation, but more importantly, each NAT connection consumes resources on the NAT device. In the case of performing NAT on the access router, all LAN connections must have NAT state information and all incoming DMZ connections must have NAT state maintained as well. Assuming that the public network is moderately busy, at any given point, there could be hundreds of NAT translations active to serve the DNS, SMTP, POP3, HTTP, VPN, and FTP servers.

Our current solution is lacking in that it may also confuse our VPN services. A great deal of detail has not been provided on the configuration of the VPN device. For example, you do not know if this device serves to terminate a remote VPN connection from another company, if it allows remote mobile users to access the corporate LAN, or if serves as a gateway device for our LAN to connect to a larger corporation or business partner. Regardless of the configuration, we will see in the VPN section that VPNs and NAT have a difficult time getting along. The crux of the problem is that a VPN does not like changes to be made to the packets once they are encrypted. NAT, by definition, makes changes to the packet. In this case, no matter the scenario, if we conclude that the VPN server encrypts information and sends it out to the Internet, NAT is in a position to certainly change the packets after they have been encrypted.

A better solution is to utilize the /28 network and subnet it further. If we subnet the /28 network into two /29 networks, we have effectively broken the network block into two smaller networks of six hosts each. One /29 network could be used to address the DMZ. For the DMZ, this would provide an address for the HTTP server, FTP server, DNS, VPN, and SMTP/POP3 servers. That would be five of the six usable addresses taken up and finally one for the firewall interface to the DMZ to utilize all six addresses — just enough. The other six addresses would be used to provide for the NAT pool for the LAN. Utilizing the port address translation feature along with NAT would provide plenty of addresses for translation.

With this design, the network would look like the illustration in Exhibit 15. Note that the subnet between the access router and the firewall is a private address space. This is allowable. As far as routing is concerned, the only function of that subnet is to provide a next hop address from the firewall to the access router or vice versa. From the access router, the /29 public DMZ and /29 public NAT pool is reachable via the IP address of the firewall interface. The access router does not care if the IP address of its directly attached neighbor is public or private. From the point of view of the firewall, it is attached to the public /29 DMZ and the /29 public NAT pool, and the rest of the Internet is reached by sending a packet to the router's IP address. The firewall is not bothered by the fact that it is reaching public IP addresses on the Internet by first sending the packet to a next-hop of a private interface.

Along with conserving IP addresses in this scenario, placing the subnet between the firewall and the router in the private address space also ensures that these interfaces of the router and firewall will not be reachable from the Internet. Because the private address space is never advertised to the rest of the Internet, packets can never reach these interfaces from the outside. Of course, the DMZ interface of the firewall is reachable from the Internet, but hopefully our access-filters will be addressing that vulnerability.

This solution is advantageous in all the ways that the previous solution was disadvantageous. The amount of NAT that needs to occur has been

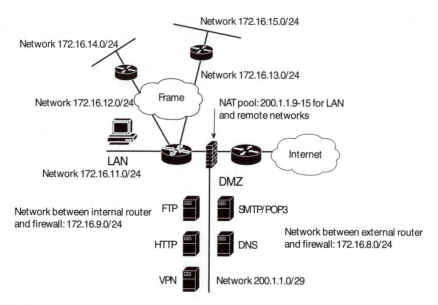

Network 172.16.15.0/24

Network 172.16.14.0/24

Network 172.16.13.0/24

Network 172.16.12.0/24

Frame

NAT pool: 200.1.1.9-15 for LAN and remote networks

Internet

LAN
Network 172.16.11.0/24

DMZ

Network between internal router and firewall: 172.16.9.0/24

FTP

SMTP/POP3

HTTP

DNS

Network between external router and firewall: 172.16.8.0/24

VPN

Network 200.1.1.0/29

Exhibit 15. Using NAT on the Firewall

minimized. Because services on the DMZ have public addresses, no translation needs to occur for them, thereby conserving both firewall and router resources and improving performance for connections to these sites. Furthermore, our VPN configuration has become easier to manage because the packets are not subject to change after they have been encrypted.

The real disadvantage in this instance is in the utilization of our addresses. We see that by splitting the 14 usable IP addresses in the /28 network in two /29 networks, we end up with two networks of six usable addresses each. We have lost two more IP addresses. Furthermore, our DMZ currently utilizes all six addresses, preventing us from adding any new services to the DMZ. At the same time, the LAN has a NAT pool of six IP addresses. Using port address translation, this is more than enough addresses for our needs.

Unfortunately, the solution to this particular problem has nothing to do with firewalling or information security. It is simply the way that subnetting works. If we wished to add more hosts to the DMZ, we would have to request a /27 from the service provider to be able to allocate the appropriate addresses.

In some cases, if acquiring additional IP addresses from the service provider is impossible, then the entire /28 network could be assigned to the DMZ subnet. From the /28, a single IP address— 200.1.1.15, for example — could be used to NAT for the private LAN using port address translation.

Care must be taken in this instance, however, to ensure that the 200.1.1.15 address is not used on any host device in the subnet. You have logically included your LAN subnet in the same subnet as your DMZ, although from a security point of view operation is unaffected because packets entering the router from the Internet destined to the LAN network are translated to the private address before they are routed.

Notes

1. War-dialing is the process of dialing a block of telephone numbers such as 1-802-555-0000 through 9999 and checking for computerized devices attached to the other end. Software to perform such scans is readily available from the Internet and easy to use. War-dialing is a popular method of circumventing corporate perimeter security by looking for a forgotten backdoor into the network via a modem.
2. SNMPv3 supports encryption. SNMP is a fine protocol with which to monitor routers, but allowing an SNMP agent to write to routers is not recommended.
3. The Session Initiation Protocol (SIP) is commonly used to initiate Voice-over-IP calls. The actual transfer of voice information, however, is done using the Real-Time Protocol (RTP).
4. Note there are many ways of using packets to map a network. Using ICMP echoes is only the most obvious way. Most scanners will not even bother with this option because it is so widely defended against.
5. The Nmap program and documentation can be found at www.nmap.org, and the Nessus server, client, and documentation can be found on www.nessus.org.
6. It is easy to argue that many security lapses in networks are the result of misconfiguration on the part of a human being. Thus, the more we let the computer do, the better the chance of a correct and secure implementation.
7. If this were a full network design, the subnet between the access router and the firewall would be ideal for an intrusion detection system. Because we are focusing on NAT in this discussion, however, we will omit this from the diagram.

Chapter 9
Intrusion Detection Systems

The goal of the network firewall is straightforward. A network firewall protects one part of the network from another by allowing or denying traffic based upon a number of criteria. With security, however, there is always a lingering doubt. How can you know that your firewall is doing its job? How do you know that you have configured the firewall properly in the first place, and how can you know that your firewall is not letting through attacks that you had not foreseen when you first configured it? The device that has traditionally served this purpose is known as an intrusion detection system (IDS).

If a firewall is the lock on your door, the IDS is the burglar alarm. The firewall is the network element that actually provides the protection. Should that protection fail, however, the IDS sounds the alarm.

What an IDS attempts to do is make an evaluation of each of the millions of packets that it might see in a normal working day. For each packet that is examined, the IDS logic determines if the packet is a "good" packet — in other words, something that might normally be seen on the network — or a "bad" packet. In this case, "bad" can mean virtually anything but normally will be construed as meaning something that should not, for whatever reason, be seen on the network. This might even mean a normally "good" packet that is seen at a "bad" time.

The actions to take when an IDS sees a good or bad packet can vary. Because it is assumed that the majority of traffic seen on a network will be good, only "bad" packets are normally attended to by the IDS. The IDS may elect to totally ignore the bad packet, log the bad packet to a log for later review by an administrator, or sound the alarms and let every one it has the ability to alert know that a particularly "bad" packet has been seen on the network.

The determination of what is a "bad" packet and what is a "good" packet has been the subject of endless discussion and a number of patents and products. To understand the choices that we can make when sorting the good from the bad, let us create an IDS of our own.

At the most basic level, an IDS is really nothing more than a packet sniffer. That is, it is a program that monitors the transmission medium and records what it detects for further analysis. So, we will start our examination of the IDS with a packet sniffer on the network. Where to place this packet sniffer for maximum effect is a subject of later discussion. For now, we are just going to plug our fledgling IDS into a hub.

For starters, we simply capture all packets on the wire and log them. After a couple of days, we realize that there are megabytes and megabytes of text data for us to sort through. In an effort to make our jobs somewhat saner, we attempt to filter the data to some extent. We can do this in several ways. The first thing we try to do is enter in all the types of "good" packets. We do not get very far before we realize that there sure are a lot of different types of good packets out there. We quickly change course. Instead, we try to find some sort of distinguishing characteristic of a number of bad packets so we search the Internet and research journals for information on various network attacks. For each attack we find, we create a matching filter in our new IDS. For example, if we notice that IP packet fragments have overlapping fragment identifiers, we include in our "bad" filter instructions for the IDS to record whenever it sees IP packets that match that behavior. If we know that we should never see an IP packet from the IP address 0.0.0.0, we add that information to our filter.

While this may take some time, the number of bad packets out there is fairly small compared to the number of good (or at the very least "not bad") packets we are likely to see on a network. Satisfied with our work, we reinstall the IDS and turn it on. Right off the bat, we notice that something is wrong. We discover a number of alarms going off — the IDS is detecting bad packets on our network right now. Leaping into action, we seek the source of this attack. After some exhaustive research and digging, we find out that some of our "bad" packets, as far as our IDS is concerned, look a lot like some good packets we normally have on our network. To respond to this, we spend several days or weeks tuning the IDS. Each time bad packets are detected, we investigate to see if they are really bad packets or just normal network traffic that has the appearance of bad packets to our IDS. Over time, our enthusiasm for the brand-new IDS begins to fade as we spend time tracking down bad packets. We may get so used to these false alarms that we may even shut off the alarm system. The odds of this happening are directly related to the number of times our pager has gone off in the middle of the night when another "bad" packet is detected.

After a break-in period, we begin to have faith in our IDS again. We note that the number of false alarms has dramatically decreased and we even catch a real honest-to-goodness bad packet on the network that we track down and eradicate. This is what makes our jobs fun and we feel that we are making a difference. As time goes by, we continue to add new rules to the IDS, saying, "look for this in a packet, it's bad!" or "look for that in a packet, it's bad too!"

Our confidence is suddenly shaken, however, as to our dismay we learn that our network had been hacked — bad. There are Trojans on several servers and host PCs, and we learn of packet sniffers that have also been installed by the Trojan software. We begin the process of restoring everything up to the last-known good backup; but because we do not really know when this attack occurred, we mostly end up installing everything from the original media. That is a long and depressing weekend, to be sure. We keep asking ourselves, where did we go wrong? Our firewall was up and running and the IDS did not find a single bad packet that we could attribute to this break-in.

That Monday, reading the information security news, we find that there is a new attack that is finding its way around the Internet — and the attack looks just like what we had been hit with. Everyone is highly recommended to update their systems and install the new rules to detect this attack onto their IDS. Now the rules are available for downloading, but just a bit too late for our network.

We have learned the hard way that our IDS, which is based on the signatures of attacks in packets, suffers from a major flaw. If there is no attack signature in the IDS, then the attack will not be recorded. By its nature, our signature-based IDS is reactive. We only know about the attacks after someone else had been attacked, noticed it, and informed the rest of the Internet community of what they found. This time, we were part of the unlucky group that gets to discover a new attack.

A bit wiser, we seek to improve our IDS. After all, it has helped us out on a few occasions, especially after we took the time to tune it properly. We decide to change our focus a bit. What if, instead of thinking of everything as good and bad packets, we instead start thinking of user behavior instead of packets? The idea is that normal users are pretty predictable. They generally use the network in the same way day after day. Our servers are the same. We have learned when creating our first attempt at an IDS that, on our network at least, there are some things that just happen all the time. We decide to categorize user traffic as "normal" and "abnormal" traffic. Tasks that users and network hosts perform all the time are categorized as "normal." Traffic that is not part of the "normal" group is considered "abnormal" and will generate an alarm or log a report.

The *piece de resistance,* however, is that instead of going through the arduous process of logging normal and abnormal traffic and entering it into the IDS, we will let the IDS itself learn what is normal and what is not normal. By monitoring traffic, we learn that we can statistically predict what type of traffic we should see between any two hosts on the network. The longer we monitor, the more accurate it becomes. To cut down on the amount of tuning we need to do, we define normal to the IDS as a small range of options. That is, we give the IDS some leeway in its definition of normal. This is so that every time users do something just a bit different, they will not summon the information security team to their desk. What is considered normal, then, is actually a small window of behavior on either side of normal as statistically defined by the IDS.

We also realize that this approach will protect us in the future against new attacks. Presumably, a new attack will set off alarms indicating that abnormal traffic had been detected, which is exactly what we would expect based on the fact that this attack would have traffic that would be considered new and not part of the statistical database of established network traffic patterns.

So the new IDS is configured and installed and we are confident in our ability to detect attacks on our network and now respond to them. We are until we sit down for lunch with a lecturer at a security conference. This expert points out that our definitions of normal and abnormal are based on the observed behavior of network traffic. We are troubled by two of her points. The first is that how do we know that someone has not actually attacked our network before we installed the IDS? They could have subsequently taught the statistical IDS that their hacking was actually normal traffic on the network. Furthermore, as a sour taste that was not part of the lunch begins to rise from the back of our throats, what if someone was patient enough and careful enough that he slowly retrained the IDS? What if he changed the behavior slowly enough and ended up changing what the IDS thought was normal? His attack could go completely undetected by our new system.

In short order, we are reminded of the general law of security. No solution is perfect. Given time, money, and motivation, any security system can be compromised. Wiser, we begin looking for another solution. We eventually strike on the idea that combines the best elements of both our ideas. We notice that most attacks are based on illegal network protocol usage. For example, we do not normally see a URL GET request (how we request a Web page) with a long string of../../../../ in it. If we do, that is normally someone trying to attempt a directory traversal. We go back to our original idea that if we simply define all the normal ways in which we would see a protocol in action, we can conclude that abnormal behavior is some sort of attack.

Eagerly, we set to coding this new IDS application. Because there is so much variation in protocols, we decide to refer to the standards in writing our protocol rules. We teach the IDS what normal protocol operations are, according to the RFC documents that define them, and configure them to alert us of any packets that violate this behavior. Shortly after installing the new IDS, we are beset with alerts of all types. Surely our network has not been under attack all this time, has it? Given our experience, we know now that we should expect some sort of tuning period to adjust the IDS sensors to our specific network environment, but the amount of alerts we are seeing far surpasses our expectations.

As we will learn shortly, observing the alerts and cross referencing traffic with a protocol analyzer, a great deal of vendor protocols do not actually work the way that the RFCs specifically define them. For example, we find that our Microsoft Exchange e-mail server uses SMTP commands in a very non-standard way. This time, to tune our IDS, we need to observe and program the IDS with all the non-standard protocol behavior that occurs transparently on our network all the time. The task seems daunting but we eventually accomplish it.

We sit down to lunch with our new security friend, beaming of our latest success, only to be dashed by her overly pessimistic (in our opinion) view that some attacks do use normal protocol behavior — for example, logging in with a stolen password at odd times or from odd locations. Back to the drawing board.

This short fable points out that IDSs, as they currently exist, are incomplete at best. No single model of IDS operation is able to conclusively detect attacks in progress all the time. They can also require a considerable amount of resources in the initial setup and tuning, because, no matter the product or the manner in which they attempt to detect attacks, an IDS will always require a learning period to learn the specific needs of your network. At the same time, they are essential tools for modern networks. As discussed above, IDSs are currently constructed to operate in one of three major ways. Each is described below in detail.

9.1 Signature-Based IDS

The most common IDS mode of operation is *signature based*. This means that attack patterns are entered into the IDS database and packets are examined by the IDS. Packets that match the attack signatures are flagged for further inspection. Signature-based IDS is very common as it is well understood and easy to implement. This form of intrusion detection can suffer from both a lack of currency and lack of signatures. The first — lack of currency — is inherent in the way the IDS operates. To detect an attack, someone needs to go through the effort of defining what that attack looks like and configuring the IDS with that information. Of course, nobody is going to know what the attack looks like until someone is actually attacked, detects the attack through some other means, and informs the rest of the Internet community of the attack. This process can take place in a matter of hours to a matter of days, depending on the nature of the attack, its scope, and the attention that the attack receives in the information security press. Normally, the more damaging attacks occurring on a massive scale are the ones that are updated the quickest. This, of course, is little consolation because it is also these types of attacks that are most likely to hit your network.

The numbers of available updates are also something to be considered. Some companies have signatures available for every conceivable attack recorded on the Internet. The size of this signature database is in the hundreds and constantly expanding. While this sounds advantageous, it can also slow down the operation of the IDS. The other end of the spectrum is a company that provides only a small subset of the "most common" Internet attack signatures. While accurate and serving the purpose of protecting your network against the most common attacks, these attacks only provide protection against the most common attacks of script kiddies. Sophisticated attacks will go unnoticed. Ideally, a compromise between the two extremes will be available. Wide ranges of attack signatures are available; but at the same time, you can implement only subsets of the signature library according to your specific needs. Therefore, if you are particularly interested in detecting packets sent by backdoor applications and denial-of-service attacks, but not FTP server attacks, as you do not have an FTP server on your network — you can configure and install only those rules that apply to your network environment.

When comparing products from this category of IDS, it is important to also consider how quickly your proposed vendors react to new attacks. Fortunately, all but the most homegrown products require you to create attack signatures on your own. This ease of use can become a liability, however, if your chosen vendor is slow to update its attack signatures. Some vendors have only periodic updates to their IDS sensors. This may be as infrequently as once a month or even once a quarter. You can be assured that, in this time period, there will be new attacks that your sensor will not detect.

9.2 Statistical-Based IDS

The second major class of IDS products is roughly categorized as *statistical* IDS. Instead of relying on attack signatures, statistical IDSs attempt to learn the normal behavior of your network and classify as noteworthy any traffic that violates normal traffic patterns. For many years, statistical IDSs were simply laboratory experiments. The idea did not meet the needs of production networks. Recently, however, IDS products have started to produce statistical IDSs that complement signature-based IDS applications. For example, one product learns user log-on patterns and generates an alert when the user log-on is outside the normal bounds.

Statistical IDSs suffer from a couple of drawbacks. The first is the need to learn the behavior of the network. It is thus possible to train a statistical

IDS into thinking that something abnormal is normal. Furthermore, to reduce the number of false positives (that is, alerts that turn out to be normal user behavior), most of these IDSs have a sensitivity level that can be adjusted, as in biometric authentication systems. The same risks that apply to sensitivity adjustments in biometric systems also apply here. Making the sensor too sensitive will generate too many alerts and annoy both users and administrators. Lowering the sensitivity too much will increase the opportunity for undetected misuse of network resources.

Closely related to statistical IDSs, but generally allocated their own taxonomical designation, are *anomaly detection systems* (ADSs), also termed *protocol anomaly detection* (PAD). These devices operate on the assumption that there are a definable number of proper ways in which a protocol should operate. Anything outside this range should be considered suspicious. Individual alerts, statistically examined, can also alert network administrators to much larger Internet attack trends. As with statistical IDSs, ADSs attempt to identify attacks prior to their widespread discovery.

Ultimately, an effective IDS is going to have elements from all three groups of IDS technologies. No single technology can successfully account for the wide variety of Internet-based attacks. As it turns out, however, even a system running all of these IDS methods still may not detect every attack. There are other factors to consider when choosing an IDS.

9.3 Host-Based versus Network-Based IDSs

In most cases, an IDS is actually a combination of products. A *sensor* is the part that actually sniffs traffic on a LAN segment. Sensors will typically send their data to a central IDS database device. Thus, a single database is able to monitor a number of sensors. On the IDS database server or as part of a separate host, the IDS may also include a console management station. The ratio of database/console management to sensors typically runs in the range of 10:1, or even as high as 20:1. This means that for anything less than a dozen IDS sensor segments, a single IDS database/management station will suffice.

9.3.1 Host-Based IDS

The first major choice that affects IDS effectiveness is the decision to use host-based or network-based IDSs. As the name implies, a host-based IDS is a system that resides on a network host. Generally, host-based systems only detect attacks directed at that particular host. The advantage of this system is that we can have fairly high confidence in knowing about every detectable attack on that host. Because the volume of traffic to the host is normally a subset of the volume of traffic on the network, we have effectively created a distributed IDS that is more likely to detect attacks due to the lower volume of traffic.

Despite this, the disadvantages of host-based IDSs are many. The first is that the host-based IDS depends on the OS of the host. In heterogeneous network environments, this may mean that several different host-based IDSs are required to cover all the hosts. Depending on how many host-based IDSs are chosen for deployment, host-based IDSs may also present a substantially higher administrative cost. This is especially true when host-based IDSs are placed on all user workstations in a network. Finally, there is the issue of managing the distributed IDS itself. Does the host-based IDS support central logging, or must each host be periodically and individually examined to detect intrusions in a timely manner? In response to these disadvantages, host-based IDSs are typically deployed only on particularly sensitive hosts such as network servers.

9.3.2 Network-Based IDS

Network-based IDSs are devices that operate on a single network segment. Operating in promiscuous mode, these devices record all the traffic they can on any given network segment. This has the advantage that a single network-based IDS can detect attacks for a great many hosts from a single spot. One or two network-based IDSs are also much easier to manage than dozens or hundreds of host-based IDSs.

Similar to the host-based IDS, however, there are a number of negatives associated with network-based IDSs alone. The first is that most networks are switched. For a network-based IDS to operate correctly, it must have access to all network traffic. Many switches, in response to this need, are configurable with port forwarding (also known as port mirroring). Port forwarding is the ability to forward traffic between other ports to a single monitoring port. Not all switches, especially the less-expensive ones, support this feature. Furthermore, even if switches do support port forwarding, they do not always support the ability to monitor both transmit and receive packets from ports.

To explain the problems of port mirroring associated with transmit and receive packets, let us simplify the problem. In Exhibit 1, we have two hosts and a port connecting to a router. We also have a fourth port reserved for mirrored traffic.

We decide to mirror the traffic sent to the router. How we can do that depends on the type of switch we are using and its port forwarding capabilities. If the switch is only able to forward received traffic (from the point of the view of the switch), then we are only ever going to see traffic that is sent from the router, and not traffic that the router is receiving from other hosts. Ideally, we would like the port to mirror both transmit and receive traffic — a function found on some but not all switches. This can be overcome by forwarding all received traffic for the VLAN or LAN, but here again,

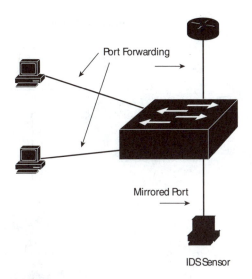

Exhibit 1. **Using an IDS with Switch Port Mirroring**

the switch must support the ability to mirror for multiple ports or on a per-VLAN basis.

Even if the switch does support this feature, there is a problem of capacity for both the network-based IDS and the switch itself. Consider the average 100-Mbps switch. Assuming that any five devices are communicating with another five devices, there is the potential for 250 Mbps of traffic being switched. We are using 250 Mbps instead of 500 Mbps, to account for the burst characteristics of packet data and the fact that it is rare to actually find hosts that will transmit information at the full 100 Mbps. Even so, if we have a single network-based IDS using port forwarding from a single 100-Mbps port of the switch, we see that the IDS is only privy to a bit less of the 100 Mbps once layer 2 headers are taken into account. More than half of the data will be unanalyzed.

One way to circumvent the problems that switches introduce into the process of intrusion detection is to avoid them entirely. This does not mean pulling the hubs out of the closet and dusting them off. A device known as a test access point (TAP) can be used to split off the signals from a standard UTP or fiber cable. TAPs have been used for some time — since switches were placed into common service. Originally, they were used to allow network monitoring devices such as protocol analyzers to examine what was happening on a particular network segment. Because an IDS is little more than a glorified network sniffer, the application of TAPs to the IDS arena followed shortly thereafter.

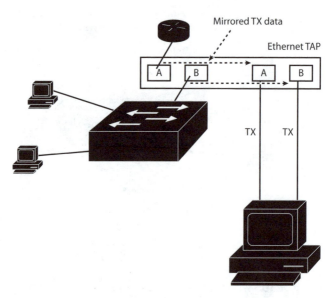

Exhibit 2. Using an IDS with a TAP

By echoing the transmit pairs in a UTP cable, the TAP would allow a single device to monitor the physical media through the use of two interface cards, as illustrated in Exhibit 2. The primary advantage of TAPs over advanced port mirroring of high-speed switches is that they do not affect the performance of the switch in any way. For all intents and purposes, they are invisible to the network. This lack of visibility also increases their security potential because the IDS itself is likewise removed from the active network traffic.Typically, a TAP is placed between a router and the switch and is able to monitor all traffic forwarded to the router. TAPs can also be placed in other strategic points on the network, such as inline between a server and a switch. To ease the deployment of multiple TAPs in a network, manufacturers offer multi-TAP units that can be rack mounted and support multiple TAPs.

While TAPs ease integration with switches, they are not ideal for all installations. As the TAP illustration above indicates, a single TAP will create two output ports, one for each TX (transmit) signal on the physical media. This is a problem because a normal network interface card will assume that there is a single TX signal and the other pair will be reserved for RX (receive) signaling. This then requires the IDS station to have at least two network interfaces for both TX signals from the TAP. As will be discussed later, some IDS devices will operate in a reactive mode, resetting or otherwise blocking suspicious connections on behalf of network hosts. To be able to perform this option, the IDS needs to know enough to associate traffic in a connection with the information it records between the two interfaces. Not all IDSs have this functionality.

As with any technical problem, there is a solution. Along with a TAP, the simplest solution is to create an IDS-specific switch. The two TX ports on the TAP are fed into two ports on the IDS switch. Port mirroring is then configured on the switch itself and all traffic is directed to the port with the IDS sensor attached. As will be discussed in the IDS design section, this arrangement of TAPs, sensors, and a dedicated IDS switch can create IDSs that are quite large and scalable.

Increasing the speeds for network-based IDSs can only increase the problems that network-based IDSs have. Vendors might claim that their products accurately detect attacks at gigabit speeds, but careful attention should be paid to the marketing literature and independent testing should be consulted. More often than not, gigabit detection speeds are only possible in laboratory environments. Real-world detection may be significantly lower at around 300 Mbps or so. The reasons for this wide discrepancy include both overly zealous marketing and the way in which these capacity tests are performed. In the lab, there may be a limited number of connections being monitored on a limited number of ports with maximum-sized packets. This softball testing will allow any product to run close to its maximum theoretical capacity.

It should not be surprising that IDSs in the real world have such a difficult time keeping up with ever-increasing network speeds. Consider that each packet must be captured and then analyzed from attack databases that can include hundreds if not over a thousand attack signatures. Even a firewall would have difficulty operating at high speeds if it was responsible for such a rule set. The actual performance of an IDS is based on a number of factors in the work environment, including the number of active sessions, the size of the packets, and whether the packets are valid to begin with. An IDS examining valid packets has far less work to do than one trying to detect out-of-sequence fragments from five million active connections. In practice, then, gigabit IDS will detect significantly less than the reported 1000 Mbps of data. What that value is will be determined by the conditions of the local network.

To compensate for degraded detection capabilities at higher network speeds, there are several options. All of them in some way relate to distributing the load of the high-speed connections to multiple IDS sensors. For installations that require them, application- or network-based load balancers can be used to split traffic onto multiple lower-speed links and allow an IDS sensor on each link to monitor what traffic it can. If this is done, it is far preferable to split traffic on a per-destination or per-session basis rather than in a round-robin scheme that is sometimes employed to accomplish network bandwidth-based load balancing. It is important that the load balancer keep associated packets together so that the IDS will have the ability to detect related packets that are part of a single attack.

The second option, which may be more difficult to manage but costs much less, is to distribute the network-based IDS sensors closer to the hosts instead of on the backbone where the higher-speed links are typically employed. While it is becoming more common for even modest networks to employ gigabit Ethernet links, many network segments operate at slower speeds. By placing IDS sensors in areas of the network that are forced to operate a slower speeds for other reasons, you can create fairly complete IDSs without the expense of application load balancers or a hardware-based gigabit IDS.

9.4   Tuning the IDS

When initially installed, an IDS will generally require some sort of tuning. This is because there will be a number of false positives. This means that normal user traffic on the network looks like some sort of attack according to whatever method of IDS you are using. The amount of tuning an IDS requires can be significant, depending on what rules are being checked and the type of traffic on the network. It is significant enough that more than one network manager has decided against an IDS altogether, as he or she perceives that the amount of work to simply get an IDS to the point of being useful to the network is excessive. The amount of work involved in tuning an IDS is also significant enough to serve as a powerful marketing tool for IDS vendors that claim that their product requires minimal tuning and can be operational virtually out-of-the-box.

Along with false positives, there is also the matter of false negatives. False negatives are attacks that do not trigger the IDS alerting system; they are undetected attacks. False negatives are even more troubling for an IDS administrator because, by definition, you do not know that they have occurred. It is also this uncertainty that keeps network administrators up at night, even when they have just installed the latest, greatest IDS product.

Part of the tuning process also involves figuring out what to do with the information that an IDS produces. An IDS, depending on the vendor, has the ability to notify network administrators in many ways. Many vendor products will support paging, e-mail, or printing output to a screen. Despite the differences between vendors, IDS information comes down to either generating an alert or logging information.

Alerts are generally events that the network administrator has determined require immediate attention. For example, an attack that the IDS classifies as a backdoor attack would generally be something that a network administrator would want to know about immediately. A port scan directed at the network would be something that has a low risk and would therefore be logged for review at a later time.

The biggest mistake that network administrators or managers make when configuring their IDS alerting system is to alert the network administrators to every network "hiccup" the sensor picks up. Generally, the volume of alerts quickly becomes so overwhelming that the alerting feature ends up getting shut off altogether. What is required to make effective use of this system is the ability to prioritize alerts.

The most common way of prioritizing IDS alerts is to use a method very similar to a risk analysis in assigning severity to the information that the IDS captures. It is a simple fact of the networked environment that your network will come under either casual scanning, the digital equivalent of rattling a doorknob as you walk down the hall, and the focused attack — someone trying to kick down the door and make off with whatever he or she can get their hands on. Because most IDSs will allow the network administrator to set the logging level for individual devices, it makes sense to do a thorough inventory of network assets prior to tuning an IDS. If you have properly created a security policy, much of this work should have already been completed during the risk analysis.

When an inventory of network services is complete, a listing of the relative priority of the services should be completed. Some systems and some applications are more important than others. For example, an enterprise resource planning (ERP) or customer relationship management (CRM) system would be considered a much higher priority than a print server. A mail server might be considered more important than a file server, or vice versa. Based on the value of this information, at some point there will be a threshold where the network administrator will wish to be alerted of a suspected attack in progress on the ERP servers while a log of a suspected attack on the print server will suffice until it can be reviewed.

Along with the priority of resources, the priorities of the attacks should be considered. For example, if you were certain that your ERP servers were patched against common IP fragmentation DoS attacks (as most modern operating system network stacks should be), then such an attack may only warrant a log. On the other hand, if a new attack vector has recently been made public and you know that your servers may yet be vulnerable, then any activity of this type should generate alerts.

In a network where security is a priority and care has been taken to cover all the bases, the network may not be 100 percent secure, but it should be resistant to the common script-kiddie attacks — precompiled, one-click, hacking programs available for downloading on the Internet. These attacks, while they will be common, should be considered a low priority — to a point. Thus, patterns that match common scripted attacks should be logged until they reach a certain threshold, at which point an alert may be in order. On the other hand, any attack that potentially gives attackers administrative access to a system should be considered a high priority and generate alerts accordingly.

The position of the IDS sensor that is capturing traffic should also be considered when determining the relative priority of alerts. In a segment of the network that serves as a server farm for internal LAN systems, alerts should receive a much higher priority than a sensor that is monitoring Internet traffic to the outside of the firewall.

Finally, the work of tuning IDS alert levels will be greatly simplified if the network itself is in good shape from the point of view of security. That is, all operating systems have been properly secured and documented as such; applications and operating systems are all at the appropriate, most recent patch level and users employ encryption and authentication in a prudent manner. Knowing that your network, as a whole, is in this state because security is a priority on the network and proper documentation procedures have been followed makes the job of administrating an IDS that much easier. It allows a great number of attacks to be logged only and minimizes the time that network administrators spend following up on common attacks that ultimately failed anyway.

The task of tuning an IDS can be time-consuming. The IDS must be taught to ignore false positives and only log low-priority alerts. The end result of this work, however, is a concise and confident view of the threats that your network has faced and, with any luck, successfully repelled.

9.5   IDS Placement

Placement of the IDS depends upon the number of IDSs that you have. If, for example, you only have resources for a single IDS, the commonly preferred method is to place the IDS between your external router and your firewall. This placement will ensure that all traffic will be inspected for attacks before it is filtered by your firewall. The hope is to have the IDS serve as an early warning system for your network and alert you to the threats that your firewall is facing. It is always nice to know if someone is trying to break into your network.

The primary disadvantage of this configuration alone is that a normal network will generate a great deal of alerts. Because you do not have any method of knowing, with certainty, which attacks succeed and which fail, the number of alerts tends to increase the sensitivity of network administrators and cause them to spend a great deal of time investigating IDS reports.

Some make good arguments that the best position for placing an IDS is just inside your firewall. The logic of this placement is that the management of the IDS will be that much less because, presumably, most of the suspicious traffic will be blocked by the firewall. Placed internal to your network in line with your firewall, the IDS serves as an important safety check on the configuration and performance of your firewall. This placement lets you know if someone's attempts to break into your network are successful.

While the placement of a single IDS internal to the network allows network administrators to concentrate only on the threats that have managed to circumvent the firewall itself, it does somewhat limit their view of what is going on outside their network. Thus, attacks directed at the firewall itself, for example, may go undetected.

Because a single management station can support multiple sensors, it is common for an organization to quell the debate on optimal IDS placement relative to the firewall by placing an IDS sensor on each side of the firewall. This allows the comparison between knowing what attacks your network is facing along with the assurance of knowing exactly what your firewall is protecting you from. If resources allow, the IDS can then be placed in other strategic locations on the network. The most common secondary locations are on the DMZ and on any server farms that may be located on the network. For maximum visibility of network traffic, IDS sensors can also be placed on host segments of the network. As with any security decision, the number and placement of IDS sensors should reflect the security priorities of the organization itself.

In all cases, an IDS should be configured in "stealth" mode. Stealth mode means omitting the IP configuration of the network interface card that performs the monitoring of the network traffic. Configuring the IDS without an IP address prevents anyone from making a connection to or even discovering the existence of the IDS. The sensor is thus protected from the very network scans and attacks it is attempting to detect.

Of course, removing the IP address from an interface prevents the interface from being used by an attacker, but it also prevents the interface from being used by a network to administer the IDS. This is of particular importance when a network has several IDS sensors placed about the network and collects the sensor information at a central management station. To protect the IDS sensor and still remotely manage the IDS itself, most IDSs have two network interfaces. One interface is used as the sensor and is configured without an IP address. The second interface usually connects to a separate LAN that has the sole purpose of collecting information from and managing the various IDS stations. An example of this configuration with three IDS sensors is shown in Exhibit 3.

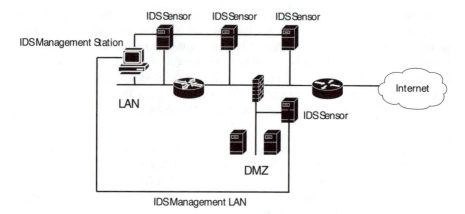

Exhibit 3. Create a Separate LAN between the IDS Sensors and Management Station

9.6 Reactive IDS

An IDS has traditionally been a passive device on the network, silently listening to traffic and providing output for analysis by the system administrator. These IDSs would support extensive alerting capabilities to alert administrators to significant threats as they occurred. Given the response time of computers compared to that of humans, however, by the time a human could realistically respond to an attack, the time for meaningful action had already passed. The best an administrator could do is examine the logs and affected systems to determine whether or not the attack was successful.

As time passed, system administrators began to realize the utility of a system that would respond to attacks for them. This is different from a firewall, in that a firewall generally has a static configuration. Packets are filtered based on address, protocols, and ports. If you wished to allow remote hosts to access the Web server, you needed to allow traffic with a destination port of 80 through the firewall. We know now, however, that there are a number of attacks that will attack the server using port 80. To protect against these attacks, we would have to filter port 80 and at the same time block all legitimate traffic to the server. Of course, there is the possibility that we could block traffic based on the source IP address if we discovered that someone was using a particular address to attack from, but this is simply reacting to a threat that we have not only discovered, but has already taken place.

It would very much be to our advantage if the IDS itself could defend against these attacks as the IDS discovered them. This would take us painfully slow humans out of the loop altogether. If someone was trying to attack our hypothetical Web server using a well-known directory traversal exploit, the IDS could send a TCP disconnect packet to the source of the attack on behalf of the affected Web server and then reconfigure the firewall so that traffic from that address is blocked. The attacker is stopped in his tracks by the IDS, and legitimate users can continue to use the network. It almost sounds too good to be true.

In some way it is too good to be true. The idea of the "reactive" IDS, while not new, has not seen wide deployment. The primary concern is that packets with spoofed IP sources can be used to perform a denial-of-service attack. If, for example, I wanted to prevent you from using a certain network resource, I could simply craft a packet that looks like an attack and make it look like it came from your computer. Voila! Your access to network resources has been limited by my actions. Imagine this scenario on a much larger scale with tens of thousands of packets and the potential for abuse is high.

Nevertheless, the reactive IDS is too good an idea to simply let die for such "minor" technical hurdles. Some of the proposed capabilities for a reactive IDS include, as mentioned above, the ability to actively reset TCP connections by sending spoofed packets of its own and to dynamically reconfigure the rules of a firewall in response to a threat in near-real-time. Other capabilities include disabling running processes on a host, locking out user accounts, and sending SNMP traps to devices.

9.7   Integrating the Firewall and IDS

Given the complementary roles that the IDS and the firewall provide each other, it should be no surprise that vendors have created "all-in-one" firewall/IDS boxes. This type of device certainly eases the integration between a reactive IDS application and the firewall application because both devices are on the same hardware.

When discussing the integration of the firewall and VPN gateway earlier in this book, several advantages and disadvantages became clear when considering the integration of multiple security devices on a single box. From one perspective, the security of the network can be more easily tested, monitored, configured, and managed when all security functions can be found on a single device. Because a major threat to information security is overly complex configuration of network services, it stands to reason that the simpler the integration of a firewall/IDS is, the more securely it can be configured with assurance.

That said, reliance on a single device for network security is a risky proposition. An IDS serves as a check on the configuration of the firewall and your logging systems serve as verification of network activity after the fact. Should all of these systems be placed in a single device, the impact of a successful attack on that device would be devastating for the network.

Not only would your firewall be compromised, a serious incident on its own, but you would also lose the ability to detect the compromise.

While dividing information security services among multiple devices increases the management overhead, it also creates the ability to discreetly ensure the integrity of the various systems — even after one has been compromised. I cannot answer whether a single security box of multiple components will be best for your network. As long as you are aware of the consequences of your decision and how it affects your security policy, you can choose the solution that is best for your network.

9.8   Other IDSs

The "traditional" concept of an IDS is not the only weapon in the arsenal of network defense. If your security policy dictates, there are other network elements that can be included as part of an overall IDS strategy.

Intrusion detection systems are beneficial in that they will alert you as to suspicious network activity. A problem, however, is determining if the detected attack was successful. Ideally, logging of all access should be performed on a separate host that is itself secure. As security goes, however, it is difficult to ever know with certainty that your system, your IDS, or your logging is secure. Furthermore, either a network-based IDS or a host-based IDS only detects attacks and other network-based behavior. It does not, however, indicate if legitimate changes have occurred to the host over the network or if someone has gained physical access to the host itself, either via the terminal or a floppy disk. Most network-based IDSs are not able to pick up such misuse or changes. If positive knowledge of network access is required, then a file integrity checker is required.

A file integrity checker is a software program that computes MD5 hash sums of all programs on a given host. For each file or executable, an individual hash sum is computed. This sum is then recorded. The purpose of file integrity software is to allow network administrators to monitor the thousands of files and executable programs that are on any given host. At periodic intervals or when the network administrator suspects some sort of network compromise, the file integrity checker can be run again. If the new MD5 hash is different from the old hash value, it is easy to surmise that some sort of change has occurred to the file.

In some instances, file changes would be expected. For example, files stored in a cache or temporary folder would be expected to have changed. Other files may have been changed during normal use, such as a database or user folders. Executable files, however, should rarely if ever change. It is up to the system administrator to determine which file changes are likely and legitimate and which are not. All commercial file integrity checking software allows configuration so that network administrators can omit certain often-used files from the checking procedure.

File integrity checkers do not allow you to determine what change has occurred. Thus, the report will not tell you that the item in column B, line 45 has changed from $401.85 to $4018.50, for example. They will only tell you that the file itself has changed. Thus, file integrity checkers are not appropriate for determining what has changed in the file, only that the file itself has been modified.

The success of file integrity checkers relies on the integrity of the MD5 hash. It therefore is not advised to store the hash values on the same host that you are attempting to protect. The reason for this is that either the file integrity checker software program itself could be Trojanized to protect other compromised programs, or the hash values themselves could be modified to reflect any modified binaries. Ideally, the hash values would be recorded on a floppy disk or CD and then stored in a secure location until the next check occurs.

File integrity checkers are essential for determining if changes are made to any given host. Network administrators can attempt to manually monitor their hosts, but this proves to be an overwhelming and, in the end, futile task. A typical UNIX installation contains about 60,000 files and even a bastion host, with all unnecessary files removed, will still contain more than 15,000 files. It would be an unreasonable use of administrator time to search through these files looking for access times and changes. Many Trojan rootkits[1] contain modified programs that hide changes to programs and often hide entire backdoor applications on the host computer by omitting the applications from directory listings and listings of running processes. Thus, even the most astute and capable network administrators will not be able to determine if their systems have been compromised simply by going over the files on their own.

While a file integrity checker may be considered a necessity in many installations to ensure the integrity of host machines, the other item to be discussed is an informative, but few would argue essential, tool for network security.

The tools that attackers are using against network systems are always evolving. Tools that exploit vulnerabilities from last year become obsolete as systems are patched. New tools are then developed to take advantage of new vulnerabilities. For network security professionals, the problem is how to determine what the new attacks are before they are used against your network to cause damage or compromise sensitive information. A novel approach to this problem is to create a system with the sole intent of it being attacked and broken into. This is known as creating a "honeypot."

A honeypot, as the name suggests, is an attractive-looking server on a network that is only placed there with the intent of it being broken into. An IP-invisible separate system, acting as a network sniffer, will be set up to record all packets destined for the host. Once a break-in occurs, the packet data will be examined to determine the method that the attacker used to compromise the system. Once the method is understood, the real network servers can then be protected against the new threat.

Honeypots are most useful against the most common types of attackers on the Internet — script kiddies. Following precompiled exploits, these users, with a limited amount of technical skill, are able to do a great deal of damage to networks and hosts. This class of threat is also the group most likely to compromise any available server — the more, the better. It is not that a honeypot cannot be used to record the actions of more experienced attackers; it is simply that the group of highly experienced attackers is more astute at investigating their targets and tend to attack hosts that in some way further their ultimate goals — not anything that simply looks interesting or is easy to exploit.

Honeypot products are available that can emulate a number of operating systems. If you need, for example, a server that emulates an Apache Web server running Red Hat Linux 6.0, then you select that as a configuration option. If you wish to change it to an IIS server, select another option. Because a honeypot is primarily a learning tool, however, one of the best ways to make one is to configure it yourself using actual server software. At the same time you are learning the attack techniques of Internet threats, you are also increasing your own skill at securing Internet servers against these attacks. The simplest honeypot is simply a server that is set up and runs no services. Because the server really does not serve any network resources, any access to the server itself should be considered suspicious. I have worked on several networks where Windows servers have been set up in exactly this manner. The administrator account was changed from "administrator" to another account, and attempts to access this server as an administrator automatically generated an alert.

To maximize effectiveness, a honeypot should be configured with some degree of network security. This accomplishes two goals. The first is that the amount of knowledge that would be gleaned from well-known attacks is minimal. Sufficient documentation can usually be found to protect your servers and it would take time better spent on other projects to determine the attack vector in any case. If you are going to go through the effort of creating a honeypot, then you will want to make sure that you get the maximum value from it.

The second reason for configuring the honeypot with a modicum of security is that a totally unprotected server may look suspicious. Although the number of unsecured servers and hosts on the Internet is still depressingly large, attackers are wising up to the existence of honey-pots and may be suspicious of a large network block and a single totally unsecured server.

The placement of a honeypot can vary, depending on the goals of the server. Most organizations will place them outside their normal firewall. This allows easy access to the server from the outside, but does not put their network at risk should the bait be taken. It is not uncommon, how-ever, to place the honeypot on the internal network in order to catch employees who may be more curious than their corporate security policy allows.

In either location, a network sniffer, or even an IDS, should be placed to capture all traffic sent to the honeypot. Because it is assumed that the host itself will be compromised, no trust should be placed in the logs of the device as a method of determining a sequence of events in the event of an attack. As with normal IDS placement, the sniffer or IDS sensor host inter-face address should not be configured with an IP address. This will allow the device to sniff traffic, but be rendered invisible from the perspective of the IP layer. Printing the logs to CD media or in hard copy may also provide interesting information regarding the actions of the attacker once your sys-tem is compromised.

While few better learning tools exist, the use of honeypots as a security mechanism can be complicated. Some organizations create honeypots for the purpose of actually trapping and prosecuting individuals and groups attempting to compromise a host. The line between enticement and entrapment can be pretty thin. Enticement is legal, but entrapment is not. Simply placing an attractive host on a network with several well-placed vul-nerabilities would be an example of enticement. It is up to the attackers to discover the host and take advantage of the situation. Entrapment, on the other hand, would be actions that "pull" the user to the host for logging their activity. For example, advertising pirated software on a newsgroup and then recording the actions of all who log on looking for such files would be considered entrapment.

Actively attracting the attention of Internet threats would generally lead to other unpleasant consequences. While the hope may be to capture and prosecute such individuals, in reality, the network administrator may find that the responsible individuals are outside the jurisdiction or reach of their local or national law enforcement agencies. This would result in a lot of work tracking down attackers, only to find an angry group of attackers in a part of the world that the network administrator cannot affect. For all their trouble, network administrators may find that they have attracted too much attention in the form of hacking attempts on production systems and distributed denial-of-service attacks on the network as a whole. While the honeypot is an interesting device for learning about network attacks and protecting network resources, it is probably not the preferred vehicle for capturing attackers. The argument could be made that it would provide the information required to determine the attacker's mode of attack, but your normal security procedures should be providing that information anyway.

Note

1. A root kit is a collection of programs that allow attackers to easily cover their activities on the host and access the host at their convenience at a later time.

Chapter 10
Virtual Private Networks

This chapter addresses the role of the virtual private network (VPN) as a countermeasure in your network. There are many different types of VPNs, but the public is generally sold on the definition of VPN that means "using encryption over a public IP network to make sure nobody can read my data." This chapter discusses the types of VPNs, including those based on the public Internet and where they may be applicable as countermeasures in your network.

The commonly used selling tactic for purchasing VPN equipment is that "someone" on the Internet would be able to read your data. Using a VPN will make it so that your data is safe. While this is true, let us put things into perspective a bit.

Most VPNs are one of two types. The first type is the remote user of corporate resources. This is formally known as the "host to gateway" model. These are users that dial up to a service provider and then route their packets to a corporate VPN server. The data is encrypted from the host device of the remote user to the VPN server at the corporate office. Once inside the corporate network, most implementations decrypt the data and forward it throughout the internal network (see Exhibit 1). Host-to-gateway VPNs are found in two different varieties. The first is known as a voluntary tunneling. This means that users have the option of connecting to the Internet or other network resources not using the VPN. For example, home users with DSL lines are always connected to their DSL providers. When they have work that specifically requires access to the company network, they create a VPN service to the corporate site. The user is allowed to make the distinction between using or not using the VPN. This can be advantageous to the company and the user because it creates less demand on company resources. VPN connections are only being utilized when users are accessing company resources and are otherwise available. A company may have 500 remote users, but because the tunneling (VPN connection) is voluntary, only 100 of those users would ever be connected during peak hours. This has a significant impact on the planning that a company needs to do for VPN countermeasures.

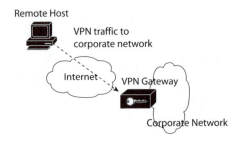

Exhibit 1. Host-to-Gateway VPN

The disadvantage to voluntary tunneling is that users are free to use the Internet outside the VPN. At least when users are using the VPN, their traffic is usually protected by the company firewall. It is entirely likely that users would download or otherwise infect their computer while they are using the Internet for general purposes and then infect the company through their own VPN once they have connected to the LAN. Furthermore, when the users are not using the VPN, the company has no control over the type of Internet usage in which the user is engaging. Depending on the security policy of the company in question, this may be an unacceptable risk.

The other option is known as compulsory tunneling. This means that the only way a remote user in a host to gateway environment can access the Internet is through the company VPN. Each time a user connects to the Internet, a VPN session is established. This provides the company using compulsory tunneling control and safeguards over user traffic but at the same time increases the use of company resources. Consider the diagram in Exhibit 1. Remote users need to use the company's Internet access to tunnel into the VPN gateway and then use that same Internet connection to send normal IP packets out to the Internet. Return traffic follows the same path. This leads to increased utilization of the company's Internet access links and increased delay for the remote user. Because all remote users will be expected to use the company VPN, the VPN needs to be sized so that all users can connect concurrently. Depending on the usage habits of your users, this can be a significant increase in the bandwidth and processing power required to support remote users.

While compulsory and voluntary tunneling have been described in the host-to-gateway context, there is no reason that the same concepts cannot be applied to gateway-to-gateway scenarios. A remote company site may have the ability to direct Internet traffic to its ISP locally, or may have to tunnel all data to corporate headquarters first and then send it out through the central Internet access connection.

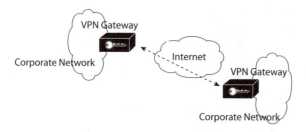

Exhibit 2. Gateway-to-Gateway VPN

The choice of which to use or which is "best" is entirely up to the company in question and is best answered according to the requirements set forth in the security policy. Maximizing security as in the compulsory tunneling example also maximizes the cost of the solution. In some instances, this may make financial sense; while in others, it is best for users to decide when to use the VPN on their own and provide other methods of protecting remote hosts (e.g., using personal firewalls, providing anti-virus updates, etc.).

In the second most common implementation of VPNs, two company locations have VPN gateways that create an encrypted tunnel between the two gateways (see Exhibit 2). Appropriately enough, this is known as the "gateway-to-gateway" model. Traffic internal to the corporate networks is unencrypted. Traffic traveling between the gateways is encrypted at one gateway and decrypted at the other. When the data is forwarded over the remote gateway, it is unencrypted.Now take a look at the vulnerabilities in the network. While it is true that someone could sniff data off the network, it is not as easy as it sounds. Consider the case of the remote user dialing into the network without using a VPN. The call is placed and a virtual circuit is set up to the local phone company and switched through their system from the POTS line to a digital circuit that is used to connect to the remote access server of the local ISP. This ISP may be a reseller of data or may be a major ISP. From the ISP, the data travels through their network and the network of a number of other ISPs. As the data passes from ISP to ISP, it is transferred through peering points — either public or private. Each of these peering points, in addition to employing much better physical controls than most corporations, also employ a high-speed switch, further reducing the risk that someone is running an undetected packet sniffer in a peering point. Finally, after traveling through one, two, or at most three (on average) ISP backbones, the data is delivered to the company network over some sort of point-to-point connection.

While the data is vulnerable inside the ISP network, most long-haul service providers' network nodes are little more than small, climate-controlled rooms with powerful switches and routers built into them. Most of the work is done by long-haul circuits that transport gigabits of data across the country every second. Fiber, contrary to popular belief, can be "sniffed," but it is much more difficult for someone to do than just plopping a sniffer onto your LAN. In fact, when considering an overall risk analysis, if you have to include threats that are willing to sniff in an ISP network or crawl into a sewer to apply expensive and specialized sniffing tools to fiber optic, you have a generally high risk factor overall for your network

For the second VPN option — that is, gateway to gateway, the same scenario applies. Where is the sniffing going to be done? Outside on a telephone pole? Under the street? While it is possible to intercept data in these locations, they generally require a dedicated threat agent to pull it off.

Even if some unauthorized agent were able to pull data off the network data that traveled from point A to point B, most attackers that are likely to affect your network; script kiddies, the curious, and vengeful individuals, are unlikely to have the resources to crack even the most basic of encryption algorithms. Encryption has been broken, but assuming that it is an encryption algorithm that has been rigorously peer reviewed, it requires the cooperation of hundreds of individuals sharing their computer time or the largest of governments and scientific computers to do so in a period of time that makes deciphering the data worthwhile.

Most people are not even going to attempt to capture and decrypt encrypted data. Most attackers will not even go through the effort of attempting to capture unencrypted packets as they travel over the Internet. There are far easier ways of getting to data. The attacker might simply attack the VPN gateway itself. Either they can DoS it or otherwise gain privileged access. An attacker might take advantage of weak authentication mechanisms and try spoofing or redirecting traffic based on DNS entries to create a VPN connection. Or the attacker might simply gain access to the company itself and install their network monitoring tools there. As pointed out in the examples above, most of the time data is encrypted as it travels over the open waters of the Internet. Traffic on the LAN, being "safe," is normally sent in plaintext. As more and more companies start employing wireless networks, the attacker may simply drive past the company with a directional antenna to pick up the information he needs.

This is not meant to undermine those institutions that have legitimate fears of someone going through those great lengths to attack their data in transit. Depending on the motivation of the attacker, the risk may be worth it. This category of risk, however, is evident in relatively few cases. What this discussion is meant to point out is that it is common to see VPNs used to solve the wrong problem.

10.1 VPN Limitations

With that in mind, take a look at what a VPN will not do for your company:

- A VPN will not ensure the integrity of the encrypted data. The most common method of encrypting, using the Encapsulating Security Payload (ESP), does include options to make sure that data is not modified *after* it has been encrypted. However, this does nothing to make sure that the data that is being encrypted is legitimate.
- A VPN will not ensure the authenticity of the host sending the data. It is terribly easy to create an encrypted channel between two hosts. Every time you create an SSL connection with your Web browser to shop online or browse your company's private Web site, you are creating an encrypted channel. The real trick is to make sure that you are really connecting to the intended on-line merchant. It may be the case that every octet of data that you send is perfectly encrypted and that you are sending it right to an attacker who is gladly accepting all that you send him.
- A firewall will not automatically make sure that your VPN traffic is safe for your network. That is, a firewall cannot do its job on encrypted information. If it could, it would defeat the purpose of encryption altogether.

10.2 VPN Solutions

A VPN will only encrypt data. To make a VPN part of a comprehensive security plan, a number of other factors must be considered. In this section we examine the different types of VPNs available and also examine the parts required to make a VPN fully functional and an effective countermeasure against threats.

Thus far, the discussion has concentrated on the common perception of the VPN: encrypted traffic over an IP backbone. This is not the only alternative, however. If a private connection between sites is required, then there are other choices to select as countermeasures. A brief discussion of each follows, along with the specific pros and cons of each solution.

10.2.1 Private Lines

Originally, when a company wanted to connect two remote locations together in a private fashion, it had two choices. The first was to install and maintain a private long-haul network. This was an option for only the largest companies or governments and was only used when connectivity and privacy were paramount. If privacy were the ultimate goal, then encryption was still required because it would be very difficult for any entity to protect every mile of a WAN that spanned the country.

More commonly, circuits were leased from phone companies. This was a virtual network only in that the facilities that connected two remote locations together were not actually a very long wire but a collection of circuits that were circuit switched in the central offices of the phone companies. The network at that time was private in the same way a phone call was private. From the point of view of two parties speaking on the phone, they have access to the entire bandwidth of the link, whether or not they are speaking.

As far as VPNs go, this is the "Cadillac" of service. Because the data is not multiplexed with data from other sites or networks, it truly is private — just as a voice conversation is. The bandwidth between the two locations is fixed and does not suffer from congestion or delay because the bandwidth is reserved for the party that is leasing the circuits. Encryption is not needed to protect data from the rest of the Internet because there is no "rest of" with which to mix up the data. From the point of view of the two remote locations, the circuit between two sites is simply an extension of the LAN.

This is also the most expensive of solutions. Due to the high costs of leasing private lines between sites, when less expensive options became available, the newer options were quickly seized upon by the networking community. Private-line networks also become very expensive, very quickly when they scale. Both full and partial mesh networks require a great many private lines to provide any-to-any or any-to-many connectivity.

10.2.2 Packet-Switched Services

The primary reason that leased lines are so expensive is because they require the service provider to dedicate resources to a particular connection. Because service providers make their money when data is traveling over their links, a leased line essentially takes facilities out of the general pool of available income generating resources.

Packet-switched networks were developed to allow multiple parties to share the same resources by multiplexing multiple datastreams, in the form of packets, across the service provider backbone. Because service providers could now, in effect, sell the same link over and over again, they were able to reduce the costs they charged customers.

The concept of multiplexing data is not new. Phone companies have been doing it for years over their digital backbone using time division multiplexing (TDM). This means that a circuit is broken up into a number of time slots, each of which is capable of holding 8K of data. This timeslot becomes available 8000 times a second, producing a total bandwidth of 64 Kbps. Incidentally, a single voice call uses 64 Kbps of bandwidth. Odd coincidence, no?[1] There are other types of multiplexing as well. Analog communications systems such as FM radio use frequency division multiplexing (FDM). In the case of FDM each channel is assigned a frequency space in the radio spectrum. Our radio receiver is able to de-multiplex and tune into only the signal in which we are interested.

The multiplexing techniques in the above paragraph are both examples of multiplexing at the physical layer. Packet switching takes the concept of multiplexing to the data-link layer. Examples of packet-switched networks are X.25, Frame Relay, and ATM.

While the frame formats and implementations of each are different, these data-link technologies all share some common characteristics. The first is that X.25, Frame Relay, and ATM are all interface definitions. This means that what they really define are the "hand-offs" between devices. A company will typically lease a circuit from a telco only to their local site. That circuit is generally the same type they would use for a private line, meaning that the physical layer of the circuit uses T-1 encoding of data and has 24 TDM slots that can be concatenated to appear to be a single link to higher layers of the OSI Model. The customer edge device will be configured to use a certain type of frame format; lets say Frame Relay for this example, to send data to the service provider access device.

Once the data has reached the service provider, the private line stops and the frame that the customer has sent enters the service provider backbone. That backbone multiplexes the customer data along with the data from other customers along a series of high-bandwidth trunks. Based on an address attached to each frame, the packet is forwarded throughout the service provider network until it reaches the point at which it is sent to the customer remote location. This remote location is provisioned with a private line that uses the Frame Relay frame format just as the sending site does. The frame is forwarded from the service provider access point to the customer edge device.

Thus far, this sounds a lot like what would happen to an IP packet — and it is. There are a few significant differences, however. The first is that this is a layer 2 technology. Only like networks can communicate. If you wanted to communicate with a remote location and you used Frame Relay, the remote location would also have to use Frame Relay. If you wanted to use ATM to communicate with the remote location, then you would have to make sure the remote location had access to an ATM network to pass data to. IP, on the other hand, being a layer 3 technology, does not care what the layer 2 protocols are. As long as the other side is speaking IP, dissimilar networks at layer 2 can communicate using layer 3.

How is this private? From the customer edge router to the service provider access router, the service is private. Inside the service provider network, layer 2 frames are switched through the network following a predefined path. In Frame Relay, frames are switched according to the Data Link Connector Identifier (DLCI) and in ATM cells (a particular type of frame) are switched according to their Virtual Path Indicator (VPI)/Virtual Channel Indicator (VCI). These identifiers are simply addresses, like IP addresses, that are used to identify Frame Relay and ATM point-to-point connections through a network backbone. Unlike IP addresses, where the numbering scheme is global, in Frame Relay and ATM, the addresses are only relevant between any two network nodes, much like the MAC address is only relevant to a particular LAN segment. From the point of view of the customer devices that send data into and receive data from the network, the connection is a private layer 2 connection. This is no different, other than the encapsulation method used, than a private line from the customer's point of view. Privacy is assured in the service provider backbone because the labels that are attached to user data keep frames from user A from becoming confused with frames from user B — although they both share the same physical facilities.

Frame Relay became very popular by companies looking to connect remote sites together in a "private" fashion. It offers the same service as an actual private line but because the service provider is able to sell the same backbone bandwidth multiple times to customers, it is offered at a cheaper price than the private line solution.

What does Frame Relay provide as far as VPN services go? It is a virtual network for sure. Sites employing Frame Relay connections essentially have a private backbone that they are leasing from a service provider. Privacy is gained through the addressing and switching mechanisms employed by the service provider.

That said, Frame Relay does not do a lot of other things we expect our VPNs to do for us. First, the only way you can create a Frame Relay network is if you have access to a service provider that provides Frame Relay access. This seems obvious, but it means that dial-in users cannot (easily) enjoy Frame Relay access and your average SOHO (small office/home office) user with a DSL or cable modem cannot create a VPN using Frame Relay. Frame Relay only works on Frame Relay networks. The same restrictions apply to X.25, a predecessor to Frame Relay and ATM, a one-time Frame Relay replacement technology.

Layer 2 VPNs, like Frame Relay and ATM, also do not encrypt data. A company's data is only protected by the integrity and security policies of the service provider from which it leases services. Because the virtual circuits, called permanent virtual circuits (PVCs),[2] that Frame Relay and ATM create are manually created by employees of the service provider, they are at a risk of "fat-fingering" the switching tables. That said, I have worked with many service providers and, while I have witnessed mistakes being made, I have never seen nor heard of customers actually receiving each other's data because of a switch configuration. Inside the service provider backbone, if someone were able to install a packet sniffer on a port, all data from all Frame Relay circuits would be readable in plaintext.

While these layer 2 VPNs do not encrypt data, the network can still be considered a VPN and, in some cases, depending on the security policy of the company interested in the service, this may be adequate. Remember that unnoticed sniffers and circuit misconfigurations are few and far between in your average national service provider. Because Frame Relay does not need to encrypt data to ensure privacy on the network, key distribution and encryption/decryption issues are not factors as well. Furthermore, this is a technology that only the service provider can configure. Other than a nominal configuration on the customer edge router, all of the provisioning of this service is done in the service provider backbone. This could be an advantage if a company has realized that, to effectively use IPSec encryption, an expensive hardware upgrade would be required and additional resources committed to the administration of the IPSec configurations.

Pulling all this together, when should you consider a Frame Relay or ATM VPN as the solution to your needs?

- Your security policy does not mandate the encryption of data.
- Your VPN connections will be gateway-to-gateway in nature.
- You lack the resources to configure and maintain your own IPSec infrastructure.
- You have concerns with throughput or latency due to the encryption or decryption of IPSec data.
- You do not wish to upgrade your hardware at all sites if they do not currently support the IPSec options you require.

A layer 2 VPN is not the solution you are looking for if:

- Your security policy requires encryption; however, IPSec encryption can be run concurrently with Frame Relay or ATM.
- You have many sites that you need to include in your VPN; however, IPSec also has serious scaling issues that make mesh configurations complicated.
- You have users who will need to work remotely and thus need host-to-gateway connectivity.

10.2.3 *Multi-Protocol Label Switching (MPLS)*

Multi-protocol label switching (MPLS) is a technology that has been around since the mid-1990s. At the time of its development, MPLS had several goals, none of which were related to VPNs. The original goals of MPLS were to:

- *Improve the speed of routing in comparison to switching.* Routers were hampered by the need to perform software forwarding on IP packets. Compared to the operations on a layer 2 header, IP packets at layer 3 required much more overhead and processing.
- *Improve the performance of Internet routing tables.* Routing tables on the Internet were growing rapidly. If router performance and memory could not keep up with the growth of the routing tables, then parts of the Internet would begin to disappear from each other. Combine this with instabilities in the routing table and the constant process of convergence, or updating the routing tables, and there was a definite need to redefine how packets were forwarded to avoid the size and complexity of Internet routing tables.
- *Improve the control of network traffic.* The IP network lacked the management abilities of ATM networks that were competing with IP in the mid-1990s. Although there is the concept of QoS (quality of service) that can be applied to IP traffic, it is not nearly as flexible as that found in ATM. Most IP traffic simply takes the shortest path between two points according to the routers. What was needed was a way to easily control IP so that less than optimal paths could be engineered as well to make better use of network resources.

Today, the original need for MPLS (i.e., faster packet forwarding) has been taken care of through increases in router technology. By performing much of the forwarding process in the hardware interface caches, routers can compete favorably with switches and offer more control as well. The work in solving the other problems of the Internet, however, created the MPLS technology and it was a short time later that engineers realized that MPLS could be used to provide a robust, secure, and scalable VPN technology.

10.2.3.1 MPLS Overview. MPLS is called a layer 2.5 technology. That means that the header information, called a label, is applied between the layer 2 frame header and the layer 3 packet header. This label is used by MPLS-enabled routers to forward frames much like the DLCI or VPI/VCI headers are used at layer 2 to forward frames. To summarize what MPLS does for a network; it provides the same services as Frame Relay and ATM networks over any type of network. While that may not have caused you to gasp in astonishment, when the implications of this are considered, they are quite profound.

First and most related to VPNs is that a network using MPLS can create the same type of service as an ATM network.[3] This means that virtual circuits can be created; and traffic engineering, the process of moving traffic around the network contrary to what the normal routing process would choose, is easily enabled. This ability, however, does not require an ATM network to work. Indeed, the entire point of MPLS is that it can create virtual circuits over any type of infrastructure that can support IP traffic. It would be possible to create an MPLS virtual circuit, called a label-switched path, between a dial-up user and a corporate site using OC-48 SONET access-links.[4] This type of flexibility is impossible on a traditional Frame Relay or ATM network.

MPLS also offers many benefits to service providers. Instead of many different protocols to control the operation of their networks, service providers can finally converge on a single technology. MPLS allows service providers with IP backbones over fiber optics and ATM backbones to be controlled using a single protocol. This offers considerable cost savings in the service provider arena. MPLS also has the ability to tunnel other layer 2 protocols inside it. Just as an example, imagine that you are a new service provider and wish to compete against the established, large service providers. To compete with all of their offerings, you would have to spend extensive amounts of money to create a voice network, a Frame Relay backbone, perhaps an ATM network to carry the voice traffic, and an IP backbone. With MPLS, you could create a single backbone of perhaps Gigabit Ethernet links and over that single network provide potential customers with voice, IP, Frame Relay, point-to-point links, and ATM, and provision the Ethernet in a way that makes each company think that instead of a WAN link, it simply has a long-haul Ethernet connection to a remote site. All these services over one network makes a service provider very competitive and cost effective.

In addition to cost savings, MPLS offers service providers the ability to offer new services to customers in a way that is scalable and cost effective for them. One service is the ability to provision different classes of customer traffic. It is possible for a service provider to sell your company "premium" links for one type of traffic and "best-effort" links for another type of traffic. This, of course, can be done without MPLS, but the cost difference in the provisioning for the service providers is considerable.

The other service that MPLS provides is the ability for the service provider to easily create large, scalable VPNs for the customer. An MPLS label-switched patch (LSP) creates a virtual circuit, which from the customer point of view looks very much like a Frame Relay PVC. Inside the network, however, routers are creating the path the LSP uses for the forwarding of traffic. Instead of manually provisioning of MPLS in the network core, as is typically done with ATM and Frame Relay, MPLS uses the existing IP routing tables to create the LSP. Again, with MPLS, a simple observation turns out to have profound implications in the operation of the network.

Frame Relay became a popular replacement for private lines because it was cheaper and provided nearly equivalent service. IPSec, to be discussed shortly, became a popular replacement for Frame Relay because the costs for IP-only links were even cheaper than those of Frame Relay.

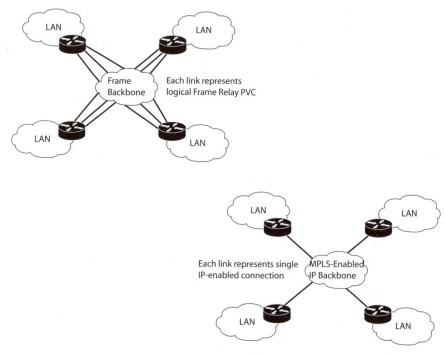

Exhibit 3. Frame Relay VPN versus MPLS VPN

The disadvantage of IPSec was the setup and maintenance of the VPNs for the customer. MPLS seeks to leverage the low cost of IP connectivity and at the same time remove the complications of configuring VPNs for customers. Let us examine how that is done.

Compare the example four-site networks in Exhibit 3. The first is a network using Frame Relay to create a full mesh of connectivity. That is, each remote site is directly connected to each other site. The second network is provisioned using a service provider core that is MPLS-enabled. From a VPN point of view, both networks provide equivalent privacy. The Frame Relay network requires the provisioning of three PVCs at each site. Any routing protocols used between the remote sites are going to have to scale for the three possible paths and peers. Adding a fifth new site to the Frame Relay configuration will require the addition of four new PVCs and the reconfiguring of all of the customer edge routers to accommodate the new site. Note as well that the Internet connection for the headquarters is a separate link that also needs to be provisioned and paid for. If any of the remote sites wish to access Internet resources, each of them needs to forward its traffic to the headquarters and, in turn, headquarters will forward the traffic out to the Internet.

Compare this to the MPLS VPN solution. First, MPLS does not need a specific data link-layer like Frame Relay. That means that only a normal IP connection is required. Furthermore, because MPLS only runs in the service provider backbone, the customer edge routers need no special configuration whatsoever for the VPN service to be established. LSPs are created from the service provider edge router to remote service provider edge routers using the backbone routing protocols.

When a packet is sent from one customer site to another, the packet is assigned a label based on its destination as it enters the service provider edge router. For the remainder of the packet's journey through the service provider network, only the label is examined and forwarding decisions are made based on that label. When the packet reaches the remote service provider edge router, the label is removed and a normal IP packet is forwarded to the remote customer edge router.

Because it is the service provider edge router that is doing all the work, the customer needs no configuration on its site to create the VPN. And because the packets are routed using normal IP destinations, the customer site only needs a single access-link to directly connect to all other remote sites. For the Frame Relay solution, recall that a separate PVC is required for each remote VPN site.

Adding a new site to the MPLS-enabled network is also a simple matter. When the fifth site is added, no special configuration needs to be done on all of the customer edge routers *or* the service provider edge routers. The new site is simply added to the routing tables used by the customer VPN and the information is automatically forwarded to the other provider edge routers hosting the customer VPN. This makes scaling the VPN very straightforward for both the customer and the service provider.

Finally, MPLS will allow each site to access the Internet directly through its own access-link. This means that each site has complete VPN access and direct access to the Internet over the same link.

It is natural to wonder — because MPLS is providing service over an IP backbone and we have been taught to equate IP with "insecure" — how MPLS can provide a VPN service simply through the use of another header on an IP packet.

The primary method is that for every site on an MPLS VPN, a private section of the routing table is created, called a VPN routing and forwarding table (VRF). Of all security mechanisms, routers are perhaps one of the most overlooked, yet most important elements of security. The routing table in a router directs packets. If there is no entry in the routing table for Host A to contact Host B, then those two hosts will never communicate. The VRF creates a subset of the global routing table for each customer site that participates in a VPN. By controlling the routing table, the flow of traffic can be precisely controlled. This type of routing table control can be done without MPLS and the VRF, but it is so complicated and subject to change that it is a solution that would never scale.

Inside the service provider network, customer VPN traffic is kept distinct from other customer's VPN traffic and normal IP traffic through the use of the MPLS label. This works much like the ATM or Frame Relay layer 2 headers. For MPLS-enabled routers, the contents of the MPLS packet are irrelevant and not examined during the forwarding process. Only the label, which associates a given unit of data with a label-switched path, is examined. Like Frame Relay or ATM headers, the MPLS label space is relevant only between any two routers. This means that someone could not "inject" false labels into the network from a remote location. They would have to be physically between two routers to insert labeled packets that would be accepted by the switches. This is not a simple proposition. To prevent the improper assignment of MPLS labels, MPLS signaling protocols can also authenticate each other using hashed passwords. This ensures that someone who has gained access to the MPLS network cannot reroute LSPs by changing forwarding tables.

MPLS, Frame Relay, and ATM all provide equivalent VPN services. The advantage that MPLS holds over the other two technologies is that it scales better for the customer, is generally cheaper, and is easier for the service provider to provision. So when should your company consider using an MPLS VPN?

- Encryption is not a required element of your security policy. MPLS does not encrypt data.
- You have a service provider that supports MPLS in its backbone. Not all service providers offer this service.
- You have many remote sites that would be difficult to connect using Frame Relay PVCs. MPLS enables one-to-many provisioning, unlike Frame Relay and ATM.
- You want to avoid the configurations of IPSec. MPLS is entirely enabled on the service provider backbone. No configuration of the customer site is required.
- You need traffic engineering or the QoS mechanisms that MPLS can provide concurrently with the VPN service.
- Your VPN connections will be gateway-to-gateway in nature.
- You have concerns with throughput or latency due to the encryption or decryption of IPSec data.
- You do not wish to upgrade your hardware at all sites if they do not currently support the IPSec options you require.

MPLS is not a technology to consider if:

- Your security policy requires encryption; however, IPSec encryption can be run concurrently with MPLS.
- You have users that will need to work remotely and thus need host-to-gateway connectivity.

In summary, MPLS offers many of the same advantages and disadvantages of Frame Relay, with the exception of scalability and traffic engineering. The fact that it is easier for the service provider to configure should not necessarily be a deciding factor for the end user of the service — unless, of course, those cost savings are passed on to the consumer.

10.3 IP-Based Virtual Private Networks

Each successive generation of VPN technology — from an actual private infrastructure, to private leased circuits, to layer 2 solutions — capitalized on the sharing of network infrastructure to reduce the overall cost of the service. Each solution was a bit less "private" than the previous one; but generally, the cost differential made up the difference for the users. An IP-based VPN takes the layer 2 solution one step further. Instead of sharing a specific layer 2 backbone with other users, IP-based solutions seek to leverage the comparatively low cost of Internet connections. Because the Internet is potentially less private than service provider layer 2 backbones, privacy is assured through the use of encryption protocols.

IP-based VPNs come in several different flavors. A description of each of the most common technologies used in the process and a discussion regarding their applicability is included in this section. Because many of these technologies rely on the concept of tunneling, this will be the focus of the first discussion.

10.3.1 Tunneling and Encapsulation

You cannot study IP-based VPNs for very long before running into the terms "tunneling" and "encapsulation." While related, there are some differences between the two terms. Recalling the OSI Model or the TCP/IP suite, the process of placing upper layer data into a lower layer is known as encapsulation. For example, an FTP application data unit is encapsulated in a TCP header. The TCP header, in turn, is encapsulated in an IP header that, in turn, is encapsulated within a data-link layer frame. For encapsulation, the normal model of the protocols remains intact.

While encapsulation occurs every time we transmit data over the Internet, it does not provide for all of our needs. Consider the instance where we need to send IPX/SPX data[5] over an Internet connection. Because IPX alone cannot be sent over the Internet, we must tunnel it inside an IP packet. If we were to follow the encapsulation process, we would see that we are taking a layer 3 protocol (IPX) and encapsulating it inside a layer 2 protocol (PPP). For the IPX protocol, this creates the illusion that the local IPX network is directly attached to the remote IPX network, a topology that IPX understands.

Of course, IPX data will not travel over the Internet; and because we do not really have a point-to-point connection between the local site and the remote site, we need to put our PPP frame inside of an IP packet so that it will be able to be routed over the Internet. At this point, we have placed a layer 2 data unit inside a layer 3 data unit. This process of placing a lower-layer or like-layer protocol inside a higher-layer protocol is known as tunneling. We have, in effect, created an envelope that can be used to deliver data that is normally not able to travel over the Internet on its own. Internet routers do not care what the contents of packets are; they only examine the outer-most packet header without regard to the packet contents.

Generic Routing Encapsulation (GRE) is known as a tunneling protocol and is the basis of many other tunneling protocols. As it turns out, simply placing a PPP packet inside an IP packet does not provide all the information required for tunneling to operate. We need some sort of framework to describe to each end of the connection what is happening inside the IP packets being sent and received. We need some way of indicating that inside this set of packets are protocols that deviate from what each side would normally expect in the process of encapsulation. GRE is one way of doing this.

Because GRE is the foundation of many other tunneling protocols, we need a brief discussion to fully explain what it is accomplishing. While there are a number of protocols that describe the tunneling of specific protocol combinations, GRE is an attempt to broadly define what is required for tunneling. A look at the protocol header from the RFC that describes GRE, RFC 2784 (see Exhibit 4) is instructive. A number of the fields in a GRE header are optional, including the checksum present bit, the reserved fields, and the checksum itself. Unless the GRE implementation is supporting RFC 1701 — which is an earlier version of GRE and supports key information, sequence numbers, and routing information — the Reserved0 field will be set to zero. The Reserved1 field is only present when the checksum field is present and is currently undefined. The version number of GRE is set to zero.

Once the final count has been performed, we see that the only real information that is consistently within a GRE header is the protocol type field (Exhibit 5). This is a value that matches the IEEE values of layer 2 protocols. In effect, and at a minimum, the IP header that transports the data indicates that the data the IP header is carrying is GRE data. The receiving host then examines the GRE header, which indicates what type of layer 2 data is found in the GRE data field. This layer 2 header will then be

GRE header format

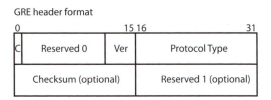

Exhibit 4. Generic Routing Encapsulation Header

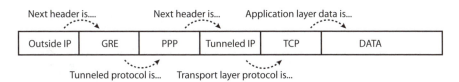

Exhibit 5. Each Header Needs to Define What the Next Protocol Header Is

examined to determine what kind of layer 3 information is found within the layer 2 frames. Simple, right? From this basic framework, tunneling protocols can become a lot more complicated. GRE itself does not provide any mechanism for authenticating tunnels or evaluating their performance. GRE simply defines which layer 2 protocol is being tunneled inside an IP packet.

10.3.2 The Point-to-Point Tunneling Protocol (PPTP)

Designed primarily by the Microsoft Corporation, the Point-to-Point Tunneling Protocol (PPTP) is designed to simulate a layer 2 connection over multiple hops in an IP network. To best understand what PPTP accomplishes, let us first consider an example without PPTP.

In a typical dial-up scenario, a home user dials into his ISP for Internet access. Through a modem connected to the home computer, the computer accesses the PSTN (public switched telephone network) and creates a circuit-switched connection to a network access server at the ISP. This connection is a point-to-point (PPP) connection and uses the standard PPP frame format. Although the home user and the ISP access server are not directly connected, from the point of view of the data-link layer, there is a single circuit between the two devices. Once the initial PPP connection is established, there are a few things that need to happen. The first step is generally to make sure that the home user has paid his bill and has the privilege of using the service provider's resources. This is most commonly done through a username/password combination sent by the home user and verified through the use of a central database server at the ISP (more on authentication methods later). Once the user is authenticated, the home user's PC needs to be configured to use the network to which it is connected. Remember when using a PPP connection that the computer appears to be a node directly connected to the ISP network. Thus, it will require, at a minimum, an IP address, subnet mask, and default gateway. Typically, a DNS server address will also be configured at this time.

Fortunately for the Internet as a whole, instead of expecting millions of America Online (AOL) users to understand how to configure these elements on their home computer each time they connect to the network, the PPP protocol has the ability to configure the host device automatically.

The same process occurs when remote users create a dial-in connection to their office's remote access server. In this case, the company has a number of incoming lines specifically reserved for data calls and these lines will terminate at some type of modem device. The only difference between home users dialing their ISP is that sometimes a corporate dial-in connection will have the requirement that protocols other than IP be used. In this case, PPP, being a layer 2 protocol, supports a number of non-IP protocols. In the case of IPX and NetBEUI, PPP also supports the automatic configuration of these protocols.

In summary, PPP is an ideal protocol for dial-in connections because it is already configured with authentication support, configuration support, and the ability to use layer 3 protocols other than IP if needed. The catch is that all of this functionality only works when you are directly connected to a PPP network access server.

Clearly, this is not possible on the Internet. What we need is a way to make two remote devices think they are directly connected over multiple IP hops. So how do we place a layer 2 protocol (PPP) inside a layer 3 IP packet for transport? Using tunneling, of course!

The ability to logically extend a PPP connection over multiple layer 3 hops is what PPTP is all about. To accomplish this, PPTP relies on the GRE header, separate control and data connections, and network devices, as illustrated in Exhibit 6.Because the GRE header does not include any type of connection setup information by default, PPTP uses a separate control connection. This control connection is used to set up a PPTP session, to negotiate protocol parameters, to control session flow, and finally, to tear down a PPTP session. Using TCP allows error checking and flow control to apply to the PPTP control session without the need to introduce more complexity into PPTP itself. TCP uses port 1723 to listen for new connection requests.

PPTP uses what the protocol specifications term an "enhanced" version of GRE. The enhancements to the GRE header are the inclusion of a sequence number field and an acknowledgement field much like that found in a TCP header. Unlike the fields in the TCP header, these fields are never

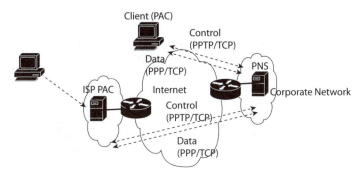

Exhibit 6. PPTP Network

used for retransmission or error correction. They are only used for flow control and sequencing information.

User data in a PPTP connection is tunneled inside a PPP header, which is, in turn, tunneled inside an enhanced GRE header. GRE simply provides protocol identification to the remote end along with some sequencing information. The GRE/PPP combination itself is connectionless. It is assumed that if error correction is important, then the user data itself will provide it.

The PPTP network server (PNS) is an application designed to operate as part of a generic operating system. Because this was a protocol primarily developed by Microsoft, the generic portion of this clearly means a Windows server of some sort. PPTP servers, however, can also be found for other operating systems. The responsibilities of the PNS include authenticating new connections, bundling PPP links if appropriate, terminating PPP control protocols for layer 3 protocols, and any bridging or routing functions required of the connection. The PNS can be summarized as the server portion of PPTP, with the exception that the PNS can also initiate a PPTP connection to a PAC if required.

The PPTP access client (PAC) can be considered the client side of PPTP. This is a device that is responsible for the interface with the PSTN, the logical termination of the PPP link control protocols (LCPs), and participation in the authentication process. The PAC is a process that in PPTP implementations is most commonly found on a host PC with dial-in software. Prior to Microsoft's L2TP VPN implementation on Windows 2000 devices, PPTP was the default protocol used for host-to-gateway VPNs on Microsoft platforms.

As indicated in Exhibit 6, a PAC can also be found within the network itself. An example of this might be when an ISP wishes to offer dial-in VPN services for its customers. In this case, remote dial-in users would dial into the PAC, which would then forward traffic from a number of PPTP connections over a single data and control channel. Used in this manner, PPTP is transparent to the client because, from their point of view, they have established a normal dial-in connection to an ISP. From the PAC, all traffic is tunneled via PPTP to a corporate PNS.

Deployed in this manner, PPTP is a very scalable protocol. Because one control and data connection between the PAC and the PNS can multiplex many different user data sessions, PPTP session information and overhead are minimal. This is not, however, how PPTP is commonly deployed. As will be discussed in the L2TP section (Layer 2 Tunneling Protocol; see Chapter 10.3.3), if an ISP wished to offer this type of service, it would be more likely to use L2TP. PPTP is most commonly deployed as a host-to-gateway type VPN instead. Because each dial-in host requires a single control connection with no chance of multiplexing either control or data sessions, PPTP in practice generally does not scale well.

So far, in discussing the architecture surrounding PPTP, has any mention been made of security? Despite commonly being sold as a VPN solution, PPTP itself does not incorporate any security mechanisms. This means that the control channel information is sent in the clear. The private part of PPTP is accomplished using the Microsoft Point-to-Point Encryption Protocol (MPPE). As its name suggests, MPPE is used to encrypt PPP data. While MPPE does support 128-bit encryption, it has suffered from a number of serious security flaws that have allowed attackers to decipher encrypted data. Most of the weaknesses have revolved around the initial generation of the keys. Each discovered vulnerability is fixed in a subsequent service pack, yet the history of the protocol has left some network security experts unable to recommend its use as a company VPN.

The early flaws in Microsoft's PPTP and MPPE encryption were based on Microsoft's support of legacy LAN Manager authentication and MS-CHAPv1. This authentication scheme is not as robust as that used in Windows domain authentication and is more easily brute-force attacked. Microsoft's PPTP authentication using CHAP was also flawed, in that the server was never properly authenticated. An attacker could pose as the server over a network and accept incoming connections. Remote users would be none the wiser. Finally, the control connection implementation had a bug in it that would allow remote users to crash a PPTP server outright by sending connection information over the control channel.

Like most protocols that rely on passwords for authentication, PPTP also suffers from users who choose poor passwords. Early implementations of the Microsoft PPTP server based the secret key used for the actual encryption of data on the user's password. This allowed easily crackable keys to be created when users did not choose strong passwords.

Lest you think that all of these flaws are old and have been resolved, versions of PPTP shipping with Windows 2000 and Windows XP have been confirmed to have buffer overflow vulnerabilities that allow a remote user to again crash a PPTP server.

PPTP has several benefits that make it an attractive VPN solution for many companies. First, it is standard on every Windows server. Client support is also built into every Windows client. This, combined with an army of MCSEs that have been trained on and tested with PPTP, ensures that it will have wide popularity. This also means that it fits into the budget of most companies. They have already paid for the rights to use the operating system, so why invest more in VPN hardware and software if the basic building blocks are already there? PPTP is not only the domain of Windows operating systems anymore. Free implementations of PPTP servers and clients can also be found for the popular Linux operating system.

The client/server nature of PPTP and the ubiquitous presence of Microsoft means that a VPN can be set up quickly. This is handy when temporary or immediate VPN connectivity is required. It is also configured totally independent of the ISP. In an effort to provide differentiating and value-added services, some ISPs offer a VPN service of their own, configured much like PPTP (see the L2TP protocol, Chapter 10.3.3). PPTP, however, can be configured without the participation of the ISP, which naturally precludes payments to the ISP as well.

Because PPTP is configured independently of the ISP, it is also a good solution for companies that have a diverse user base. If you purchase PPP-based VPN services from an ISP, then to be cost effective, your users need to be dial clients of that ISP as well. With PPTP, if you have a remote user base that is connecting to the Internet in many different ways such as through cable modems, DSL, and multiple dial-up accounts, PPTP can easily accommodate them all.

Due to the virtual layer 2 PPP connections that PPTP creates between the remote user and the PPTP server, PPTP is also ideal if a company has non-IP data that it must transmit over the VPN. This is most commonly the case with corporations that are still running Novell's IPX on their LANs, or even Banyan Vines. PPTP allows remote users to tunnel these normally non-Internet protocols over public networks.

There are also several reasons why you might decide to pass on PPTP as your VPN solution. The first of these reasons is security. Most of the examples previously discussed in this chapter regarding flaws in the PPTP implementation have been fixed. Despite this, the fact remains that Microsoft is a favorite target of the Internet underground. It is not that Microsoft is necessarily any less secure than other options out there; it is just that those who would harm your network more often target it. It is a safe bet that new PPTP flaws will be found (just as new security flaws will be found in any Internet application), and there will be hordes of individuals out there who are anxious to try out any new PPTP holes.

Also related to security, the encryption used for PPTP packets is not as robust as other options such as IPSec. At the very least, PPTP does not offer any encryption of the control channel information. To an attacker trying to learn more about the network, captured control packets provide a wealth of information. With IPSec, after the first few packets of negotiation, all information exchanged between hosts is encrypted. The encryption algorithms in IPSec are also more robust. Not all 128-bit encryption schemes are created equal. Even those that use the same encryption algorithm depend on the use of securely generated secret keys used to encrypt and decrypt the data.

PPTP also adds quite a bit of overhead to IP packets. Consider that, in addition to the normal TCP data that you are sending to the company LAN, you add an internal PPP header, a GRE header, an outside IP address, and another layer 2 header, most likely PPP again. This adds about 37 more octets of data to each packet. While header compression can reduce this somewhat, over dial-up links these effects are noticeable. While this overhead is required for the functionality that PPTP brings to the VPN, if you are always going to pass IP traffic only, then the overhead to allow other layer 3 protocols to be tunneled is unnecessary.

The scalability of PPTP has always been an issue with the protocol. While the PPTP specifications outline a very scalable protocol when used with a network PAC and local PNS, the common implementation of PPTP with multiple remote clients means that for every user connection there is an associated control connection. This is contrasted with the original standards that suggested many remote users sharing a single PAC, thus allowing a single control connection to coordinate many user sessions. PPTP in the Microsoft implementation also has limitations as to how many remote clients can connect at one time. At last count there was support for 255 connections. While this sounds plentiful for the small network, I have never seen a server in common networking environments able to handle nearly that many connections.

Finally, for some, PPTP means Microsoft. While there are plenty of implementations of PPTP clients and servers out there that are not Microsoft products, the association between PPTP and Microsoft is strong. Some may disagree with Microsoft business practices and choose not to use its products — although these exceptions are few and far between. The association that PPTP has with Microsoft causes some to look elsewhere for alternative protocols.

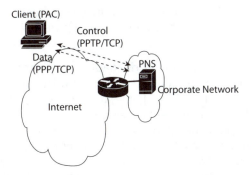

Exhibit 7. PPTP Operation Example

Now that we have an understanding of the parts that make up PPTP, let us examine it in action (see Exhibit 7). For this discussion we assume the most common configuration of PPTP, which is that a remote user is accessing a company network. The remote user's computer will act as the PAC and a Windows server on the company network that is accessible from the Internet will operate as the PNS (PPTP network server). First, the user will establish a regular dial-up connection to the Internet via any ISP. After the authentication process, this will create a PPP connection to the ISP itself that will configure the user's computer with an IP address and other IP-related information. So far, this is the exact process the user would follow if he wished to surf the Web or download files.

Once the initial PPP connection to the ISP has been established, the user will then open another connection. For the most part, this is a connection that is configured much like a normal dial-in connection except, instead of dialing a phone number for a connection, the configuration indicates a remote IP or DNS name to which to connect. This should not be surprising, considering that PPTP simply creates another tunneled PPP connection. When the user initiates the second connection, the PPTP software on his PC attempts to create a TCP/PPTP control connection with the PPTP server software located on the company network. Depending on the configuration of the network itself, the firewall protecting the company network will have to be configured to allow TCP port 1723 and the GRE protocol through the firewall to the company's PPTP server for this connection to be successful.

The first packets sent will attempt to set up the control connection itself. Once this has been accomplished, information specific to the PPTP data session will be exchanged. The outer layer is now up. PPP and key exchanges will then be performed to bring up the virtual PPP link over the GRE data session. Key information will provide for the encryption process applied to the PPP session. The PPP authentication process will also validate the user and configure the remote user's host PC with another IP address. Yes, the remote host will now be configured with two IP addresses and that point bears some discussion.

PPTP will create a virtual network adapter on the remote host. This virtual adapter will be the one that is configured with IP information specific to the tunneled PPP connection. The real network adapter — the one that dials the ISP in the first place — is assigned an address and IP information specific to the ISP. This allows packets from the remote host to be routed across the Internet. Once the GRE PPP connection is created using PPTP, the virtual adapter allows the remote host to look like it is directly attached to the company LAN. Because the IP addresses used inside the GRE PPP connection are never examined or seen by the Internet routers (the whole point of GRE and tunneling, right?), the inside IP addresses can be private addresses that are not normally routable over the Internet.

At this point there is a TCP control connection between the remote user and the PPTP server. This control connection, once set up, periodically sends a keep-alive packet between the two hosts. This is simply to ensure that the remote side was not suddenly disconnected and resources are being saved for a connection that no longer exists. There is also an enhanced GRE tunnel between the remote PPTP client and the PPTP server. Data sent over this traffic appears to the two devices to have traveled over a PPP connection. In effect, the remote PPTP client has become a virtual part of the company LAN. While PPTP itself does not support any encryption, during the setup of the PPP tunnel, MPPE was configured based upon the username of the remote user. This provides up to 128-bit encryption for the traffic over the GRE tunnel only.

Because the user has an Internet IP address assigned to him by his local ISP when he dialed in to the Internet, the remote user is also able to access Internet sites at the same time he is using the PPTP tunnel. This process is known as split tunneling and will be discussed in more detail when we consider the overall security implications of VPNs. Suffice it to say at this point, a split tunnel is the ability to access the VPN tunnel and non-VPN sites at the same time.

When the user no longer has a need for the PPTP tunnel, the control connection begins the process of first terminating the remote PPP connection, and then the PPTP connection. Finally, the TCP session that has established the control connection is torn down between the PPTP client and the PPTP server. If the user has no need for Internet access at all, he will then disconnect from the ISP or is able to continue using the ISP's Internet connection to continue working online.

Based on all this information, we are ready to make some recommendations regarding the use of PPTP as a VPN protocol. PPTP should be considered when:

- *A company has limited needs for VPN connections.* PPTP on the Microsoft platform is not as scalable as other solutions.
- *Remote connectivity is more important than encryption.* PPTP will protect data, but not as securely as other options available.
- *There is an immediate need for VPN connectivity.* PPTP can be deployed very quickly without the involvement of other parties. Typically, PPTP can be ready for access within a couple of hours at most.
- *Windows domain integration is desired.* PPTP uses existing user names and passwords for authentication on the Windows network. This makes managing users a straightforward process for Windows shops.
- *Non-IP protocols must be supported.* The PPP extension that PPTP provides allows for non-IP protocols to be tunneled over the Internet.

PPTP also has a number of reasons that it should *not* be considered, including:

- Microsoft is moving away from the PPTP model as well. The option we will discuss next (i.e., L2TP) is the preferred method of layer 2 VPN connectivity for dial-in and remote clients on Windows 2000 and XP operating systems.
- It does not scale as well as other options.
- The security of the protocol according to Microsoft's implementation has been compromised several times in the past; including the encryption.
- It is primarily a Microsoft-only protocol. While there are other implementations of PPTP available, the major support for PPTP has been through Microsoft.
- This technology is primarily to enable dial-in, or host-to-gateway VPN connections. Gateway-to-gateway tunnels are possible, but normally not configured using PPTP.

10.3.3 *Layer 2 Tunneling Protocol (L2TP)*

Like PPTP, the Layer 2 Tunneling Protocol (L2TP) is used to create an extended PPP tunnel. We will see that as we explore L2TP, it shares many similarities with PPTP and there is a reason for this. Prior to the development of L2TP, there was another layer 2 tunneling option known as Layer 2 Forwarding (L2F). Developed by Cisco, this protocol was used in routers to create virtual point-to-point connections and competed with the Microsoft-developed standard PPTP. Knowing that confusion in the marketplace is bad for technologies, the IETF requested that Microsoft and Cisco work together to merge their tunneling protocols. The result of that work is L2TP. Currently, the most widely deployed version of L2TP is L2TPv2. Most of the discussion below refers to v2. There is an emerging standard known as L2TPv3 that provides many of the benefits of MPLS without the need for an MPLS-enabled network. This protocol, along with its pros and cons, are discussed after the initial L2TPv2 discussion.

The major difference between L2TP and PPTP is that L2TP does not use GRE encapsulation for data. Instead, the protocol specifies an L2TP header designed specifically for the needs of the protocol. The second major difference and one more relevant to implementation of the protocol is that L2TP does not attempt to provide its own encryption of the PPP tunnel as PPTP does. Instead, L2TP relies on the IPSec protocol to apply encryption if it is required.

Before explaining these two points and examining the protocol in greater detail, it is worthwhile to point out while we are on the subject that both L2TP and PPTP do not have to provide encryption of data. Encryption adds additional overhead and latency to packets due to the encryption/decryption process. In some cases, it may be more important to simply establish an extended PPP tunnel between two points as in the case of tunneling non-IP protocols.

While PPTP was developed with the average Windows office network in mind as the market, L2F and its derivative L2TP were developed with the ISP market in mind. Thus, while many of the features and pieces of the protocols are similar, we will see that their implementations are different. This, however, is changing, with L2TP working its way into the small-office market as recent Windows operating systems include L2TP as the default tunneling protocol.

L2TP networks (Exhibit 8) are designed around two primary components: the L2TP access concentrator (LAC) and the L2TP network server (LNS). The similarity to the PPTP components PAC and PNS should not be overlooked. Other than the name, the devices provide similar functions in both protocols. The LAC is the remote side of the connection. This can be a remote client, but is just as often an actual device that sits on the ISP's network. Deployed with the LAC as part of the ISP, L2TP is an ideal example of compulsory tunneling. Clients dial-in to the LAC and their calls are forwarded in a multiplexed L2TP tunnel to the LNS. Clients are unaware of, and do not have to configure, any element of the VPN tunnel. They dial what to them seems like a normal ISP dial-up connection. The LNS is the corporate-based network server. In a managed solution, however, this does not even need to be located at the company site, but can be at the ISP. L2TP uses a data session and a control session. The control session is used for the establishment of the PPP connection in the data session and for feedback about the quality of the link. The L2TP control channel is fairly low bandwidth once the connection is set up and therefore can be used to multiplex many data sessions. When employed as originally designed, with the

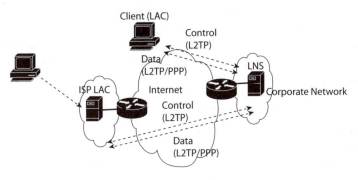

Exhibit 8. L2TP Network

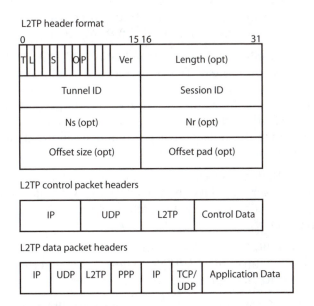

Exhibit 9. L2TP Header Format

LAC part of the ISP network, this leads to a very scalable solution with one control session being able to manage numerous user sessions. Of course, used in a host-to-gateway solution like PPTP typically reduces the usefulness of this option.

For both the control and data session, L2TP has its own header that it encapsulates inside a UDP datagram. For reliability, the L2TP control channel has its own built-in sequencing and acknowledgement of packets. The entire protocol header for discussion is shown in Exhibit 9, along with the encapsulation model of the control and data sessions.

The first bits of the header, the type (T), length (L), sequence (S), and offset (O) are primarily used to differentiate between control and data sessions within a stream of multiplexed L2TP messages. The priority (P) bit is used to indicate the relative importance of the L2TP packet in a local dequeuing and transmission scheme. This bit is only used in data messages. The version field is always version 2, unless of course this is one of the rare circumstances where the emerging version 3 is being introduced.

If the length bit (L) is set, the length field will logically enough contain information as to the length of the L2TP message in octets. Like other fields indicated with the optional (opt) term, these fields may or may not be present in any given L2TP message. The most common differentiator is that control messages have more options set and data messages have less. The concept is that the control messages have nothing assisting them with flow control or reliability, whereas data transmitted will have the encapsulated data itself to provide flow control and resequencing if necessary.

Of the most interest for us in our examination of L2TP are the tunnel ID field and the session ID field. The tunnel ID is a locally significant value exchanged during the creation of a control session. Locally significant only means that the value does not need to be agreed upon between remote points of an L2TP connection; it only needs to be communicated. If an LNS has multiple control sessions active, the tunnel ID allows the LNS to identify control information as it is received.

The session ID identifies a session within a particular tunnel. This is the identification of user data. Like the tunnel ID, this value is only locally significant, determined by the local host and transmitted to the remote host for use in packets sent back to the local host.

Nr and Ns are both sequence numbers indicating what has been sent (Ns) and what has been received (Nr). These fields together are used by control sessions to ensure reliable communications.

Turning to the issue of security, L2TP does not make any attempt to secure data on its own. Instead. it uses IPSec as its means of encrypting data. The benefit of this approach is that IPSec is mature and well tested. Any security flaws have been identified. IPSec also has many vendors that support and implement it, increasing the chances of interoperability in a heterogeneous environment.

When describing L2TP encryption with IPSec, the question is often asked, "If I'm going to use IPSec for encryption anyway, why use L2TP at all?" A good example of this is in the Microsoft implementation of its IPSec VPN intended as a replacement for PPTP. Although it is an IPSec VPN, it uses L2TP as the protocol to transmit data. Although we have not discussed IPSec in any detail yet, we will share just enough to make sense of this discussion.

IPSec provides encryption for IP protocols, as the name implies. It also has the ability to encapsulate data so that all information in a packet, other than the IP header required for routing is encrypted. Notice the use of the term "encapsulate" rather than "tunnel" in this instance. By default, IPSec will not allow you to tunnel layer 2 data — only IP data. So far, this is not a problem. L2TP is transmitted inside a UDP header, making its operation with IPSec seamless.

IPSec, however, cannot support layer 2 protocols. That is, IPSec will not provide the illusion of an extended PPP tunnel. If you need to include other non-routable protocols across the WAN, then L2TP is required for the tunnel. IPSec on top of that tunnel is then required for encryption.

Many companies will then note that they only transmit IP data anyway, so there is no need for the PPP connection enabled through L2TP. That may be true for data transmission, but PPP also provides another important function for remote users: the ability to authenticate users and configure the PPP adapter of remote users with IP addresses, subnet masks, default gateways, and DNS servers. Referring back to the Microsoft IPsec VPN implementation, L2TP provides authentication and configuration services that are essential to the seamless deployment of a host-to-gateway VPN solution even if IP is the only protocol that the remote user will ever be sending over the connection.

In the end, it is not so much a matter of L2TP lacking functionality as the reason that IPSec was included as the encryption protocol. It was the lack of capability of IPSec at the time that L2TP was being developed. The protocol designers realized that IPSec lacked important functions for host-to-gateway deployments where IP address would change frequently and it would be a duplication of effort to include another encryption protocol for L2TP. Instead, the protocols were joined. As we discuss in the IPSec section (Chapter 10.4), many of the problems with the remote configuration of IPSec and authentication of roaming users have been fixed. The future of L2TP, like that of PPTP, may be limited as understanding and operating implementations of IPSec shrink over time.

In summary, L2TP is a VPN solution to consider if:

- *Compulsory tunneling is required.* If an ISP is going to offer a managed dial-in solution for VPN services, L2TP is most likely to be the protocol in use.
- Non-IP protocols need to be routed over the WAN to remote gateways or hosts. The PPP connection created by L2TP enables this.
- *A managed VPN service is desired.* As noted above, PPTP is a Windows-based solution and L2TP is a service provider-based solution.

- *Strong encryption is called for in the security policy.* L2TP's integration with IPSec ensures that the strongest available encryption and authentication methods can be used.
- Your site decides to completely manage the VPN on its own. L2TP, like PPTP, does not require the assistance of a service provider to enable it.
- *Dial-in users can use multiple ISPs and accounts to access your VPN.* Just because L2TP is ideal for service provider provisioning does not mean that this is the only way to provision it. L2TP can be provisioned just as PPTP is in a host-to-gateway scenario.

There are few reasons not to use L2TP. Most of the reasons not to use L2TP revolve around redundancy of features with IPSec. L2TP would not be an ideal solution if:

- *Only IP-based protocols are ever going to be required on the VPN.* In this case, L2TP only adds more complexity and overhead to the VPN.
- *Packet overhead is an issue on low-bandwidth links.* L2TP does add overhead to IP packets. If all that is required is encryption then it is more efficient to simply use IPSec.

10.3.3.1 Layer 2 Tunneling Protocol, Version 3. While much of the discussion thus far has focused on L2TPv2, there is a new VPN protocol on the horizon that might fit your security needs as well. Although related to L2TPv2, L2TPv3 is significantly different enough in its implementation to warrant its own chapter section.

While L2TP was a technology that allowed the extension of a PPP tunnel across a network, L2TPv3 removes the PPP-specific information in the header of the L2TP packet. This, with further modifications to the header, allows L2TPv3 to tunnel layer 2 protocols other than PPP. Thus, L2TPv3 could tunnel Ethernet frames across a network, giving a company the appearance of a global LAN. Other protocols that operate with L2TPv3 are HDLC, 802.1q VLANs, Frame Relay, and Packet over Sonet (POS). The header has also been modified to support rapid encapsulation and de-encapsulation, allowing L2TPv3 to operate at high speeds.

In many respects, L2TPv3 is much like MPLS but without the need for a network core that has been reconfigured to support MPLS. Only the endpoints of the tunnel need to understand that there is an L2TPv3 tunnel present. All other network nodes route IP traffic normally. To some service providers, wary of investing too heavily in a fairly new technology like MPLS, L2TPv3 tunnels are the perfect solution. Customers receive the same layer 2 protocols using L2TPv3 that they would receive if the carrier were utilizing MPLS layer 2 VPNs, yet the service provider does not need to globally provision an MPLS network. L2TPv3 can only be rolled out between the customers that desire the service.

So far, much of the discussion of L2TPv3 has focused on the carrier backbone. This is because unless you are a large enterprise customer, L2TPv3 is not something that you are going to be able to provision on your own. Currently, L2TPv3, while on a standards track with the IETF, is Cisco proprietary. Furthermore, the L2TPv3 feature set is available only on some of Cisco's most powerful (and expensive) routers. This alone limits the implementation of L2TPv3 to only large service providers and large corporations. If you are a small company that is interested in the benefits of L2TPv3, then you need to find a service provider that supports this service.

When considering if L2TPv3 is the solution for you, many of the same pluses and minuses that are applied to MPLS can also be applied here. First, L2TPv3 alone does not provide any type of encryption service. IPSec is used as in L2TPv2 to provide encryption services. The privacy of L2TP is still up in the air. MPLS takes a number of steps to ensure that data cannot be inserted into the label-switched path. Because L2TPv3 is simply IP encapsulated packets, the ability to restrict traffic to the level of an MPLS, Frame Relay, or ATM network is limited to current IP controls. To help protect against data being inserted into an L2TPv3 session, an L2TPv3 header uses a 64-bit "cookie" field that serves as an incrementing sequence number. As in a TCP session, remote ends of the L2TPv3 tunnel will only accept data that is within a certain range. Without the ability to sniff the data, it would be extremely difficult to guess the value of these sequence numbers and insert bogus L2TPv3 data remotely. Data captured in transit can be read. Remember, however, that L2TPv3 is generally a provider technology. Your data is much more likely to be captured on your own LAN than in the backbone of a single, large service provider. In summary, if you want the private element of L2TPv3, make sure that IPSec is being employed on sensitive data.

10.4   Internet Protocol Security (IPSec)

Layer 2 tunneling protocols such as PPTP and L2TP are not the current state-of-the art in IP VPN technology. Currently, this is the domain of the Internet Protocol Security (IPSec) suite of protocols. By combining tunneling and encryption, many users are able to realize cost savings, flexibility, and confidentiality for their data.

IPSec is a mechanism used to encrypt data. Using encryption and tunnels, a virtual private network can be created over the Internet. As mentioned, this is often a preferable solution to companies for a single reason — cost. Internet access alone is generally cheaper than a leased layer two VPN through a service provider. This should not be the only consideration, however. Some service providers are marketing their layer 2 solutions with much lower costs to prevent customers from making the switch to a pure

IP/VPN solution. This is because the second major advantage of an IPSec VPN is that the service can be provisioned completely independently from the service provider. This freedom is another powerful incentive for those who are frustrated by the sometimes long provisioning cycles of service providers.

The primary disadvantage of IPSec for some time has been interoperability. IPSec is a complicated set of protocols spanning several RFCs. In fact, the primary criticism of IPSec has been that it is too complicated, with too many options to consider when deploying it. These options and disagreements about the standards for implementations have led many vendors to develop incompatible IPSec solutions. This landscape has changed in recent years and, although interoperability is not perfect yet, an understanding of the IPSec protocol and the most commonly encountered options will go a long way in ensuring you have a painless VPN rollout.

To understand where to use IPSec in our networks, we first must discuss how IPSec operates. To protect traffic, IPSec uses two different types of protocol headers, the Authentication Header (AH), which as its name suggests is used to ensure the integrity of data that has been transmitted, but does not encrypt data. The other header is the Encapsulating Security Payload (ESP). ESP is the header that is used to encrypt data and provides the confidentiality service that we commonly associate with a VPN. The IPSec standards also call for two *modes* of operation: tunnel mode and transport mode. Of the two, tunnel mode is more common, but we will examine uses for each mode.

We will discuss the AH and ESP headers in more detail shortly, but for now let us introduce the concepts so that we can establish a baseline vocabulary for further discussions. While IPSec is commonly associated with encrypted data, this is only one of the features that the protocol suite offers. The AH only ensures that the data that has been transmitted has not been altered. That means that if Host A sends a message to Host B over a shared network, someone could sniff the data and see the contents of the packet. Use of the AH would mean, however, that the person in the middle could not alter the contents of that packet without alerting the receiving end. Furthermore, if proper authentication of the session has occurred, Host B would have a very high assurance that it was indeed communicating with Host A.

What is the point of all this IPSec complexity if data cannot be encrypted? Is that not what we want IPSec for in the first place? Readers in countries other than the United States might more quickly appreciate this; in some places, the encryption of data is illegal. In this case, the AH at least provides the assurance that if someone is observing your data, they cannot change it without alerting you. In short, the AH provides integrity, but not confidentiality.

The ESP, on the other hand, lives up to what we commonly associate with the confidentiality requirements of a VPN. The payload of the packet is encrypted and is encapsulated by the ESP header and an ESP trailer. Typically, the ESP header provides confidentiality, but not integrity. That means you can be fairly sure that someone has not been able to read your data, but you cannot be completely sure that someone has not sent you a fake encrypted packet inserted into your communications with a remote host. However remote this possibility may be, ESP does have an authentication option that can be configured if required. It should also be noted that ESP does not *need* to provide encryption at all. Null encryption can be used. That means that the ESP header is attached to data, but the data is not encrypted. Remember this if you are ever troubleshooting an IPSec connection.

In addition to the two major header types, IPSec also uses two modes of operation, each of which is discussed in some detail here, along with suggested implementations of each mode.

The easiest mode to work with if you are new to IPSec is the transport mode. In this case, the data being transmitted is simply encapsulated in an AH or ESP header and transmitted. In a sense, IPSec just becomes another header layer in the IP suite of services and, as data is passed down the stack it is encapsulated just as it is at any other layer. The packet diagram in Exhibit 10 shows an example of TCP data being protected by an ESP header in transport mode (upper) and another diagram showing the AH header providing integrity to a packet (lower). In this case, the IP header on the outside of the packet contains the same IP address header of the originating host. Tunnel mode means that an IP packet carrying user data is tunneled inside another IP packet. If you recall the previous discussion of tunneling and encapsulation around PPTP and L2TP, you will see that the same process is occurring here. Exhibit 11 shows a tunneled packet.

In the case of PPTP, the "tunnel header" field was a GRE|PPP header combination. In the case of L2TP, the tunnel header was an L2TP| PPP header. IPSec is not interested in the extension of a layer 2 header and so the tunnel header is an AH or ESP header.

There are several significant elements of tunnel mode operation. The first is that the IP headers on the packet do not need to match. This means that Host A can send out normal unencrypted data, and a router or another VPN gateway device could accept the packet and then tunnel it inside another IP packet over the Internet using an IP address from the gateway. The packet that the Internet sees has the IP address given to it by the VPN gateway device. Eventually, another VPN gateway device would receive the packet and remove the outermost IP header and then decrypt the data. The now-unencrypted IP packet will have the IP address of Host A. This

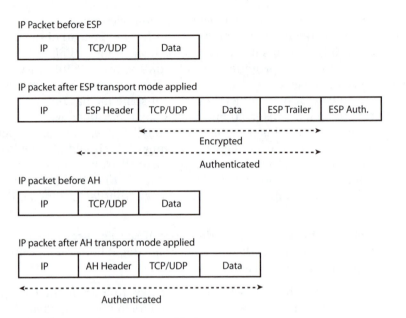

Exhibit 10. ESP and AH Transport Mode

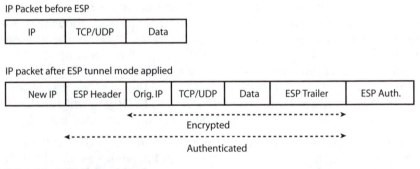

Exhibit 11. ESP Tunnel Mode

unencrypted packet can now be forwarded on to Host B as a normal IP packet. This process is diagramed in Exhibit 12.

While the data is traveling over the local LAN, it is unencrypted and viewable to anyone with a sniffer. When it travels out over the Internet, the packet is encrypted by the gateways. Using this method, entire networks behind the gateways can communicate with each other using only one IPSec connection between the gateways. Anyone monitoring traffic on the Internet would only see a lot of traffic passing between the two gateways, but would not be able to read any of the data nor have any clues as to

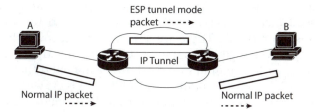

Exhibit 12. Gateway-to-Gateway ESP Tunnel Mode

which LAN devices on each network were communicating with each other. This ability to multiplex many user sessions into a single tunnel is a powerful ability of IPSec. The traffic patterns between internal LAN hosts are hidden to any interloper.

Because the internal IP header is not visible to any Internet traffic, these addresses can also be in the private range. My 192.168.1.0/24 network could be connected to your 10.0.0.0/8 network with no problems, as long as the gateways that we were using had at least one public address to "wrap" the encrypted traffic between our networks.

Taking this concept one step further, it also means that a remote client could connect to a company gateway using a public Internet address, as is done with L2TP or PPTP solutions. Inside the tunnel, a virtual interface could be created for the remote client and the remote client could be assigned a company internal or private address to use for communications over the tunnel. This allows the remote gateway to configure the client using extensions to DHCP and eases the configuration of roaming IPSec clients. From the point of view of the virtual tunnel interface, the remote client looks like it is part of the company subnet.

Together, transport mode and tunnel mode cover just about all the requirements for connectivity that could possibly be presented. Of the two, tunnel mode is the more commonly employed, for three reasons. The first reason is that the majority of IPSec implementations are of the gateway-to-gateway type, although this is changing as IPSec alone becomes more widely available for host-to-gateway configurations. This type of deployment naturally fits with tunneled data for reasons explained above. All traffic between the gateways can be encrypted with a single IPSec tunnel. This greatly increases the simplicity of deployment and improves the performance of the IPSec gateways.

Remote clients also commonly use tunnel mode because of the ability to use private addresses on the internally tunneled IP header. This greatly simplifies firewall configuration for tunneled packets and address allocation issues for network administrators.

Using tunnel mode with remote clients also has another important benefit that is explained in greater depth shortly; it works better with network address translation (NAT). There are a number of reasons why IPSec and NAT do not work well together; but let it suffice for now that of all the problems, the ones with tunnel mode are more easily fixed than those with transport mode. Because a popular use of IPSec VPNs is with SOHO (small office/home office) users who connect from their home networks using NAT to the corporate office, NAT issues were a serious impediment to the adoption of IPSec as the VPN protocol of choice.

Transport mode is best suited for direct data transfers between two hosts. For this reason, it is less likely seen in host-to-gateway implementations because the reasons for these connections are not to access the gateway itself, but to access services behind the gateway. Transport mode, however, does have an application for LAN hosts. On a local network, there is no need for the additional overhead of another IP packet and the benefit of hiding inside another IP packet would be questionable. The LAN, however, is where data is most likely to be sniffed or otherwise exposed. If this would be a concern in your organization, then the IPSec transport mode would be an ideal solution.

Having discussed the basics of IPSec, we can now begin to look at the protocol in a bit more detail. While a general overview of IPSec is helpful, when considering interoperability, troubleshooting, and implementation choices, it is best to know the protocol suite to some level of detail.

10.4.1 Authentication Header (AH)

We begin this discussion by examining the authentication header (AH). This header provides integrity, but not confidentiality of data. While use of the AH is not widespread, it will provide the opportunity to examine several common elements of IPSec headers. The first element to understand about AH is the integrity it provides to IP packets. This will be an important issue when we examine the operation of other protocols that like to change packet headers and data, such as NAT.

AH, unlike the ESP authentication option, provides integrity to the entire IP packet, including the IP header itself. Thus, if anyone tried to spoof the IP header or even modify information in it, then the authentication of the packet would fail.

A careful examination (see Exhibit 13) of the operation of the IP header through multiple hops will show that the IP header itself, during normal operation, is not a static entity. If the IP header is changing throughout the lifetime of the packet, how can authentication on the IP header itself be performed? Although the TOS flags — fragment information, time-to-live (TTL), and checksum values — change as the packet travels from hop to

AH header format

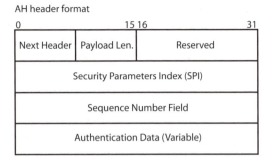

Exhibit 13. AH Format

hop, the AH does not include those fields in its calculations. So, AH does not authenticate *every* bit of a packet, but it would be difficult to modify the TTL or checksum without affecting the deliverability of the packet to begin with.

The AH is always found immediately after the outermost IP header.[6] Protocol ID 51 in the IP header indicates to the receiving device that the next header is an AH. Like most protocols, the AH has a field that indicates what the protocol header *after* the AH header will be. This allows the receiver to correctly interpret the bits as the packet is read.[7] The next header can be any IP protocol. One of the primary advantages of IPSec over other IP-based solutions like SSL is that IPSec works on every IP packet, not just those of a particular higher-layer protocol.

Because the authentication data at the end of the packet is a variable, the length of the packet as a whole needs to be described to the receiver so that it is aware of when the AH information ends and the Next Header begins. This is the purpose of the Payload Length field (Payload Len.), which describes the AH in 32-bit words (four octets). Note that this is the same value that is expected by the IP and TCP headers.

The Reserved field is currently not used and should be set to all zeros.

The "security parameters index" (SPI) is the first significant new term that we find in the AH. It is worth a thorough discussion because the concept of the SPI is critical to the operation of the ESP and IPSec in general. Consider the following example. A VPN device is terminating a number of IPSec connections. Each one of these connections has a number of parameters associated with it, such as the encryption algorithm to be used, the keys, the mode (tunnel/transport), the header option used with that neighbor (AH/ESP), and any initialization vectors that may need to be shared. This data is all kept internally to the VPN device in a security policy database (SPD). The SPD contains information specific to each security association (SA) that the gateway currently has active. There needs to be some

NETWORK PERIMETER SECURITY: BUILDING DEFENSE IN-DEPTH

way for the VPN gateway to associate an incoming packet with the agreements that the gateway has previously made with a remote host. Depending on the implementation, the VPN gateway may also have multiple associations and multiple connections with a single remote host, thus eliminating the possibility of simply using the source IP address of the packet to distinguish between them. Instead, each packet is labeled with a unique security parameters index. When the VPN gateway receives packet with an AH header and needs to check the security association to make sure the integrity is valid, the SPI is the value that tells the gateway which SA should be compared against. The SPI is a connection identifier for the IPSec protocol.

SPIs are unidirectional. That is, the SPI that Host A uses when it sends to Host B is different than the SPI that Host B uses when it sends to Host A. As previously seen in the discussion surrounding PPTP and L2TP, keeping these values locally significant reduces the complexity of making sure that values are unique. Instead of Host A asking Host B what value is OK to use, Host A simply chooses an SPI value that it knows it is not using with Host B. Because the IP address is also included in the packet header, if two remote hosts happen to send the same SPI to Host B, the source IP address can still be used to distinguish the IPSec connections from each other. Between the source IP address of packet, the mode/header in use, and the SPI, every IPSec packet can be uniquely identified and referenced in the security database on the VPN gateway.

Back to the AH itself; the sequence number field is used to protect against replay attacks. If an attacker is able to capture a packet from Host A to Host B, he could not change it without affecting the integrity of the packet, but he could send the packet again. In some cases, this attack may have the desired effect. IPSec peers can use a sliding window algorithm that essentially says, "Only packets in this sequence number range will be accepted at this point." The window is sliding because as packets are received, the expected sequence numbers will likewise increase. This is an optional feature and not all implementations have the interpretation of received sequence numbers enabled. Its use does, however, increase the integrity offered by the header because not only can individual packet tampering be identified, but any potential alterations of the traffic flow can potentially be detected.

The actual work of the AH is found in the authentication data field. This is the integrity check value (ICV), which is essentially a Hashed Message Authentication Code (HMAC) with either the MD5 or SHA-1 algorithm. The ICV covers all but the mutable fields in the IP header and the ICV value itself in the AH. Otherwise, the contents of the entire packet are protected against tampering by this value.

When an AH packet is received by a remote device, the packet is first evaluated against the existing security associations database (SAD) by

ESP header format

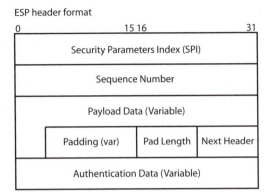

Exhibit 14. ESP Header Format

looking up the packet source, operational mode, and SPI in the database. If no existing security association is found for the packet, then the packet is discarded and the event logged. If the SA does exist and the sequence number is within the expected range, then the packet is considered valid and the receiving host runs an identical hash on the packet. If the SA tells the host that the sender is using HMAC-SHA-1 to calculate the ICV, then the receiver will use the same algorithm. If the computed value matches the ICV in the received packet, then the packet is valid and further processing can occur.

10.4.2 Encapsulating Security Payload (ESP)

The Encapsulating Security Payload (ESP) header is primarily used to provide confidentiality to transmitted data. It will also, however, provide some origin authentication in the manner of the AH and anti-replay protection when using sequence numbers. While the packet header is somewhat more complex in order to accommodate this, many concepts we have already covered while discussing the AH and will be familiar.

The ESP header (Exhibit 14) is inserted in the same position as the AH in an IP packet. When the outermost IP header next protocol field is set to 50, then the next header is an ESP header. Unlike AH, ESP also uses at least one trailer field — and possibly two. The first ESP header itself contains the SPI and the sequence number. The first ESP trailer, which is always included, has information on any padding that might have been inserted into the packet to facilitate the encryption algorithms and the next header for the encrypted data itself. If the authentication option is chosen, then ESP will include a separate trailer describing that information.

The first field of the ESP header is the SPI. As with the AH, the SPI is a connection identifier. It is used by the security association database (SAD) on the host to map a packet with specific connection information in the security association (SA). Use of the SPI ensures that each IPSec connection can be identified based upon the source IP address, mode/header, and SPI.

The use of sequence numbers is mandated by the ESP RFC, but only by the sender. The receiver can choose to accept or discard the delivered sequence information. If the anti-replay protections are being used, which is generally a default setting, then the information is processed. The sliding window is used to ensure that only packets within an acceptable range are processed.

Payload data is either the entire tunneled IP packet, or transport, and other upper layer data. From this field to the end of the next header field, all data is encrypted using one of a number of encryption algorithms.

Some encryption algorithms only work on blocks of data of a given size. Because the data sent by upper layers is unaware of these requirements, there is sometimes the need to pad the data to give the encryption algorithms the proper amount of data to encrypt. If there is a pad, then the receiver of the data needs to know how many bits at the end of a packet are parts of that pad so that they can be removed before forwarding the real data up the stack. This accommodation to the encryption algorithms is responsible for the presence of both the padding field and the padding length field.

Padding can also be used for other reasons. IP protocols generally require that data be sent aligned on four octet boundaries. Regardless of the needs of the encryption protocol, the upper layer data may need to be padded to meet these requirements.

Perhaps the most interesting use of padding, however, is to further hide data. Assume that you were able to sniff data encrypted using ESP over a network. Of course, the data itself would not be accessible to you without the proper decryption key, but a little knowledge of the TCP/IP suite, and the length of the packets themselves would enable you to make some pretty good guesses about the function of the hosts that were passing data back and forth. Padding can be used to reduce this information by padding all packets to a uniform size. Traffic analysis is still possible but becomes more difficult.

The final field of the ESP trailer is common to most TCP/IP protocols. This is the indication of the next header in the packet. The position of the ESP header is interesting, however. We see that it is applied after the data itself; that is, the receiver of the data will not be able to tell what the next header is until it has already read the packet. While not intuitive, it makes sense if we consider the decryption process by a remote receiver. To encrypt as much data as possible, the ESP covers all data in the packet except the SPI, sequence number, and any authentication data that may be present. The only reasons that these fields are not encrypted as well is that they are required to either determine if the packet is valid or not and to associate the packet with the keys that are used to decrypt it in the first place.

Once the receiver deems the packet a valid ESP packet, the decryption process occurs. The front of the payload is decrypted first and stored as the rest of the packet is decrypted. When the user data has been entirely decrypted, the next hop header is decrypted. This gives the IPSec device the information it needs to immediately forward the packet up the protocol stack without having to revisit the information at the front of the packet. After all, the reason that most next headers are included at the front of the packet is only for convenience's sake. Packets are read as they are received. In the case of an encrypted packet, nothing can be read until it is decrypted anyway. Placing the next header at the end of the packet allows the packet to be decrypted a bit at a time and then a forwarding decision made without having to re-read the entire packet.

While authentication is an option in the ESP protocol, it is commonly used to ensure that encrypted packets have integrity in addition to confidentiality. In a case of using network address translation (NAT), the ESP authentication trailer is the only way to apply authentication to a packet. Note that, according to the packet header, the authentication mechanism of the ESP protocol does not authenticate anything in the IP header of the packet like AH. Instead, only the encrypted data itself and the SPI are authenticated. In most cases, the authentication that the ESP header uses is enough although it should be noted that there is no reason that the ESP and AH could not be used in combination for certain very sensitive installations.

The authentication process for the ESP protocol, other than what information is protected, is the same as what occurs in the AH protocol. That is, a hashed message authentication code (HMAC) is used with a common hashing algorithm such as MD-5 or SHA-1. The value in the authentication data field of the ESP trailer is simply the hash value of the covered information or, in IPSec terms, the integrity check value (ICV).

Use of the authentication trailer is advantageous in an ESP environment because it reduces the effect of a denial-of-service attack on an IPSec device. Consider this: you wish to deny service to the legitimate users of a VPN gateway. Knowing that the decryption process is the most intensive portion of receiving IPSec data, you send a series of invalid packets that look like they should contain encrypted information but actually are just garbage characters. Because you know that an SPI stays the same through the duration of a connection and that sequence numbers increment one per packet, capturing a few packets will give you a valid source and anti-replay window in which to send packets. Without attempting to decrypt these packets, the receiver has no way of knowing whether or not the packets are valid. Because the authentication option uses a hashed message authentication code based on an asymmetric signature, the origin of the packet can be confirmed. Presumably, your forged packets would not have the proper signature and would be discarded.

This, of course, would only work if the authentication data was examined prior to or in parallel with the decryption process. In the typical genius of protocol designers, this is exactly what happens. Packets that do not pass the authentication test are discarded without attempts at decryption.

So far we have covered the basics of an IPSec connection. When considering the basics, we can see why some have criticized IPSec for being too complicated. We have discussed options for using the transport mode versus tunnel mode and for using the authentication header versus the encapsulating security payload. It does not help that an ESP transport mode packet can be tunneled inside an ESP tunnel or that the ESP tunnel can also have AH applied to it to ensure the integrity of the IP header or you could just apply the ESP authentication option, or both. The flexibility of IPSec leaves many heads spinning. Fortunately for those of us who need to implement the protocol, there are really only a few combinations of options that really make sense for daily use. Most of the time, unless IPSec is going to be used on a LAN, the ESP tunnel mode is the option most often seen. There are some VPN vendors that support *only* this option, with no chance of configuring others.

Although we may have sorted out these options, we are only a small way into the overall discussion of IPSec operation.

10.5   Key Exchanges

One of the strengths of IPSec is that it is based on encryption algorithms that have been thoroughly peer-reviewed and tested. Instead of relying on a "super secure, private" encryption scheme, IPSec uses algorithms that can be viewed and dissected. This leads to the exposure of vulnerabilities and threats in a much more thorough manner than any private encryption scheme. The strength of these algorithms lies not in them being secret, but in the quality of the keys used in the algorithms. Thus, no discussion of IPSec would be complete without a discussion of key exchange protocols.

When considering IKE (Internet Key Exchange) and the key exchange protocols that define IKE, it is generally helpful to define what is needed in a key exchange. In this manner, all the protocols and packet exchanges that occur can be understood in the context of some straightforward requirements.

Encrypting data over the Internet has some particular problems associated with it. The actual encryption of data is pretty straightforward once you understand the different methods of operation for IPSec. Because the actual encryption algorithms used in IPSec are well-known, the security of an IPSec encryption is based on the quality of the keys being used. The question, then, is how do two parties on the Internet share keys with each other in a secure manner?

With some thought, a couple of solutions present themselves. We can manually set the keys. That is, we know what the key lengths are and can create keys manually. This process, however, would be tiresome, would not scale, and people would tend to create poor keys. It would be better to let the computers mindlessly churn through possible keys and look for "good" keys to use. Once a key has been generated, how do we tell the remote side of the connection what key we are going to use? Recall from our earlier material that most data encryption is done using symmetrical encryption algorithms. That is, the same key that is used to encrypt data is also used to decrypt data. We cannot just send the key over the Internet in a packet. Presumably, we are encrypting our data because we are concerned about someone intercepting it. If this is the case we have a chicken-and-egg problem. "I cannot encrypt data until I get my key across the Internet, but I need encryption to protect my key as it is sent!"

Just figuring out a way to get the key across does not solve all of our problems either. If you wanted to exchange sensitive information with someone you knew in person, you would have some way of validating who you were about to exchange information with. Because you know Joe, you could use Joe's visual appearance to provide the proof you need that you are really talking to Joe. This is not a simple matter to do over the Internet. One famous early cartoon describing the Internet culture noted that one of the primary benefits of the Internet was that, while online, nobody knew you were a dog. That is, we cannot meet face to face with the entities with which we want to communicate. It would be straightforward to create and exchange secret keys with a hacker site that was posing as a legitimate business. If this were the case, I could be encrypting all my financial data to the hacker, thinking that I was encrypting all the data to a legitimate investment site. Based on this, we need some way of securely identifying ourselves to anonymous computers over the Internet, to make sure that "Investments R Us" is really the site where my 401K is managed — and not a hacker site posing as a banking site.

However, the problems have not been all addressed yet. Now that I have figured out a way to exchange the secret key to use in our secure connection over the Internet and a way to prove that the other side is who they say they are, how do I negotiate all the options that are available in IPSec? Depending on the IPSec implementation, at the very least, the two sides of a connection will have to agree on whether to use AH, ESP, or ESP-Authentication, transport, or tunnel mode. But there is more. IPSec supports multiple encryption algorithms and multiple hash algorithms. Which ones out of these options do the two sides support? Which options available with the algorithms are also supported? There needs to be some initial negotiations to determine all of this information.

Once the secure connection is set up, our problems are still not resolved. Somone capturing our encrypted data could, in theory, break our encryption keys if they were to capture the data for a long enough period of time. This is because although it looks like random data, the encrypted data itself is not random. In tunnel mode, there is going to be another IP header and possibly a transport layer header that is encrypted. In the IP header, at least there are going to be fields and addresses that may be guessed at. Through a number of packets, someone with the aid of a very powerful computer may be able to piece together the secret key. To combat this threat, we are going to want something that allows us to change our keys without having to go through the entire key exchange process again. There also may be limitations on the lifetime of the security association that is used to identify the connection. These are all other options that need to be negotiated during connection setup.

We can see that the process of exchanging keys, to be fully functional in an Internet IPSec environment, needs much more thought than simply the generation of "nice" keys. This is the reason the IKE process can be somewhat complicated.

Understanding the key exchange process is more than just academic. If you are considering an IPSec VPN as a countermeasure for your company, understanding IKE and what goes on with each stage of the IKE negotiations will go a long way in helping you better evaluate the protection offered by an IPSec VPN. Not all options and devices are created equally. Knowing the keying process will also help you quickly troubleshoot any VPN connectivity issues as, most of the time, it is not the encryption process itself that is failing; rather, IKE has failed to operate in the normal manner. If an IPSec VPN is going to fail, it is generally going to fail during the initial key exchange phase. Even if it does not, being able to understand the key exchange phase will help you to quickly eliminate this as a possibility and focus on other common failure instances.

For many, one of the most confusing elements in understanding the key exchange process is simply understanding the relationship between the four protocols that are commonly referenced when talking about key exchanges. The high-level view is this: the Internet Key Exchange (IKE) is the protocol used to exchange keys between IPSec peers. Then why is it so complicated? The answer is that IKE is not really a single protocol, but like

318

IPSec itself, is a combination of protocols, each of which contributes its own elements to IKE.

The protocols that make up IKE are the Internet Security Association and Key Management Protocol (ISAKMP, pronounced eyesa-CAMP), Oakley, and the Secure Key Exchange Mechanism (SKEME). Each one of these describes a certain function of the IKE protocol itself.

Because we are primarily interested in the operation of IKE, we will discuss the other contributing protocols in only enough depth to explain their relationship to IKE. The first protocol is ISAKMP. ISAKMP is a protocol that defines the process of exchanging keys over the Internet and the method of authentication, but does not define the actual process. Alone, ISAKMP does not do much for us. ISAKMP is similar to the concept of "house." When someone says, "We need to build a house," this conjures an image of the final goal of the project. We think, "OK, we need a foundation, a roof. Some doors and windows would be nice." However, we do not have enough information to actually build the house. We need to determine how big the windows are going to be, what kind of doors are required, how many corners are in the foundation, if there will be a walk-out basement, etc. To actually build the house, we are going to need some more detailed blueprints with information specific to the house we are trying to build. With ISAKMP, we have determined what goals need to be reached, but not how to actually implement them. In fact, most of what ISAKMP does for our IPSec key exchange protocols is lend a convenient header format and order of packet exchange.

Oakley is a protocol that helps provide those specifics. To continue with the house analogy, Oakley is our blueprint. It tells the parties in an IPSec key exchange how to authenticate each other and how to exchange the secret keys in a secure manner to create a security association. Oakley also defines what methods of authentication are acceptable and how to authenticate a remote party using certificates.

Once the connection is established, SKEME provides a mechanism to be used in the re-keying process. Re-keying is the periodic refreshment of keys used to encrypt data. Although the algorithms used to protect data are thought to be secure, to improve their security, the keys are periodically changed in order to cause anyone who is trying to break the keys based upon capturing data to have to start their work over again each time the key is refreshed.

In summary, the IKE protocol is a specific implementation of the ISAKMP/Oakley and SKEME framework. While each of the associated protocols include guidelines from the general to the specific, none of them need to be used specifically with the IPSec protocol. ISAKMP/Oakley and SKEME can be used with other protocols that require key exchanges. IKE simply defines the specifics when using those protocols with an IPSec key exchange. To put the finishing touches on the house analogy, IKE is the detailed blueprint, including wiring, heating, air conditioning, and measurements, that you would use to create a very specific house. Now that the relationship has been explained, for the rest of this discussion, we will be using the terminology "IKE" to describe the key exchange process, but you will know that we are really borrowing from parts of other protocols to enable all that we want in an Internet key exchange protocol.

10.6   Internet Key Exchange (IKE)

It is best to start the examination of IKE at a high level and then revisit it to examine the details. IKE has two main phases of operation. The first one is conveniently known as phase one and the second as phase two. During the first phase, no secure channel exists between the two Internet hosts. The primary goal of phase one is to create an encrypted session between the two hosts so that the exchanges of IPSec-specific information can then occur in phase two.

In phase one, IKE operates in one of two modes: main mode or aggressive mode. The primary difference between the two modes is simply the number of packets that are exchanged and the amount of protection offered to protect the exchange itself and the ability to verify the identity of the remote host in a secure manner.

Main mode is the original specification of IKE. It does not, however, mean that it is the default mode of operation for a given VPN device. By default, some VPN gateways expect the packet exchanges to occur in aggressive mode and others expect them to occur in main mode. Both sides need to agree for the IKE protocol exchange to go any further than the first packet. Once the secure channel has been created, IPSec negotiations will begin. This will be a series of IPSec-specific proposals between the two hosts. To put it nontechnically, it is one side saying to another, "OK, I can support the RSA algorithm with 128-bit keys with an SHA-1 160-bit hash. I would like to do this in tunnel mode using ESP if you could. If you cannot support that, then here is my next idea...."

Once phase one has been completed using either main or aggressive mode, a secure channel now exists between two remote hosts across the network. Furthermore, the IPSec specifics as far as encryption algorithms have also been established. All that is left to do in phase two is to actually exchange the keys to be used to encrypt data.

Once this combination of events has occurred, IPSec is ready to begin the actual transmission of data. Now that we have a high-level view of what needs to go on with IKE, let us look at the specifics of the matter and see where things can go wrong and what we need to be careful of.

When we stop to consider the ways that one host can authenticate itself to another, two general cases arise for both main mode and aggressive mode. The first method is that we can use digital signatures. The second is that we can use public key encryption. These methods imply that there is some way to share the digital signatures or the public keys of course. If the infrastructure does not exist to support this, we can simply pre-share the keys. This is another way of saying that each side will agree on a password to use in the process. The danger of the second option is that the encryption will only be as strong as the password. It is, however, a very simple way to exchange authentication information from one host to another and is very commonly used in gateway-to-gateway implementations.

Each of these authentication processes has a separate phase-one IKE packet exchange. It would not be beneficial to go through each one of them in detail — that is what RFC 2409 does; but it would be helpful to examine one of the packet exchanges. Although the exact information in the packets is different for each method of authentication, there are enough similarities between them so that lessons drawn from one can be applied to others. In our case, we will examine the protocol exchange used during public key authentication.

While IPSec itself uses IP numbers 50 and 51 to identify IPSec traffic, the IKE process is a UDP packet sent on port 500. Normally, the source and destination port of IKE is 500; but if NAT is used, the source port may be different. This also is the first point of failure when setting up a VPN connection. If IKE never has a chance to initiate, odds are that either the network itself is broken with regard to routing, IP addresses, etc., or there is a firewall that is preventing UDP port 500 from being forwarded. Some broadband service providers, eager to market their own VPN services to SOHO users, will actively filter out port 500 UDP to prevent home users from successfully establishing an IKE exchange with the branch office. Before committing to a VPN solution as a countermeasure for your remote connectivity needs, make sure that your users will not be using such a service provider.

The first decision that needs to be made when initiating IKE connection is which mode will be used in phase one of the connection. The first example we will examine here is based on main mode negotiations (Exhibit 15).

The first two packets in Exhibit 15 are simply the "hello" between the two hosts. During this process, the security association (SA) that is going to be used for the remainder of the IKE process is negotiated. The SA is a term that we have seen before associated with IPSec. While IPSec does use the concept of the SA, it is not an idea that is unique to IPSec. IKE, like IPSec, has a number of variables that need to be kept track of during the key exchange process. Some of the information that needs to be associated with a particular IKE session will include the encryption algorithm to be

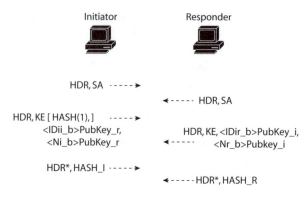

Initiator   Responder

HDR, SA ----►

◄---- HDR, SA

HDR, KE [HASH(1),] ----►
<IDii_b>PubKey_r,   HDR, KE, <IDir_b>PubKey_i,
<Ni_b>PubKey_r   ◄----   <Nr_b>Pubkey_i

HDR*, HASH_I ----►

◄---- HDR*, HASH_R

Exhibit 15. Main Mode IKE Operation

used in the phase one setup, any type of hash algorithm included, authentication, and typically Diffie–Hellman information.

To create a secure channel over an insecure medium, without compromising the integrity of the session, the Diffie–Hellman protocol is used. Discussed in a previous chapter, Diffie–Hellman is a protocol that can be used to exchange keys over an insecure medium to create a temporary secure channel. It is the second packet exchange of IKE that exchanges the Diffie–Hellman values, the identification of the remote side (normally its IP address), and a nonce. Nonce is a new term, but a simple concept. A nonce is simply another term for a pseudo-random number[8] that each side generates and then encrypts. The theory is this: if Host A is able to encrypt a nonce with Host B's public key, the only host on the Internet that should be able to decrypt that nonce and send it back to Host A would, of course, be Host B. This exchange proves to each side of the connection that the other side is who they claim to be and that the packets are not being intercepted and modified as in a man-in-the-middle attack.

Once the Diffie–Hellman values have been exchanged and the identity of the remote side established, a channel using the secret keys communicated during the Diffie–Hellman process has been established. Now that nobody can see what is going on, the two parties can then begin to transfer the important information. The final packet in the phase one exchange is a hash of several pieces of information, including the keys used in the protocol exchange, the Diffie–Hellman information, cookies from the ISAKMP header, proposals exchanged during the first packet exchange, and an identification payload. This information is not actually sent, but is hashed. The logic behind this is that this is all information that only the two legitimate participants in the IKE session would know in their entirety. By sending the hash of this information to each side, a final check is done on the authenticity of the remote participants.

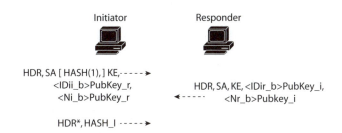

Initiator   Responder

HDR, SA [HASH(1),] KE, - - - - ➤
<IDii_b>PubKey_r,   HDR, SA, KE, <IDir_b>PubKey_i,
<Ni_b>PubKey_r   ◄ - - - -   <Nr_b>Pubkey_i

HDR*, HASH_I - - - - ➤

Exhibit 16. IKE Aggressive Mode

As mentioned, this process is slightly different, depending on the authentication method being used. For example, in the case of pre-shared keys, there is no ability to encrypt information using the remote host's public key. The end result of each option, however, remains the same. At the end of phase one of the IKE session, an encrypted session has been established that will allow the exchange of IPSec SA information in phase two of IKE.

Aggressive mode is similar to main mode except that it does not provide the identity protection exchange, which is the purpose of the second and third packet exchanges in main mode. While the extra steps of verifying identity are not performed prior to creating a secure connection, the advantage of aggressive mode is that it can accomplish the phase one exchange in only three packets. The exchange for public keys is shown in Exhibit 16.

We see that much of the same information is exchanged in terms of IKE security association information, Diffie–Hellman keys, and identification of the local host encrypted with public keys, but identity protection for the participants is not established because the identities are exchanged before a secure channel has been established between the two parties.

The distinction between aggressive mode and main mode is important to understand — not necessarily because the packet format is important, but because the two formats are incompatible with each other. There is no place in the ISAKMP header for the negotiation of the two different modes to occur. This means that each side must be preconfigured with the appropriate modes in order to communicate. Furthermore, we noted that there are at least three different ways to authenticate remote hosts to each other: using digital signatures, public keys, and shared secrets. The packet exchange for each of these is slightly different. As with the mode, there is no opportunity to describe how the authentication should occur in the ISAKMP header itself, so the authentication modes must be predefined as well.

If the phase-one IKE transaction should fail, it is generally for one of the above two reasons. There is a third possibility, however; during the establishment of the phase one encrypted session, a number of variables need to be agreed upon between the remote sides. These include things such as the Diffie–Hellman key length and the hash algorithm that is going to be used to hash data in the payloads. If these values are different between the two hosts, then the phase-one authentication attempts are doomed to fail.

To summarize IKE phase one, its goal is to create an encrypted channel between two hosts so that IPSec security association information can be transferred. Common trouble spots that prevent this from happening include differing modes configured on the two hosts, different authentication methods configured on the two hosts, and the hosts not agreeing upon the algorithms used to create the secure proposal.

Phase two negotiations establish the parameters that are to be used during the actual transfer of data and the re-keying process. This means that secret keys to be used during the encryption process and other session parameters that need to be established are exchanged. By this point, all traffic between the negotiating hosts is encrypted.

One of the more important parameters to be negotiated is the re-keying parameters. A common configuration option is whether or not to configure perfect forward secrecy (PFS). Perfect forward secrecy means that new keys used for the encryption and decryption of data are generated from scratch with no reuse of prior keying material. Normal re-keying, in an effort to be efficient, may use some of the same data from key to key. This implies that someone who is able to compromise one key might be able to compromise any keys related to the compromised one. With PFS, this possibility is eliminated. The disadvantage of configuring PFS is that re-keying is more computationally expensive than normal re-keying. Generally speaking, however, PFS provides greater assurances of confidentiality and is preferred. If a VPN gateway seems to suffer from performance issues, try disabling PFS and observe the result.

Any PFS that may be desired is a product of the phase-two negotiations. With no PFS, as illustrated in Exhibit 17, the keying material is derived from the phase one negotiation. If PFS is required, new keying material will be generated and exchanged during the phase two negotiations. Phase two of the IKE process is described in Exhibit 17 in packet format.

In the exchange in Exhibit 17, the first hash value from the initiator is a reiteration of much of the information that was established in the phase-one exchange. The SA information exchanged in phase two, however, relates to the IPSec SA that is being established. Again, the nonce is used to prevent replay attacks and the key material is the Diffie–Hellman material used to establish the key material for the IPSec encryption. To establish

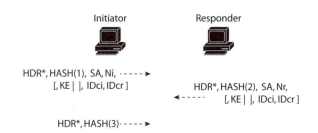

Initiator   Responder

HDR*, HASH(1), SA, Ni, - - - - ➤
[, KE | |, IDci, IDcr]

HDR*, HASH(2), SA, Nr,
◄ - - - - -   [, KE | |, IDci, IDcr]

HDR*, HASH(3)· - - - - ➤

Exhibit 17. Phase Two IKE Exchange

authenticity for the exchange, the IDs of the participants are also included. The packet from the responder echoes much of the initiator's material in its own hash and then provides the same material as the initiator for the SA establishment. Finally, the initiator hashes the information received from the responder and resends it as a final verification of the SA that has just been established.

Failures that occur at phase two are difficult to decipher. Remember that the packets are encrypted so you cannot tell what is going on by capturing them in a packet sniffer. But know that the IKE process will help you quickly debug the problem. We know that if phase one has established successfully, the two sides have successfully authenticated to each other and have IKE operating in the same mode with the same authentication. If there is a failure in phase two, it must mean one of two things. The first is that the IPSec proposals that are being exchanged are incompatible. This means that the initiator is saying, "I would like to do IPSec in this way…" and the responder is replying with an, "I don't understand any of those methods." The other common failure point is that one side is requesting PFS and the other side is not. Both of these failures are a matter of examining the configuration options on the VPN devices themselves.

10.6.1 Just Fast Keying (JFK)

IKE is tried and tested and found in most IPSec implementations. Over time, three key complaints about IKE's operation have been voiced. The first is that it takes too many exchanges. Using main mode, there is a minimum of four exchanges between the two phases, for a total of eight round-trip times. Even if serialization delay due to the bandwidth of the links were not an issue, at a minimum, end-to-end delay from one end of the United States is bound at a minimum of 30 ms by the laws of physics. The number of exchanges increases the time it takes to initiate the IPSec connection.

To address these concerns, another keying protocol has been proposed by the IETF. Known as Just Fast Keying (JFK), this newer key exchange protocol attempts to counter the implementation issues that haunt IKE.

Due to the fact that IKE requires the server to maintain information about the connection request, IKE can also become the victim of denial-of-service attacks in the same manner as a TCP SYN attack. This means that attackers can send many requests for key exchanges, yet never follow through with them. Because the servers are holding information about connections that will never be used, legitimate users have fewer resources available for their own connections.

Finally, IKE is complicated. This is a general criticism of the IPSec suite of protocols in general. We have seen in our discussions that there are several places where IKE sessions must agree before the session is allowed to complete. They must agree on the authentication method, the hashing algorithm to be used, Diffie–Hellman key lengths, perfect forward secrecy, and IPSec proposals. This wealth of configurable information makes the protocol robust but most have found that there are many options that are not used and in the end only configuration errors are increased.

JFK addresses each of the criticisms of IKE. The first is that JFK reduces the overall packet count between devices. As the exchange below shows, the packet exchange is reduced to just two packets per device. The first exchange of packets is to exchange the Diffie–Hellman information that will provide the information needed for encrypted packets. The second exchange of packets contains all the information needed for the establishment of an IPSec session.

To keep the exchange brief and to lessen the chance of misconfiguration, JFK supports fewer options than IKE. The benefit of this is that the negotiation of options does not need to occur at the start of the key exchange.

To lessen the chance for denial-of-service (DoS) type attacks utilizing resources on the server side, with JFK, it is the client that is responsible for maintaining the state of the key exchange during packet transfer. It is not until the last packet is sent from the responder to the initiator that the responder needs to start keeping track of the IPSec connection information. As an additional step to protect against DoS attacks, it is the client that is burdened with the computationally expensive process of generating the session key to be used with the IPSec SA.

To ease configuration issues, in the second packet in the exchange, the responder directs the initiator as to which proposals are acceptable for the encryption of traffic. This reduces the complexity of the exchange by putting the burden on the initiator, which is acting as a client to match the responder's configuration options. Additionally, the number of options has been reduced with regard to authentication and negotiation to reduce the overall complexity of the protocol.

Based on the advantages presented by JFK, it seems that this would be a protocol with which you should become at least casually familiar as you evaluate VPN solutions.

10.7 Integrating Network Address Translation (NAT) and IPSec

A common issue that must be considered when considering a VPN solution is the integration of IPSec with network address translation (NAT). While many purists feel that NAT disrupts end-to-end connections on the Internet and thus breaks one of the primary intents of the Internet standards, the fact is that NAT is here to stay. It is useful as part of a firewall and it allows organizations to number their internal networks as they desire and use a minimum of IP addresses. In the United States, blessed from the beginning with an abundance of IPv4 addresses, the eventual transition to IPv6 has been somewhat forestalled by the prevalence of NAT. For most network administrators, NAT is a proven technology that has minimum impact on the configuration of their networks, unlike IPv6.

As a quick refresher, NAT is the process of changing a packet sent from the inside of a company network to the Internet. The source of the packet is changed from the original private address to a public address that allows the remote Internet host to respond back to the original client. Unfortunately, the process of changing the IP header will break certain modes of IPSec.

NAT's problems with IPSec can sometimes be difficult to diagnose if you are not familiar with the IPSec process. Remember that IPSec needs two separate processes to occur before a connection can be established. The first of these is the key exchange process with IKE. Then the actual data is sent using AH or ESP. It is common for the IKE process to succeed; but because NAT is attempting to modify information protected by the AH or encrypted by the ESP, the packets containing data fail. This presents itself as a situation where an IPSec SA has been established but traffic between the two hosts fails. This problem is normally due to one of several circumstances that depend on the operation of IPSec that is being attempted. The first major issue is that of using either the AH or the ESP. The second issue is the decision to use transport mode or tunnel mode.

To begin with, NAT and the IPSec AH will not interoperate. This is because the entire purpose of AH is to make sure that the entire packet, including the IP header, has not been altered in transit. Because this is exactly what NAT does, any attempt to authenticate the header by the remote side will fail. Tunnel mode and transport mode will both fail equally. Thus, if your security policy dictates that authentication of packets must be done, yet your network requirements suggest the use of NAT, then some other method of authentication must be performed. ESP with the authentication options enabled is a good place to start.

With ESP, the possibilities of proper NAT operation allow the use of tunnel mode or transport mode. Recall from our earlier discussion the operation of the TCP/UDP headers and the operation of NAT. TCP and UDP packets contain a checksum that is not only a check of the TCP data, but also the pseudo-header. The pseudo-header contains information found in the IP header, including the IP addresses. When NAT changes the IP header, it must also reach into the transport layer header and change the checksum; otherwise, the receiving host will discard the packet as an error because the checksums do not add up. If ESP encrypts the transport information, however, the checksums cannot be changed. Likewise, if the ESP authentication option is used, and the checksum could be changed, authentication of the packet at the IPSec level would fail due to the packet having been altered after being sent.

With the above options eliminated, really the only hope we have for NAT and IPSec working together remains the use of ESP and tunnel mode. Because tunnel mode completely encapsulates the original packet, NAT only needs to work on the outermost IP header, which of course does not affect the original packet that has been encrypted by the ESP.

Alas, if only it were that easy. Even using our one best hope for IPSec and NAT to work together, we will see that there are a number of places where things can go wrong. First, the common NAT implementation of port address translation (PAT) will not work. Remember that the protocol headers for tunnel mode ESP are as shown in Exhibit 18.

This means that the port information that NAT relies on for one to many translations between public and private IP addresses will fail. Recall from our NAT discussion that NAT really affects the ability of traffic to return to the original sender more than it affects the ability of traffic to be sent over the Internet. When there are ten hosts internal to the company that are being NAT'ed by a single gateway to a single IP address, the NAT device needs some way to associate *return* traffic with the original sender.

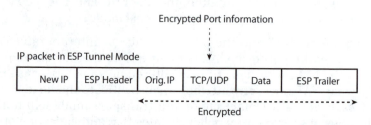

Exhibit 18. NAT Cannot Operate Correctly When Port Information Is Encrypted

Normally done with transport layer ports, when these ports are encrypted, this technique is not available.

If we examine this problem a bit more closely, we see that using ESP in tunnel mode with NAT would allow at least one VPN connection. After all, if one internal host is using IPSec through the NAT device, the NAT device only needs to associate a single incoming connection with a single internal host. That is straightforward enough to do, especially because IPSec has its own IP protocol numbers.

Although a "one IPSec connection only" rule would work to solve our NAT/IPSec interoperability problems, this solution is not going to be attractive to many. Most will want multiple VPN connections through the NAT device. For this to work, we are going to have to find something that will allow the NAT device to keep track of packets returning from the Internet and be able to associate them with internal hosts. But what would we use?

Looking at the packet structure, we see that any useful information to be used for telling one packet from another, other than the SPI and the sequence number of the ESP header, is encrypted. The sequence numbers are going to be changing constantly, so it may not be a good candidate for distinguishing packets. The SPI, however, is a possibility. The SPI is a unidirectional identifier for each IPSec SA. This seems to fit the bill perfectly.

To make this work, we would simply need to get the NAT device to use the SPI value as the unique identifier for each connection instead of a transport layer protocol identifier. Because this is just a programming issue, that is not a problem. While the main hurdle has been overcome, there are still some minor issues that remain with using the SPI of an ESP packet.

The first issue is that the SPI is a unidirectional identifier. The SPI that Host A uses to send packets to Host B is not the same SPI that appears at the NAT gateway when Host B returns traffic to Host A. To overcome this, some guesswork will be necessary. The NAT gateway must also be programmed to take a look at the IKE exchange when the initial phase one, unencrypted SAs are being exchanged. This tips off the NAT device that these two hosts are creating an IPSec session and to pay attention to any packets that start to flow between these two devices. The NAT device is going to guess that, because it saw an IKE exchange between Host A and Host B, the first IP packets that show up with the ESP protocol coming from Host B on the Internet are the ones with the incoming SPI to associate to internal Host A.

This process is not always perfect and sometimes is incorrect. Let us expand the scenario a bit and say that Host C is also internal to the NAT domain and it wishes to create an IPSec connection to Host B on the Internet at the same time that Host A wishes to. The NAT device will see both Host A's and Host C's IKE requests be sent and start to pay attention; but

IP packet in ESP Tunnel with UDP Wrapping

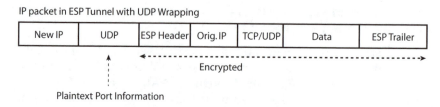

Plaintext Port Information

Exhibit 19. UDP Wrapping Adds Extra Port Information for Proper NAT Operation

when Host B sends the first encrypted packet, how is the NAT device going to know with which internal host to associate it? It is not. The NAT device will have to "guess" correctly or the process will fail. Typically, this guessing is limited to the first packet seen in response being associated with the first host to send the request or the NAT device simply refusing to make the association due to the ambiguity.

Although a stumbling block, this process is not as failure prone as it might seem. Consider the most common application of NAT that needs to employ this solution. A remote user or SOHO user is connecting through a shared home LAN connection to a work VPN. The router that the home user has is almost always a NAT device and the IPSec client software is on the home user's PC. Unless there are extenuating circumstances, most of the time there will not be multiple users on the SOHO network attempting VPN connections at exactly the same time. This, however, cannot be said for a large office with dozens of users utilizing a VPN connection to a corporate office at once. As a benefit, most cheap home routers already support SPI mapping, but be sure to check before purchasing 50 of them for SOHO users.

While a workable solution, SPI mapping is not perfect and can make mistakes. Ideally, what we would like is a fool-proof solution. Reexamining the problem, we see that it is the encryption of the transport layer protocols that prevents us from distinguishing one packet from another. What if we were to simply insert another transport layer header between the IP packet header and the ESP header, like that in Exhibit 19?

With this solution, any NAT device can operate normally because the transport layer header is the furthest they ever look into a packet. UDP is the preferred header in this case because all we need are port numbers and none of the overhead associated with TCP connections.

While clever, this solution clearly is not part of the original IPSec protocol suite. In fact, for it to work at all, both hosts that are participating in the IPSec session must be aware that it is happening. It would not do to have Host A wrapping an ESP tunnel in UDP, only to have Host B receive the

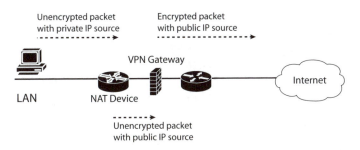

Exhibit 20. NAT before Encrypting for Best Results

packet and say, "What is going on here?" Currently, these solutions are vendor proprietary. If your vendor does support this option, however, other than the extra eight octets of packet overhead, this solution is fairly straightforward.

Fortunately for most of our VPN implementations, when deploying a host to gateway or gateway-to-gateway VPN, tunnel mode is normally the mode deployed. Because most are interested in encryption of sent data, ESP is also deployed in preference to the AH.

The easiest way of making sure that NAT and IPSec do not step on each other's toes is to simply make sure that any address translation of IP packets is done before any IPSec encryption occurs. Examine Exhibit 20. If the NAT device is placed before the VPN device relative to the outbound flow of packets, the addresses can be translated and then the IPSec encryption applied.

Because no changes need to occur to the packet after the IPSec encryption takes place for outbound packets, authentication of the packet by the receiver does not fail. NAT does not need to worry about identifying encrypted packets because either outbound or inbound traffic is not encrypted when it reaches the NAT gateway. Alternately, the IPSec/NAT function can occur on a single device such as a combination VPN/firewall or VPN gateway. Presumably, the manufacturers of such a device will apply the proper encryption/translation order internally to the device itself.

This solution only works when a gateway is being employed, however. For SOHO/remote users who have VPN client software on their host PCs, they often do not have the choice to be able to apply NAT before the IPSec encryption. In this case, the solutions discussed above must be taken into consideration or another alternative to IPSec considered.

10.8 Integrating the VPN and Firewall

A VPN can either be an asset to your company's security policy or a big gaping vulnerability, depending on its relationship with your organization's firewall. All that a VPN does is protect traffic that is in transit. It does nothing to protect the hosts that generate the traffic or to verify that the information that is being encrypted is actually good for your network. As far as a firewall is concerned, a firewall can only make forward or drop decisions on traffic that it can read. If all data is encrypted in an ESP session, then the firewall will have no way of making a decision on the contents of the encrypted data. When this is taken into consideration, it becomes much easier to determine the relationship between the firewall and the VPN.

As a general rule, you will want to consider all VPN traffic to be untrusted. Remember that just because it has been encrypted does not mean that the traffic is safe. Therefore, you will want all possible VPN traffic to be decrypted by the firewall and examined before being allowed into your network. This, of course, is not always possible. Consider the case of an HTTPS server that provides secure client connections to Web pages that it serves. Because the SSL connection that provides this encryption is established between the two hosts, it will be impossible for the firewall to examine this data without affecting the SSL session between the client and the server. Exceptions such as this can be remedied by placing such devices on DMZs created specifically for the services. In this way, even if the server is compromised by an encrypted session, the amount of damage or access to the remainder of the network can be minimized.

Exhibit 21 displays several network configurations that can be used in a gateway situation to enable VPN traffic and the firewall to interoperate with maximum protection for your network.

We see that in each of the topologies in Exhibit 21, the VPN traffic is decrypted and examined by the firewall before being allowed into the internal network. If your security policy mandates that VPN traffic be allowed through the firewall, then it is advisable to have a separate DMZ for the VPN gateway. The key is that there is something checking the traffic as it enters your LAN. In some cases, this may even require host-based firewall systems, especially in the case of remote clients.

The interaction between a VPN and a firewall can be between two specialized devices: one acting as a VPN gateway and the other acting as a firewall, or between a single VPN/firewall appliance. When considering the relative security and performance of these two models, be sure to consider what would happen to your network security if your VPN device were compromised in some manner. The best security model, as cannot be mentioned enough, is defense in depth. Realistically, nobody short of a government or the ISP itself is going to spend a lot of time trying to capture your data as it crosses the Internet. Even fewer people are going to spend the time and effort to decrypt data that is captured. The far more likely and easier target is going to be the VPN gateway itself. Although we hope this is not the case, any VPN gateway (and firewall, for that matter) that we

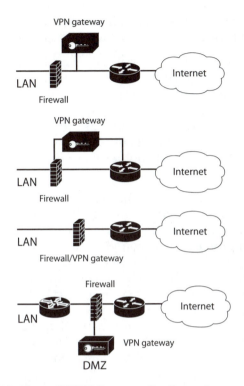

Exhibit 21. Possible Firewall/VPN Gateway Configuration

build or purchase has to be assumed to have a security flaw that allows an attacker access. Historical data has shown us time and time again that "secure" solutions have some sort of vulnerability that is just waiting to be discovered.

By placing the VPN and firewall functions into a single hardware appliance, we are making a large gamble that when vulnerability is found with our product, we will find out about it and have a fix available before anyone can damage the network. An attack against the device could render all of your perimeter network security worthless. With different devices housing your VPN and firewall functions, there is still the risk of compromise, but we have split our eggs into different baskets. Hopefully, one of those baskets will hold together long enough for us to fix the other.

There are also reliability issues associated with creating a single VPN/firewall appliance. A failure in that device will shut off Internet access until the device can be repaired. How long that timeframe is depends on the vendor of the product and the support agreement that you have signed. Unless a spare, identically configured box was already available, you can count on at least four hours of downtime in such an event. When separating the devices, a firewall failure may still be a show-stopper, but a VPN failure would still allow some useful work to occur.

Finally, there are performance issues to consider. A VPN/firewall appliance has that much more work to do than a stand-alone device. I agree wholeheartedly that vendors can produce combination devices with enough horsepower to serve both functions; the question is whether it would be a better investment to purchase those functions separately. When considering the overall cost of stand-alone or separate solutions, remember to include redundancy requirements and growth into any equation.

That said, it is difficult to resist the deployment of a single VPN/firewall appliance. Because the functions are tightly integrated, the issues surrounding filtering encrypted traffic and NAT are neatly taken care of. In fact, most integration problems between VPNs and firewalls are neatly taken care of. It is also alluring to be able to walk into a remote site and simply insert a preconfigured VPN/firewall box in-line with the egress access link and walk out. Installation of such devices can truly be a breeze when configuring many remote offices and can often be handled by nontechnical staff. Once again, there is no right solution to offer. The right solution is the one that most closely reflects the needs of your security policy and an intelligent budget that takes all circumstances into account.

The performance of a VPN device is often a point of discussion. Two questions that I am frequently asked inlcude, "How can I make sure that I get the best performing VPN?" or "How can I compare VPN gateways?" Comparisons based on vendor information are always tricky. Make sure you read the fine print. When citing the packet transfer rate, make sure that you know the size of the packets they are quoting and the type of encryption being used when making the comparison. Also, be sure to examine the number of concurrent connections that can be supported and any options for user management, especially in the case of a host-to-gateway VPN.

To discuss what makes a VPN device perform, let us pretend that we are going to make our own VPN box. This may not be an entirely philosophical discussion. When you open the lid, you will see that most VPN devices are just repackaged computers running on a UNIX or even Linux platform with a nice GUI (graphical user interface). There is nothing stopping you from building the same on your own.

The first item on the shopping list is the network interface card (NIC). Nothing will affect the performance of a VPN device like a NIC that supports hardware encryption. The process of encryption and decryption is cumbersome on a CPU that is also responsible for many other functions in a general-purpose computer. Even the occasional interrupt to another process will slow the encryption process. An NIC with built-in VPN support performs the processor-intensive mathematical transformations involved in encryption in hardware. This is not only always faster than software encryption, but it also frees up the CPU of the gateway device itself for other functions.

Once the hardware encryption is considered, most other elements in the VPN box are more than adequate for common WAN connection speeds. Consider that some of the most popular VPN devices on the market can support 280,000 concurrent connections — this is on hardware that is a 600-MHz PIII, 256-MB RAM, and 40-GB hard drives. Most of these items can be found at commodity prices if you can manage to dig up a processor as "slow" as 600 MHz at an online bargain site.

Even the choice of hardware encryption cards, which can be quite pricey, may not be necessary, depending on your connection speeds. What you are primarily concerned about is how fast you can decrypt and encrypt packets. If you have a full T-1 line to the Internet that runs at 1.544 Mbps, then that is the most speed you need to squeeze out of your VPN box. I have successfully created VPN devices out of 486 processors with 128 MB of RAM that can keep up with a T-1 line. This is using 3DES encryption. Any type of modern processor (PIII 800 MHz) can easily encrypt and decrypt traffic at up to 20 Mbps. This is without any form of hardware encryption whatsoever. Unless you are encrypting traffic on the LAN at 100 Mbps or over aggregate T-1s and T-3 (45 Mbps) links or higher or plan to upgrade soon, money spent on hardware encryption cards is not necessary.

10.9 Quality of Service (QoS) and the VPN

Quality of service (QoS) is a topic that is typically found in books on network design — not network security. However, because VPNs inherently increase the delay of traffic through the encryption and decryption process, a word or two is appropriate here.

QoS is an issue that is often sidestepped when designing networks. It is a myth that IP does not support QoS, but true end-to-end QoS can be difficult to achieve. While it does not solve all problems, most network engineers simply address QoS by adding more bandwidth to the network. While this is common, it makes networks more expensive to operate than they need to be and still does not address all QoS issues. Variable delay and queuing delays caused by link aggregation are two common failures of simply adding more bandwidth to the network.

Many times, the issue of QoS will be outside your ability to control, unless you also happen to be a network administrator of the ISP backbone that you are going to use to transport your VPN traffic. Even then, it is unlikely that you will have control over your competitors' QoS solutions if your VPN traffic should need to traverse another backbone. This is not to say that it is a lost cause. The information in this section will give you what you need to discuss QoS requirements and solutions with your service provider and offer suggestions for the traffic that you can control. We will see that the most effective place to apply QoS is normally at the edge of the network, which is exactly where your access-link is located.

While QoS can be complicated to implement, the concept of QoS comes down to a simple idea. You have two packets that need to be sent out a particular interface. Which one goes first? Intuitively, we know that if we want one packet to go before the other, we have to be able to tell the router, firewall, switch, or VPN gateway which one it is. To do this we are limited to information that is already in the packet. There needs to be some way to say to the hardware, "This packet is the more important of the two. Send it out first."

For a VPN, which is a security countermeasure, understanding QoS will typically allow the network to reduce the costs associated with the Internet access. As the above discussion points out, there are two ways to take care of the QoS dilemma. The first is to add more bandwidth. When we are evaluating countermeasures for cost effectiveness, increasing the bandwidth speed to account for any VPN performance issues must also be considered. This might be fine for an ISP, but for most companies, the cost of upgrading their Internet access to higher bandwidths can be high. A cheaper, more sensible solution is to create a way that makes it look like you have more bandwidth available — without having to actually purchase it. This good business sense will translate to a security policy that is secure and cost effective.

A VPN has no special needs or requirements for QoS beyond that for normal IP traffic. To put another way, there is nothing special about how to provide QoS for VPN traffic; all of our normal IP tricks are available to us. It will be the content of the VPN traffic that will determine the specific requirements for any QoS.

The one exception to the above paragraph is the process of differentiating between traffic within the VPN. All QoS relies on a simple premise. There must be something about the packets that allows the device performing the QoS to be able to tell one from another. Without this marking, there is no way to selectively process one packet ahead of another. As an example, Host A is sending to Host B two types of traffic over the Internet with no encryption applied. One type of traffic is a normal file transfer going on in the background. The other type of traffic is a Voice-over-IP (VoIP) session that two users at the host are having. Clearly, the QoS requirements of these two streams are different. Because it is normal IP traffic, there are plenty of ways to tell one type of traffic from another. Although both streams are to the same IP addresses, we can use the IP precedence bits to mark one type of traffic higher than the other. We can also use Diffserv, which simply uses the same IP precedence bits and marks them in a different (but compatible) way. If our network supported it, we could also use the Resource Reservation protocol (RSVP) to reserve a certain amount of bandwidth along the path between the two hosts.

Now encrypt the data and the voice traffic between Host A and Host B and place it in a tunnel between two gateways. Suddenly, this is a lot tougher. Host A and Host B can mark the packets when they leave the host to indicate priority, but those marked packets are then placed inside another IP header at the gateway. Unless the gateway has some method of marking the priority of the outside packet as the inside packet, the differentiating information on the traffic is lost. After all, it is now encrypted. Routers on the Internet know that they are seeing VPN traffic, but do not know that there is data and voice in the packets; each of which requires different service on the network.

The simple yet inelegant solution to this is to create two VPN sessions at the gateway and sort traffic based on transport layer protocols for forwarding down a particular session. One VPN session, the voice, is marked for high QoS. The other, data, is marked for less demanding QoS.

The choices you have for QoS normally rely on the transport technology that you utilize. If you are using multiple protocols over Frame Relay, you are limited to two priorities: high or low. ATM, of course, supports a wide range of priorities being one of the original driving forces for the protocol. It is common to find service provider backbones transporting both toll-quality voice, video, and data over a single network. If you are transporting all of this data encapsulated in an IP packet, then you have protocol identifiers available at that level as well.

MPLS is often touted as the solution to quality-of-service problems. In truth, the MPLS protocol itself does not provide any QoS. What it does is provide a framework that makes it much easier to implement the same QoS techniques that we already use for IP. It becomes so easy that service providers can do it on a large scale. Remember that it is not that QoS with IP is impossible; it is that it is difficult to implement consistently and get it to scale. MPLS allows both consistency and scalability.

QoS in MPLS is typically provided in two ways, both of which can be employed at the same time. The first method is the "pipe." This means that RSVP is being used to create a label-switched path through the network with certain bandwidth reservations. For example, you could create a VPN between your main office site and a remote office. You could also request that the service provider guarantee that the bandwidth of that VPN remains at 1 Mbps, or 10 Mbps, or higher. The service provider would then use the RSVP to reserve the requested bandwidth between the two sites to the exclusion of other traffic if needed. If the network between the two sites should change, RSVP would be able to automatically find another path that guaranteed the bandwidth for the traffic.

The "pipe" reserves bandwidth between two points. Inside that pipe we may wish to treat one traffic type with a priority over the other. If our hypothetical central and remote sites above were also doing video conferencing or VoIP between these two sites along with normal Web traffic and e-mail, then in addition to the bandwidth reservation, we would want to make sure that our high-priority data never gets stuck behind our own low-priority data. To this end, MPLS also supports integration with the Diffserv and IP precedence protocols. Both of these allow the marking of traffic in the MPLS header. The effect is that if two packets sent out the same port between the two company sites over the RSVP reserved pipe, the proper QoS can be applied to each. Inside the pipe, the MPLS label switching router can determine that, "Hey, this MPLS packet is marked with a high priority; I should make sure it gets sent before that other MPLS packet."

Neither RSVP nor Diffserv requires MPLS for operation. The benefit of MPLS, however, is that it becomes much easier to implement. What that is, however, is most likely the subject of another book.

For VPN traffic sent over a LAN technology such as Ethernet, the 802.1q standard applies to Ethernet frames. This is a sorting mechanism that allows Ethernet frames to be marked with much the same priority levels of an IP packet. All of the traffic grooming at the IP level will be useless if the switches used to connect the routers together become congested. While the 802.1q standard applies eight priority levels to traffic, be aware that most switch manufacturers only support two levels of QoS — high and low. While this may seem inflexible, in reality it is more than adequate and prevents the hardware from being bogged down sorting out incremental priority levels. Sometimes, the best QoS solution is a limited one. Too much processing can slow down high-speed QoS.

Depending on your service provider, you will have limited options for VPN traffic sent over their backbone. What should really concern you more is the service level agreement (SLA) for your traffic. How the service provider maintains that SLA and at what cost to them are irrelevant to you as long as their service and prices are comparable to the competition.

While much of the backbone QoS may be out of your hands, it does make sense to think about QoS with regard to your VPN (and other traffic) at your access router. At this device you can control the order in which packets are being sent onto the service provider backbone. Note that you cannot control the return of that traffic — that is what your ISP will do. I have seen, however, noticeable responsiveness to VPN and user traffic by simply configuring QoS on a single site. When considering a network as a whole, this makes sense. Most LANs now operate at 100 Mbps or more.

Most company access-links to the Internet are still at T-1 speeds, on average. When you have the potential for 100 Mbps of data trying to fit over a 1.544-Mbps link, there is going to be congestion. A couple of simple QoS techniques for prioritizing your VPN traffic on the single interface link going to your ISP should result in noticeable improvements in this case. If you can get your ISP to configure its interfaces pointing back toward you in a similar manner, the quality of the link increases significantly. Applying QoS at these two points and no place else has such a profound impact because for most traffic, this T-1 link is the slowest link in the chain. Traffic coming from the ISP is generally not congested or delayed on the ISP backbone itself. Any reasonably competent ISP will have bandwidth to burn and its own sophisticated QoS mechanisms on the backbone. The congestion hits when it gets to the link to the customer.

In summary, while the VPN does not have any specific QoS needs above and beyond that which you have assigned to the traffic being encrypted, knowing your options will assist you in creating a VPN service that is secure, robust, and meets the needs of your users.

Notes

1. This bandwidth itself is related to the frequency range of the human voice. The evolution of the telephone system is fascinating but beyond the scope of this book.
2. Frame Relay also supports a switched virtual circuit (SVC) that creates on-demand virtual circuits. This product has never been widely deployed in the United States.
3. MPLS does currently fall short compared to ATM in the ability to precisely control traffic delay and jitter as an ATM network can. MPLS, however, does offer great improvements in the provisioning of traffic engineering and quality of service in an IP network.
4. Do not go asking your service provider for this. The example is just to point out the options that are available for provisioning MPLS and do not reflect current MPLS offerings.
5. Diminishing in popularity, IPX/SPX is the network layer protocol used by the Novell operating system for best effort and reliable transportation of data on LANs.
6. One confusing element of IPSec in general is that the standards describe the ability to use AH and ESP together in the same packet. While possible, this is not widely employed and will not be further discussed here.
7. One of my colleagues likes to describe a host reading a packet using a Pac Man analogy. The Pac Man eats the bits one at a time — but always likes to know what the next meal (header) is to get psyched up for it.
8. "Pseudo-random" itself is a term that requires some explanation. Computers have a difficult time coming up with true random numbers. To indicate this for the detail oriented, the term "pseudo-random" is used to indicate a number with the "appearance" of randomness. Try using this term at your next party. It will be a big hit.

Chapter 11
Wireless Network Security

The very first time I used a wireless card in my laptop, I knew that I had seen the future of computing. Being part of that group that marketing departments all over the world call the "early adopters," I had set up a wireless node as part of my test network. From there it was a short leap to apply it to my own home network. Honestly, there is nothing like sitting out on the deck with a nice iced tea answering e-mails.

The allure of wireless networks has always been their ease of use. In Vermont there are many old farmhouses and Victorian mansions that eventually are converted into small business offices. For years, the standard operating procedure was to either remodel the building to support cat 5 wiring or to run the wiring in exposed conduit — or even worse, along the floor. Wireless networking changed all that. Install a single access point and the entire building is network enabled.

Not only is the entire building network enabled, but many times you have also just network enabled the other tenants in the building and half of the parking lot. Unlike modern switched cat 5, the 802.11 IEEE standards that define wireless LAN communications act like a big repeater. Anyone within range of the access point is able to intercept network communications or utilize network resources.

From the security perspective, there are two different problems that must be overcome. The first is one of confidentiality; the second is one of availability. When network information is available for reading, this is a concern. When the other businesses in your building are able to use your network resources, there are fewer resources available for your users.

The original 802.11 standards attempted to address the confidentiality issue. Known as Wired Equivalent Privacy (WEP), the goal of WEP was to provide privacy equivalent to a wired network through the use of encryption. The story of how this fell short of the goal is a study in security and how good marketing cannot make up for a bad implementation. This is not to say that somehow WEP was "sold" to an unsuspecting public. On the contrary, the developers of WEP believed they had a secure solution to the problem of confidentiality on wireless networks. When I say "sold," I mean that WEP was designed with two default key lengths (40-bit for WEP version 1.0 and 128-bit for WEP version 2.0). The public has been taught that the longer the key, the more secure the encryption. In this case, this is simply not true.

Rather, this is a case of how key length is not the whole story when considering the overall strength of an encryption scheme. Just as an overview, WEPv1 uses 40-bit RC4 encryption, a popular secret key algorithm that operates as a stream cipher; that is the actual key is a stream of bits that is XOR'd with the plaintext to produce ciphertext. The advantage of RC4 and stream ciphers in general is that they are very fast encryption algorithms. From the beginning, the 802.11 community admitted that the 40-bit encryption may have not been adequate. To increase the security, the key length was increased to 128 bits, the standard for most commercial-grade encryption. This is the same encryption strength that you are most likely to use when shopping online over an encrypted session.

Unfortunately, increasing the key length did nothing to improve the security of WEP. This is because the primary flaw with WEP is not the length of the key at all; rather, it is the encryption key, called the initialization vector (IV), which is flawed. The IV is a 24-bit value that is appended to each packet that is sent between an access point and a wireless host. The combination of IV and the key stream generated by RC4 creates a per-packet key that is used by the remote host to decrypt the incoming packet.

The WEPv1 IV key space of 24 bits only allows a rather limited number of unique IV keys. This allows an attacker to sniff the network and, when enough packets have been sent to cover all the possible combinations that 24 bits allow, the attacker has essentially created a dictionary of keys (IV and RC4 streams) that allow them to decrypt the traffic on the network in real-time. Depending on the size of the packets and the activity of the access point, this amount of traffic can take an hour or less to collect from a single access point. Information collected from a multi-access point network takes even less time than this to collect the required number of packets.

The ability to decrypt the information from a collection of IV and RC4 key streams is due to the ability to employ a common method of compromising cryptographic algorithms. Using what is known as a *known plaintext* attack, attackers can compare what they know the unencrypted data should look like with what the encrypted data is and thus derive the key. For example, a PING packet has a fairly standard structure to it. Attackers could send a number of PINGs and record their own encrypted ICMP traffic. Knowing what the unencrypted data should look like allows them to determine the key for that packet. This normally would not be such a huge crisis; plaintext attacks are well-known cryptographic attacks, but the fact that the same key that encrypted that traffic will be reused in the future will allow attackers to create a dictionary of keys and decrypt traffic in near real-time. Each time the reused IV is detected, the attack can correlate that with the associated key for that IV. If attackers are unable to send their own traffic, they can also perform a partial known plaintext attack. After all, protocol headers are fairly constant in appearance.

The solution would be to change the base key (typically a password) frequently. The problem with the WEP implementation is that there is no way to perform this operation. First, the base key would have to be changed very frequently; and second, this is infeasible to do on a large network with many remote stations, given the manual key changing requirements that WEP currently has. WEPv2 attempts to use a larger IV value but this is of limited use. WEPv2 remains ineffective in the changing of base keys and allows plaintext attacks to succeed.

While WEP has problems assuring the confidentiality of data, it also has issues that need to be addressed regarding availability. Under normal circumstances, anyone with the proper service set identifier (SSID) can join the network via a wireless access point. The SSID is simply an identifier for the access point. Unfortunately, the SSID itself is often broadcast, allowing anyone with a wireless sniffer to read and use the SSID. In short, it is difficult to prevent unauthorized users from using an access point, especially if the network is configured to provide DHCP addressing for all requests and WEP encryption is not enabled on the wireless portion at all.

Given these problems, the prospect of installing wireless on your network and maintaining the goals of your information security policy seem to be at odds. There are, however, many ways that 802.11 can be included in your network infrastructure, as long as the risks are understood and compensated for. Let us examine our options.

The first option is to ignore WEP and design your wireless installation around the insecurities that are inherent in wireless communications. This would allow several options. The simplest solution would be to place the access point in your company where the ability for outsiders to access the signal is limited. Instead of placing the access point on outside walls, simply place it toward the interior of your building. Other simple steps include enabling WEP. We have established that it does not protect the confidentiality of information very well, but it is a small incremental step that may persuade the curious to move on to another target.

Be sure to change the SSID and access point key from the manufacturer's default. Based on MAC addresses, most wireless sniffing software can quickly identify the manufacturer of the access point and compare that with well-known default values for both. While DHCP is convenient, you might also consider disabling DHCP and using static IP addresses. These steps at least prevent someone from casually connecting to your access point, but will not stop the determined.

Many access points, like switches, also allow the network administrator to restrict access to the device on a MAC address basis. For each allowed remote device, a corresponding MAC address entry would be added to the access point database. This too can be effective in preventing casual use; but practically speaking, most hosts can change their MAC address and it is easy enough to sniff a MAC address out of a packet. Attackers can simply find a MAC address that is being allowed and reconfigure their host with the same MAC address.

The above options do not provide much with respect to guarding your network against misuse. Even placing the access point in the middle of the network will not do much to deter a determined individual. Directional wireless antennas can be built from Pringle's cans for a couple of dollars worth of parts. This greatly extends the range of 802.11 reception. One of the workshops I offer focuses on wireless technology and, as a demonstration, I use a homemade directional antenna and simply point it at nearby buildings and observe the signal strength increase as the antenna focuses on the wireless LANs in the remote office buildings. Because security is about reducing risk in a cost-effective manner, it can be argued that the risk is indeed reduced using the above options — just not very much.

Configuring the wireless network to be a distinct subnet from the rest of the network can increase the security provided to a wireless network (see Exhibit 1). Traffic from the wireless network is then filtered through a firewall as if the entire wireless subnet were untrusted (which it should be considered). If your corporate firewall will accommodate an additional port, this is a fairly straightforward option to consider. It will not address the confidentiality of encrypted data or the ability for the determined to gain access to the wireless network, but it would at least reduce the risk of your internal network being attacked via the wireless subnet.

It is also possible to disregard the protection offered by WEP and utilize higher layer encryption protocols. In most networks, it is a simple matter to configure common services such as POP3 and SMTP to be encrypted via SSL/TLS. Encrypted access to your company intranet may also be possible via HTTPS, the same protocol used to secure online transactions. If the infrastructure has already been created to support these protocols, then the threat of somone intercepting important company information is further reduced.

In some cases, it is possible to utilize the company VPN to encrypt all traffic from the wireless LAN using IPSec. Consider the case of a number of mobile users coming in from the field and setting up in a conference room for a meeting. These mobile users will have any host-based VPN client

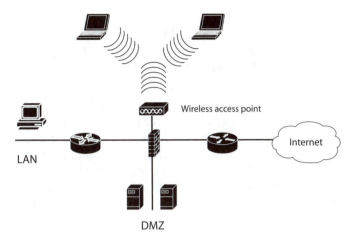

Wireless access point

LAN

Internet

DMZ

Exhibit 1. Treat All Wireless Communications as Untrusted and Plan the Network Design Accordingly

already installed on their laptop. The firewall protecting the wireless network will only allow traffic to the VPN gateway from the wireless LAN. Wireless users would then establish a VPN session to the corporate VPN gateway, and all traffic sent from their hosts would be encrypted using IPSec, a much more secure and reliable encryption algorithm. This reduces the risk of unauthorized access and loss of confidentiality the most, but admittedly requires proper network design and implementation.

Instead of licking their wounds received from the WEP problem, Internet engineers in conjunction with the IEEE have begun working on a number of new solutions that address the problems of WEP encryption. Although the IV length is an issue, the real problem stems from the fact that there is no easy way to change keys in WEP. Recall that it was only long-lived keys (long-lived being a number of minutes in this case) that allowed the encryption to be easily defeated. The IEEE, in response, has drafted the 802.1x protocol. This protocol uses the Extensible Authentication Protocol (EAP), a protocol designed by the IETF to authenticate users to a RADIUS server and provide key management functions for users. EAP itself is very similar to PAP and CHAP, which are currently used to authenticate dial-up clients all over the world. The major difference is that EAP, as the name suggests, allows the inclusion of user-defined extensions, essentially allowing vendors and standards bodies to increase the authentication options of the protocol beyond that of CHAP or PAP.

The 802.1x standard is officially known as the Port Authentication Protocol (PAP) and is intended to only allow network access to a device that has authenticated itself on the network. From a security standpoint, this is significant because it would reduce the risk of sniffers and unauthorized network hosts. This application also makes it attractive to wireless networks. An 802.1x-enabled device would not allow any access to a device on a port-by-port basis until the device has authenticated with a remote server. Only then would users be able to surf the Web or check their e-mail.

802.1x is an attempt to overcome the inherent weaknesses of the WEP protocol. Using 128-bit encryption with the larger IV value, EAP passes an authentication request to a RADIUS server that authenticates the user and then provides a temporary WEP key on a per-user basis. This alone is a great improvement over the earlier WEP implementations in that the WEP key was shared between all users. It is only after the user is authenticated that an IP address and access through the access point is granted. Furthermore, a new key is provided at regular intervals, most often every ten minutes. This prevents someone from collecting enough data to be able to decrypt large amounts of data.

While this would seem to be just the solution required to solve the wireless problem, and indeed address a number of other network security risks, 802.1x has some issues of its own that need to be considered. Some have criticized 802.1x authentication as being too limited, in that only the client is authenticated, not the access point as well. Furthermore, although 802.1x can be used to provide key management, the standards do not define how that key management is to occur, thus allowing vendors to implement their own solutions. The use of EAP is also flexible, meaning that the method of authentication while using EAP can vary from vendor to vendor. In the real world, this means that incompatibilities between vendors are going to exist.

Despite these shortcomings, 802.1x is gaining acceptance in the networking community. I would not recommend trusting your entire wireless infrastructure to this standard at this point and would continue to advise segmenting the wireless subnets and filtering traffic with a firewall, but it seems that 802.1x will become more common in the reduction of risk for wireless networking.

Chapter 12
Network Penetration Testing

There are few subjects that can perk up a tired audience quicker than a discussion of network penetration testing. This is the chance for the good guys to act like the bad guys for a short period of time. Secretly, this is what most network administrators wish they could do, but for whatever reason, they have not joined the "elite" of the "information Wild West." Having a chance to "hack" a network as part of their job is something that most people will jump at. It is interesting, it is dramatic, and it is the reason (at least initially) that most people become interested in the information security field. While management and government rally the public about the danger of computer crime, it is a fact that many in the information security field, on either side of the fence, regard the process of breaking into and securing computer networks as a challenging test of skill and experience.

Network penetration testing, like network security and hacking, is part art and part science. Using the same tools that the average attacker will use in trying to circumvent the security on the network, the goal of a network administrator is to discover the errors and omissions of their own security policy implementation before the bad people do.

Despite the intangible qualities of the art of network penetration testing, for our purposes, we want a process that has definable goals and achievable outcomes. Our ultimate goal is to provide information that will allow us to create a more secure network. Therefore, before beginning any work on network penetration testing, it is important to take care of some paperwork.

The network penetration test should begin with clear goals. These goals would then be affected by a number of constraints on the test itself. This is crucial because, sometimes, it can be difficult to tell the difference between a penetration test and a real attack. When your testing crashes an important server, many would argue that there is no real difference.

At a minimum, your plan of action should define the following from the outset:

- *Goals.* An idea of what the network penetration will attempt to accomplish. For example, "To test for vulnerabilities on the corporate network by testing the administrative, physical, and technical controls that affect information security. This information will then be used to prioritize any corrective action that may be required to align the state of the network with the published information security policy of this company."
- *Scope.* What is to be tested should always be defined. This serves as a statement of work for the project and can include a specific checklist of tests to be performed, or can provide a broad description of the testing procedures. Statisticians would say that we are what we measure and, in this case, we will only be able to evaluate the security of what we have tested. This portion should leave no confusion as to what will be examined and what will not be examined.
- *Off-limits.* Closely related to scope should be an explicit list of what is off-limits. Services or vulnerabilities should be clearly listed; for example, "In no event shall the physical security of the building be attempted to be circumvented or disabled." or "The server at 192.168.1.11 is to be exempt from all testing." In many cases, someone from outside your organization may be the one performing the actual testing. Some information may be sensitive enough that even the testing of the security by an outside entity can be suspect. Other times, the service is important enough that automated scanning, with the possible result of a host crash, may be unacceptable. If either of these cases apply, these exceptions to the policy must be clearly stated.
- *Time of execution.* In most instances, a network penetration test is going to look a lot like a network attack. To protect the person doing the testing and to allow the organization to detect a real attack, the time of the test should be clearly defined.

Ultimately, for the network penetration testing to provide any value to the company that orders it, a thorough report should be made at the conclusion of the testing. Whether you are performing the test yourself or employing the services of a third party, you should expect, at a minimum, the following from the final report:

- *Executive summary.* A manager is going to expect to see the results of the testing. An overview should be written that is sufficient to convey the findings of the testing without going into too much detail.
- *Technical presentation.* For those who actually need to implement the findings of the testing, a technical report should be included;

this report contains details of the testing process along with descriptions of the vulnerabilities.

Both the technical presentation and the executive summary should also include the following sections:

- *Results sorted by priority.* It would be the rare penetration test that returned the result of "A+" and nothing more. When action needs to be taken in response to discovered vulnerabilities, it is crucial that these be prioritized for the benefit of management and network administrators.
- *Risk exposure.* What is the potential effect on the company if the identified vulnerabilities are not addressed?
- *Resource requirements.* What would it require to reduce the threat from any risks discovered during this process?
- *Recommended actions.* Finally, a recommendation as to the course of action that should be taken to address the issues revealed through the testing process.

When the report has been generated, reviewed, and acted upon, the final step is to evaluate the company's information security policy. Does anything in the report suggest that it was an oversight in the security policy that must be addressed? A security policy is not a static document. It is to be expected that as the result of a test, it would change to reflect the changing nature of the network and the threats that put it at risk.

Ideally, the time for network penetration testing is after the security policy has been implemented. In some cases, a simple penetration test has also been used to convince management of the importance of a proper information security policy. Once the initial testing has occurred, it should then be scheduled for regular testing in the future and after all significant changes to the security policy or implementation in the enforcement of the security policy.

To properly perform network penetration testing, it is important for network administrators to change their perspective on their network for a time. They must look at their own network from the point of view of a determined attacker.

Whether or not a particular attacker knows it, there is a certain series of steps that occur in more or less detail before an attack is actually launched. The first and most important step is to understand the motivation for someone to attack your network. Understanding this step will help define the goals of the various groups of attackers and to better understand their targets.

Many attackers are simply out to gain recognition or admiration from their peers. Hackers motivated in this manner may increase their virtual tally through the number of systems that they compromise or rank their prestige vis-a-vis their peer group based on the perceived difficulty of attacking the target. Many attackers in this category are the stereotypical "hackers." That is, they are (usually) young males with a great deal of time and an incomplete understanding of the technology they are using. Attackers in this category are the most likely to use vulnerabilities discovered by others that have been made simple to use through the use of exploit scripts — programs that execute a series of precompiled attacks. The lower skilled of this group are commonly referred to in a derisive manner as "script kiddies" due to their reliance upon other, more experienced attackers for the actual knowledge required to successfully launch an attack.

Unless your network presents a particularly attractive target for attackers in this group — that is, your network represents some sort of "crown jewel" of possible targets — most attackers looking for prestige in their peer group are most likely to attack the most clearly vulnerable sites. Normal expenditures on network security will be sufficient to deter these attackers because, sadly, there are plenty of easier targets out there for them to set their sights on.

"Hacking" has not always carried the negative connotations that it does in today's language. At one point, it was a symbol of respect to be referred to as a "hacker" in any technology. This is because the original hackers were simply people who sought to fully understand the workings of any technology. Thus, a hacker was simply someone with a great deal of knowledge and curiosity regarding technology. The second primary motivation for attacking networks still reflects this basic premise of hacking — curiosity.

Many people in the security industry are there because they are motivated by curiosity. Just as some people are attracted to being expert chefs, musicians, mechanics, or fighter pilots, the curious hacker simply seeks to understand how networks work and what information can be learned about any given network. Simply put, they hack because it is something they have a talent for and because they like it. Like those seeking prestige, many curious hackers will move on if a given target seems to be unyielding in its secrets. On the other hand, the curious hacker will also be more tempted than those looking for prestige to stick with a particular target if it proves to be an especially tough nut to crack. It does follow. after all, that a well-protected network must have a great deal of interesting information.

The curious hacker is especially valuable to the rest of the security community because it is their drive to understand how programs and protocols work that often leads them to discover what breaks a particular application of network technology. The product of the curious hacker's skill and dedication is what allows the majority of the hacking community access to lesser-known exploits.

Hackers motivated by either prestige or curiosity have the ability to wreak havoc with your network but, commonly, these attackers are looking for the easiest target they can find — because in most cases they do not have any particular motivation to specifically attack your network, they will move on to an easier target if it appears that your network is following good security practices in the same way that burglars move on to homes with owners who do not secure their windows and doors with secure locks and place burglar alarm decals on their windows. These homes are not impossible to break into; it is just that easier targets exist that will make their own efforts that much more productive.

From the point of view of your network's security, the more dangerous motivations are yet to come. In some cases, your network specifically will come under attack because of what an attacker thinks or knows about the information they are likely to find there. In this case, the attackers are primarily motivated by gain. When an attacker steals the account information of your customers, they are hoping to use that information to increase the money in their own pocket. This motivation is particularly dangerous to your information security because attackers specifically know what they want. It is only by bypassing your information security systems that they can specifically access what they want.

In this case, the same network security systems that keep out the egotistic and curious may not be adequate to keep out those specifically looking for your information. Attackers in this category may be more than the rogue individual hacker or even a group of hackers; they may be part of a large crime syndicate or even government organizations. This means that we can assume that the attackers in this category have the time to sufficiently test your network defenses, the expertise to know what to attack and how to carry out the attack in an effective manner, and the money to finance their efforts. It is defending your network against this group of attackers that the value of the security policy becomes clear. You cannot assume to have the same budget to allocate to network defense that attackers have to circumvent those defenses. Thus, you need to understand the value of what you are trying to defend against versus how much to spend defending against an adversary who potentially has much greater resources than you.

The final type of motivation is revenge. Hackers may have many reasons to strike back at a company. They may feel that the company has slighted or otherwise belittled their skills or a cause that they are particularly close to. The motive of revenge can also be based on political ideology. Ideology is behind a number of political attacks known as "hacktivism," in which the political ends of an individual or group are furthered through network attacks.

Revenge is often found as a motive of employees of a company, be they current or former. Perhaps an employee feels that he passed over for a promotion, unfairly terminated, or "downsized." With an inside view of the network and knowledge of targets that would be particularly damaging to the health of the company, this type of revenge can be particularly dangerous to a network.

Understanding the different motivations that an attacker might have is important when planning your network penetration test. Based on what we now know, attacks based on prestige or curiosity will most likely be deterred through straightforward security testing. Because the threat is simply looking for the easiest target, the solution is to configure enough security so that the attacker will simply get tired or bored with trying and move on to an easier victim. Threats that seek some sort of gain are more difficult to thwart because they usually have a specific goal in mind. What on your network would most likely serve as a target for someone with motivation? If you identify a resource, then it would be a good use of your time to try to penetrate your network resources to "break into" that resource yourself. Finally, assume that someone outside your company is simply interested in causing you damage. These types of attacks are generally denial-of-service attacks, either based on application flaws or simply bandwidth-based denial-of-service. How can your company protect against this? If the attacker is a knowledgeable employee of your company, what would be the likely target?

Understanding the motivation of the different classes of attackers should give you a better idea of the likely targets and scope of any likely attack against your network. Once the motivations of attackers are understood, the next phase is the information-gathering phase of an attack. During this phase, attackers seek to learn all they can about your network for the purpose of selecting appropriate targets. Granted, not all attackers are sophisticated enough to fully examine all the information on your network; but when performing penetration testing, it is a good idea to assume that they are. What information can someone who has no idea of your information systems learn about your company? Can he learn about the type of business you have? Most likely, because letting people know your business is part of being *in* business. Can they learn the operating systems that your servers run? The release versions? The types of network applications that support your network and their release versions? The IP addresses of your servers and the configuration of your firewall?

People who are good at network penetration and hacking in general know that information is valuable. Thus, any serious threat is going to begin with "casing the joint" before an actual attack is launched. In network security terms, this is known as *footprinting* and is an attempt to obtain a detailed description of the security procedures of an organization. This is an attempt to understand where the likely targets in a network are, and what kinds of defenses are protecting them.

The process of footprinting has its own methodology, which you can emulate while conducting your own penetration testing. While you may know your network, it may be useful to begin the network penetration test with only the knowledge that an outside person may obtain. To do this, start thinking like a hacker.

First perform a through search on all the information that you can find out about your company. Go through your company's Web site, taking notes on all the information you can pick up about your company. Some things to look for include:

- *Corporate organization.* Does the corporation have any remote branches, subsidiaries, or strategic business partners? It can be assumed that each of these corporate entities will have some type of network. Perhaps they even have their own Internet access outside that of corporate headquarters. Are the links between headquarters and branch offices or partners IP-based VPNs or circuit-based VPNs such as Frame Relay? The hope is that one of these remote sites or business partners may be easier to break into and thus provide a backdoor to the main site.
- *Personnel information.* This can reveal quite a bit about a company. E-mail addresses, phone numbers, and personnel structure all can work together to give an attackers information they can use for the most powerful attack method known — that of social engineering.
- *Technology information.* Note any information on your company Web site that may provide a clue as to the actual technology you are using on your network. This may be information about security policies, vendor alliances, Web site hosting, user help pages for accessing corporate resources, etc. This information also includes any domains that are associated with your company. While there may be the primary domain that people associate with your organization, be sure to look for other domains that might suggest to an attacker information about corporate or technical structure of your network.

Make sure to also include a Web search on several different search engines, looking for information about your company. You never know when an industry writer, ex- or current employee, or your own advertising copy may post something to the Internet that is of significance to your information security. A common method of digging up particularly juicy information is to search for the e-mail address or domains of your company in Internet newsgroups and Web-based bulletin boards. A support engineer may be in need of some quick help and post details of a problem on a board — information that may seem innocent but, when combined with other information that can be found about your company, may be enough to suggest likely avenues of attack.

Many Internet search engines also allow you to search for Web pages that link back to your site. For example, on the Google search engine, if you type "link:www.proteris.com." it will provide a link of all Web pages that link back to your site. This is a quick way to turn up some information about where else on the Internet your company has visibility.

Once your notes are complete, examine them with an eye toward information security. What in your research can be used to give attackers some direction? This is the same information that attackers would use to begin their own work. The goal of this information is to try to find actual hosts that will serve as targets.

The next step in the footprinting process is to determine the IP ranges that your target network uses. This is a fairly straightforward process, in that the American Registry for Internet Numbers (ARIN)[1] maintains a complete database of network numbers correlated with the business units that own them. By entering in a company or business unit name into the ARIN database, a range of network numbers that have been assigned to that company are returned. This information can then be correlated with IP addresses that can be found for publicly accessible resources such as Web servers, DNS, and mail servers. This will give attackers clues to the network ranges that can be used for servers, if they are hosting the servers on their own network or another network.

During this time period, a serious attacker will also begin the process of social engineering. This may mean calling any available telephone numbers and posing as an important member of the company. It would not be unheard of for an attacker to physically go through a company dumpster in an attempt to find important memos that relate to information security policies or likely targets. Companies that are in the process of mergers or transitions are especially vulnerable to this type of probing, as it is more than likely that the confusion and uncertainty that make social engineering successful will come into play. An attacker might also attempt to learn the local exchange telephone block that has been assigned to the company and use a tool known as a wardialer to dial each of the numbers in an attempt to find modems attached to phone lines that may serve as a weakly protected backdoor into the corporation.

DNS is also a very useful tool for attackers. As noted in the previous paragraph, this allows an attacker to use a domain name and translate that into IP addresses. The amount of information given out by DNS can vary. In some poorly configured DNS implementations, the DNS entries for an entire network can be delivered to any host that requests them. Fortunately, this practice is disappearing as many network administrators realized they were essentially providing an entire network topology to the curious every time a DNS request was made. Today, DNS is typically configured to be much more guarded in the information that it provides to the outside world; but even so, the DNS information that you need to have available for others to be able to access your network resources is a clue that attackers can use to identify potential targets.

Attackers will use the information they learn from the IP addresses to then perform some network reconnaissance. This is most likely done through the use of a network scan. This can be a direct scan of the network through the use of any number of freely available network scanning tools. An attacker or security professional places a network range of IP addresses into a software program and the program then "tests" each IP address in that network range to see if it is an address that is "live," that is, assigned to a host. Reconnaissance may also take place using tools such as Traceroute, which trace the path of a packet from the attacker's site to your site. Multiple iterations of this program will allow an attacker to create a fairly detailed view of the network topology, including any type of load balancing that may be occurring due to multiple Internet links by your company. This is also an excellent method to use when trying to determine the likely position of a firewall or other security device in the network between the attacker and yourself.

Most of these scanning attacks are not very subtle and are akin to walking past a building with a placard saying, "I'm going to attack your network now!," but alone, network scanning is so common that it is easy to miss these signs. An attacker can also be very discreet when performing these types of scans, breaking them up into small chunks over a time period of weeks and sourcing them from multiple hosts, all in an attempt to cover or at least obscure their tracks from those less vigilant.

Scanners themselves have varying levels of sophistication. The simplest scan is to simply use the PING application to send packets to an IP address to see if it is active. When network administrators discovered this application of PING in the scanning of their own networks, ICMP packets, the type that PING uses, were thus blocked at most firewalls. Scanning software responded to this change in network security by using other types of packets in an attempt to bypass the ICMP filters. For example, scanning software may try to create a TCP connection on a number of ports. If the connection is successful, the scanning software has a good idea of what applications the host is serving. If unsuccessful and an error message is returned from the scanned host, then this is useful information as well. It lets the scanning software know that, at the very least, there is indeed a live host at that address.

Network administrators responded to this use by filtering out which ports allow incoming connections through the firewall. Thus, a host PC in a network may be able to create connections to resources on the Internet, but hosts on the Internet trying to make a connection through the firewall to the internal host are blocked. Scanning software again responded by sending TCP segments without a connection request. This, of course, would generate an error; but again, the presence of an error is information that an attacker could use to launch further attacks against your network.

This process of attack, defend, new attack is one of the elements that makes information security an interesting profession. This escalation of attack technologies and security technologies continues endlessly. I am never at a loss for respect for the ways that people figure out how to attack or circumvent a security policy. I do not agree with their goals or methods, but a certain "geeky" technical side of me appreciates the thought and creativity that goes into such attempts. Nevertheless, for every defense, you can assume that someone is thinking of a counter-attack. Discovering what your network is defending and what it is allowing through is one of the primary purposes of performing network penetration testing.

Through this escalation, scanners have developed to the point where they can send IP fragments, send a range of spoofed source addresses to obscure the real source of the scan, guess the remote host operating system, and identify any running applications that happen to be listening on the ports.

Originally, scanning a network was the final step in determining the likely targets to attack. Once the hosts were found, the real research would begin. An attacker would attempt to determine what applications were available over the network, along with the version or release level of the application. Once this information had been obtained, the attacker would then try to correlate known attacks against the version of the operating system. If, for example, a network scan had detected a Cisco router with an operating system version 12.2(1) and the scan also revealed that the router was acting as an SSH server to allow remote administration, with some research, an attacker could learn that this version of SSH was vulnerable to certain types of specially crafted packets generated by the SSHredder application. This would lead the attacker to perhaps execute this attack or determine that the router itself was not the primary target of their hack. This cross-referencing could be a great deal of work.

Many scanners today include additional resources to "helpfully" interpret and organize all the research and vulnerabilities that attackers previously had to do on their own. A scanning program today will not only include the scanning software, but also a database of applications, vulnerabilities for the various release levels of the applications, and a guide on how to take advantage of them and perhaps fix them.

The cynical among us may be disgusted that such resources are available for anyone to download from the Internet and use against our networks. For just a few minutes worth of work once the target network has been identified, an attacker may have a complete printout of the network vulnerabilities suitable for presentation at a board meeting. On the other hand, having these tools is incredibly valuable for those trying to protect our networks. Because we know that some of the primary motivations for attackers is to simply choose the path of least resistance in accomplishing their goals, these tools provide a way for network administrators to perform their own tests and as well as see exactly what a possible hacker would see. No network penetration test would be complete without scanning your own network from the inside and outside with these tools.

The ultimate goal of network footprinting is to identify targets for a likely attack. Once accomplished, an attacker will move on to the next step — attacking. The database of vulnerable systems is used to allow the attacker to work his way into the network. Most of the time, the initial goal of an attacker would be to gain administrative privileges on a system, preferably a domain controller or other device central to the network. With administrative privileges, an attacker would then install software (sometimes known as a "Root kit") that would allow the attacker unrestricted access to the server should his original attack vector be removed and at the same time allow the attacker to cover his tracks by removing or obscuring data that would reveal what he had done to the system.

Once administrative access has been gained, attackers would then be free to perform whatever action suited their motivation for the attack. They might change the Web site, remove important files, shut down the servers, or use the host as a stepping stone for another attack. During the process of your penetration testing then, any evidence that points to a way for attackers to gain administrative access to a host should constitute the top priority for fixing.

Network administrators rarely take the process of network penetration testing to this extreme. Simply knowing that an attacker could access your network through a previously unknown vulnerability is typically enough for the administrator to take action. Only in extremely rare circumstances should the actual execution of the attack be carried out on a live system. It is, however, acceptable for learning or demonstration purposes to create a test network that closely mirrors the production network in terms of operating systems and applications. This will allow proof of concept testing on any suspect vulnerabilities.

The vast majority of the time, penetration testing is going to reveal vulnerabilities that can be fixed in one of three ways:

1. *Patch the affected system.* A surprising number of network security vulnerabilities can be completely eliminated by applying the proper patch to the application. The reason that network administrators do not always do this in a timely manner is that the company may be releasing patches at such a rapid rate that it is difficult for network administrators to keep up, or the patch itself may adversely affect a business-critical application in its own right.
2. *Reconfigure the firewall or other security devices.* All packet filtering devices should follow the rule that all traffic not permitted is otherwise denied. However, it is easy to make mistakes when many applications are concerned. Furthermore, rules on the packet filters may have been applied in a manner that has unforeseen consequences for IP traffic. Reconfiguring these devices is usually straightforward.
3. *Change access control permissions for applications and operating systems.* Most out-of-the-box operating systems are designed for ease of use by inexperienced network administrators, not security. Network penetration testing often reveals that permissions are more liberal than they need to be. Changing the access controls of shares and other network resources will assist in reducing these vulnerabilities.

Simply running a network scan, however, cannot be construed as complete network penetration testing. The scan is the starting point. Clearly, if there is an obvious way for someone to gain administrative access through the network, then this must be dealt with immediately.

Many vulnerabilities that allow your information to be compromised are not purely technical in nature. It is difficult for a network penetration test that is based solely on IP packets to understand that users expect help-desk personnel to ask for passwords over the phone or that the key to the server room has been lost and replaced several times. Thorough network penetration testing includes examining administrative and physical security procedures in addition to the technical information that network scanning provides. The primary goal of this additional testing is twofold: to ensure that users are following your documented security policy and that these policies are sufficient to protect your network from unforeseen circumstances.

For example, is it possible to log in with an account from a former employee? If it is, is it possible because the employee's account has not been disabled in accordance with the security policy of the company or because the implementation rules of the security policy do not specify that this is a step that must be taken? Is it possible to recover company information from magnetic media tossed into the dumpster because someone has not taken the time to properly sanitize the media in accordance with the security policy or because the security policy does not address the actions that must be performed on hard drives before they are disposed of? Are all devices on your network accounted for, and can the source of all traffic be identified? Or has someone walked in the front door of your company and installed another PC on an available port that is acting as a network sniffer?

As you can see, thorough network penetration testing means that you need to be creative. Many times, the easiest way into a company network is not through the firewall, but through the front door.

12.1 Outsourcing Network Penetration Testing

There are good arguments to be made for hiring a third party to provide network penetration testing for your organization. The first is that it is always helpful to have another set of eyes that do not share your prejudices and assumptions about your network. The second is that when testing the complete information security policy, outside individuals may be a better indication of your company's susceptibility to social engineering than if you just tried to disguise your voice over the phone. Third, because this is the primary business of such firms, they have the tools and knowledge to quickly isolate and identify threats.

Even among network professionals, our own experiences affect the way that we see threats. We are likely to spend much of our time focusing on elements of network security that we are really good at, such as configuring a firewall or adjusting user privileges across the network domain. Sometimes, without even consciously realizing it, we address only lightly other security countermeasures on the network. This is behavior that commonly manifests itself through folk wisdom; "You don't know what you don't know." It is difficult to be an expert in all areas of information security, no matter what credentials or certifications an individual's resume may purport. If employing an independent third party to perform the penetration testing is not an acceptable option, at the very least, another set of trained eyes within the company should perform the penetration testing along with the network administrator.

As previously discussed, penetration testing is more than just footprinting the network and performing a scan. The most common vulnerabilities of information security are often exploited through the process of social engineering. Despite what the evening news tells us about ourselves, most people want to be helpful when they can be. This may cause them to inadvertently give out more information than they should. Ideally, this important element of information security should be performed by someone outside the company. Otherwise, a situation similar to the following may result.

(Network Administrator): Uh, hello. This is David Hasselhoff from Acme Electric. I understand you have an electrical problem in the server room. It will just be a minute for us to clear that up.

(Receptionist): Jim? Is that you? Why are you talking funny and wearing those silly glasses?

Finally, the third-party security firm most certainly has the benefit of experience. If a security expert spends the majority of your billable time looking for vulnerabilities, then it stands to reason that the security expert will be attuned to common vulnerabilities that seasoned network administrators who need to deal with many aspects of network operations may overlook. That said, do not necessarily buy into overly negative assessments of your current state of security. Remember that, for many groups like this, penetration testing is just the first step in what they hope will be additional work adjusting the security infrastructure to be more secure. I am aware of more than one security consulting firm that keeps a few "aces" in the hole to be used to secure a contract. They seem to miraculously pull some very serious vulnerabilities out of a hat when most needed.

This may remind us that the process of selecting a security consulting firm to perform penetration testing is one that we should treat like any other contractor or vendor contract. Examples of the testing and reporting that the company offers should be made available for prospective customers. Likewise, a number of references from companies in your same market sector would be ideal. Any company that cannot provide these references should be avoided. Remember that you are going to trust an outside firm with the most important data in your business. Any company that uses "hacker" themes in its advertising or contact information such as Web page information, company brochures, and e-mail addresses should most likely be avoided. This is not to say that these firms do not possess adequate talent, only that for an operation of this importance you will want to make sure you are dealing with a company of the appropriate professionalism and maturity.

There is a final consideration in hiring outside firms that was not listed above. I did not list it because I do not fully agree with the motives; but for the sake of completeness, I will include it here. It may, at times, be advantageous to hire an outside firm to test the performance of your network administrators. It may also be advantageous to hire an outside firm if there is suspicion surrounding the network team regarding its own actions with respect to the network security policy.

I find this reasoning flawed, simply because of the damage that it would inflict on the management–employee relationship. Imagine showing up to work on Monday morning to find that your manager had called in outside help over the weekend because he or she did not trust you or your work. At best, this creates a poor working environment. Unless there is an indication of illegal behavior on the part of the employee, the network administration staff should be involved in any decisions regarding outside help in penetration testing. Most good network administrators would welcome this because it allows them to improve their security — but when sprung upon them, it has been my experience that the staff treats this as a threat to their integrity and professionalism.

There are also disadvantages associated with hiring an outside firm for network penetration testing. The first is that it is unlikely that the firm will fully understand the strategic importance of all the elements of your network. Few can approach the level of understanding of your network in a short time that your network administrators have gained from months or years of working on the network.

12.2 Putting It All Together

Network penetration testing should be viewed as an essential part of network security. It should be performed when the implementation of the security policy is complete and at regular intervals thereafter.

Good penetration testing will have clearly stated goals of testing and improving the existing security policy of the network. It will also end with a detailed report of the findings and recommendations for resolving any issues uncovered as a result of the test.

The first step in penetration testing is to footprint the network with the purpose of determining likely targets. To do this:

- Obtain written permission from management to perform such research.
- Research electronic and print media for information about the company.
- Record all information about the company that you can find, including business structure, news of mergers or acquisitions, operating systems, preferred vendors, domain names, servers, services offered, individuals, phone numbers, and service provider information that can be found about the company.
- From the above information, determine available IP ranges from ARIN or another address registry, resolve all servers to IP addresses, and Traceroute to servers. Attempt to reconstruct the network as best you can with the clues provided from your earlier research.
- Scan the networks based on your findings from the previous steps. Use a variety of scanning tools and options in an attempt to force your way past any firewalls or other filtering devices.
- Connect to all available services and record what information you have learned about them, including operating systems, application names, release numbers, etc.

- Correlate this information with vendor releases regarding vulnerabilities in the given operating systems or applications by version number.
- Optionally, attempt to exploit these vulnerabilities. Do this with caution — or not at all — to avoid damaging important systems.
- Attempt to circumvent or otherwise test administrative and physical security countermeasures.
- Prioritize your results in terms of severity and possible business impact and present your findings along with a recommended course of action.

Note

1. ARIN is the Internet Number registry for North America and is accessed at the Web site www.arin.net. There are registries for other continents, such as RIPE (Europe/Middle East), APNIC (Asian Pacific region), and LACNIC (Latin America and Caribbean region). All of these registries can be accessed through the IANA homepage at www.iana.net.

Chapter 13
Incident Response

There is no single indicator of computer crimes that has shown a decrease in the amount of computer incidents over the past ten years. In some cases, the number of reported computer crimes is increasing exponentially and one can only guess at the number of unreported crimes.

By using the information in this book and through the use of other resources, you will create a network that can be called "secure" by the current state of the technology. Remember, however, that this term is simply relative. Your network will never be "totally secure," no matter what vendor marketing may try to convince you in an effort to sell its products. Just the opposite is true; you will periodically experience "computer incidents" and at some point your network will be the target of a computer crime.

To react to this eventuality, you need a computer incident response team (CIRT).[1] Successfully responding to an incident will require a group in place with an established plan of action. There are several advantages to having a plan in place when an incident occurs. The primary objective of establishing an incident response plan is to prevent the loss of life or the loss of data because of the incident. It also ensures that resources are efficiently allocated. If two network administrators respond to a computer incident by performing the same actions, then that is a waste of time that could have been otherwise better spent. Having an established plan also allows the team to practice its response. It would not be a good idea, for example, to require a team to practice its evidence handling procedure during its first case of suspected computer crime. Finally, speaking of computer crime, if it does turn out that a computer incident is indeed the result of a crime, then having a trained team with a response plan that has been practiced and followed greatly increases the chance that the criminal will be successfully caught and, just as importantly, tried and convicted based on the evidence that your team has gathered.

By the end of this chapter, we will have covered the steps required to ensure the following:

- Why an organized incident response plan is important
- How to create your own company incident response team
- How to craft your incident response policy

- How to respond to an incident in a manner that minimizes network disruptions and provides consistent positive results for your network, its users, and the security of your information

While talking about incident response, we will also spend some time discussing the forensic process — due to the importance of the forensic process in a complete incident response plan.

Computer crimes have been growing at a phenomenal rate. While early numbers may have been somewhat lower due to companies' reluctance to speak about incidents on their networks, every major indicator of computer crime, from the FBI to global computer emergency response teams, has shown an incredible increase in the number of computer crimes over the past ten years.

Law enforcement often states that crime follows the money. Given the amount of money that is invested in and relies on our global information infrastructure, it is no surprise that computer crime trends have been rising so dramatically.

In the communications industry, we have spent enormous sums of money to protect our networks. We train our network administrators and end users in the art of information security. We establish security policies that lay out the expected behavior for network users, and we place our trust in fascinating technologies such as firewalls, virtual private networks, encryption, and intrusion detection.

Despite our best efforts, however, statistics tell us that it is just a matter of time before our companies will need to respond to a computer incident. How we react when this happens can often make the difference between a minor hiccup in network activity or considerable downtime and lost productivity. How we react when this happens can make the difference between the successful resolution of a computer crime and lost data, trade secrets, and trust on the part of our network users and investors.

The key to successful incident response is preparedness. Like any team, the best plays are executed when every member of the team knows his or her part and practices the execution of the play until it is perfect. When the big game comes, the best-prepared team is the one that wins. Inside the organization, the same analogy holds true. While creating an incident response team is going to cost some money and energy, having a team in place can offer a significant return on investment.

When an incident response team is called into action, its actions benefit the company in several tangible ways, including:

- The incident response team that has practiced its response can most importantly prevent the loss of life or critical data. This is irrespective of whether data or lives are at risk due to software failure or a computer crime in progress.

- Like every good team, each member knows the role that he or she plays in supporting the team. This allows rapid response and maximum utilization of company resources. This benefit pays big dividends when a team is allowed to practice its responses prior to an incident occurring.

- Good incident response teams are good public relations teams as well. Whether individual investors or network users, people are happy to know that a crisis that might put the company at risk can be professionally managed.

- Finally, but certainly not the least in importance, professional incident response may be the best countermeasure to criminal actions directed at the company. Digital data, like any type of evidence used in a crime needs to be handled in a specific and legally correct manner. When a company attempts to prosecute a computer crime, its chances of success are greatly reduced if it has not taken the proper steps in the acquisition of evidence. The best way to ensure success in the courtroom is to make sure that professionals trained in the science of evidence gather the evidence in the hectic first moments of a computer incident.

With that in mind, let us start thinking about incident response.

The discipline of incident response can be broken into nine major categories, each building on the previous one.

1. *Planning.* This is where to spend the most time. A good planning process will ensure that the rest of the elements of incident response fall smoothly into place.
2. *Prevention.* The best offense is a good defense. Special care should be taken to ensure that your network is secure and up-to-date with regard to a good security policy. When the network is secure, the detection and evaluation of real network threats are made much easier.
3. *Detection.* Many computer crimes occur right under our noses, so to speak. Someone could be using your computer right now over the network without your knowledge. Without some way to see what is going on in the network, responding to an incident you do not know is occurring will be difficult.
4. *Evaluation.* Not all incidents are crimes. A great deal of the time, suspicious behavior on your network can be accounted for by either software or hardware problems that have nothing to do with hackers in a small room thousands of miles away. Before sounding the alarm, we need to make sure that the behavior we are witnessing is indeed the result of a computer crime.

5. *Containment.* In general, the first rule of incident response is to get a handle on the incident and ensure that neither your network users nor your information is at further risk.
6. *Investigation.* Once the affected systems have been contained, it is time to examine the incident. During this time, any evidence that might be used in criminal proceedings is collected. At a bare minimum, the incident response team will seek to understand the cause of the incident so that a repeat event can be prevented in the future.
7. *Eradication.* The cause of the incident is removed.
8. *Recovery.* Finally, the updated, repaired, and safe system is brought back online. This might require a complete reinstallation of the software controlling the machine or it might require less drastic methods, depending on the number of steps taken during the planning and prevention stages. Once again, good planning pays off.
9. *Post-mortem.* Every incident should be followed up with a meeting of the team to discuss what went right and what needs to be improved the next time around. Documentation produced during the incident should be reviewed and the incident response process should be refined to improve performance.

As previously mentioned, the most important step of incident response is the planning stage. There are several major objectives of this stage. Primarily, we are looking for buy-in from management that an incident response process is valuable to the company as a whole. This applies not to just the incident response team specifically, but to a corporate network security policy as a whole. Indeed, the incident response team is only a part of an overall security policy. Once approval for creating an incident response team has been granted, the next step is to assemble the team and develop the response plan.

Because an incident response team is part of an overall information security infrastructure, the same business benefits that can be made for selling security policy can also be made for the selling the incident response team. There are various ways to justify this expenditure, but they all hinge on the value of the assets that the security policy and the team are protecting. You would buy insurance to protect your house, right? This is an asset that you wish to protect. For the same reasons, you implement an incident response team — because your business depends on the network and the data that the network houses.

There are several ways to put an incident response team together. Many times, the team can be constructed from interested parties within an organization. Do not limit your search to just people who work on the IT staff. There are many roles to play on an incident response team. Your team will most likely include members of the IT staff, but it should also include members of human resources, the legal department, and administrative staff. It might also include some members who are not directly employed by your company if expertise in a given area is lacking from the in-house pool of talent. For example, in-house staff may not have the expertise to adequately investigate digital data. If company employees are trained in how to collect evidence and data correctly, an outside forensic expert with whom you have a professional relationship can do the actual forensic examination of the data.

There are several options to consider when choosing the composition of an emergency response team. Several years ago, it would have been acceptable to request the services of a public CIRT, such as the Carnegie Mellon Computer Emergency Response Team (CERT). When an incident was suspected, the concerned network administrator would contact the CERT and alert them of the incident and seek advice for resolving the issue. This arrangement was often advantageous not only because of the price, but also because the public teams responded to a great many incidents. This global perspective would mean that public CIRTs had an accurate view of overall incident activity and could maintain extensive databases of incidents and resolutions. The Internet as a whole, however, was a much smaller place and the number of incidents reported was nowhere near that of of today's numbers. While public CIRT teams are available, companies typically use them simply as places to record data. They are no longer a serious option for first responder roles.

Instead, a company can choose to use a commercial incident response vendor. These companies contract to monitor the network security of an organization and are empowered to respond to any incidents that might occur. Like the public CIRTs, these companies have a wealth of experience in forecasting and detecting incidents. While network administrators for a single organization may not have the perspective to recognize that problems on their network are occurring on a great deal of other networks at the same time, commercial CIRTs have just this ability.

A commercial CIRT may be advantageous to a company in that it allows the organization to better utilize its own resources. Most organizations cannot afford to keep someone on staff with the training and sole duty of responding to incidents. Many times, it is clear that outsourcing this function is good cost management.

Other organizations prefer to maintain their own incident response teams. While it is logical to presume that the team would be made up primarily of IT staff, this is not always a requirement. Many times, large organizations will split incident response teams so that they better mirror the business roles rather than strictly IT roles. The presumption is that each department knows its own needs best.

This intimate knowledge of the network and business needs of a company is the primary advantage to creating a CIRT utilizing your own resources. In large companies, where the incident response team and security groups might be independent entities, an in-house incident response team generally has an easier time than an outside vendor working with the security group to ensure that the incident does not re-occur.

The final option is not really an option, but necessity sometimes makes it so. An ad hoc incident response team is better than having no formal team in place at all. At a minimum, an ad hoc incident response team composed of whoever is available at the time would have a set of documented procedures to follow to assist in the timely response to an incident. This ad hoc team would also have documentation to and aid in the investigative and recovery portion of incident response.

When establishing the team, it is important to establish the chain of command and who has what responsibilities. This is a crucial element of incident response. While a democracy works well when there is time to deliberate actions, in a crisis, there needs to be a single person coordinating the actions of the other team members.

Some thought should also be given to whom the team as a whole reports to within the organization. This is where the understanding of the political climate of your organization will be important. There may be times when the team discovers inappropriate behavior on the part of individuals working within the company. Knowing that they can act upon such behavior without fear of backlash will be important for the proper operation of the team.

Once the team is established, it is time to work on response plans. These are the steps of who does what in a crisis. The major outline of the plan should follow the steps that we have already discussed. That is, there should be clear guidelines regarding how an incident might be detected, meaning what behavior should alert users to a possible computer incident; what the process of evaluation will be; and how an incident is distinguished from other network behavior. Once it is clear that there is a computer crime occurring on the network, how is the system contained? How is evidence collected? How is the system cleansed and protected from future attacks? Finally, how is the system brought back online?

The most difficult part of planning these steps is going to be the degree of subjectivity that most computer incidents have surrounding them. While it may be clear that a computer incident is in the works, it may not always be clear as to how the incident should be responded to. For example, consider the common event of someone scanning your firewall for vulnerabilities. This happens so often that a passing scan would be a waste of time and resources on everyone's part. What happens if one scan becomes ten from a single source or network? When does this nuisance activity become something to be concerned about?

One way to deal with such ambiguity is to create a threat list that categorizes potential incidents according to the degree of severity. For example, one such organization's list might look like this:

- *Critical.* The Critical level might include only those threats that put human life and safety at risk. They might also involve threats that could potentially and irrevocably destroy critical data. Because every organization should have a comprehensive backup and recovery plan in addition to an incident response plan, it is hoped that the number of threats that could affect their data in this manner is quite minimal.
- *High.* Threats in the High category might include attacks that have a very high potential for damage to critical network resources. Such threats might include attacks or vulnerabilities that allow an attacker root or administrative access to servers or the domain. Others might be attacks where system damage is imminent and classified or sensitive data is at risk. As a general rule of guidance, threats that affect the confidentiality or integrity of data should fall into this category. Our example of someone gaining root access to a system would allow this to occur.
- *Medium.* Threats in the Medium category are those that are significant but do not directly threaten critical systems or data. Examples might include attempts at unauthorized access to user accounts, unusual user account activity, or the impairment of noncritical network resources. Many Web-site defacements might belong in this category as well. While the Web site has been attacked and this is a serious event, critical data has rarely been altered, lost to, or obtained by an attacker. Another generalization might be to include threats that affect the availability of resources but do not affect the confidentiality or the integrity of data. The Web-site defacement or a denial-of-service attack would qualify as threats to availability.
- *Low.* A low threat is someone attempting to pass the Klez virus through your e-mail server when you know that your server is scanning for and removing these viruses. When you know that the system has been prepared for such an incident and that no harm will result from it, then the threat is low. Many "script kiddie" attacks, especially the older, well-established ones fall into this category as well.
- *Minimal.* As a normal part of business, your network will be the target of a great deal of half-hearted "doorknob rattling." This group of minimal threats might include such things as PING scans, SYN scans, and the normal high-volume, low-threat activities that make the Internet such an interesting place.

These are, of course, just examples. Many companies like to use obtuse or important-sounding, threat-level categories like "alpha-orange-1" and "fire-left-down." Furthermore, what your company prioritizes may differ from the suggestions offered above. Whatever you like to use, the important element is that you have established that not all threats and incidents are created equal.

At the same time you are establishing threat levels, you should also examine your network resources. Prioritize them in terms of importance. There are surely some servers that are more important to the overall business than user end-stations, just as your customer relations management software is more important than a misbehaving e-mail client. The relative importance of your assets will also help your team make the right decisions during a crisis.

Once your team has established threat levels and defined critical network resources, it is time to define some response options. There are four major options that provide guidance on how to respond during an incident.

The first of these choices is: *Do nothing!* And that is right. You might decide that the most effective way to address some incidents is to do nothing at all. This is most often the case when the severity of the threat is low or minimal and the relative value of the target is also low.

One of the major reasons that incident response teams fail, in addition to lacking proper planning, is that they try to respond to too much. Properly following the eight steps of incident response requires a great deal of energy and time on the part of the incident response team. Throwing all these resources at every script-kiddie that comes your way will be a sure way to burn out your team members. Do not be afraid to "do nothing" when it is justified.

The second choice of incident response is to simply defend against the attack and future attacks. This may mean configuring the firewall to block such attacks or installing application or operating system patches that render the attack harmless. Not every organization is interested in investigating and pursuing computer criminals. Sometimes, the most effective use of time is to identify the threat, eradicate it, and prevent it from threatening your network in the future. This is a good choice for low to medium threats against most of your company assets.

In some specialized cases, one option may be to perform surveillance or gather additional data on the threat. This may mean confining the system to prevent the attacker from further damaging the network, but at the same time installing monitoring software or hardware to follow the attackers. Most of the time, this information is used to collect evidence in the eventual prosecution of the attacker, but it can also be used to educate the incident response team as to the attacker's methods and goals.

The final of the four response options is to defend the network against further attacks and at the same time seek the arrest of the perpetrator or otherwise demand satisfaction through the civil court system. This is the most costly and time-consuming of all options and should only be considered when the threat level and asset value are high. While there is a growing awareness of computer crimes, catching and successfully prosecuting a criminal for computer crimes can still be a long-shot proposition. Nevertheless, your incident response team members should be trained for this decision because the actions they take in the first few minutes of response can determine the eventual outcome of any legal action.

The final step of finishing the policy is to establish some guidelines as to the involvement of the incident response team members. For example, you do not necessarily need to involve the members of the team who are part of the legal department or those who are primarily concerned with the examination of forensic evidence for every incident. The level of threat, asset value of the target, and chosen response should dictate the involvement of team members on an as-needed basis.

Part of creating a CIRT is ensuring that the team has the resources it needs to accomplish its tasks. To further this end, a couple of "incident toolkits" should be prepared ahead of time so that during the response, when time is of the essence, all needed materials are at hand.

A single-incident toolkit typically includes a well-prepared laptop that has at a minimum the following features:

- Sniffer software/protocol analyzers.
- *Network adapters for the various media on your network* — typically Ethernet, fiber, and perhaps Token Ring if you are still fortunate enough to be employing this technology. Be aware that most Token Ring adapters do not work in promiscuous mode, thereby making them difficult to operate with sniffing software.
- *CD-RW drive.* The laptop may be required to capture and store media. Ideally, these captures will be stored directly to a CD-RW to minimize the argument that someone had altered the data after collecting it.
- *Disk imaging software.* There are a number of software products available for the direct copying of information from one disk to another. This is useful in the acquisition of data from active hard drives.
- *Forensic disk reading software.* This specialized software allows a user to view the contents of a disk drive by viewing the surface of the drive itself. It is ideal for finding information that is otherwise hidden through the directory services of an operating system.

The above tools will, in combination, create a minimal forensics station capable of troubleshooting computer incidents and, if need be, collecting data to be used for further troubleshooting or an actual investigation. The laptop will not be as versatile as a dedicated forensics station, but will be adequate for a first response role. Companies that are serious about incident response and have the on-site expertise to be able to perform their own forensic investigations upon captured data should also invest in a dedicated forensics station. Introductory desktop forensic stations normally start around the price that you would pay for a decent laptop computer. Mobile stations start at about double that cost.

Impressive hardware with lots of bells and whistles, however, is only the start of a good incident toolkit. Other materials that assist in the troubleshooting and recording of data and actions are also helpful. Also consider including the following:

- Removable media such as a JAZ or ZIP drive for quick removal of information from a system hard drive or volatile memory.
- Spare, large-capacity drives, including IDE, SCSI, and tape drives. These are useful when a direct dump of all drive information is required. Retaining the same format as the original drive is especially important if you wish to boot the copied drive to recreate the environment on the original machine. Along with these drives, include a number of adaptor cables for each drive type, as well as spare power couplers. It is typical of Murphy's Law to be out of couplers from the internal power supply just when you need them for disk imaging.
- *Spare power strips.* You can never have enough outlets.
- *35mm flash camera or digital camera.* Much of the documentation that must be performed in an investigation is greatly assisted through the use of a camera of some sort. The original environment can then be documented to film, along with the specific steps taken during any investigation.
- *A collection of bootable floppy disks.* At a minimum, this should include boot disks for the operating systems that are used in your network. A number of single-disk Linux distributions are available that can provide a complete RAM disk-based operating system with network utilities if required.
- A generous supply of write-once CDs, along with markers and labels for documentation.
- *Complete documentation for all operating systems, applications, and hardware likely to be found on the network.* In general, this information is stored electronically on a number of CDs. Otherwise, your network response team is going to have to include weight training in its response planning.
- *Notebooks and pens.* Documentation is crucial while investigating computer incidents.
- *Personal voice recorders.* These can either be the cassette or MP3 variety. Ideally, CIRT members work in pairs, with one member taking

notes and one recording events. A personal voice recorder, however, can allow one investigator to work while recording actions for later transcription if need be.

- Evidence labels.

One item in the above list merits further explanation (i.e., the evidence label). Every piece of information gathered during an incident should be treated as if it would someday wind up in front of a judge. In the majority of cases, this will not be true; but for those times that it is true, collecting the evidence with a clear chain of custody will be preferable to trying to reverse-engineer the evidentiary chain of custody. The evidence labels we are referring to mean that, at a minimum, the following information is recorded on them: date and time the evidence was collected, a unique incident number, a unique item number within the incident, who the evidence belonged to before it was collected and where it came from, a complete description of the evidence, who collected the evidence, and who received the evidence from the person who collected it. Additionally, space should be included to record any information pertaining to use or movement of the evidence after it has been collected. This includes information as to where the evidence was moved from, where it was taken, and who removed the evidence, along with the date, time, and reason for moving it.

Once the team has been set up, it is time to drill. Ideally, there is time to drill, based on threats of various levels. Each team member should have the chance to practice his or her roles several times before there is an actual incident. Persons who are responsible for recognizing incidents should have full training with any logging software, intrusion detection devices, and troubleshooting tools that are available on their network. Persons responsible for the gathering of evidence or data should practice creating a clean copy of a hard drive several times before the outcome of an incident hinges upon it.

13.1 Prevention

Key to any incident response plan, once the initial planning process is complete, is the implementation of a complete security policy. Not only is a security policy a good idea from the point of view of network security, but it also assists the incident response team in evaluating the difference between a real incident and a false one. Furthermore, if the security on the network is up-to-date, it also reduces the number of high-priority threats that response teams need to address, thus making better use of their time.

13.2 Detection

The setting up of the security policy will also introduce several technologies that will be key in the detection of possible incidents on a computer network. The firewall can often serve as the first warning sign of attacks or network activity from outside the company's own network. With the firewall, any intrusion detection systems (IDSs) will also flag known attacks found in packets on the network. This allows not only efficient detection, but also rapid evaluation of the threat.

It should be noted that an IDS will not serve as a perfect detection device. There are ways to fool an IDS, and even an IDS can miss new or novel attack patterns on the network. Another clear attack that the IDS might miss is someone discovering the password of a user or administrator. To the IDS, the activity may look normal. There is no substitute for knowing your own network and the vigilance of your network team.

Most applications support robust logging. They may record significant operational conditions or user actions such as log-in times and activity while connected. Each logging device should be capable of being time-synchronized with other devices and, if possible, all log information should be collected and stored on a central server such as a syslog server. The ability to store the information in a central location, along with time-stamping, will make it much easier to reconstruct a sequence of events along with providing easier management and easier detection of possible computer incidents.

In fact, so many applications and operating systems support logging information that it is sometimes a challenge to know what to collect. A good forensics investigator will recommend that the more information you are able to collect and store, the better. A network administrator who is responsible for the collection and storage of those logs might argue otherwise. In active networks, the amount of logging information that is collected can be enormous. Furthermore, logging everything that is capable of being logged and shipping it over the network can affect the performance of your system. At a minimum, logs should collect information regarding user log-in times, unsuccessful log-in attempts, and any attempts to change security policy. From there, the amount of logged information depends on the cataloging system available for the logs (extra information does you no good if you cannot find it), the performance of the network itself, and the ability to store the logged information for a reasonable period of time.

Finally, there is no substitution for common sense. Incident response teams, network administrators, and end users should all be trained to identify unusual behavior on the network. It may be changes to an important database that cannot be explained, problems with operating systems or servers, and the gradual or sudden use of network resources that occur without other explanation. Any of these symptoms and more may be the early warning signs of a computer incident.

13.3 Evaluation

Once an incident has been detected, the next step is evaluation. Throughout this discussion we have used the term "incident" rather than "crime" or "attack" for a reason. Information systems are complicated. There can be any number of causes that explain strange behavior, not all of which qualify as a crime or attack. The purpose of this stage of incident response is to make that evaluation.

Sometimes, it will be clear that a computer incident is in progress. For example, the firewall and IDS may both be generating alerts that packets known to be associated with a particular attack have been detected. Or, a user may experience a screen message that says something helpful, such as, "j00@r3 0wNZ0R3d," a clear indication that something is amiss. Many times, however, the evidence is not so clear. A good deal of research may be involved to rule out possible explanations before the cause of suspicious symptoms can be ascertained.

It may even be the case that evaluation, containment, and investigation become one and the same step. If no other solution suggests itself, the same tools that are used to examine evidence can also be used to examine the state of your system during the behavior in question. Most of the time, however, a computer "crime" should be suspected only when there is conclusive evidence or all other possibilities have been eliminated.

The importance of this step cannot be overestimated. I have worked with more than one customer that was determined that every problem on their network was the result of some network attacker ruining their systems. In the long run,this fixation on a hoped-for cause is detrimental to speedy resolution of any incident. If you are convinced that there is a hacker, you will spend all your time looking for evidence of the attack and miss the fact that a simple configuration setting is causing your problems. Good incident response is logical and methodical and does not leap to conclusions.

Once an incident has been identified, the next step is to determine the scope of the incident as part of the evaluation process. This includes determining the number of affected systems and even the number of affected sites. At this point, the sensitivity of the target and the degree of threat that is brought against the target must also be evaluated. Initial estimates of the suspected cause of the incident, what the potential damage of the incident is, and the required time and resources should all be noted at this point. This information will lead to a decision being made with regard to the response strategy to choose.

After determining the scope of the incident, it is time to bring in any members of the incident response team who have not already been activated and whose skills are required for the resolution of the incident. In some cases, this may mean that the HR person deals with the press, the forensics expert begins the examination of any collected data, and the legal expert begins to consider the implications of the incident for the company and any satisfaction that can be obtained through criminal or civil courts.

When spreading the word of the incident, it is important to keep information about the incident as professional, clear, and concise as possible. There is a tendency when something big has occurred for people to react in an emotional way. This is not an advantage when working through an incident. Conclusions about what the cause of the incident is, if not known, should not be speculated. The "sky is falling" type of statement only tends to excite people and does nothing to keep people focused and attentive to the details that are important in successful incident resolution.

The rules of incident response must be made especially clear to anyone who needs to interface with the public or the media. While it is good policy to provide information to the media about an attack that might affect your company's image to the public, it is also important to be conservative regarding the information provided. There are several rules to assist you in this process, to include:

- *Interview only on your own time.* Reporters will like to contact you at odd hours in the hope of receiving an unprepared report that may have exclusive information. All relations with the media should be through mechanisms that your company controls — such as prepared press releases.
- *Keep technical information to an absolute minimum.* This serves two purposes. First, the person responsible for the attacks may be listening for information regarding their success; and second, too much information may motivate other copycat attackers to try their hand.
- *Avoid any speculation as to who is causing the incident.* This will only serve to politicize the situation and may interfere with any investigation that occurs.

13.4 Containment

Once an incident has been established as genuine, the next phase, containment, begins. The role of containment is simply to ensure that the affected system is unable to affect other systems on your network. This can be most readily accomplished by disconnecting it from the network, isolating the affected system via a firewall or other device, or simply shutting down the system.

If more information is required about the attack, then isolating the system from others via a firewall or VLAN (Virtual LAN — a network logically divided using switch software) might be the simplest option. Network monitors can then be attached to the device to monitor packets.

Of all the options, shutting down the affected system to preserve data is one of the most contentious issues in incident response. While shutting down the affected system is a sure way of ensuring that no other parts of your network are affected, it often destroys important evidence. At the very least, the contents of the volatile memory will be lost and the file system of the hard drives will be changed upon start-up. If catching the attacker is the primary goal, then shutting down the system may not be the best option. On the other hand, if critical data is at risk, then shutting down the system may be the best way to protect it.

At this point, the training of the incident response team will be crucial. The optimal compromise when in doubt about shutting down the system is to quickly image the contents of the volatile memory and preserve the integrity of the hard drive after the system is shut down.

13.5 Investigation

With the evidence in hand and the rest of the network secured from the affected systems, the process of investigation can begin. Because investigation relies on information, the first rule in investigation is to get your hands on everything you legally can as soon after the incident as you can. This means requesting logs from any remote servers as well. Due to the amount of information they collect, service providers generally do not retain information for extended periods of time. While they may not hand over the information without the involvement of law enforcement, they can at least be notified to keep a copy of a particular log until the proper permissions can be obtained. Again, training will improve the response time in this case.

The incident response team must act quickly to preserve the contents of volatile memory in affected systems, secure any logs that they are able to, including those from any network service providers they believe are relevant, image all hard drives to backup drives for analysis, and capture any relevant network traffic they can.

There are five[2] primary places that information can be stored on a computer, and each one should be considered for collection during the investigation phase. The first and most volatile piece of information is the actual memory contents of the system. Depending on the operating system, the method of capturing the state of the RAM information in a system varies, but is possible through the use of common administrative utilities such as dd in UNIX or through specialized forensic applications. The most important thing to remember while copying the RAM is that the process of copying the RAM utilizes the RAM and therefore changes the contents of this evidence. This should not discourage anyone from copying volatile information, but it should serve as a reminder that documenting all steps in the incident response process is important. If asked in court, it is a small matter to explain that the evidence presented as RAM is an accurate reflection of the state of the device during capture, with the exception of resources allocated to the copy program itself.

After RAM, there is other important information that can be lost if the computer were to be powered down. The most important of this information is both the state of running processes on the system and the state of any network connections. Both can be captured by running standard system utilities. The information here can often be the most useful in determining the cause of an incident. It is, however, not fool-proof because hacked versions of the applications can hide information about their own processes. This situation is rare enough that it is always a good idea to collect this information before powering down the system.

It should be noted that performing a live system review is not always absolutely necessary. If, for example, there is suspicion that an employee is harassing someone via e-mail, then examining the running system and network processes will not necessarily provide any useful evidence. When the cause of the incident is unknown or is network based, then this information is critical.

With the volatile information secured, the system can then be powered down and the more permanent information from the hard drives and any removable media can be obtained. The cardinal rule of collecting evidence from storage media is to always obtain and perform your analysis on a copy of the original. At all costs, modifications to the original should be avoided.

Imaging information from a production hard drive to a backup hard drive can be accomplished using either system utilities or forensic software created specifically for this task. Most of the time, a direct copy can be performed; but if it is desirable to be able to boot from the imaged drive on a remote host, then the drive geometry must be maintained.

Even when examining a copy of the original data, no changes should be made to the storage medium. Depending on the operating system, it is possible to mount or use a drive in read-only mode. This allows investigators to examine data on the drive without changing the content. Another option is to use forensic software that allows data drives to be mounted in a read-only state for examination.

Examining a large hard drive can be a very tedious process. While forensic software allows pattern searches and may even index the contents of the drive for the benefit of the forensic investigator, this functionality still requires quite a bit of time to perform an extensive analysis on a hard drive of many gigabytes. This is especially true when the investigator does not know what he or she is looking for. If inappropriate pictures or e-mails are the only target of the search, then this can be performed in short order.

If the evidence is going to be used for a criminal or civil trial — and all evidence should be collected in this manner — then steps need to be taken to show that the contents of the imaged drive are identical to the information found on the original drive. This is most often performed using hash algorithms. As we learned about cryptography, hash algorithms are often used to verify the integrity of data. The hash algorithm, commonly MD5 or SHA-1, is run against the content of the original drive and the content of the imaged drive. If the imaged drive is indeed an exact replica of the original, then the hash values should match as well. Considering that hundreds of gigabytes of data can be reduced to a single expression of 160 bits is fairly remarkable and much easier at proving integrity than manually examining the two drives.

Once all the data has been secured, it is ready for investigation. There are numerous software applications favored by forensic examiners that allow the examiner to catalog, sort, and search through the stored evidence. What the software does not provide is an inquisitive mind and an understanding of the protocols, applications, and the experience that forensics investigators acquire over time.

While what to collect may be rather straightforward, the manner in which the information is collected may make or break an investigation. Digital data suffers from the particular disadvantage that it is possible to easily change. This creates the requirement that data be collected and preserved in a particular manner.

The first such requirement is the presence of witnesses. The more people present during the acquisition of data, the better.

The second such requirement is documentation. The entire process of collecting data must be clearly documented. The easiest way for this to occur is for one person to narrate the steps they take and a second person to record those steps. Documentation includes providing the initial state of the system prior to any evidence gathering. This means recording serial numbers, all cables and hook-ups, and any screen display that is present. Providing documentary evidence such as photographs is helpful in this regard. Recording the time that each step has taken will be important in a legal case as well.

One issue that is sure to come up in any criminal investigation is the chain of custody. Because digital data can be easily modified, a defense attorney will attempt to cast doubt on the truth of the data. To avoid having your evidence thrown out, be sure to document in your incident response plan the proper rules regarding chain of custody — who had access to the data, when they had access to it, and for what reason. At a minimum, be sure that the following is recorded for all evidence collected:

- Who collected the evidence
- How and where the evidence was collected
- Who took possession of the evidence
- How the evidence was stored and protected from tampering in storage
- Who removed evidence from storage, and why
- Anything that can be stored in a sealable container should be stored in such

The use of evidence tags, as previously described, will help ensure that these important steps are followed.

Securing evidence is usually where most mistakes are made during the incident response process. The most common mistake is to underestimate the importance of the incident or the scope of the investigation. This causes investigators to treat collected information in a haphazard manner — behavior that cannot be reversed when it is suddenly discovered that the information is indeed important. While it has been mentioned before, the importance of documentation cannot be understated. Every command entered, and every person with access to the media must be documented. Remember that a court of law has different standards than most network administrators are used to operating with.

Other common mistakes involve failure to observe the proper chain of custody rules. This means that the evidence must be stored in a secure location, not in or on your desk, and that all access to the evidence must be recorded. Another mistake is either failing to report an incident altogether or failing to report the incident in a timely manner to either management or law enforcement. When an investigation begins, time is of the essence, especially when persons are to be interviewed or temporary information secured.

The above mistakes might be procedural in nature, but there are also a number of common technical errors. The first and most important is altering the evidence before recording the state of the evidence to a backup drive. This may mean that the file system was altered, the date and time information on programs changed, or even new programs installed during the course of the installation!

13.6 Eradication

Once the evidence has been secured, the process of eradication can begin. In some cases, where the entire affected system is being used as evidence, eradication can also mean replacement.

The most pressing issue concerning eradication is that a system that has been compromised in any manner can no longer be trusted. While the incident response team may be confident that it has found the cause of the incident, it is difficult to establish that nothing else has been modified. Thus, the most common method of eradication is either restoring the affected system from a known good backup, or restoring the system from the original media and restoring saved data from known, good backups.

Restoring a system can be time-consuming and troublesome in its own right. Once again, having an incident response plan in place prior to the incident can make this process much easier. During the prevention phase, a common step in prevention is to create a cryptographic hash of all files and executables on a given system. When done during the installation of a system, incident response teams can ascertain with some certainty what has been affected on a system. This is one of the rare exceptions to the "reinstall rule" and may greatly reduce any downtime.

Finally, the recovery phase can begin. This is the process of reintegrating the system into a production network. Ensure that the cause of the incident has been addressed before reintroducing the affected system. This means reviewing the security policy, adjusting any packet filtering rules, reviewing user permissions, and installing vendor patches to the affected systems as required.

13.7 Post-Mortem

Incident response planning is an iterative process. The final step in resolving any incident is the post-mortem analysis. Here, the incident response team must meet and review the cause of the incident, the resolution, and recommend any steps that must be taken to either improve response time in the future or prevent similar incidents from occurring again.

Some things to consider during the post-mortem phase are any additional requirements that the incident response staff may require, such as:

- Additional training in response time
- Additional training in troubleshooting or evidence collection techniques
- Methods of improving team communications
- Methods of providing additional resources to incident response team in a timely manner
- Formally requesting changes to security policy as appropriate

The goal is not only to improve the response of the incident response team, but also to document the evidence as much as possible so that similar incidents can be more quickly resolved.

As a last step, the total monetary costs of the incident should be tallied. This includes any loss of data and the estimated value of that data, any hardware damage that may have occurred, and the total cost (in manpower hours) that response to the incident cost.

No matter how thorough your information security document may be, it is essential that proper attention be paid to the steps that will be taken when things go amiss — because they will. Incident response is typically written as a separate part of the overall information security policy because the process of incident response can change without altering the rest of the security policy. Due to its crucial role in the resolution of unforeseen circumstances, the incident response plan is just as important a step to overall information security as the security policy itself, an acceptable use policy, or a disaster recovery document.

Notes

1. CIRT is also used interchangeably with the other common acronym, CERT (computer emergency response team). Since every incident may not be an emergency or a crime, I prefer to use the term CIRT just for the sake of logical consistency.
2. Some might argue that the actual registers and cache of the CPU itself contain information. This is true, but it is not common practice to collect this information during an investigation. The crux of the problem is that the very process of trying to capture the information will change the information contained therein.

Chapter 14
Disaster Recovery and Continuity Planning

An important component of the information security policy is the section that describes the steps that the business will take if a disaster were to strike the company. There are two essential questions that a disaster recovery plan must answer. The first is what are the immediate steps that must be taken during or immediately after the disaster to ensure the safety of our employees and ensure that the company is able to resume critical business functions in the shortest time possible? The second question relates to the longer term. Now that the disaster has struck and we have recovered to a minimally operational state, what steps do we take to bring the business back to the state it was prior to the disaster? The first step is the disaster recovery process and the second step is commonly referred to as business continuity planning.

Almost by definition, a disaster is an unplanned event that may cause the entire company location to be unusable for a day or longer. This is compared with nondisasters that are simply service interruptions and local device or software failures. The nondisasters are hopefully addressed in the main security policy and have been identified during the risk assessment phase of developing the security policy.

The companies that recover from a disaster are the ones that plan ahead and create and implement a disaster recovery plan prior to the disaster striking. This means that the company has taken steps to identify their most important assets, estimate the risks that a given disaster may present, and implement steps to ensure a speedy recovery from any exposure. It is a sobering statistic that more than 40 percent of companies that experience a disaster never recover, and an additional 30 percent of companies experiencing a disaster of some sort close within two years. Altogether, that adds up to 70 percent of U.S. businesses closing within two years of a disaster. Some studies put that number much higher. If your business is important, then disaster recovery is a critical component of the information security policy.

Unfortunately, many companies underestimate the impact of a disaster on their organization if they even consider it at all. Sadly, many companies fail to even reopen after a disaster that puts them out of business for more than five days.

If you read the chapter on creating and implementing a security policy, then much of what is being said here should sound familiar. Identify assets, perform risk analysis, and implement solutions. The primary difference here is that the scope of the risk has changed. Instead of considering a single system, as is often the case when evaluating nondisaster scenarios, the disaster recovery plan attempts to evaluate the business organization as a whole and identify critical interdependencies between systems. Another comparison might be that the security policy is interested in what happens if a server goes down or the effect that denial-of-service attacks might have on the goals of the security policy. The disaster recovery plan attempts to plan for the contingency that the entire building is wiped off the map.

Nevertheless, the process is very similar to the overall process of the security policy. In fact, much of the risk analysis can occur at the same time or at least use the same data. Like the incident response policy, management initiates the disaster recovery plan by creating a disaster recovery team, providing the leadership for setting goals, and making available the required resources. Once this has been accomplished, the process of creating a disaster recovery policy is a series of defined steps like most other elements of good information security.

The first step is to identify any major legal or policy constraints that must apply to any disaster recovery planning in the same way that there may be legal or regulatory influence in the creation of the information security policy as a whole. Is there the requirement that patient or customer data remain confidential even in the face of a disaster? Do executives have the legal responsibility to perform due diligence regarding disaster recovery? Does the company's own security policy make any particular requirements regarding the treatment of data? It is these high-level considerations that will impact the steps implemented in the disaster recovery policy just as they do the information security policy as a whole. This will help define the overall goals of the disaster recovery plan.

The next step is to perform a risk analysis. Most of the time, if a company has taken the process of information security to heart, this step has already been taken. While most people remember to consider such natural disasters as fires, floods, earthquakes, tornados, and hurricanes as potential threats, it is important to recall that threats can also be technological or human in nature. A riot or civil unrest can damage your business just as much as a flood. More so than the risk analysis that is performed as part of the information security policy, the emphasis for the disaster recovery risk analysis should be on numbers. It will be important when planning contingencies to know the total dollar value of assets to the organization. What is the potential financial impact of a disaster on an organization? How much money would the organization stand to lose per day that it could not operate? How many days could this go on before the business is unable to open again?

Many disaster planning models use what is known as a time-loss graph. This tool allows the disaster planning team to describe the dollar effects of an extended outage over a period of time. Simply put, it describes the amount of cash that is lost on a per-hour or per-day basis when information is not available. This may reveal that significant losses are not realized until the third day of nonoperation. This information, of course, is then used to plan the recovery strategy. If your information reveals that the most significant losses to the company occur within the first three days of an outage, then this is the timeframe that must be considered. Knowing your own business cycle will greatly impact the values and timeframes that are determined. Does your business have a critical customer that requires its orders on a certain day of each quarter? What if you suffered a loss two days before that order? What if the loss occurred six weeks before that critical date?

As with the risk analysis that occurs for the information security policy, the intangible monetary effects of a disaster must also be considered. How will this affect your market share or competitive advantage? How long can you be out of production before suppliers start looking elsewhere? Are there any possible legal fees or regulatory requirements that would affect your loss estimates?

With a clear idea of the likely threats and assessment of possible losses, it is time to perform what is called a business impact analysis (BIA). The BIA uses the information from your risk analysis and attempts to identify the interdependencies that exist between departments and systems. The goal of this step can be broadly summarized as "knowing what needs to happen to get the products to the consumers." To obtain this knowledge, the essential business functions and departments that support these functions must be identified. Not only must they be identified, but also the order in which they must be brought back online must be prioritized. Some business functions are going to be critical to the survivability of the business and must be prioritized; other functions can wait a bit longer.

With this information, it is time to begin the process of developing the standards and procedures that will be implemented before disaster strikes and after the unfortunate event. While the exact implementation of the disaster recovery plan will vary from company to company, there are some common threads that appear in almost every plan and should be considered.

The first is the chain of command. Like incident response, in a crisis there needs to be a single knowledgeable person, with good leadership qualities who is responsible for the oversight of all other disaster recovery activities. Make sure that it is very clear who is the "go-to" person when a disaster strikes.

It is this person who will also be responsible for declaring a disaster. From there, the notification chain should be established. The disaster recovery manager calls two managers; they call more managers and so on, until all affected employees are notified.

Some consideration must also be given to the scale of disaster recovery that will be required. Some organizations may have the requirement to be up and running within hours after a disaster. The only way that this will realistically occur is for the company to maintain a parallel site. If the company has multiple offices, this may mean mirroring business-critical operations in near-real-time at multiple sites.

If the company does not have such stringent recovery requirements, then a hot site may be an acceptable option. A hot site is a remote facility that is close enough to the primary site to be easily accessible, but not so close that it would likely be affected by the same disaster that struck the main location. A hot site has equipment on hand and copies of all data ready for production. In practice, this requires that the hot site operating environment closely mirror that of the primary site. Hot sites are often maintained by the organization itself; however, some companies that specialize in disaster recovery solutions will maintain an organization's hot sites for a fee.

Hot sites have the primary disadvantage of being expensive to maintain. More often, companies are interested in warm alternate sites. Warm sites may include the critical data or simply servers and basic networking equipment ready for configuration by the company IT staff during a disaster. Unlike a hot site, which is essentially a remote office, the warm site has only the materials on hand to supply the business functions described as most critical. Warm sites allow a reasonably rapid response to a disaster, but they cost less to maintain than hot sites.

With hot and warm sites, it should be no surprise that the final option for recovery sites is known as the cold site. The cold site is little more than storage and has only the most basic of business needs such as power and cabling. Of all the options, this is the cheapest, but it will also require the most time to bring up. Imagine if the hardware of the main site is destroyed. How long would it take for replacement hardware to be shipped to the cold site, configured from scratch, and brought online to replace critical business functions? Full recovery may take several weeks at best.

The final option is known as a reciprocal agreement. This is a business agreement with another organization that if some disaster should strike one company, then the other would provide a temporary alternate location during the recovery process. While this sounds like a good, inexpensive idea, careful consideration should be devoted to this idea before it is implemented. Most offices do not have excessive extra space or cabling to comfortably support more than one organization. Tensions will rise as the hosting organization attempts to fulfill its business objectives while the business in recovery is scrambling to get back on its feet. Remember that time you thought it would be "no problem" to have that old college roommate stay with you for a "few days" until he got some things sorted out? Apply that scenario to two businesses and you can see the potential problems.

Like incident response, training is a critical component of any disaster recovery plan. Some training is self-evident, such as CPR and emergency first aid training. Other training would apply to how the employees can ensure their own personal safety and the safety of others, and then the safety of the organization's information infrastructure. All of this training should be brought together in organizationwide testing of the disaster recovery plan. While having a plan is a good start, it does little good to the organization if in the first minutes of a disaster you realize that you have made no provisions for emergency communications when the phone system has been disabled.

14.1 Types of Disaster Recovery Plans

There are various levels of testing that can occur to test a disaster recovery plan. The first is the most intensive, which is known as the full-interruption test. This is a full-scale drill that simulates shutting down the company site and attempting to bring up an alternate site. This is of course very intrusive to the organization as a whole, but provides the best feedback as to the effectiveness of the disaster recovery plan.

Just a bit lower on the accuracy meter, but still high on the complication and expense meter, is the simulation test. Unlike the full-interruption test where the entire organization is involved, the simulation test only involves those who are either on the disaster recovery team itself or those who support critical systems. The simulation test is an attempt to test the responsiveness of the team to a specific disaster scenario.

Most companies cannot afford or otherwise justify such extensive testing. Usually, they are interested in something that is not quite as intrusive. Another effective, but not quite as disruptive, test is known as the parallel test. During a parallel test, the disaster recovery team ensures that only critical systems can be brought online at an alternate site. Once the alternate site has been brought online, the results of any work done there are compared to the original site's output. This comparison will hopefully point out any changes that need to be made to the disaster recovery planning.

Depending on the scope of the disaster recovery plan, at a very minimum the plan should be examined and critiqued. This can be a matter of simply distributing the plan to the different departments and having them examine the plan as a whole. This helps ensure that major elements of the plan have not been omitted. The same process can also occur during some sort of face-to-face meeting where the department leaders meet and review the plan and hash out any differences in priorities or interdependencies, or simply critique the plan from the perspective of their department. The key in either situation is that if extensive testing is not possible, at the very least, review and input by as many knowledgeable people as possible will help minimize any shortcomings in the plan. Unlike the incident response plan that will have a chance to be tweaked over successive incidents, disasters are hopefully few and far between for any organization. The chance for iterative tuning of the disaster recovery plan will be quite limited.

While the chances to fine-tune the plan based on practical experience will hopefully be limited, the disaster recovery plan, like the rest of the security document, should be considered a living document and be regularly reviewed and updated. Changes to the business focus, the infrastructure, software applications, personnel changes, etc. can all affect the viability of the disaster recovery plan. For best effect, ensure that the disaster recovery document is treated in the same manner as the security policy as a whole. Schedule regular reviews and review the document when significant organizational changes occur. Include maintenance of the document in the regular review of disaster recovery team members and be sure to regularly test, train, and drill.

Here is to hoping that you never need to use the disaster recovery document. If, however, you do need to use it, make sure that you are not blowing dust off the top of it — keep the plan up-to-date and make sure you and your team know what to do when bad things happen.

Chapter 15
Acceptable Use Policies

Not every security control is technical in nature. The acceptable use policy (AUP) is a portion of the information security document that clearly describes to network users the boundary between acceptable and unacceptable usage of network resources for your company.

A quick search of the Internet will provide any number of sample acceptable use policies for your perusal; but like the security policy, in the end it is important that the AUP specifically address your network environment. Copying and pasting an AUP from another organization will only cause confusion and headaches for the IS team when users begin to either do their job and find that their normal job functions are somehow in violation of the AUP or challenge the AUP in some manner.

The primary objective of the AUP is to support the goals set out in the information security document. Although you should welcome input in the creation of the AUP, the document should not contradict or otherwise come into conflict with the goals of the information security policy. At the same time, users should know that the AUP is not to simply take the fun out of their jobs, but to ensure that the information security policy, which supports the objectives of the business, is upheld.

Every AUP is going to be different, but successful AUPs share a lot of common characteristics, including:

- They involve as many people as possible. This means that department managers as well as end users of the network are able to provide input into the content of the AUP.
- The policy is unambiguous. It is simply going to amaze you how Matt down in technical support, who cannot seem to finish any project in less than four days, is able to point out every inconsistency and ambiguity in the AUP. The rules should be well-defined and concise, with the penalties for noncompliance clearly stated.
- Address data privacy and user's rights, along with a process for settling grievances and requesting changes.

With that in mind, what follows are some suggestions for items to consider when creating an AUP. Some of these items are fairly cut and dry; but when appropriate, flexibility and compromises are also discussed.

- Are users allowed to conduct personal businesses using company resources? Generally, the answer to this is "no." It is difficult to keep the users' business requirements from interfering with those of their employer. This also means that users may not set up unauthorized services on the network such as Web servers, file servers, etc. It may also include accessing e-mail from another account and using company network resources to send and retrieve it.

- Is there any time that a user can use information resources for personal use and, if so, when or where can they do this? What restrictions are placed on them? Remember that even if users are staying late at night to use the network or respond to e-mails, their use of the company resources will reflect on your company. Is it OK for them to send personal e-mail but not surf the Web, or vice versa?

- Users must comply with the appropriate laws and policies regarding harassment, libel, copyright infringement, etc. at all times. Be sure to explain what these are in the AUP for those users who may be unclear.

- Closely related to the above rules is policy regarding sexual or pornographic images or other material from being retrieved, stored, viewed, or forwarded by the users of the system. Many organizations expand that to include chain letters, jokes, etc.

- Users must not install any type of unauthorized software on their PCs. Such software might include games, personal programs, distributed computing clients, peer-to-peer file sharing programs, etc. The environment that runs only those applications necessary to the success of the business will be the most secure environment.

- Users must obey all copyright laws while using network resources. This means they cannot store their MP3s on the company hosts.

- Users will make no effort to eavesdrop, sniff, or otherwise monitor the communications of other staff members. This usually also includes the installation of sniffing software on their computers, impersonating another user, and attempting to circumvent established information security procedures.

These are just the tip of the iceberg, but they should give a good idea of the types of topics that an AUP should address. Some AUPs simply lay out these rules while others attempt to organize them according to task or network usage such as "Email AUP," "Web Use AUP," etc. in an attempt to make the rules as specific as possible. Again, this decision will be based on your operating environment and user needs.

Chapter 16

The Final Word

This book explains much of the technology that goes into creating a secure network. It is true that this technology can be used to provide a sense of trust in your information, but it would be unwise to pretend that a single box or line in an information security policy can provide all that is required for "security." Information security is an iterative process. You create the policy, implement the policy, enforce the policy, and review the policy when things go wrong. Notice the emphasis on *policy*. The cycle of information security is not written as, "You create the firewall, you implement the firewall, you ...." You get the idea.

That said, it is indeed important to understand the technology so you will have a good idea of how a particular solution will reduce the risk to information on your network. I cannot tell you what is a good acceptable use policy (AUP) for your network or what are the value of your assets, but I can provide the information required to make an intelligent choice of countermeasures when you are looking for the way to enforce certain provisions of your information security policy.

Now that we have made it this far through the book, let us just take a couple pages to sum up the steps required to "secure" your network.

The very first step? Convince those in charge that this process is worthwhile to your organization. There are numerous ways to do this. You can point to virtually any newspaper and say, "This could be us!" You can bring out a book of the appropriate state federal laws and say again, "This could be us they come after!" Indeed, these are both reasons to support information security. Either of these techniques, while emphasizing the importance of information security, are sending the message that information security is a necessary evil, an add-on that drains revenue and produces no return. Instead of opting for the sensationalistic method of convincing management, however, attempt to persuade them using business logic. You have the knowledge to create the information security policy in a manner that supports the business and *adds* to the bottom line in increased network efficiency, decreased downtime, and perhaps shareholder confidence. You can do this because you can create an information security policy that not only complements the corporate mission, but is cost-effective as well.

You should no longer be concerned about providing the very best security that money can buy. You now know that this is, in practice, impossible. Your goal is to provide security in a manner that is appropriate to the *likely* risks your information will face and the *relative* value of your assets.

The best security process starts with an examination of the company mission statement. Answer the following questions:

- What keeps your company in business?
- What keeps everyone working?
- What does the future hold for your organization?

Finally, using the information above, answer this question:

- How does the information assist your company in realizing its goals?

The answer to this question starts you on the process of creating a security policy that enhances the overall mission of your organization. During this process, identify the information system assets that are critical to supporting the overall corporate goals.

Create the high-level information security policy. Get as much input as you can and make sure that everyone is on board — it will prove critical to your long-term success. In particular, this means getting the input of users of the information and not just the wish-list of your IT staff.

Based on the high-level security policy requirements and the assets that you have previously identified, perform a risk analysis. Attempt to identify and quantify, either formally or informally, all of the combinations of threats and vulnerabilities that can put the goals of your information security policy at risk. This can be a complicated process, especially when you attempt to quantify the intangible elements of your information assets.

Only when this process is done, and the likely risks to your information have been identified, is it time to start playing with the toys. The process of selecting countermeasures can now begin. The proper selection of countermeasures should not be based on what a sales rep tells you a device is capable of doing. Because you have done a risk analysis, you know what capabilities you require of countermeasures. Remember that each selected method of risk reduction must be cost-effective; that is, the cost of the control does not exceed that of what it is trying to protect. Furthermore, different countermeasures can provide varying value to your information systems. Be sure to compare the possibilities completely. In many cases, the advertised price is not the best estimate of the real value of any countermeasure.

During this process is where the information in this book will be the most important. There are many ways to protect the information on your network. The guidelines in this book should allow you to make an informed decision as to which solutions are best for your situation.

From the policy, create a number of documents that provide the standards and procedures that will be used on your network. At a minimum, you should include the following standards and procedures documents:

- Technical (network)
- Administrative
- Physical
- Incident Response
- Disaster Recovery and Response
- Acceptable Use Policy

Each of these documents should outline the specifics of the "do's and don't do's" for your environment. They may include rules that human resources must implement for the hiring and firing of employees or an outline of the way in which encryption will be used to protect the confidentiality of data.

From these documents, the actual configuration guides will be created. These guides are used by the staff to implement the standards and procedures. These should be quite detailed and provide all the information required for each aspect of the information security policy.

Begin the implementation! Implement the various countermeasures you have selected. Enforce them as necessary. Provide training to your users, positive feedback, and refresher courses as required. Practice your disaster recovery and incident response plans so that your teams are experienced when the time comes to use them.

Things are going to happen after your implementation. Do not view this as a failure of your security policy. Accept that this is a normal part of the networked environment and be confident that, most likely, your preparedness prevented the situation from being much worse. In fact, this is a perfect time to estimate the actual dollar value of what your security policy may have saved you versus what the incident has cost you.

When things have calmed down, begin the process of reviewing your information security policy and any associated parts of that policy. Modify the information security policy and begin the process again.

People have been trying to secure themselves for hundreds of thousands of years. Some of the earliest uses of technology were an attempt to increase this protection. History teaches us that this approach has never been completely successful; but by understanding and following the process of security, you can be confident that you are employing the technology in the most effective manner possible. Good luck, but remember that luck favors the prepared!

Index

A

Acceptable use policy, 16, 43, 49–50, 389–390
Access control, 147–165
  AAA, 147
  accounting, 152–154
  assigning administrative status, 37
  authorization, *See* Authorization
  central servers (RADIUS/TACACS+), 163–165
  default to secure state, 37
  discretionary (DAC), 148–149
  mandatory (MAC), 149–150
  passwords, *See* Passwords
  physical countermeasures, 45–46, 54
  role-based (nondiscretionary), 150–152
  security labels, 149
ACK bit (TCP header), 104–105, 107, 192, 214
  SYN attack, 111–112
Address Resolution Protocol (ARP), 74, 82–84
Administrative countermeasures, 42–45, 49, *See also* Access control; Passwords
Advanced Encryption Standard (AES), 130
Alerts, 35–36, 264–266
Alias, 141
Annualized loss expectancy (ALE), 27–28, 32
Annualized rate of occurrence (ARO), 26–27, 31–32
Anomaly detection systems (ADSs), 259
Apple Talk, 72
Application layer, 72
  filtering, 199, 226
  proxy, 196

Application security, 137–146
  patches, 137–138, 244
Asymmetric encryption algorithms, 130–134
Asymmetric keys, 121–122
ATM, 64, 72, 281–282
  packet prioritization, 337
Attributes standard (PKCS), 182
Auditing
  penetration testing, *See* Network penetration testing
  router/firewall configuration, 221–222
Authentication, 147–148, *See also* Passwords
  biometric identification, 32, 160–163
  certificates and certification authorities, 123, 167–168, *See also* Public key infrastructure
  Internet Key Exchange, 321
  IPSec ESP options, 315
  public key infrastructure function, 184, 185
  trust models, 172–177
  Web servers, 183
Authentication header (AH), 306, 307, 310–313
  NAT interoperability, 327–328
  security parameters index, 311–312
Authorization
  discretionary access control (DAC), 148–149
  mandatory access control (MAC), 149–150
  nondiscretionary access control, 150–152
  privileges, 150
  security labels, 149
Autonomous system, 96–99

F